The Marquis de Sade

THE
MARQUIS de SADE
A Biography

GILBERT LÉLY

Translated by
ALEC BROWN

GROVE PRESS, INC., NEW YORK

Contents

CONTENTS

CONTENTS

Chapter Sixteen

Chapter Seventeen

Chapter Eighteen

Chapter Nineteen

Index

CHAPTER ONE

The Ancestors

THE SADE family originated in Avignon, where we find many of its members mentioned in documents dating from the 12th century on. They appear as Sado, Sadone, Sazo and Sauza. The surname indeed may derive from an early suburb of the city situated along the Rhône and known as Saze.

The earliest mention of the Sades is a document granting certain privileges to the priory of Franquevaux drawn in 1171 by Hugues, lord of the manor of Baux and bearing the signature of a *Bernard de Sade*. And if we accept the word of Nostradamus in his *History of Provence*, we find a Bertrand de Sade in 1216 attending an assembly held at Arles. This Bertrand may well have been the father of Raimond de Sade, after whom we have an unbroken pedigree in the form of a continuous list of marriage contracts and wills. Perhaps the glow which the personality of their illustrious descendant sheds over all those who preceded him will do something to lighten the monotony of that long list. It makes rather dull reading, but we need only glance at the essential.

Raimond's grandson, Paul de Sade, was one of four dignitaries of the city of Avignon appointed to welcome the new Pope Jean XXII when on October 2nd 1316 he sailed down the Rhône from Lyons. Paul was re-elected *Syndic* of the city many times over, and let us note that the municipal office of *Syndic* was then a most important one. Thereafter for several generations the Sade family was to provide the papal capital with outstanding governors. The Sades also gave the church a good many dignitaries. The first of a long line of clerics was Raimond's third son, Jean de Sade, who was Papal Chaplain at the close of the 13th century. Paul's great-grandson Pons de Sade was first *Abbé* of Saint Eusèbe d'Apt, and then (in 1445) Bishop of Vaison, in which capacity he was present at Martigues when what Provence maintained were the earthly remains of St Marie Jacobeus and St Marie Salomé were removed to a new place of burial. In 1465 we find the same Pons, in recognition of his fervour, being appointed Avignon's ambassador to Pope Paul II.

Paul de Sade had eight children, one of whom was Hugues (known as Hugues the Elder), whose first wife, whom he married on January 16th 1325, was that delicate flower of the Comtat, Laure de Noves, that "Laura" famous for her beauty and for the love which she inspired in Petrarch. She was a daughter of the late Audebert de Noves, knight, and Lady Ermessende. Eleven children were born of this marriage : Paul, or Paulon, Dean of the metropolitan church of Avignon, Audebert, doctor of law, Provost of the collegiate church of Pignans, Hugues, known as Hugonin, who continued the line, Pierre (to whom Pope Innocent IV granted a canonry at Avignon), Jacques, Joannet, Philippe, Augière (who married Bertrand Milson-di, esquire), Ermessende, steward of the Convent of St Laurent, Marguerite, and finally Garsende, or Garsenète, who was thrice married and still alive in 1406.

"I first set eyes on Laura, famous for her virtue and long sung in my poems, in the flower of my youth, in the year of our Lord 1327, on April 6th, in the morning, in the church of St Claire in Avignon. . . ."

Thus begins a note which Petrarch made in his manuscript of Virgil. So incomparably unassuming, these words, glowing with Provençal warmth, seem as worthy of admiration as the finest of his sonnets. Did Laura never once yield to the poet who so loved her? That is what legend would have us believe, as well as Petrarch himself, who time and again in his work lamented the relentlessly firm morals of his mistress. Yet in the *Canzones* there have been noted certain contradictions, for Laura does seem sometimes to be described as a source of physical delight. And is it really likely that, being both young and impressionable, she was able throughout twenty years to withstand the persistent attentions of a lover of whom she was fond, and whom all Christendom admired—this in the heady atmosphere of 14th-century Avignon, which was a pleasure city, a city of love-making, where the greatest liberties were regularly taken, even in convents?

Hugues de Sade was certainly not at all sure. He could not look on the friendship between his wife and the author of the sonnets without suspicion. Indeed—Petrarch's dialogues tell us so much—there were occasions when his jealousy took a violent form. Whatever the truth, is it too much to say that a complaisant Laura shocks our imagination less than that chilly, idealised figure which all the historians of Provence have vied with one another to depict?

Laure de Sade died on April 6th 1348, a victim of the plague, on the same day, in the same month and at the very same hour that Petrarch had first set eyes on her. She was buried in the monastery church of Avignon, which contained the Sade family tomb. When passing through the city in 1533, King François I had her grave opened. In the coffin were found some bones and a lead casket containing a medallion and an Italian sonnet. The sonnet recorded that these were the remains of the woman whom Petrarch had made famous. The King thereupon wrote another epitaph himself, in eight lines of French verse, added this to the medallion and the sonnet in the lead casket, and had the tomb re-sealed.

According to a tradition in the Avignon country, which all the earlier genealogists accepted, Laura came of the Sade family, Paul being claimed as her father and Hugues the Elder her brother. It was however the paternal uncle of the Marquis de Sade—Jacques François Paul Aldonce, titulary Abbé of Ebreuil—who was by incontrovertible documentary evidence to establish the real relationship of fair Laura to the house of Sade. For this Abbe de Sade had the good fortune to find the marriage contract of "Laure de Noves" and Hugues the Elder in the family papers, and further the wills of both Hugues and Laure and also of Paul de Sade, giving the full list of the children and confirming that Laura, who had been taken to be Paul's daughter, was in fact his daughter-in-law, being the wife of his son Hugues. The Abbé's work *Mémoires pour la vie de François Pétrarque* contains all the details of the proof, including the supporting documents. There can be no question about it, "Laure" was Paul de Sade's daughter-in-law, and she was also the "Laura" of the sonnets.

Seven months after Laure de Sade's death, Hugues took a second wife, Verdaine de Trentelivres, whom he married on November 19th 1348, and by whom he had six more children. The first son of this marriage was Baudet, from whom the lords of the manor of Saumane began, a line ending in the mid-16th century with Joachim de Sade, hereditary Captain of the town and lord of the manor of Vaison. Hugues' third son Paul was first appointed Counsellor to the King of Aragon by letters patent dated April 19th 1397, then secretary to Yolanda, Queen of Naples and Countess of Provence, and her minister at the Court of Avignon, finally, on May 24th 1405, becoming Bishop of Marseilles.

In recognition of his military achievements, Hugues' grandson Jeannon was given the command of the fortress of St André de Villeneuve by King Charles VI. A document in his hand in 1349 shows that Hugues the Elder possessed a considerable fortune, with various manorial rights in Avignon, and also rights to Rhône toll charges, salt tax and so forth. In 1355 he donated 200 gold florins towards the rebuilding of the first three arches of the St Benezet bridge, which still bears the rough-hewn family arms. On November 14th 1364, he made his will, indicating the chapel of the Holy Cross in the Church of the Minories in Avignon, which he had built and in which he had established his vault, as his eventual burial place.

FROM HUGUES THE YOUNGER, SON OF LAURA, TO
GASPARD FRANÇOIS, GRANDFATHER OF THE MARQUIS DE SADE

Hugues de Sade, known as Hugonin or Hugues the Younger, founder of the line of the lords of the manor of Mazan, was Consul of Avignon in 1373. His second son, Elzéar, Groom, then Cupbearer to Pope Benoît XIII, as reward for his services to the Empire was granted, by Emperor Sigismond of Luxembourg, for his own enjoyment and that of his descendants the privilege of surmounting the family arms with the two-headed imperial eagle, the limbs, beak and diadem *gules*.

The diploma is dated January 11th 1416. Since then the Sade family, whose original arms were *Gules with eight rays or,* has always surmounted them with a two-headed eagle draped with sable.

The eldest son of Hugues the Younger was Jean de Sade, Doctor of Law, Chief Justice of Provence in 1406 and Counsellor to Louis II of Anjou, King of Jerusalem and Sicily, Count of Provence, who as reward for his services made him lord of the manor of Eyguières. When the High Court of Aix was set up, Hugues was made its first president. Thus it was a Sade who first opened that *parlement* of Provence, a court which among its members was to number those most implacable judges of Donatien Alphonse François de Sade (our Marquis), whom they condemned to decapitation and burning for having made some prostitutes of Marseilles eat aniseed balls doctored with Spanish fly.

Girard de Sade, Hugues' son, who bore the titles of lord of the manor of Eyguières and lord of the manors of Saint Jeurs, Majastres and Creyssel, and co-lord of the manors of Mazan, Venasque and Saint Didier, by deed of May 10th 1444 gave the Church of Our Lady of Eyguières the relics of St Catherine, on condition that every year on the day following the feast of St Catherine a solemn mass should be served for the house of Sade. At the close of his life, he was invested with the office of First Consul of the City of Avignon.

His eldest son, Etienne de Sade, had three children, one of whom was Guillaume, who was the father of Gabrielle de Sade, who towards 1550 married Jacques de Beaune de Samblançay, Knight of the Order of the King, Gentleman in Ordinary of the Bedchamber, Ambassador to Switzerland, Chamberlain of the Duke of Anjou, brother of Henri II. The marriage brought Gabrielle de Sade the titles of Baroness de Samblançay and la Carte and Viscountess of Tours. Her husband was the grandson of the famous Jacques de Samblançay who was Superintendent of Finance under Charles VIII, Louis XII and François I, and finally hanged at Montfaucon on August 9th 1524, victim of a shameful trial instituted by the Queen-Mother, Louise de Savoie.

The author is in the possession of the original manuscript of a bond to the advantage of her farmers signed in 1599 by

Guillaume de Sade's daughter. The document bears the signature of the Viscountess of Tours twice—*Gabrielle de Sade*—and this is supported by that of her daughter, *Charlotte de Beaune*. Their handwritings are of incomparable nobility and grace.

Charlotte de Beaune was a favourite of Catherine de Medici, her first husband being Simon de Fizes, Baron Sauve, minister and secretary of state under Charles IX and Henri III. He died in 1579. Her second husband was François de la Tremouille, Marquis of Noirmoutiers. Celebrated for her beauty and her liaisons, first with Henri IV, then with the Duke de Guise, Charlotte had points in common with the exuberant heroines to whom the imagination of the author of *Juliette* gave birth. At a banquet at Chenonceaux on May 15th 1577, Gabrielle de Sade's daughter and Lady de Retz waited on Catherine de Medici without a stitch of clothing on. This however was quite a usual demand of Catherine's. Brantôme attests to the fact, and also tells us that the Queen did not insist on nakedness merely to wait at table, but also used to subject her girls to mild flagellation. And, says Brantôme, by this means she "so excited their appetite that afterwards she often had good reason to hand them over to a gallant with the necessary constitution and vigour."

Girard's second son was Balthazar, founder of the line of Eyguières, which, after having linked up with the Mazan branch by the marriage of Gabrielle Laure de Sade d'Eyguières to Donatien Claude Armand, son of Donatien Alphonse François, Marquis de Sade, petered out in Count Xavier de Sade, in 1846.

Girard's fourth child, Pierre, who continued the Mazan branch of the family, married Baptistine de Forbin, widow of Raimond de Glandèves, Grand Seneschal of Provence, who was her first husband. Girard's marriage was concluded in secret, without banns, by special licence of the Pope, on December 23rd 1493. There were three children of this marriage. In the will which she made on June 4th 1528, Baptistine de Forbin left her son Joachim 1,200 florins and a house and garden in Avignon, but made Pierre de Glandèves, her son by her first husband, her heir. This Joachim, son of Pierre de Sade, a doctor of law and lord of the manors of Mazan, Vénasque and

St Didier, was by letters patent of François I issued at Amboise on October 22nd 1530 appointed Councillor of the Court of the Parliament of Provence.

Joachim became known as Joachim the Younger, to distinguish him from his cousin and godfather Joachim de Sade, who was the last of the Saumane branch, and, having no issue of his marriage with Madeleine de l'Artissut, by a will dated October 22nd 1530 made Joachim the Younger heir of all his lands and other property. In this way the Mazan branch added to all it already enjoyed the manor of Saumane and the office of hereditary Captain of the town and castle of Vaison. On his way to Aix on September 13th 1538, Joachim de Sade was drowned crossing the Coulon (or Calavon), and was buried at Mazan in the church of St Nazaire, beside his spouse, *née* Clémence de Gérard, who had preceded him by nine years.

Joachim de Sade's eldest son, François, died in childhood, and it was the younger Jean, born on November 8th 1522, who continued the line. He was lord of the manor of Saumane and co-lord of Mazan, Cabanes and Istres, as well as hereditary Captain of the town and castle of Vaison. He studied law in Paris under the famous Alciat. He followed his father-in-law, Claude de Jarents, in the offices of First President of the Chamber of Accounts and of Guardian of the Seals of the Chancellory. His mansion at Mazan was laid waste in August 1562 when Baron des Adrets invaded the Comtat. He died on December 15th 1599.

Jean's eldest son, Balthazar, "that grand and illustrious lord", married Diane de Baroncelli-Javon on May 14th 1600, and had two sons, Jean Baptiste and Richard, and a posthumous daughter, Catherine. A doctor of theology of the University of Avignon, Richard was granted a pension of 1,200 *livres* by King Louis XIII, in 1634, and by a Papal Bull of October 6th 1634 was given the canonry of St Laurent in Damaso, in Rome. He became Chamberlain to Pope Urban VIII and Vice-Governor of Tivoli and Ravenna. Appointed a Grand Vicar in 1562 by letters granted by Cardinal Barberini, he was raised to the office of Bishop of Cavaillon by a Papal Bull the following year. He returned to Rome in 1663 as representative of the county of Vence and died there on June

27th of the same year. He was buried in the church of St Laurent in Damaso, where Cardinal Barberini had a magnificent tomb erected in his honour.

It was by the marriage of Balthazar's eldest son, Jean Baptiste, to Diane de Simiane (contract of April 12th 1627) that the castle and lands which bear the name became part of the Sade family possessions. Jean Baptiste de Sade was Colonel of the light cavalry of the Pope in the County of Vence, an office which was transmitted from father to son in the Sade family through three generations, down to the father of the Marquis. Jean Baptiste died on September 17th 1687.

Of his union with Diane de Simiane ten children were born, four sons and six daughters, five of whom became nuns. His third son, Richard, a knight of St John of Jerusalem, distinguished himself in the Candian war and captained one of the Pope's galleys. In 1719 he became Grand Prior of Saint Gilles. His fourth son, Jean Baptiste, born at Mazan on July 14th 1633, was first Prior of Bonnieux and Cucuron, then followed his uncle Richard as Bishop of Cavaillon on September 4th 1665, being formally inducted on March 14th 1666. He died on December 19th 1707. To him we are indebted for a number of religious writings, in particular *Edifying Christian Comments on Various Passages of Holy Writ,* and a *Eulogy of the Sacrament of the Eucharist.*

Côme de Sade, Jean Baptiste's eldest son, on February 11th 1669, by a special licence granted on February 9th, married his cousin, Elisabeth Louët de Nogaret de Valvisson, daughter of Jean Louis, Marquis of Calvisson and Marshal of the Garrisons and Armies of the King and of Françoise Bermond de Saint Bonnet du Caylar de Thoiras. Côme and Elisabeth obtained permission for the consecration of their marriage by their uncle, Jean Baptiste de Sade, Bishop of Cavaillon.

Of this union were born six children : Jean Baptiste, Prior Knight of the Order of St John of Jerusalem, Captain of the Galleys of that order (he was drowned in 1700) and Jean Louis, Prior of Sainte Croix de Maulsang and Provost of the church of l'Isle.

It was Gaspard François de Sade, the eldest son of Côme, who was the first of this family to bear the title *Marquis.* He was occasionally referred to as the Marquis de Sade, but more often documents refer to him as the Marquis de Mazan. This is the title we find in his marriage contract, in his will and in the Bull of Pope Innocent XII of April 3rd 1693 giving him the office for life of Colonel of the light cavalry of the *Comtat*.

In 1700 Gaspard François was appointed the Comtat's envoy to Pope Clement XI, to compliment him on his elevation. Appointed Provost of Avignon on June 4th 1701, in this office he invited the Dukes of Burgundy and Berry to honour the city by their presence. On September 25th 1699, he married Louise Aldonce d'Astoaud, daughter of Jean, Marquis de Murs, Baron de Romanil and Lord of the Manor of Séderon, and of Marie Thésan de Vénasque.

Gaspard François drew up a will on October 16th 1722, in the presence of an Avignon notary named Giraudi, adding a codicil to this on February 9th 1734, and died on November 24th 1739. He had had five sons and five daughters.

It was of the union of his eldest son, Jean Baptiste François Joseph and Marie Eléonore de Maillé de Carman, a blood relation of the Royal family of Condé, that on June 2nd 1740 was born Donatien Alphonse François, Marquis de Sade, celebrated by reason both of his misfortunes and his genius and destined to enrich his ancient family with the highest of all distinctions, those of fine language and fine thinking, bequeathing to his descendants the real magnificence of their name and their title.

CHAPTER TWO

From Birth to Marriage

(part one)

1740 - 1754

HIS FATHER AND MOTHER

THIS SECTION will be restricted to biographical generalities. We shall try to elucidate the relationship between Donatien Alphonse François and his parents.

Jean Baptiste Joseph François, Count de Sade, lord of the manors of Saumane and La Coste and co-lord of Mazan, Colonel of the Pope's light cavalry in the County of Vence, was born at Avignon in 1702. Commencing his career as a Captain of Dragoons in de Condé's regiment, in 1730 he was appointed ambassador to the Russian Court, but the death of the young Tsar Pierre II and the Austrian policy of the new empress, Anna Ivanovna, made his mission pointless. In 1753 Cardinal de Fleury intrusted him with clandestine negotiations at the English Court. He next campaigned as *aide-de-camp* to Marshal de Villars in 1734 and 1735, after which he purchased the office of Lieutenant-General of the provinces of Bresse, Bugey, Valromey and Gex from the Marquis de Lassay for 135,000 *livres*, the office being transferred to him by letters patent of May 29th 1739. On November 9th 1740, he paid homage to the Pope from his estates of Saumane and Mazan.

When the Emperor Charles VI died, he was despatched as minister plenipotentiary to the Elector of Cologne, to win him over to the cause of the Emperor's brother, the Elector of Bavaria, who was backed by France and elected emperor under the name of Charles VII. It was thanks to the Count de Sade that the new emperor concluded a treaty of alliance with France and Spain in May 1741 at Nymphenburg. On his return, the Count de Sade relinquished his office of Colonel of the Pope's light cavalry to the Marquis de Crochans, and in the ensuing years was charged with fresh diplomatic missions. In 1760 he bore the title of Marshal of the Camp of the Royal Armies. He died at Monteuil, a suburb of Versailles, on January 24th 1767, not far from his Glatigny estate.

In the *château* of Condé-en-Brie, now owned by the Marquis Xavier de Sade, can be seen his portrait by Nattier. Maurice Heine describes it as follows :

" . . . A man of about fifty-years of age in appearance, his hair dressed and powdered in the Louis XV style, with tight curls, wearing a cuirass partly concealed by a voluminous cloak, with a nose that was long and, as far as one can judge from what is almost a full face portrait, slightly aquiline, a well drawn mouth, the oval of the face somewhat modified by profound furrows running on either side from mouth to nose, and eyes which seem to have been light in colour. The general appearance wilful and rather noble."

On November 13th 1733, Count de Sade was married in the chapel of the Condé mansion to Marie Eléonore de Maillé de Carman, who was on this occasion designated as Lady-in-waiting to the Princess de Condé. Born in 1712, Marie Eléonore was cousin in the fifth degree to Claire Clémence de Maillé de Brézé, who was a niece of the Cardinal de Richelieu and who had married the great Condé.

Thus by his marriage the Count de Sade became united by marriage to the younger branch of the royal house of Bourbon, thereby introducing a new element into the family of the Sades, who had originally been Italian and up to then exclusively Provençal.

The first child was not born till 1737. This was Caroline Laure, who had the Prince and Princess of Condé for godparents; she lived only two years. On June 2nd 1740 the Countess de Sade gave birth to her second child, Donatien Alphonse François, and six years later, to a third, Marie Françoise, baptised on the same day in the church of St Sulpice. No author has ever made mention of this little girl. The author came upon a reference to her birth in the *Mercure de France* of August 1746. Marie Françoise, whose name does not appear in the genealogical tree of the house of Sade which was kept at the Condé-en-Brie *château*, must have lived for only a week or two.

After the death of the Princess de Condé, which took place on June 14th 1741, one year after that of the Prince, the Countess de Sade, whose functions as lady-in-waiting were now over, nevertheless stayed on in the Condé mansion, where she no doubt helped to bring up the young Louis Joseph de Bourbon, orphaned by the death of his father and mother. Towards 1745 she seems frequently to have been absent from Paris, no doubt accompanying the Count on his diplomatic missions. About 1760 she retired to the Carmelite convent in the rue de l'Enfer, and died on January 14th 1777.

THE UNCLES AND AUNTS

Gaspard François, Marquis de Sade, had had ten children by his wife, Louise Aldonse d'Astoaud de Murs.

1. There was Jean Baptiste Joseph François, Donatien Alphonse François's father.

2. There was Richard Jean Louis, born in 1703 and made a Knight of the Order of St John of Jerusalem in 1715. He served in the war in Italy in 1732 as aide-de-camp to the Marshal de Villars and the Count de Broglie. Later he was appointed Commander of his order, then became Bailiff and Grand Prior of Toulouse.

3. Next came Jacques François Paul Aldonse, known as the Abbé of Sade, and born in the Mazan *château* on September 21st 1705. Vicar-General of Toulouse in 1733, then of Narbonne in 1735, he received a pension of 2,000 *livres* from the Archbishop of Arles by Royal decree of August 20th 1741, and was entrusted with a mission at Court by the Estates of Languedoc. In 1744 he was granted the monastery of Ebreuil in the diocese of Limoges.

In 1762 we see that the Abbé was imprisoned for some days because of a bout of debauchery, for on May 25th of that year we find the King ordering "the release of Paul Aldonse de Sade, aged 50, priest of the diocese of Avignon, commendatory abbot of the monastery of Ebreuil, taken in Paris in the house of the woman named Piron, given to debauchery, together with the prostitute named Léonore".

The amorous propensities of the Abbé, who lived in Paris for a considerable period in intimate relations with Mme de la Popelinière, mistress of the Marshal de Saxe, did not escape his friend Voltaire. On November 25th 1733, the author of the *Henriade* addressed the following to him:

"I hear you are going to be priest and vicar general. What a lot of holiness all at once in one family! So that's why you tell me you are going to renounce love-making.

> So do you really persuade yourself
> that when you once possess
> the dismal title of vicar-general
> you will all at once turn your back
> on love and the great art of pleasing?
> Oh, however much a priest you may be,
> you, my dear sir, will still make love;
> were you bishop or Holy Father
> you would make love and take your pleasure,
> that is your real ministry,
> You will make love and you will take your pleasure
> and always be most successful
> both in the church and in Cytherea."

By a deed dated March 7th 1760, the Abbé de Sade acquired the life enjoyment of the lands and mansion of Saumane from his elder brother, for an annual rent of 2,700 *livres,* payable from 1764. But from 1745 on we find him equally at Saumane and Ébreuil, accompanied by his young nephew Donatien Alphonse François, with whose education he was charged. Later he established himself at la Vignerme, a dependency of the *château* of Saumane. It was under the same vault of heaven that illuminated the love between Laura and Petrarch that the Abbé wrote his graceful *Notes for the life of François Petrarch* (1764-1767), which no doubt enlivened the gloomy solitude of the prisoner of Vincennes. Both in the Bibliothèque Nationale and in private collections there are a number of unpublished letters of the Abbé de Sade which, like his *Petrarch,* reveal the rare delicacy of his style and the purity of his language, which is often extremely moving.

In the course of this work we shall gradually sketch in the outlines of that aristocrat of an Abbé, learned and of highly cultivated tastes, who in his Saumane retreat never tired of unravelling the story of that great romance in the county of Vancluse. The marquis's uncle finally died at his Vignerme residence on December 31st 1778.

4. After Jacques was born Jean Baptiste Henri Victor, a Maltese Knight, who must have died before his father, since he does not appear in the latter's will.

5. Next there was Antoine Félix Toussaint, who died in infancy. After him came :

6. Gabrielle Laure, born in 1700, later to be Abbess of St Laurent of Avignon. The Bibliothéque Nationale possesses a number of letters exchanged between this nun and her brother the Count de Sade.

7. Gabrielle Eléonore, abbess of St Benoît of Cavaillon, followed, and after her

9. Marguerite Félicité, a nun in the Convent of St Bernard of Cavaillon.

10. The last child was Henriette Victoire, who in 1733 married Ignace, Marquis de Villenueve, lord of the manor of Martignan and of St Maurice. There were three daughters of that marriage, Lady de Raousset and Julie and Henriette de Martignan. It was for Lady de Villeneuve-Martignan that the Avignon architect J. B. Franque built that delightful mansion which today houses the Calvet Museum.

BIRTH AT THE CONDÉ MANSION

The Condé mansion, which occupied almost all the ground enclosed today by the rue de Condé, the rue de Vaugirard, the rue Monsieur-le-Prince and the Odéon intersection, was originally built out in the country, outside the walls of Philippe Auguste's Paris, by Antoine de Corbie, first President of the High Court of Paris. Under Charles IX it belonged to Albert de Gondi, the royal favourite, who let it to Catherine de Medici for two or three years. Philippe Emmanuel de Gondi, father of the famous Cardinal de Retz, became bankrupt and his mansion was seized. In 1610 it was given to Henri de Bourbon, Prince of Condé, by Marie de Medici, to reward him for marrying Charlotte Marguerite de Montmorency, with whom

King Henri IV was in love, and the mansion was restored and largely rebuilt by its new owner. The Condé family kept it till the reign of Louis XVI. In 1773 the ground was sold for 4,168,107 *livres*, streets were driven through it and it was split up into building plots.

"It was a vast conglomeration of buildings which were already old, with wings separated by cramped inner courts," writes Maurice Heine, "with awkward enclaves under different ownerships, but the main block of buildings opened on to a huge garden in French style, divided from the parade court-yard by an iron railing which rose in three stages to face the Palace Luxembourg in the rue de Vaugirard."

This garden was so spacious that when the Luxembourg had to be closed, the gates in the Condé railings were opened and the crowd easily found room inside.

It was in this palace, where the young Countess de Sade had her apartment, as lady-in-waiting to her relation, the Princess de Condé, that on June 2nd 1740 Donatien Alphonse François was born. His father was away at the time, having been sent as ambassador to the Court of Cologne. The very next day, June 3rd, with neither of his godparents (his maternal grandfather and paternal grandmother) present, the newly born babe was held out over the font of the parish church of St Sulpice by two servants.

"Today, June 3rd, Donatien Alphonse François, born yesterday, was baptised, son of the eminent and powerful Lord Jean Baptiste François, Count de Sade, Lieutenant General of the provinces of Bresse, Bugey, Valromey and Gex, lord of the manor of Mazan and other places, and the eminent and powerful Lady Eléonore de Maillé de Carman his spouse, resident at the Condé mansion. The eminent and powerful Lord Donatien de Maillé, Marquis de Carman, grandfather of the child, represented by Antoine Bequelin, officer of the Marquis de Sade, the mother-in-law Alphonse Dastuaud de Murs, grand-mother of the child, represented by Silvine Bedié, wife of Abel Le Gouffe, officer of the house, the father being absent not signing.

[signed] Bequelin, Bedié, Bachoud (Vicar)."

Donatien Alphonse François—of these three Christian names, only the first was the choice of the family. The Countess de Sade had asked the two servants who represented the godparents to have the child christened Louis Aldonse Donatien. But the ancient Provençal name of Aldonse was unknown in Paris and either the servants or the priest transformed it into Alphonse, while Louis was quite plainly forgotten altogether on the way to church and replaced by François, which was one of his father's names.

However, the Marquis de Sade was not going to allow this to deprive him of the names originally designed for him; in the great majority of the official documents which he signed subsequent to being invalided out of the army no regard whatever was had to the names with which he was actually baptized. Thus, to choose from the many examples, in his marriage contract he appears as Louis Aldonse Donatien, while in the record of his interrogation on June 10th 1768 (the Rose Keller case) he is recorded as claiming to be known as Louis Aldonse Donatien de Sade. His letter of April 19th 1792 to the Constitutional Club of La Coste is signed *Louis Sade* while in his arrest warrant of March 22nd 1794 (in the Madelonettes records) he had himself described as François Aldonse Donatien Louis! We shall see later that these caprices of nomenclature were to be cause the Marquis de Sade considerable trouble, when after the Revolution he sought to be struck off the list of *émigrés*.

THE CHILD

We have only one single record of those early years when little Donatien Alphonse François lived with his mother in the Condé mansion and was playmate of Prince Louis Joseph de Bourbon, his senior by four years.* It is autobiographical, and we find it in the novel *Aline and Valcour*.

*The son of Louis Henri, Duke de Bourbon, Prince de Condé and Princess Caroline de Hesse-Rheinfels-Rothenburg. Born in Paris August 9th 1736, married May 3rd 1752, to Charlotte Godefride Elisabeth de Rohan-Soubise, widowed March 4th 1760. He served with distinction in the Seven Years War and helped to win the battle of Johannesberg (1762). When the Revolution began, he was one of the first to leave France and in 1789 began to assemble on the bank of the Rhine that *émigré* army known as "Condé's army." After the restoration, he returned in the suite of Louis XVIII, who made him his Grand Chamberlain and Colonel-General of Infantry. It is to him that we owe the erection of the Palais-Bourbon. He died at Chantilly in 1818.

Allied through my mother with all the grandest in the kingdom, and connected through my father with all that was most distinguished in Languedoc—born in Paris in the heart of luxury and plenty—as soon as I could think I concluded that nature and fortune had joined hands to heap their gifts on me. This I thought because people were stupid enough to tell me so, and that idiotic presumption made me haughty, domineering and ill-tempered. I thought everything should give way before me, that the entire universe should serve my whims, and that I merely needed to want something, to be able to have it. I will relate only one incident of my childhood to convince the reader how dangerous were the notions which, with such utter folly, they allowed me to foster.

As I was born and brought up in the mansion of the distinguished nobleman whom my mother had the honour to serve, and who was approximately of my age, the family made every effort to bring him and me together, so that by reason of our having known each other since infancy I might enjoy his support at every turn in my life; but such was my impetuous wilfulness, in my utter ignorance of this scheme, that the day came when in our boyish games I took offence because he would not give way to me in something, and still more because—no doubt with very good reason—he thought himself justified by his rank in what he did. I replied to his obstinacy by hitting him time and again; nothing could stop me, and it was only by force, indeed, by quite violent means, that I was finally separated from my opponent.

On August 16th 1744 the municipality of Saumane sent its consuls and secretary to Avignon to represent it and "offer its compliments to My Lord the Marquis de Sade, the Lord Count of this place, on the occasion of his happy arrival at Avignon, and to wish him long years and good fortune as the titulary successor of his father". This clearly indicates when Donatien-Alphonse François was sent to the County of Vignon. The paragraph of *Aline and Valcour* immediately following the passage quoted above tells us what prompted the Countess de Sade to send her son away. "About this time my father was employed on some diplomatic mission and my mother travelled to join him. . . . I was sent to my grandmother in Languedoc and her blind affection for me fostered all the defects I have just confessed."

Was it to the exclusive care of his paternal grandmother, in the old Sade mansion which still rears its 15th century Gothic front in Avignon, that the future author of *Juliette* was consigned? Most likely his five maternal aunts—Madame de Villeneuve-Martignan (mother of three daughters), the Abbess of St Laurent d'Avignon and the Abbess of St Benoît de Cavaillon and nuns Anne Marie Lucrèce and Marguerite Félicité—also craved to have their turn each with the fair-headed child who was the only male representative of their ancient line.

It was most likely towards the end of 1745 or early in 1746 that the Abbé de Sade d'Ebreuil took the place of his mother or his sisters in the education of Donatien Alphonse François, for now it was the biographer of Petrarch who provided the boy with two homes, one at St Léger d'Ebrueil and the other at Saumane, where he led the life of an aristocrat with an avid curiosity about everything, but especially the ancient world rather than that of a servant of Holy Church. But by the time the young marquis had reached his tenth year, the Abbé de Sade no doubt thought it would be difficult for him to teach his nephew beyond the rudiments of knowledge, and it was decided to send the boy back to Paris, where he continued his studies in the Louis le Grand College (formerly Clermont College), a Jesuit institution in the rue St Jacques. In addition, the boy was provided with a personal tutor, the Abbé Jacques François Amblet, a tonsured priest of the diocese of Geneva. Here is how the marquis describes his teacher, in those few autobiographical pages of *Aline and Valcour*: "I returned to Paris to study under the guidance of a man who was both severe and intelligent and who would probably have exerted a good influence on my youth, but unfortunately I did not keep him long enough."

Of the four years that Donatien Alphonse François spent in the Louis le Grand College we know absolutely nothing. No family letters relating to these years have been discovered, and when the Jesuits were expelled in 1762 most of the records relating to pupils perished. It is always possible that the archives of the Jesuit order contain some information on the pupil who was to write *Juliette,* but unfortunately these are not open to the public. Failing any such records of this period of de Sade's life, we are obliged to be content with giving a brief outline of what the Louis le Grand College was. From a strict biographical standpoint we can be precise about only one point : in the list of end-of-year prizes, to be found among the *lycée* records, not once do we find the name of the young Marquis de Sade between 1750 and 1754.

It must have been in 1682 that Clermont College, said to be a royal foundation, acquired its present name. It had been instituted in 1563 by Guillaume de Prat, Bishop of Clermont, who had observed the fine qualities of the first spiritual sons of Ignatius de Loyola and provided them with a home in his own mansion in the rue de la Harpe. When the Bishop died the Jesuits and their pupils moved to the rue St Jacques, in the heart of the school quarter. In the mid-eighteenth century there were as many as 3,000 pupils, about 2,500 day boys and 500 boarders. Most of the latter slept in dormitories, each under the charge of a *praefectus cubiculi,* some score of them living together. Other more fortunate boarders had their own private rooms, in which they lived with their valets, their tutors, or their private prefects. The daily time-table of the school was :

MORNING	AFTERNOON AND EVENING
a.m.	p.m.
5.30 Rise	1.15 School work
6.00 Prayers	4.30 Snack and
6.15 Study of Holy Writ	recreation
7.45 Breakfast and	5.00 School work
recreation	7.15 Supper and
8.15 School work in studies	recreation
or class-rooms	8.45 Prayers
10.30 Mass	9.00 Bed
11.30 Private Study	
12.00 Dinner and	
recreation	

A list of plays presented at the school during the years 1750-1753 suggests that there were more recreations than the somewhat austere time-table would imply. They may also account for the interest the marquis was to show later on in the art of comedy and in dramatic literature as a whole.

In all probability the young Marquis de Sade entered the College in 1750 as a day-boy, for it would seem unlikely that his father's financial misfortunes would have permitted private apartments. But on the other hand, if he had joined in a common dormitory, it is hard to see how his private tutor, the Abbé Amblet, fitted in. We presume that Donatien Alphonse François lodged either with his tutor in the rue des Fossés Monsieur le Prince, "across the road from the wheelwright's", or else in the Condé mansion itself, which was not far from the rue St Jacques, in the countess's own apartments, whether she was constantly in residence at the time or mainly absent from Paris because of her husband's negotiations at foreign courts.

CHAPTER THREE

From Birth to Marriage

(part two)

1754 - 1763

THE SOLDIER

ALTHOUGH WHEN one turns to this period of de Sade's life one is not in such impenetrable darkness as that which envelops his four college years, the fragmentary records which come into our hands concerning the Marquis de Sade's military career scarcely offer more than a series of transfers and a few details of his private life when on leave. The Sade file in the French Army Records offers merely a dozen fragments of varying interest, four of them dating from after his retirement in 1763 as cavalry captain. To those one should add an autobiographical passage in *Aline and Valcour,* a highly impersonal account of the 1758 campaign, a somewhat more vivid letter in his hand written from camp at Obertistein and sparse indications in various works of his in manuscript and among his father's letters.

1754

Scarcely fourteen, the Marquis de Sade left the Louis le Grand College. On May 24th the genealogist Clairambault furnished him with a certificate of nobility which enabled him to enter the cavalry training school founded towards 1740 by a M. Bongars and in 1751 attached to the Light Horse Regiment of the Royal Guards, garrisoned at Versailles. This school cost three thousand *livres* a year. It accepted only young men of the most ancient nobility, and was a rival to a similar establishment attached to the Musketeers. As with the latter discipline and teaching were rigorous. The pupils trained on foot as well as in the saddle and manoeuvred in battalions as well as squadrons. The King had a soft spot in his heart for the Light Horse College and often inspected it.

1755

On December 14th 1755, after serving twenty months in the Light Horse School, de Sade was appointed unpaid sub-lieutenant in the King's own infantry regiment.

1757

On January 14th 1757, de Sade was granted a commission as Cornet (standard-bearer*) in the Carbine Regiment of the Count of Provence (St André Brigade), commanded by the Marquis de Poyanne, and took part in the war against Prussia.

"The campaigning began," wrote the Marquis de Sade, in an autobiographical passage of *Aline and Valcour,* "and I have no doubt but that I gave a good account of myself. The natural impetuosity of my character, that fiery soul with which Nature endowed me, served but to enhance that unflinching savagery which men call courage and which—quite wrongly, I don't doubt—is regarded as the one indispensable quality in our make-up."

On April 1st, still with the rank of Cornet, he was transferred to the Malvoisin brigade of the Carbine regiment.

1759

On April 21st 1759, Sade was promoted captain in the Burgundy Horse, one of a number of replacements of captains taken prisoner.

The Bibliothèque Nationale possesses a document of four pages (annotated in three places in the Count de Sade's hand) containing the copy of a letter from his son the marquis, and another from a M. de Castéra, no doubt a young officer who was the Marquis's travelling companion. These letters, although undated, can be attributed to April 1759, when the Marquis was on his way back to the army in Germany after a long spell of leave, perhaps six months, which had preceded his appoint-

*This rank had just been re-introduced by the King, in the preceding January.

ment as captain in the Burgundy cavalry. This letter, which gives us interesting information on the beginnings of the Marquis's love life, is at the same time the earliest piece of writing of our author that we possess.

In the Count de Sade's hand we read : "Copy of a letter which he (*sc. the Marquis*) wrote to the Abbé (*this must be the Abbé Amblet*)* which has greatly annoyed me, for I did not want anybody to know what he had done."

And here is the letter, copied in an unknown hand.

"Saint Dizier, the 25th inst.

All the misdeeds I committed while in Paris, my dear Abbé, and the way I treated the fondest father in the world make him regret ever having caused me to be at all. But my remorse at having displeased him and the fear of having lost his affection for ever may be sufficient punishment. Now all that remains of those pleasures which I thought real is the most bitter grief at having outraged the fondest of fathers and best of friends. I rose every morning to run in search of pleasure and the thought of it made me oblivious of all else. I believed myself fortunate the moment I found it, but what seemed happiness evaporated as quickly as my desires, leaving me but regrets. By evening I was desperate and saw my mistake, but that was the evening; with a new day there were my desires back again, and back I flew to pleasure. I would quite forget what I had thought the evening before. At the suggestion of a love bout I accepted, thought I enjoyed myself, then saw I had merely committed follies and not enjoyed myself at all in my heart of hearts. Now the more I think about my conduct the stranger it seems to me. I see how right my father was when he said that three-quarters of what I did was just showing off. Oh, had I but done only what really gave me pleasure, I would have spared myself much anguish and would have hurt my father's feelings less. Was it indeed possible that I thought the girls I saw would really be able to afford me pleasure? Alas, does one really enjoy the happiness that one buys, and

*These copies of de Sade's letters were probably sent to the Count's Abbé brother in Provence.

can love-making devoid of delicacy ever be truly heartfelt? Now my pride suffers when I tell myself that they only loved me because I paid perhaps a little more generously than the others.

I have just received a letter from my father. He wants me to make a general confession. I shall do so, and, I assure you, it will be sincere; I have no more intention of pretence with so fond a father, especially since he is ready to forgive me if I admit all my misdeeds to him.

Goodbye, dear Abbé, give me your news, please, though I shall only get it late, for as I cannot stop anywhere, I can only get your letters after I'm back in the army. So, my dear Abbé, do not be surprised if you get no news from me till I get there."

There follows another note in the Count's hand : "Copy of a letter from M. de Castéra, from Saint Didier." Another letter in the same unknown hand as the other follows.

"The dear son is very well indeed, he is charming, gentle, entertaining, but [*three indecipherable words, as the top of the page is worn*] that he might possibly want while we are staying here—partly on trifling business of my own and partly through his goodwill. Travelling is filling him out again and putting colour back in his cheeks, which the pleasures of Paris had somewhat changed; [*indecipherable*] is a treasure which I implore him to value. Our mounts harass us each in turn; he eats badly and is lame (shoe trouble); he declares it to be malice, because when it can break free it leaps about like a goat. Mine is withergalled, but I have hopes we shall pull through all right. He [*sc. Sade*] leaves behind him and himself carries away regrets from every halt. His little heart or rather *body* is frightfully inflammable : 'ware the German wenches! I shall do all I can to prevent his doing anything silly. He has given me his word not to gamble more than a *louis* a day in the army. But that's a secret I will not tell you. Your kindness and the flattering signs of your friendship, etc."

Here the Count comments : "Just imagine, the young rascal has a *louis* a day to lose [*two indecipherable words follow*]; he promised me he would not gamble a *sou,* but whether he said so or not it is all the same. Still, there's no need to get worked up. This M. de Castéra is but twenty and has never done anything silly; he is so surprised he should be a libertine that he bears no grudge.

"I have received a letter from a man from Sault which I send you. Since he is bearing the costs, there would be no risk in going ahead with the matter. I enclose a proxy for it. Write and tell him I have his letter."

March 4th 1760. By letters patent the Count de Sade relinquished his office of Lieutenant-General of the King for the provinces of Bresse, Bugey, Valromey and Gex.

1762

The Marquis de Sade acquired the right to a gendarmerie pennant, but was obliged to decline it, owing to lack of funds for the purchase of the right.

February 2nd 1763. The Count de Sade wrote to tell his brother the Abbé that on discharge cavalry captains get only 600 *livres,* which is retained to pay the debts of the unit, and this affects his son. He also says that the Marquis (no doubt now on leave pending discharge, since the preliminaries to the peace treaty had been signed at Fontainebleau the previous November 3rd) "never misses a ball or a show : outrageous"! He had not been to see his father, being involved in some sort of rustic carousing. The major of his regiment had told M. de Saint German "frightful things" about him.

February 10th 1763. Signature of the Paris Treaty ended the Seven Years' War.

March 16th 1763. The Marquis de Sade was discharged with the rank of cavalry captain. It was customary to discharge a large number of officers and soldiers in this way at the end of every war. Officers thus discharged did not thereby lose their rank and if in good health could ultimately either rejoin their unit or enter some other. This is how the Marquis de Sade came to serve again as officer from 1767 to 1770.

LADY LAURE DE LAURIS

For some years now the financial position of the Count de Sade had been most unsound. Despite their number and extent, his Provençal estates must have brought him in much less than they brought his farmers and managers,* nor does it seem that his diplomatic achievements brought any very tangible recognition from the King. In his letters the Count often complains of his health, and he seems to lack that modicum of energy which might have helped him to restore his fortunes. He was now a misanthropic hermit, living separated from his wife (she in a Carmelite Convent, he in the Foreign Missions building in the rue du Bac). This does not mean that husband and wife had quarrelled. It was merely that the Count found it hard to bear anybody near him, except his personal valet. At the end of 1762 his affairs were in a particularly sorry state. "Everything here has been seized," he wrote to his *abbé* brother at the time, and in another letter, no doubt dramatising the situation a little, he complained that he was dying of poverty and obliged to do without even necessaries.

But there were other causes for worry, caused by his son's conduct, which daily added to his melancholy concern about health and money. We have already seen in the letter of February 2nd 1763 how the dissipated life that the Marquis led exasperated him. The young fellow had the worst of reputations. He was a gambler, he was a spendthrift and he was profligate. He hung round stage doors and frequented the houses of procuresses. To make it worse, he had not a thought for the future and omitted to pay his respects to the King. Because of a duel with M. de Soyecourt he had had to borrow money. He was capable of the worst extravagance. The Count had had "a

*The revenues of the Provence estates amounted to about 18,000 *livres* and the office of Lieutenant-general of Bresse brought in 10,000, so good management ought to have enabled the Count to spare himself those financial worries of which his letters are full. Was not his impecuniosity subsequent to 1750 due to either his mismanagement or his prodigality, as P. Bourdin suggests in the following excellent portrait? "He was a meticulous and rather grim person, a great lord aloof to the point of extreme frigidity, stiff in both manner and language, as pompous to his family as to his servants, most jealous of his rights, rigid to the point of narrowness, yet liberal to prodigality. He ruined himself with compunction and modesty without seeming ever to have had a notion what he was doing . . ."

terrible letter" from "M. de Ch." to whom his son had written things most unseemly for a man of his position.

His patience exhausted, ever apprehensive of some new outrageous escapade of "that young rascal", the Count sometimes contemplated leaving Paris altogether, so that he might hear no more talk about Donatien Alphonse François. Yet he knew only too well that to remove himself physically from his son's neighbourhood would in no way protect him from the consequences of the young man's conduct. There was only one possible way of freeing himself from this son "who has not a single good feature in him", and that was to find him a wife. Then he would no longer depend on his father. Besides, marriage might make him mend his ways.

The Marquis never showed any objection to such a proposal, though for some time now he had been saying that he would never marry save "whom his heart dictated". There had already been talk of an engagement with a girl of Hesdin whom the young captain must have met when his regiment was quartered in that city, and more recently a Mlle de Cambis, another country girl, had been in the running. But to this person the Count preferred Lady Renée Pélagie de Montreuil, who was a daughter of the President of the Taxation Court and whose fortune and connections seemed much more profitable. In any case, Paris was no place for a spendthrift husband to live in.

But let us leave the story of the engagement to Lady de Montrueil to the next chapter and turn for the moment to something hitherto undisclosed—the Marquis's love affair with Lady Laure de Lauris, whose hand he was still hoping to win a mere fortnight before his actual marriage to Lady Renée Pélagie! In 1948 a stroke of luck led to the discovery of this other *fiancée* in unpublished correspondence of the Sade family which Maurice Heine left to the Bibliothèque Nationale and never had time to examine. Soon after that discovery, chance again guided the author to fresh sources, which brought still more information about Lady Laure de Lauris, the young lady of the manor of Vacqueyras. She was one of the most seductive heroines in the love life of the Marquis de Sade!

Born at Avignon on June 8th 1741, Laure Victoire Adeline de Lauris was the daughter of Louis Joseph François de

Castellane de Lauris des Gérards de Vassadel, generally known as the Marquis de Lauris, *Syndic* of the nobility of the County of Avignon, and of Marie Madeleine Gabrielle de Rivière de Bruis. The house of Lauris, one of the most illustrious in Provence, goes back to the 13th century. In 1233 Hugues de Lauris, the first of the name, was in that famous duel when one hundred noblemen selected by Charles I of Anjou fought the King of Aragon's men. His arms were *in a field argent three bars, two gules and the centre one sinople.* The author has had the pleasure of meeting the present-day representative of this ancient family, Marquis Georges de Lauris, author of novels and reminiscences and sometime friend of Marcel Proust. Unfortunately, the present Marquis was unable to offer information on his ancestor, but it seems certain that after her liaison with de Sade she never married. She had a brother, Louis Joseph Marie André Gabriel, born at Avignon on November 30th 1738, who was a talented painter.

References in two unpublished letters of the Count de Sade to his Abbé brother, and two others, also unpublished, to his sister the Abbess of Saint Laurent, go to show the following : 1. Towards the end of February 1763 the Marquis de Sade was engaged at the same time to Lady Montreuil and to Lady Laure de Lauris; 2. That he preferred the second; 3. That the Count his father was most displeased to see the Marquis following the promptings of his heart and preparing to renounce the financially profitable alliance to the Montreuils; 4. That at the end of April 1763, that is to say, a fortnight before the date fixed for his marriage to Lady de Montreuil, the Marquis was still at Avignon, still trying, despite news which had reached him of her breaking off the engagement, to win the consent of Lady Laure.

The manuscript collection of *Miscellaneous Works* includes a long letter which he wrote to Lady Laure. It throws a vivid light on a love affair which all but ended in marriage and shows us the young marquis the victim of jealousy which was terrible but certainly fully justified, and the violence of which is some excuse for the actual threat of blackmail which he finally made as a desperate last measure.

"To Lady L. de L. . . .

Avignon, April 6th, 1763

Perjurer! Wretch! What has happened to those assurances of life-long devotion? Who has prompted this inconstancy? Who obliges you to break the bonds which were to unite us for ever? Did you take my departure for flight? Did you think I could live and run away from you? I must suppose that you judged the feelings of my heart by your own. I obtain my parents' consent; tears in his eyes, all my father asks of me as a last favour is to come to Avignon and be married there. I leave; I am assured that efforts will now be all concentrated on getting your father to take you to Avignon. I arrive, Heaven alone knows how urgently, in this place which is to witness my good fortune, a lasting good fortune, a good fortune that nothing will ever trouble again. . . . But what becomes of me—dear God, can I ever survive this blow?—what becomes of me when I learn that, inspired by great-hearted emotion, you fall on your knees before your parent to ask him to abandon all thought of this marriage, to tell him you have no desire to be forced into an alliance with some other family. . . . Meaningless reason, dictated by perfidy! You, graceless deceiver—you. Afraid to be united to one who adored you! The bonds of an everlasting chain became burdensome to you and your heart, which only inconstancy and frivolity can seduce, was not sensitive enough to realize all the charms of that bond. It was the idea of leaving Paris that frightened you; my love was not enough, nor was I the one to inspire constancy in you. Well, you can stay there for ever, monster, born to make my life wretched! May all the deceits of the wretch who will take my place in your heart make it one day as loathesome to you as yours have made it in my eyes. . . . But whatever am I saying? Oh, my dear love, oh, my divine love, sole support of my heart, sole delight of my life, is it this that my despair has brought me? Forgive the expressions of an unhappy man who is beside himself and for whom, after the loss of what he loves, death is the only solution. Alas, I draw near to it, to the moment which will free me from the day I loathe; my only desire now is to see that day come round. What can hold me to life, of which you were the sole delight? If I lose you, I lose my existence, my life, I die, and by the cruellest of deaths. . . . I wander, dear love, I am no longer myself; let the tears which blind me flow ... I cannot live with such misfortune. What are you doing? What has become of you? What am I to you? Something horrible? Something you love? Tell me, how do you look upon me? How could you justify your conduct? Heavens, perhaps mine is unjustifiable in your eyes. Oh, if you still love me, if you love me as you have always loved, as I love you, as I adore you, as I will adore you all my life, weep for our misfortunes, weep over the killing blows of fortune, write to me, try to give some reason for what you have done. . . . Alas, the task should not be beyond you : the real torture of my heart is the knowledge that you can contemplate so tragic a mistake. Even to acknowledge your fallibility is some relief! If you love me, I am absolutely sure you have chosen convent life. Do you remember telling me, the last time I saw you, the day of our misfortunes, how you would be delighted if they put you in a convent? If you want us to be able to meet, you know it is the only step you can take, for you know very well that it will be impossible for me to visit your house. When he told me what you had done my father left it to me to stay as long as I chose or to join him at once. What I decide depends on your reply; do not delay it; I shall count the days. Give me the possibility of seeing you when I arrive. I do not doubt for a moment that I shall seize it. If there is nothing definite I shall take it as refusal, refusal will be clear proof of your inconstancy, and your inconstancy will be my death sentence. But I cannot believe you have changed. What reason could there be for it? Perhaps this journey of mine frightened you, but do please try to see that I had genuine *reasons* for it. They blinded me, they made me believe I was running into the embrace of happiness, and all the while they were trying to take me far from it. . . . My dear love, do not leave me, I implore you, ask at once to be placed in a convent. The moment I get your letter, I leave and am at your side. What sweet moments will be born again for us! ... Look after your health; I am doing my best to restore mine. But whatever the state of yours, nothing shall prevent me from giving you the fondest proofs of my love.* In all our affair I think you have reason, and will still have, to be satisfied with my discretion. After all, I have only done what I should, I take no credit for it. ... Beware of inconstancy; it is something I do not deserve and, make no mistake, I should be very angry indeed, there would be nothing too awful for me to do in revenge. The little business of the c—** ought to make you go carefully with me; I assure you I shall not conceal it from my rival, nor will that be the only secret I shall tell him. I swear it, there is no awful length I would not go to. ... But I blush to think of such means of keeping you. I do not want to talk of aught but your love, nor should I. Your promises, your oaths, your letters, which I read incessantly all the time, should be enough to keep you mine, I refer to nothing else. I insist, I implore you not to see ... ; he is unworthy of your even seeing him. ... So now, my dear love, can I count on your constancy? I shall not be away long, I only await a letter from you to leave. ... Let it be a kind letter, I beg you, and let me find the means of seeing you when I get there. There is nothing I crave, or think of, or dream of, but you. ... No, I am not afraid of being effaced from your heart, I have not deserved it. Go on loving me, dear love, and let time do all. Perhaps the time will indeed come when you will no longer fear to enter my family. When I am head of it, my wishes alone will determine my choice, and perhaps I shall then find you more decided. I need consolation, need reassuring, need proof of your constancy; everything frightens me. Your heroic act has been a death blow to me. I assure you that I give you my word

*See note below.
**This may stand for the picturesque term still used popularly for gonorrhea. In a letter (unpublished) the Count wrote to his sister, the Abbess of Saint Laurent, the Marquis is said to be more amorous in love than ever with Lady Laure, who had "made him ill." There seems little doubt, when we remember the advice to look after her health etc., about the truth of this.

of honour that nothing is more certain than what I am now telling you : one word from you and I start out. My father has sent for me again; don't think it is for a marriage. I am very determined not to make any marriage, and would never want to. I am going to use all the means necessary to be sure you get this letter. Don't fail to give the woman who brings it a receipt in these terms : *I acknowledge receipt of a letter from the hand of so-and-so.* Do this exactly, as she is only going to be paid what I have promised her when she brings me the receipt. Don't delay your reply if you want to see me. I count the days. Try to see that I get it very quickly and that when I come I am able to see you. Love me always, be faithful to me unless you want to see me die of sorrow. Adieu, my dear child, I adore you and love you a thousand times more than my life. Away with you, you will say, but I swear to you that we shall never really exist except with one another."

It would appear that Sade's love for Lady Laure de Lauris lasted a long time after his marriage to Lady Renée de Montreuil. The incredible humility of the following letter to her father can hardly be explained but by his longing at all costs to see his former fiancée again on the occasion of a ball which her father gave.

Letter written to the Marquis de L. because for a certain reason he did not invite the author to his ball. "It is as compatriot and relation that I ask what once I would have asked as a friend. The irreproachability of my conduct since eternal bonds prevented my forming those which would have made my life happy did not merit the exception which you seem to have made of me when you gave M. de Vignole your list yesterday. I did not want to importune you in public, but content myself with speaking in private. I beg you, do not make me suffer the mortification I have in no wise merited of being excluded from the party you are giving on Tuesday. The constant cast of my thoughts will always give me claims on your friendship of which misfortune would apparently wish to deprive me but which I will never willingly renounce.

With impatience I await your reply and beg you to believe me, Sir, to be your most humble servant."

The Calvet Museum of Avignon possesses an autograph letter of Lady Laure's. Dated January 11th, and written in an exquisite hand, it is addressed to Lord de Salamon, State Secretary of the Papal Legate at Avignon. In this unpublished letter Lady Laure requests an immediate interview about a matter which she does not state but which seems to move her greatly. In the same museum we have also found a letter of her mother's dated January 10th 1775, addressed to a magistrate of Avignon. This other unpublished document mentions a term of imprisonment to which a Consul of Vacqueyras had been sentenced for gossip which had harmed the daughter of the lord of the manor. And finally, there is a song of that Provençal troubadour Sade about his love : Day and night he sees her in the slightest thing, a rose has her complexion, her feet have trodden the ground where it grows, at night thought of her seduces him with the semblance of love. That love wakens him in the morning and he sees how vain his sacrifice has been. Sometimes he thinks he hears her, he cannot keep the sweet sound of her voice from his ears, and in his heart is nothing but her portrait. Thus, lascivious but brief, the Marquis de Sade's passion for his sometime fiancée, Lady Laure Victoire Adéline de Lauris, soon ended, but left in its wake for long after the overpowering fragrance of what might have been.

HIS MARRIAGE

It would seem to have been early in 1763, and thanks to the intervention of one of Lady Renée de Montreuil's uncles who was at the head of the *Invalides,* that the first marriage negotiations took place between the Count and the family of his future daughter-in-law. What was the social position and what was the material position of that family? Here let Maurice Heine speak. It would not be easy to emulate the delicate precision of the picture he offers of the comparative positions of the Sades and the Montreuils.

"At first glance the choice the Count de Sade made for his son may somewhat surprise us. The man who by his own marriage became allied to the Royal blood has no

bones about accepting for his son a family of the minor
nobility whose origins it would be vain to seek earlier than
the beginning of the 17th century. But was not the disproportion of rank outweighed by the inverse disproportion of their fortunes? The future bride was wealthy, not
in actual dowry, for that was modest enough, but in well
founded prospects. Above all, her parents had good contacts and relations who were particularly powerful at
court. Thus the Count de Sade could hope that, once the
age of passion was over his son might expect certain favours
of the régime. Till that time he would have to live
modestly and economically with a sensible, gentle wife
whose character had been shaped by a mother whose qualities of intelligence and character had proved themselves.
Finally, it might well prove sound policy to ally a family
which till then had lived almost exclusively by the church
and the sword to a family of politicians and magistrates.

The wealth of the Cordier family seems to have been
due to Jacques René Cordier, war treasurer of the towns
of Berghe and Furnes. . . . Born at Strasbourg November
23rd 1683, Jacques René Cordier, squire of Launay, on
May 25th 1711 married Anne Thérèse Croëzer. . . . It
was of this marriage that Claude René Cordier de Launay
was born who on August 22nd 1740 at Saint Eustache
married Marie Madeleine Masson de Plissay, herself of a
family of equally recent nobility. The Massons became
allied to the Baguenauts, the Partyrets and the Boillots,
then on June 4th 1719 Jean Masson de Plissay, son of
Antoine Masson, Groom, Counsellor and Royal Secretary, married Marie Pélagie Partyret, born at Versailles.
Marie Madeleine Masson was their daughter."

Here we must note that in a number of letters to his wife
written from Vincennes and from the Bastille, the Marquis—
being justifiably furious with the spouse of the President of the
Court of Taxation who was responsible for his long captivity-
did not hesitate to set down regrets which were not only super-
cilious, but even insulting, about a marriage which he now
made out to consider a real social mistake. Thus in 1783 we
find him addressing his wife as follows:

"Do please inform me if it is my Cordier mother-in-law or my Fouloiseau father-in-law who is against my having a change of shirts. Prisoners at the *Hôpital* can be refused a change of linen, not me. Both your own low origin and that of your parents comes out in everything! My dear, when I forgot what I was even to the extent of being prepared to sell you what I am, although that may have been done to provide you with a shift, it was certainly not in order to be deprived of one myself. Do not forget that phrase, you and your crowd, till I have had it printed."

In the same year that his son and Marie Madeleine de Plissay married, Jacques René de Launay bought the baronial estate of Echauffour in Normandy and also the dependent manor of Montreuil-Largillé from the Marquis de Pont Saint Pierre. It was the latter title that Claude René assumed. On May 24th 1743, he was appointed President of the Taxation Court of Paris, a dignity he retained till July 17th 1754, when Jacques Charpentier de Boisgibault succeeded him. When his daughter and the Marquis de Sade were betrothed, Lord Montreuil was already merely Honorary President.

The *Dictionary of the Nobility* published in Paris in 1772 and even La Chesnaye-Desbois' famous list fail to tell us what descendants the President of Montreuil and Marie Madéline de Plissay had, and today we can only record precisely four issues of their union. Yet it seems that they had more at least if we judge from a passage in one of the Marquis's letters to his wife—"The Montreuil Président's good lady," he said, "who has presented her husband with seven or eight bastards. . . ."

Those of whom we know for certain are Renée Pélagie, the Marquise de Sade to be, born in Paris December 3rd 1741 and baptised next day at the church of Saint Eustache, Anne Prospère, known as Lady de Launay, whom we shall have to discuss at length in Chapter 6, Françoise Pélagie, born October 12th 1760, who married the Marquis de Wavrin towards the end of January, 1783 and died February 9th 1837, and Marie Joseph, who served in the army.

Claude René de Montreuil himself was the most obscure of men. He was never to play any part in the life of his son-in-law, and was completely under his wife's thumb. Of the lady herself P. Bourdin (who excels as portraitist when those he describes are not above his comprehension) would have given us a faithful picture "had he not unfortunately", as Maurice Heine puts it, "been stirred by the appalling malice which constantly ruled the mother-in-law". We shall therefore take only the most reliable touches of that portrait, since we are going to see Lady Montreuil in action, when she came to take an inhuman revenge which neither the pleas of the *Marquise* her daughter, nor the desperate appeals of the prisoner of Vincennes and the Bastille were capable of softening.

> "It is she who runs it all and she to whom everybody, even including the Marquis, turns. . . . She makes the decisions and acts with all the prejudices of her kind, and she rules the motives which prompt her to action too. She does whatever is necessary to attain her end and is never worried by the rights or the troubles of anybody else. . . . She turns a blind eye to or scorns whatever does not suit her plans, but the methods she uses are as elastic and varied as her aim is clearly defined. She is capable simultaneously of seducing, browbeating and bribing, using everybody else's influence, but sparing her own. All the resources of trickery are at her disposal and she never fails to make rapid progress over any obstacle. Her great word is 'security', and none knows better than she what provides this without endangering success. . . . She always thinks of everything at the right time and never needs to regret a setback or find a culprit. What is past ceases to mean anything to her. She is without regrets and without remorse. . . .
>
> . . . She uses simple unstudied language which make one aware what ought to be and what can be, without drawing particular attention to herself. The correctness of her stratagems and the unaffected wisdom of her way of seeing things put everything in the place required by custom and good manners, by maintenance of appearances, by the proprieties to be observed and by the advantages to be sought. . . ."

The wife of the President of Montreuil, in fact, was

dazzled by the thought of a marriage which would ally her family to a house connected with the Royal blood. The brilliance of such a union made her close her eyes to the bad reputation of the proposed son-in-law and become indulgent to a young man's peccadilloes. Here it may be added that it was precisely because of that evil reputation that many a previous proposal of marriage had come to nought.

However, the Count de Sade did all he possibly could to deceive the Montreuils as to the real character of his son. In a letter to his sister the Abbess we find him reproaching himself for this lack of honesty. The young Marquis was only apparently a gentle creature; in reality he was obstinacy itself. In March and April 1763, madly in love with Lady Laure de Lauris, who had not shrunk from becoming his mistress, he went so far as to compromise his father's negotiations with Lady Montreuil.

Despite all her good will, the wife of the Taxation Court President soon became rather cool about her future son-in-law, especially when certain news reached her from Avignon, for she was all at once informed that the Marquis was dallying in that city in order to prepare to marry the de Lauris girl! It needed all the diplomacy of the Count de Sade—who had himself decided to agree to this latter marriage, then discovered that if it took place it would be likely to produce a number of embarrassing repercussions—to convince the President's lady that he had thought all arrangements with the Montreuils were firm, and this was the reason why he had sent his son to Avignon. The Marquis had gone to prepare the house there since he proposed to live in that city. And no doubt because the Count foresaw the young man's stubbornly staying on in Avignon, hoping against hope that Lady Laure would join him there, he asked his brother the Abbé to write him a fictitious letter telling him that the young Marquis had gone down with an attack of fever and he did not propose to send him back till he was really better!

But at last, despite the costliness of such a mode of travel, there at the very last moment was the *fiancé* coming in from Avignon by post chaise, though we should add that he also brought with him two or three dozen artichokes, produce of Saumane or La Coste, and a pot of tunny paste bought cheaply, which could be set against the terrible cost of the journey.

The letter already referred to, which Donatien Alphonse François's father wrote to the Abbess of Saint Laurent, serves well to acquaint us with the state of mind of the Sade and Montreuil families only a few days before the marriage of their offspring.

"I think the latest mail from Avignon has told Lady Montreuil everything. This and the other business have made her terribly frigid regarding my son, but there's no going back on it now : Whatever face he puts on it, I keep things going a bit by my efforts, my courtesies, my little attentions. The whole family seems to like me. I dine and spend every day with one or other of them. They see nobody else and you cannot imagine how attentive they are to me. I cannot help regretting the acquisition they are about to make, and reproach myself for deceiving them about their future son-in-law's character. In his last letter the Abbé agrees that nothing is less gentle than he is. When I told him that before, he wouldn't believe me and kept assuring me that he could do whatever he liked with my son. The only gentle thing about him is his voice, but from the smallest things to the biggest, you can't make him change. I expect I shall be in a hurry to leave Paris the moment he lives there. . . ."

"Whatever face he puts on it," wrote the Count of his son. It was the face of a *fiancé* who did little enough to hide his mortification and who was heartbroken for Laure de Lauris. But at any rate the marriage was certain to take place. On May 1st at Versailles it was honoured by the consent of the King and Queen, the Dauphin and his consort, the Dukes of Berry and of Provence, and Princesses Marie Adélaïde, Sophie Philippe and Louise Marie, the Princes de Condé and de Conti, and Lady de Sens. A glorious, but exhausting day. The Count de Sade returned to Paris with "swollen legs".

On May 15th the contract was signed by the bride and bridegroom-to-be in the Montreuil mansion in the *rue Neuve du Luxembourg,* and the following day the parents and friends, among them sister-in-law Lady Anne Prospère, also signed. There had indeed been a spot of trouble with the Montreuils, because of the avarice of the Countess de Sade. She had refused to part with her diamonds. "A terrible woman," the Count wrote to his Abbé brother, on the wedding day. "Her son takes after her." As for the Count, to get rid of his son he was obliged to do something he never would have done merely from fondness of heart—he borrowed 10,000 francs by mortgaging his property—to dress the bridegroom and his party and to purchase him a suitable carriage with two horses. His sister the Abbess of Saint Laurent, whom he had begged to find the money, had replied by a page full of figures and talk of how she would send the cash, but forgot to complete the transaction! . . .

A lawyer's record of the conclusion of the marriage contract of the Marquis de Sade gives us considerable information, though mainly the business side—the bride's settlement and that of the groom. First, Lady Renée's part. Let us summarise:

1. From her father: 80,000 *livres* on the death of her parent, 10,000 in cash and 1,500 in rents, to be raised to 3,500 on the death of her paternal grandmother.

2. From her mother: 50,000 *livres* on the death of this parent.

3. From Anne Thérèse de Croëzer, widow of Jacques René Cordier de Launay, paternal grandmother of the bride : (a) 120,000 *livres*, of which during the donor's lifetime a rent of 6,000 *livres* was payable and (b) 25,000 *livres* on the inheritance of the main sum, but only after her father's death.

4. From Louise Catherine Cordier de Launay, widow of Henri Louis, Marquis d'Azy : 25,000 *livres* after her demise.

5. The bride's parents to board and lodge the young couple and their two servants both in their Paris mansion and on their estates during the first five years of the marriage, or failing this, to pay them 2,000 *livres* per annum.

6. At the termination of the above five years, the bride's parents to provide 10,000 *livres* for the young couple's household fittings.

Secondly, on the Marquis's side:

The Count de Sade undertook to give his son :

1. His office of Lieutenant-General of the Provinces of Bresse, Bugey etc., bringing in an annual revenue of 10,000 *livres*, a post he had relinquished on March 4th 1760 in favour of a

revenue, the proceeds of which he would pay as from that date. In this respect a certificate of credit of 60,000 *livres* was granted the Marquis by the King.

2. The bare ownership of his lands and manors of La Coste, Mazan, Saumane and Mas de Cabanes, with annual revenue of 18-20,000 *livres,* as of all his other property present or future, the donor nevertheless reserving the freedom to dispose of 30,000 *livres* of the above property.

3. 10,000 of the 34,000 *livres* owed him by the Count and Countess de Béthune, the Marquis de Sade to receive the interest on this as from the date of his marriage.

Finally, the Marquis de Sade granted his wife an annual income of 4,000 *livres,* as dowry, subject to transfer of the capital in favour of any issue of the marriage.

"An interesting contract indeed," wrote Maurice Heine, "since it reveals not merely the state of the young couple's fortunes, but also the intentions of their families." He goes on to remark that "clearly the Count de Sade, as father of a prodigal, libertine son, was concerned not to allow him to amass any sum of capital, a concern which excellently matched the marked miserliness of the Montreuils, who were infinitely more disposed to pay the young couple an allowance than to provide them with a real endowment."

On May 17th 1763, the marriage of the Marquis de Sade and Mlle de Montreuil took place in the church of St Roch.

PHYSICAL PORTRAIT OF THE MARQUIS DE SADE

The Marquis de Sade shares an unusual distinction with that other aristocrat of language, Count de Lautréamont, a distinction unique in the history of the last three or four centuries of literature : to this day not a single portrait of either the author of the *Songs of Maldoror* or of the author of *Juliette* has been found.

We know that Mlle Marie Dorothée de Rousset (who will preoccupy us greatly after 1777), basing herself on a canvas by Van Loo (was it Carle or one of his three nephews?), made a portrait of the Marquis which was in Sade's possession in Vincennes prison. What else do we know about the fate of that picture? It eventually followed the Marquis to his Carmelite apartment and that of Sainte Aure. Most likely, notwithstanding the separation pronounced in 1790 between the spouses, after that the *Marquise* clung to it, for we note that to her dying day she also preserved even the most outrageous of the letters that her husband had written her. What happened to the picture after her death on July 7th 1810 at the family seat of Echauffour? There are three possibilities: (a) Sade's portrait remained at Echauffour, (b) it passed to the second son of the marriage, Donatien Claude Armand (the first son, Louis Marie, having been killed in Italy on the 9th June preceding), or (c) it passed to his daughter, Lady Madeleine Laure de Sade, who died January 18th 1844. We may add that if the portrait did pass to Donatien Claude Armand, we can be fairly sure that in his lack of respect for his father he had no hesitation about burning it, just as he made sure that the police burned the invaluable manuscript of the *Journées de Florbelle*.

Lacking that adaptation of Van Loo's canvas, for the present we must content ourselves with the few facts that follow concerning the outward appearance of the Marquis during fifty years of his life.

April 25th 1759. A note from M. de Castéra to the Count de Sade, written on the road back to the Seven Years War, said (we repeat): "The dear son is very well indeed, he is charming, gentle, entertaining. . . . Travelling is filling him out again and putting colour back in his cheeks which the pleasures of Paris had somewhat changed. . . . His little heart or rather *body* is frightfully inflammable: 'ware the German wenches!'"

May 16th 1763. Lady de Montreuil to the Abbé de Sade: "Your nephew could not be more charming or more desirable as son-in-law, with that genial intelligence of his and that tone of good education that your care seems to have instilled in him."

June 27th 1763. Extract from the minutes of the Marseilles trial: "Shortly afterwards the servant reappeared, with another young man who he said was his master, of medium height, rather fully fleshed, fair haired, wearing a sword, dressed in a grey surcoat and breeches of marigold-coloured silk, and carrying a gold-knobbed stick."

From the same source: " . . . Two men, one of them tall . . . the other smaller, handsome, rather full faced, in a grey surcoat, wearing a sword and carrying a stick. . . ."

December 8th 1793 (Frimaire 18th, Year II). From an arrest warrant: "François Sade, aged 53, native of Paris, author, domiciled at 871, *rue de la ferme des Mathurins*. 5 foot 2 ins, hair and eyebrows fair and greying, high open forehead, clear blue eyes, medium nose, mouth small, chin round, face oval and full. . . ."

May 25th 1787. The *Marquise* de Sade to Lawyer Gaufridy: "He is well, but getting very fat. . . ."

April 20th 1790. Sade to Gaufridy: "While there [Vincennes prison and the Bastille] through lack of exercise I got terribly fat, so I have difficulty in moving."

1802. (A portrait in Charles Nodier's *Memories, Incidents and Portraits of the Revolution and the Empire*, where he deals with the Saint Pélagie Prison.)

"One of these persons rose very early, because he was to be transferred and had been warned of this. All I could see at first was a frightful obesity which so hampered the man's movements that he could not display a vestige of that grace and elegance, hints of which are to be seen in his general comportment. Yet the weary eyes still preserved a hint of brilliance and subtlety which flare up from time to time like a dying spark in a dead coal."

From the same source:

"I have said that this prisoner merely passed under my gaze. All I recall is that he was obsequiously polite, effusively affable and spoke with respect of everything that is respected."

November 1814 (Charenton). From Dr L. J. Ramon's *Notes on the Marquis de Sade, 1867*. "I often came upon him, walking alone, with heavy, dragging gait, most carelessly dressed, in the corridors near the room which he occupied. I never once saw him talking to anybody. When I passed him, I would salute him, and he would respond with that icy sort of courtesy which at once disposes of any thought of entering into conversation. . . . Nothing could have made one suspect that this was the author of *Justine* or *Juliette*; the only impression he made on me was that of a haughty, morose old gentleman."

The arrest warrant of the Year II of the Revolution shows him to have been just over 5 foot 2 ins in height.

*   *   *

More than this we do not know, beyond one tentative detail. His direct descendant, the Marquis Xavier de Sade, relates that in 1939, before German troops pillaged the family mansion of Condé en Brie, there was in their possession a certain miniature of Donatien Alphonse François. The Marquis says it depicted a young man with blue eyes and a small mouth set in a charming countenance. It is still the author's hope that after so many lucky finds connected with his subject, he may yet come upon either that miniature or some other genuine portrait.

CHAPTER FOUR

From Sade's First Imprisonment to the Eve of the D'Arcueil Affair

1763 - 1768

THE FIVE years which lay between Sade's first imprisonment on October 29th 1763 and that Easter Sunday of 1768 (April 3rd) when he accosted a woman who was begging in the *Place des Victoires* constitute the first stage of his libertine life, and the subject of this chapter.

Here is the main outline: four months after his marriage the Marquis de Sade was imprisoned in Vincennes Fortress for excesses committed in a bawdy house. We do not know exactly what these excesses were, but no doubt they resembled what he was later to do to Rose Keller. For any distress which Donatien Alphonse François may have felt during that fifteen days' incarceration left no trace in his mind or at least did not prevent his giving way to his frenzied cravings the following year. On November 30th 1764 Inspector Marais felt obliged to tell a procuress named Brissault that she should stop "furnishing the Marquis de Sade with girls". It is much to be doubted that Brissault paid any attention to this. The Marquis was one of Brissault's best clients. But her house at *la Barrière Blanche* was not this libertine's only paradise. A girl named Dorville who was "big and complaisant" and in January 1766 agreed to sell Sade her favours for ten *louis* a month belonged to the seraglio of a procuress named la Huguet, while the Royal Academy of Music, of which La Mettrie said "lust has no more splendid or more frequented temple", furnished Sade with victims not only as complaisant but also more exciting. These were Mlle Riviére, auxiliary ballet-dancer, and Mlles Leclerc and Le Roy, two other ballet dancers. There were also two other amateur courtesans who inspired him with real passion, Mlle Colet, or Colette, a young actress of the Italian Theatre whom he loved "with frenzy" (according to Lady de Montreuil) and Mlle de Beauvoisin, one of the most expensive of them all, who seems, however, to have been less concerned with the proceeds than with the heights of passion to be obtained. This girl Sade took down to his La Coste estate during the summer of 1765 without any qualms, passing her off, if not as his wife, at least as a near relation of hers.

But besides these liaisons, most of which were not the sort a man would speak publicly about, Sade was never tired of hunting society women capable of stirring his emotions and we find him writing to assure a certain Lady de C——, whom he had met in the best company, how sorry he was he had not known her earlier; he would have married her.

To give himself a free hand while carrying on several affairs simultaneously, he rented flats or houses of convenience, both in Paris and out at Versailles or Arcueil. "A collection of receipted bills indeed most mischievously eloquent," cried Paul Bourdin, as he listed some of them. The Marquis indeed spent far more time in the beds of his five or six clandestine lodgings than in his wife's in the *rue Neuve du Luxembourg* or at Echauffour House in Normandy. Moreover, whatever the circumstances, he was never daunted even by long journeys. We have already seen how he took the Beauvoisin girl down to Provence. On April 20th 1767 again we find him leaving his young wife in Paris, five months gone with child, to hare off to Lyons to join the same actress. Despite his fondness for the *Marquise*—he certainly declared he would be "brokenhearted to upset her"—he could never bring himself to spend long with her. He found her "too frigid and prim" in her morals.

During these five years of furious loose living, what sort of figure did Sade cut in the eyes of his contemporaries, and how have most of his biographers seen him? As a fop who was already a problem case, a libertine who went beyond all bounds and would soon be resorting to flagellation and to sweets doctored with aphrodisiacs if he had not already begun to do so. . . .

But at the same time the future author of the *120 Days of Sodom* was beginning to assemble, partly from the confessions of prostitutes, partly from observation of his own delirium, the first items in his infernal dossier; and the dawn of a tragic knowledge, the laws of which no thinker before him had ever deciphered, was gradually breaking in the depths of his soul.

A RECORD

June 2nd 1763. The Count de Sade wrote to tell his brother the Abbé that he had been to Marly with his son and the Montreuils to see the parade of the Royal household. Lady de Montreuil, he said, "is crazy about the Marquis, though he is all wild ideas and craving for pleasure, which he finds nowhere". He complained that though living next door to him for a week his son has not yet visited him and he had a foreboding that Master Donatien Alphonse François was not going to do so till he wanted to make a fool of his father.

September 21st 1763.   In a letter either to his Abbé brother or to his other brother, the Commander, the Count complained that the Marquis was demanding payment of the emoluments of his office of Lt-General of Bresse and Bugey since 1760, and refused to agree to set off any cost of upkeep. What was worse, his son had "quite turned the head" of the good lady of the President of the Taxation Court and was actually trying to make her dislike the Count. The Count begged his correspondent to write to Lady Montreuil and get her to see reason.

October 20th 1763. Lady Montreuil wrote to the Abbé de Sade at Saumane to tell him the latest about her "little son-in-law" who, she now wrote, was "a queer boy"!

"That's what I call him my little son-in-law. I sometimes take it upon myself to give him a scolding. Then we quarrel, but we make it up at once, it's never very serious or lasting. . . . He's a scatterbrain, I admit, but marriage is settling him down. Unless I'm much mistaken, you will notice the difference in him when you see him. As for your niece, however much she wishes to please you and obey you, she will never say a word of reproof to him. She will love him as much as you like. That is very easy to understand; so far he is nice to her, very fond of her, could not treat her better." But, she adds, her daughter is nevertheless "still much put out", for the Marquis went off to Fontainebleau on Saturday. He was apparently to ask de Choiseul for a place, and after that he was going to try to get the Dijon high court to receive him—which in fact only took place the following June 26th. To conclude, Lady Montreuil hoped next summer to entertain her correspondent at Echauffour. Such a visit would crown her delight, and the Abbé would be able to read his life of Petrarch out to her!

October 29th 1763. It was now nearly a fortnight since Sade had allegedly gone to Fontainebleau, with the intention of going on to Dijon. But one wonders whether he ever left Paris. Since June he had been tenant of an "establishment" which he had furnished on credit, and in the seclusion of that little nook he had been indulging in one perversion after another with prostitutes, although regular enslavement to all this had long since robbed him of any pleasure in it. But now the mercenary hussies whom he had used had been arrested by the police officers set to watch Sade when in Paris, and though these girls had done all that Sade had wanted of them, they now found it right and proper to give evidence against their client to a magistrate. The report on all this was passed to M. de Saint-Florentin, Minister of the Royal Household, and de Saint-Florentin assured His Majesty that such excesses deserved the most rigorous punishment. On the King's orders, the Marquis de Sade was now arrested and taken to Vincennes Fortress.

November 2nd 1763. We find the young prisoner requesting the Governor of the jail to transmit a letter to his mother-in-law. What he most fervently craved was—to see his wife! That was a mercy he dared to beg on his knees, tears in his eyes.

> "Give me the solace of making my peace with one who is so dear to me and whom I have been weak enough to outrage so grievously. . . . Sir, I beg you not to refuse me a meeting with the person I hold dearest in all the world. Had you the honour of her acquaintance, you would see that more than anything else a meeting with her is likely to put a wretch whose mortification at having gone off the right road exceeds all else back on that road."

The same day he makes a similar application to the Lieutenant of the Police Sartin:

> "For all the wretchedness of my position here, Sir, I make no complaint about my fate; I have earned the wrath of the Almighty and I am experiencing it; all I do now is lament my ill deeds and loathe my errors. Alas, God might have destroyed me before I had had time to recognise them and know them for what they were; what acts of grace I owe him for allowing me to come back to myself again. Give me the means to perform them, I beg you, Monsieur, by allowing me to see a priest. It is my hope that with his good guidance and my sincere repentance I may soon be in a position to come to those holy sacraments the complete neglect of which had become the first cause of my fall."

November 13th 1763. The King signed the order to free the Marquis, but ordered him to withdraw to the Montreuil estate at Echauffour and stay there.

January 21st 1764. Lady Montreuil to the Abbé de Sade from Echauffour:

> "I take an aversion from any who bears your name, Monsieur? Far be that from me, indeed! You alone would dispel any such thought and inspire its very opposite which would grow all the stronger, had I the honour of knowing you better. I confess I did lack the courage to tell you the facts which you already know. I thought you were lucky enough to be so far away as to have heard nothing.
>
> It is entirely up to your nephew to repair the past by irreproachable conduct in future. Now he is restored to us, we are happy. But this is not the place for regrets. Besides, for all the effect this has had on him, making him think, I still feel only time will convince me. My husband and I have done what we would have done for our own son and what we thought suitable to save him from the scandal which might harm him, persuading ourselves, for that matter, that such behaviour on our part must surely have its effect on a soul of such gentle birth. As for my daughter, you can imagine what mortification

she felt. She has behaved exactly as a lady of virtue should. It is not for me to sing her praises. I leave it to those to whom she has the honour to belong to judge of her...."

April 17th 1764. A private theatre, with Donatien Alphonse Françoise as producer, was founded at Evry *Château,* the country residence of the uncle of the *Marquise* de Sade, at which Regnard's *Unexpected Return* and Bruey's and Palaprat's *Crafty Lawyer* were produced. These two farces were interpreted by the Marquis himself, assisted by de Launay, de Lionne and de Rupière and the *Marquise* de Sade, her mother, and Lady Bourneville.

June 26th 1764. The Marquis de Sade made his address to the High Court of Burgundy at Dijon on the occasion of his acceptance as Lt-General of the King for the Provinces of Bresse, Bugey, Valromey and Gex.

July 15th 1764. Sade was introduced to Mlle Colet or Colette of the Italian Theatre and after the show took the lady home to her lodging.

July 16th 1764. Sade addressed a declaration of love to Mlle Colet. He could conceive now no other bliss but to spend his whole life with her and share all his worldly goods with her.

September 11th 1764. The Minister of the Royal Household informed Lady Montreuil that His Majesty has completely revoked the order restricting the Marquis's residence to Echauffour.

December 7th 1764. Inspector Marais reported:

"The Count de Sade, whom on His Majesty's orders I took to Vincennes a year ago, on his last journey to Fontainebleau and then to his father-in-law's estate, where he had the opportunity to save a little of his income, received permission this summer to go to Paris, where he still is and where to occupy his time he has found fit to give Mlle Colette, an actress of the Italian theatre, 25 *louis* monthly, she being the kept mistress of M. le Marquis de Lignerai, who has turned a blind eye to sharing her with others whenever it suits her pocket. He is not ignorant of her affair with Lord de Sade, but the latter has begun to realise that the girl is making a fool of him and this week he went to La Brissault's brothel to take his pleasure, and persistently asked La Brissault if she did not know me, to which she said no. I have strongly advised this woman, without saying why, not to provide the Marquis with girls to go to any private chambers with him."

December 21st 1764. Inspector Marais reported that the Marquis de Lignerai had felt obliged to quit Mlle Colet and had given her up to the Marquis de Sade, "who for his part is most embarrassed, as he is not affluent enough to support an actress all by himself".

December 28th 1764. Inspector Marais reported that the Marquis de Sade was finding it extremely difficult to cut loose from Mlle Colet, "but nevertheless has slept with her three times this week".

February 20th 1765. Sade wrote to "de C——", a young society lady whom he had fallen in love with at a ball. He expressed regret at not having met her earlier, or he might have married her.

March 29th 1765. Lady Montreuil wrote to the Abbé de Sade at Saumane to tell him that the Marquis was on the point of leaving for Provence [in fact he did not go till May 9th], where he said he had business. She wondered if this journey was really necessary, yet reflected that the Marquis would profit by staying with his uncle. She had received the second volume of *Petrarch,* which had been quite a success, but she had not yet read it.

April 26th 1765. Inspector Marais reported : "The Beauvoisin girl is making up to Lord Douet de la Boulay as much as she can and he is showering favours on her. Lord de Pienne is still the favoured young fop but it is Lord de Sade who is burdened with the costs of her dresses and shows, which come to a good twenty *louis* a month.

Early in 1765, just before she became the Marquis' mistress, la Beauvoisin must have been about twenty-two years old, counting that she was probably sixteen when in 1759 she started out as the maid of a *Mr Cadet, Surgeon,* of the *rue Mont-*

martre, before being initiated (being a "very charming young thing") to the delights of prostitution by the famous Count du Barry.

May 20th 1765. Lady Montreuil wrote to tell the Abbé de Sade at Saumane that on May 9th the Marquis had at last left for Avignon. He was to take over some property due to him. The Count had been against his son's journey. Nobody had so far had any news of the Marquis. She trusted the Abbé's good counsel will steady the young man a little.

June-July 1765. This period the Marquis de Sade spent at La Coste House with la Beauvoisin. We are not quite sure whether he passed her off as only a relative of his wife's, or boldly as his wife herself, since the *Marquise* had never been down to La Coste, so nobody there knew her. Even Lady Montreuil in her letter of September 8th was not at all sure about the position, but the Marquis himself, replying to his aunt the Abbess of Saint Benoît, was quite positive that he had never allowed, suffered or authorised anybody to assume that the lady staying with him was his wife.

All we can say is that it is hard to believe that all the gossip about la Beauvoisin's sojourn at La Coste with Sade was not enriched by a host of details on its tortuous route by way of Ménerbes, Oppède and Cavaillon, after with an initial loop *via* Apt and the hill village of Bonnieux, to the ancient city of the popes. . . . But whatever the truth of the matter, the private theatre at the Château was certainly restored at great cost and all the nobility of the district responded to the Marquis' grand invitations and flocked in to his productions. There was a round of balls, pageants and banquets. The Abbé de Sade came and stayed a whole week, and was one of the first to honour these parties with his presence. If, as Lady Montreuil later suggested, he could put up with the "outrageous impropriety of the Marquis' passing off a whore as the *Marquise*'s relation or as the *Marquise* herself," this was no doubt to spare Donatien Alphonse François the humiliation of seeing all his guests depart as soon as they came, scandalised by being imposed upon. Certainly the Abbé's passing goodwill gave rise to much comment, so that when he got back to Saumane Sade's uncle found himself obliged to be as much annoyed as anybody by the trickery of which so many had been victims. Indeed he even went so far on occasion as to deny flatly ever having been present at the outrageous comedy which the Marquis and la Beauvoisin added to those they enacted on the stage! "I refuse to see my nephew at all," he now declared, "and I should be most vexed to see anybody else behave as badly."

Or at least, so the Marquis said he said! But the Abbé de Sade certainly felt himself obliged to inform his Cavaillon sister about the Beauvoisin business, and Sade's aunt lost no time writing him a letter of reproach which he was far from receiving with the contrition the old lady hoped. Indeed, his reply was one of studied insult. He went so far as to call in question Lady de Villeneuve-Martignan's own conjugal fidelity. He gave vent too to all his rage against the Abbé for giving the game away, and revealed the Abbé's own peccadilloes in the most shameless terms.

In October the following year, however, we find him trying to make his actress responsible for his having written such a letter. Alas, he could only have sent such a missive under the "dictation of the siren who at the time had turned his head". How could that genuine respect he felt for his favourite uncle ever have prompted him to write such terrible things?

But however much the Marquis protested and however sorry he might now be, it was more than the Abbé could do (to whom his sister had "maliciously and unwisely" sent the shocking letter) ever to forgive his nephew's outrageous language.

But are we to conclude the story with the rage of uncle and aunt? Rather let our imaginations turn to the fervour with which the altars of Comus and Momus, Thalia and Terpsichorea, and also that of Aphrodite Kallipygous, Sade's favourite goddess, must have revelled in the heady atmosphere of the incense of all their worshippers on that ancestral stage, during that divine summer of 1765. Its fragrance seems still to haunt those long-silent stories!

August 8th 1765. In the postscript of a letter from Echauffour to the Abbé de Sade at Saumane Lady Montreuil gave very detailed indications on what should be done to effect a rupture between the Marquis and Mlle la Beauvoisin. At the same time she intimates that she could not contemplate her son-in-law's return to Paris without some disquiet. He would be pursued by his creditors, he would at once make new debts, and even if he did get tired of la Beauvoisin, some other courtesan was sure to take her place. Indeed, she would really rather he got himself tied up with "some woman" down there in Provence. "Such a liaison would be less dangerous than that of a kept mistress."

August 20th 1765. Sade's valet arrived in Paris, *rue Neuve du Luxembourg,* with the trunks, and announced that his master would be there at any moment. The news was brought to Lady de Montreuil out at Echauffour and she suspected that the Marquis had in fact already reached the capital, but was co-habiting with "his wench"—namely, la Beauvoisin. If she were only sure of this, she would come to Paris herself to grab him at the woman's door and remove him from her, as she had done at the door of another, a year previously.

August 21st 1765. Lady Montreuil had indeed hit the nail on the head! The Marquis had arrived in Paris on the 20th, together with la Beauvoisin, in fact, at just the same time as his valet!

Early September 1765. It was not till about ten days after his clandestine arrival in Paris, where he spent more time with his mistress than at home, that the Marquis de Sade finally let his wife and mother-in-law know where he was. But even then he said that he was still unable to go down to Echauffour to see them.

Two important pieces of business retained him in Paris. First, he had to find the money to settle debts amounting to 4,500 *livres* that he had incurred in Provence, secondly, he had to help Lord de Baujon draw up a genealogical tree to present to His Majesty,—in the eyes of Lady Montreuil scarcely a valid excuse for not going to see his wife after four months' absence!

Meanwhile, Sade had also written to his wife, who was still ignorant of the La Coste scandal and her husband's partial cohabitation with la Beauvoisin, that as soon as he had concluded this urgent business he would join her in Normandy.

September 15th 1765. At last, late one evening, Sade did reach

Echauffour. Lady Montreuil only caught a glimpse of him, and this in the presence of his wife, so was unable to get from him anything that really interested her. Nevertheless, from a letter from the Dowager *Marquise* she gathered that by his behaviour and his attentiveness the Marquis wanted to have the past forgotten, though on the other hand he was very concerned that his wife should know nothing about it. Above all he wanted her still to have a good opinion of him.

November 7th 1765. Lady Montreuil wrote to the Abbé de Sade to inform him that "a mishap that person" (namely, la Beauvoisin) had suffered—which in fact was an advanced pregnancy—had sent the Marquis flying to the woman's succour. He had gone to Paris, where "he remains confined to his prison"—that is, to the lady's dwelling. But the Montreuils were returning to Paris on the fourteenth, and the Marquis was going to welcome them at the *rue Neuve du Luxembourg* house.

December 13th 1765. Having given birth to her child, la Beauvoisin shortly before this date had appeared again on the boards of the Italian Theatre "like a new star in the firmament". So reported Inspector Marais. And added :

"Her confinement has improved her, and young Lord de Saint Conta was immediately on her heels and for him she has sacked de Louvois and de la Boulaye. Lord de Raconis has dealt with a score of creditors for her and parted with fifty louis on her account. In a word, all our fashionable young fops vie to please her, not one missing, even Baron de Saint Cricq, officer of the French Guard, who has declared himself ready to give up the Lafoud girl for her, but the most dangerous of all is the Chevalier de Choiseul, and yesterday I noticed him ogling her. I saluted him and he replied 'I caught a glance of hers just now which convinces me that in no time she will be mine'."

January 3rd 1766. Generously maintained by the Marquis de Saint Conta and enjoying the sweetest pleasures of Venus thanks to the efforts of young de Choiseul, la Beauvoisin had now broken off all relations with the Marquis de Sade, and the abandoned lover was now busy seeking consolation in a girl named Dorville, "a tall, charming creature who quite recently broke away from the Huguet woman's brothel." Her he paid only ten *louis* monthly, but as assistant paymaster he had M. Elchira, esquire, who visited the girl quite once a week, paying her at least four *louis* per visit. But the Marquis made up this by being a regular visitor of a stand-in ballet-dancer of the *Opéra* named Le Clair!

There exists a letter which Sade wrote to la Beauvoisin. It is full of bitter rage and was probably written at this time. Yet despite the situation at this moment, the rupture was still not complete. In the latter half of January 1767 the Marquis was once again snug in his fickle mistress's bed and on April 20th that year he was off to Lyons to join her on tour. By that time he was once again completely under her spell.

End of April 1766. On his way to Avignon the Marquis de Sade halted at Melun for four days, spending his time there with a woman whose name was not recorded.

May 21st 1766. Travelling from Lyons, the Marquis reached Avignon, where his uncle the Abbé was awaiting him, having left Saumane for this purpose on the 15th.

June 1st 1766. The Abbé de Sade informed Lady Montreuil that his nephew had arrived. He advised on the way he thought this hothead should be treated and intimated the feelings the Marquis had for his spouse, mentioning great friendship and respect, together with great anxiety lest she should learn of all the foolish things he was doing.

July 6th 1766. The Marquis was in Paris, paying sixty *livres* for the hire of a *cabriolet*.

September 26th 1766. Inspector Marais began a report:

"A fortnight since the Marquis de Sade left Mlle Le Roy of the *Opéra* without attempting to renew his union with her. M. de Sénac, Farmer-General of Revenues, is negotiating with the girl's mother and aunt about keeping her,"

but in secret, as he would like to conceal the liaison from his young wife. . . .

November 4th 1766. A Mr Lestarjette received 200 *livres* from the Marquis de Sade as four and a half months' rent of a furnished house in the *rue de Lardenay* at Arcueil which he himself was leasing from a Mr Gallier.

January 23rd 1767. M. de Jeancourt, *Knight,* official lover of Mlle la Beauvoisin, learned from Inspector Marais that this person was deceiving him "with a number of men", among them "little Tomboeuf", an officer of the Guards, and—the Marquis de Sade! Sade now seems to have completely restored his old relationship with her. He "armed" her in public!

January 24th 1767. Jean Baptiste François Joseph, Count de Sade, died at Montreuil, near Versailles, aged 65.

Six days later Lady Montreuil wrote to give the Abbé de Sade some details of the Count's demise. During the last month his health had taken a distinct turn for the better, and his son and the Count de Crillon, who saw him together only five days before his death, had said that he seemed to be in a normal state of health. Yet on Saturday the 24th he suddenly departed this world! The way the Marquis had taken this loss had moved Lady Montreuil greatly and "completely reconciled her to him".

April 16th 1767. The Marquis de Sade was promoted Captain Commander in the du Mestre cavalry regiment, with orders to assemble his company without delay. Lady Montreuil was delighted with this, for, she says, "it means at least a brief period of peace".

April 20th 1767. Having in all probability obtained from the Colonel of his new regiment a postponement of the order, to form his company, the Marquis went secretly to Lyons, to join la Beauvoisin. The actress was now believed to have reestablished all her former influence over him, and now that his father was dead, she was making the most of it.

The *Marquise*'s pregnancy had now reached its sixth month.

June 21st 1767. The Marquis went to La Coste. Here he demanded due recognition of his rank and insisted on a memorial service for his father in the church.

August 27th 1767. In the parish of the Madeleine de la Ville l'Eveque in Paris Louis Marie, first son of the Marquis, was born.

October 16th 1767. Inspector Marais reported :

"You will be impatient to hear my report on the frightful goings on of the Count de Sade; he is going all out now to persuade Mlle Rivière of the *Opéra* to live with him and has offered her 25 *louis* a month on condition that whenever she is not performing she will spend her time with him in his maisonette at Arcueil. She has rejected the proposal,* because she is in receipt of the favours of M. Hocquart de Coubron, but the Count is still pursuing her and while waiting for her to yield he has this week done all he could to persuade la Brissault to provide him with girls to sup with him in his little house at Arcueil. Brissault has steadfastly refused, having some notion of what he is capable of, but he has approached others who are less scrupulous or who do not know what sort of man he is, and there is no doubt we shall soon hear talk of him."

January 24th, 1768. Louis Marie de Sade was baptised in the private chapel of the Condé family, the Prince de Condé and the Princess de Conti being godparents.

February 1st 1768. For an annual rental of 800 *livres* Gallier leased to Sade the maisonette at Arceuil which he formerly leased to Lestarjette.

If we are to believe rumours which reached the ears of Constabulary Lieutenant Gersant, who commanded the Bourg la Reine Brigade, Sade one day brought four prostitutes to his house and flogged them, after which he gave them dinner and had his valet pay them a *louis,* out of which the valet kept a crown "for the trouble he had going to find them in the Saint Antoine suburb". This incident was according to the same officer "nothing out of the ordinary". For the past fifteen months

---

*A report of the Inspector's dated March 18th 1768 shows that Sade was not invariably unsuccessful with Mlle Rivière who was listed in the *Guide to the Shows* (Almanach des Spectacles) for 1767 as one of the reserve ballet dancers of the Opéra.

the Marquis had been causing much scandalous talk at Arcueil "bringing persons of both sexes to his house there, by day and by night, for wild debauchery with them".

March 18th 1768. Inspector Marais reported :

> "It is now some time since the Count de Sade left Mlle Rivière, who since then has made a number of persons a nice little love present, and it is said that with a view to getting her for himself eventually the Prince de Conti has been so moved by her condition that he is providing her with medicaments. It is indeed true that his Aesculapius, Dr Guérin, is to be seen visiting her every day. She would be a pretty woman if only she were healthy."

CHAPTER FIVE

The Arcueil Affair

1768

SADE'S OBSESSION WITH PAIN

THE FOLLOWING portrait of the sad Bacchus of John Cleland's *Fanny Hill's Memoirs* might well be a description of Sade himself, surely, as he must have appeared to his mistresses on the eve of the Arcueil affair. For there could not be a better prologue to the examination which follows than this sensitively drawn description of a man infected with *algolagnia*:

"As he was under the tyranny of a cruel taste; that of an ardent desire, not only of being unmercifully scourged himself, but of serving others so, in such sort, that though he paid extravagantly those who had the courage and complaisance to submit to his humour, there were few, delicate as he was in the choice of his subjects, who would exchange turns with him so terribly at the expense of their skin; but what yet increased the oddity of this strange fancy, was the gentleman's being young; whereas it generally attacks, it seems, such as are, through age, obliged to have recourse to this experiment, for quickening the circulation of their sluggish spirits.

"He seated me near him, when now his face changed upon me with an expression of the most pleasing sweetness and good humour, the more remarkable for its sudden shift from the other extreme which I found afterwards, when I knew more of his character, was owing to the habitual state of conflict with, and dislike of himself, for being enslaved to so peculiar a guest, by the fatality of a constitutional ascendant, that rendered him incapable of any pleasure, till he submitted to these extra-ordinary means of procuring it at the hands of pain, whilst the constancy of his repining consciousness stamped at length that cast of sourness and severity on his features which was in fact very foreign to the natural sweetness of his temper."

(from letter No. 2 of the Memoirs)

In this chapter, before touching on the affair of the flagella-tion of Rose Keller and that other affair—the aphrodisiac sweets at Marseilles, it may be well to provide the reader who does not know much about such things with an outline sketch of the impulses to which the Marquis de Sade was subjected during those events. Before discussing sadism at all it is essential to make it quite clear that because of the ambivalence of the sadistic impulse, which has constantly been confirmed by psychoanalysis, this neurosis is never found in any individual without being accompanied by its inseparable opposite, masochism.

This twin nature of masochism and sadism should surprise us only at first sight. In sadism just as much as in masochism the basic principle, as we know, is that of a connection, either real or symbolical, between cruelty and sexual satisfaction. Whether we vent our cruelty on a woman who excites us or that woman submits us to her own cruelty, the result is the same, the only difference being so to speak a technical one, the replacement in masochism of the original object by oneself.

This transformation of the active into the passive or *vice versa* should however not seem mysterious to anybody who knows much about the remarkable plasticity of the human mind when under the influence of the sexual urge. The trans-formation sometimes seems to take place without any transi-tion, without any emotional disturbance at all, and the bond between the two opposites is apparently so close that it was possible for Freud to declare that this inversion "never has any effect on the totality of the instinctual emotion" and that the original impulse goes on more or less side by side with the new one, "even when the process of transformation has been very intense".

A hundred years before the term *algolagnia,* from Greek *algos*—pain, and *lagneia*—enjoyment, was forged by

Schrenck-Notzing, so as to have a single word for the not contradictory notion of pain received as well as inflicted in enjoyment of the sexual act, there was not a single important character, male or female, born of Sade's imagination (except, as
we shall see, Justine) who had not already in his or her behaviour shown the invariable appearance of both sadism and
masochism together in the same person. The Noirceuils, the
Saint-Fond who asks Juliette to strangle him while he submits
to flagellation, seek an intrinsic sexual enjoyment, rarely any
physiological advantage.

The most varied features of masochism are to be found in
countless instances in these cruel creatures. Open a volume of
Juliette at random and we at once have two : in one episode
Saint-Fond asks Juliette to strangle him while he commits
sodomy with Palmire; in another Juliette says to Delcour, the
Nantes executioner : "You must beat me, you must crush me,
you must flog me. . . ." And while he subjects her to this harsh
treatment, she cries : "Oh Delcour, divine destroyer of man-
kind, you whom I adore, by whom I shall finish now [i.e.,
obtain a sexual spasm], lash your bitch harder still, mark her
with your blows, you can see she is burning to bear those
weals. . . ."

In the exceptional case, Justine, it is however impossible to
see any definite link between the two forms of *algolagnia*. At
first sight it seems to be solely a form of masochism, a social
masochism, a neurotic attraction towards whatever is fatal for
her, that we seem to observe. However, enquiry shows that it
would be a mistake to speak of masochism at all, even theoretical,
in this heroine, for the simple reason that Justine is almost
entirely devoid of psychological importance, at least in her reactions as a whole, if not in the relevant details. Justine is a
mere concept, an abstract construction, who would seem only
to have been thought up by the author to prove his pessimistic
thesis about the consequences of virtue. And we should note
that in the corresponding novel, the *Prosperities of Vice,*
Juliette is not at all cast in that rarefied psychological atmosphere which makes her young sister a mere automaton planted
by the Marquis among his living creatures.

Of all neuroses, sado-masochism, or *algolagnia,* is without
question the most widely distributed. The person is rare who

has not a trace of it in him or herself. Perhaps we all have. We should at once add of course that as a rule, at least in times of peace, sado-masochism shows in such attenuated form, or else is hidden by a symbolism apparently so remote from its subject, that it is so to speak not visible at all to the naked eye. The many forms it may assume are all embraced by Dr Eugen Dühren's definition, the exhaustive brevity of which could not be surpassed: "Sadism (sado-masochism) is the relationship deliberately sought or arising by accident between sexual excitation and the realization of enjoyment, real or symbolical (imaginary illusory) of events that are terrible, of horrible facts or of acts of destruction which menace or destroy the life or the health or the property of man or of other animate creatures and endanger or destroy the continuity of inanimate things. In all such instances the man who obtains sexual pleasure therefrom may himself be the immediate cause or may induce others to be the cause, or may be only the spectator, or even willingly or by force the victim of these agents."

Basing ourselves on the Freudian doctrine (and the psychiatry of the schools has certainly been obliged to adopt its basic assumptions) we may admit that there are three ways out for neurotics. The gravest cases may end in crime or lead to the threshold of psychosis. The solution by suppression (the most usual) produces obsessions or phobias. But there is also a third solution in which in theory repression is rejected. This consists in the sublimation of the a-social instincts, and sometimes takes the form of works of literature or art. There would indeed seem to be not exactly a fourth way out for sado-masochism, but a sort of auxiliary form, which would reduce the degree of perversion, and might even remove it altogether; we have in mind the normal sexual act. For there can be no doubt but that during sexual union the behaviour of the man and of the woman are related respectively to sadism and masochism. The two impulses, though appearing only in barest outline, or even purely physiological, are none the less unquestionably there. This state of affairs indeed completely fits in with the nature of the two sexes, and one might even assert that it is only the presence of these slight elements of sadism and masochism that give the act of love its peculiar quality of perfection.

One's first impulse is to classify Sade's neurosis as capable of the third solution, that of sublimation, in his case in literature. But this choice (as for that matter either of the two others) would imply a deliberate technique of suppression which seems quite incompatible with everything we know of the Marquis. Sade was quite well aware of his own *algolagnia,* for it showed in acts which were completely indicative of the state of mind, but yet—this cannot be said too often—were still very far from seriously threatening the health, let alone the existence of his "victims".

This means that we should have to formulate a special type of sado-masochism for the Marquis, however close this may have been to sublimation. But, first, the sublimation here was not unconscious, and secondly, it was a sublimation in the realm of science, Sade's literary work, although among the most striking of modern times, coming into it solely as a record and quite independently of his neurosis.

As we see him, Sade was a man above all else gifted with a scientific imagination amounting to genius. What after all is imagination, in its highest form? Not the re-creation of fictitious matter, but the use of a fragment of reality to create the whole of reality. Just as Cuvier the naturalist, from a mere fragment of fossilised bone, was able to re-establish the very articulation of the bones of an animal, so Sade from only the rudimentary elements of his own mild *algolagnia* (supplemented, of course, by any other acts he may have witnessed) constructed a vast museum of sado-masochistic perversion. Unaided by any precursor, in one great act he attained perfection in a work which, while endowed with all the advantages of poetry and eloquence, remains none the less an example of the most conscientious and most effective scientific enquiry.

We must conclude this brief outline with remarks somewhat outside the limits of pure theory in order for the first time to draw attention to the great feature of objectivity which, despite the *algolagnic* learnings which were the initial prompting, we find in the great erotic novels of the Marquis de Sade.

INTRODUCTION

In the preceding chapter we glanced at the five years which preceded the Marquis de Sade's marriage. It was the first stage in his libertine life. The Arcueil affair with which we are now to deal opens the second stage, which covers ten years, running from the flagellation of Rose Keller on April 3rd 1768 to the gates of Vincennes Fortress on February 13th 1777. These fifteen years, during which the Marquis' insensate intoxication with life was interrupted solely by a few months of detention in Pierre Encise prison and Miolans fortress, were described by Maurice Heine in the following words:

> "For fifteen years Sade was to be the victim of the most complete liberty of the senses—no convention, moral, social or religious was to be an obstacle and he came to know a restless, fervent, persecuted sort of existence, above good and evil, triumphant and pitiable by turns. Rebelling against the laws of God and man, he was to combine the pride of the wicked angel and the anguish of the outlaw."

* * *

The publication, some fifteen years since, of an account of the Arcueil affair gathered those snippets of information of unequal value, with which those who discussed Sade had formerly been obliged to be content, into a strange chapter. If the two letters of Mme du Deffand's on the subject or the story given by bookseller Hardy to give details which at least bear witness to the good faith of their authors, the same could never be said for Rétif de la Bretonne's fantastic inventions, written in the Marquis' lifetime and revived fifty years later with horrifying details by Jules Janin and medical jurisprudent Brierre de Boismont. Yet it is on the lies of such a man as de Bretonne, the disgusting outburst of a type like Mirabeau, the scurrilous horrors of a Dulaure and the ridiculous inventions of some other nineteenth century authors, about both the Arcueil flagellation and the "Spanish Fly" sweets of Marseilles, that for one hundred and fifty years the reputation of the Marquis de Sade has been founded. Even today for the average reader his name still suggests the picture of an erotic maniac who dissected living women. And such a legend has of course not failed to excite real prejudice against his work, to the great detriment of fine literature, philosophy and science, for the popular essayist, always unwilling to take the trouble to find out what Sade really wrote, still invariably treats it as a collection of monstrous rhapsodies born in the imagination of a criminal lunatic.

* * *

There was a sense of unity about the little psycho-sexual drama enacted at Arcueil which was lacking, for years later, in the Marseilles debauch. The *dramatis personae* of the story of June 27th 1772 consists of as many girls as there are seasons, a valet to provide the intoxication of both observing and being observed, and the Marquis himself, about his brow a garland of cantharides and brandishing in his hand the double algolagnic thyrsus of *amanita impudica* and some heads of aniseed. But on Easter Sunday, 1768, there was only one object of indulgence and the plot was most simple, just the use of an ordinary cat-o'-nine-tails. We are inclined to agree with Maurice Heine that "the sincerity of the victim, her genuine tears and the sight of her mutilated buttocks provided the Marquis de Sade in his super-sensitivity with sufficient of what he needed for an orgasm". He adds that this seems all the more likely if we consider the mention in Rose Keller's evidence of "the terrifying cries of the Marquis just before he untied her". On the other hand, we should also notice that Sade's active *algolagnia* here was further transmuted into the mental torment of his victim, for when she cried out too loudly to suit him he showed her a knife and said he would kill her and bury her in his garden; and shortly after this, when she begged him not to flog her to death because she had not made her Easter confession, he refused to give her any assurance and offered to confess her himself.

Dr André Javelier has diagnosed the protagonist of Arcueil as suffering from "minor sadism with anti-social reactions mild however in form", adding that "the torture chambers of modern brothels daily witness similar scenes, and it scarcely even enters the victims' heads to complain". This diagnosis, which reduced the matter to its true proportions, its very language implying a difference of degree in sadistic acts, may well be set beside a well known pronouncement of Sade's which was more outspoken than subtle. He put it into the lips of his

Juliette. Juliette said : "If you whip me, you are cruel; flogging in a libertine is merely his ferocity reaching its peak, it is to get some relief that he resorts to it, he would do something else if he dared." True, some flagellators would go farther if they were not afraid of the law, but some are completely satisfied by their act, though even if untouched by any sanction, they would still not go beyond the point which marked their limit of *algolagnia*.

The Marquis de Sade is to be grouped with these latter, though we should not forget that, by reason of the sort of sublimation discussed earlier, the excess of his perversion found its own outlet in the products of his pen.

*   *   *

The following account is in the main based on Rose Keller's evidence given before the la Tournelle Court of enquiry. The allegations about cuts and burns have been left out, since the reports and interrogation of surgeon Le Comte show them to have been untrue. In addition, when drawing on the evidence of witnesses for details, we have been consistently cautious, particularly regarding the account given by Marie Louise Jouette, wife of the Arcueil Registrar, for that is itself clearly hysterical in places. The important question of the Marquis' degree of moral responsibility in the matter, that is, whether before he took the victim to his maisonette he really gave her to understand that he proposed some kind of an orgy or whether, as the woman insisted, she only went with him because he proposed "an honest job of work", nobody will ever be able to answer. But since, despite the exclusion from a plain account of what happened of anything like critical discussion (the case for and against comes immediately after, in a commentary from the standpoint of medical jurisprudence) one has had to decide on either one or the other version, it was felt that here Rose Keller's story should be accepted.

It will also be noted that in order to be quite fair, (if that is how to put it), both the cane and the cat-o'-nine-tails are included in the story, since Rose Keller spoke of the first (adding the detail that it was a "stout stick", which has been left out)

and Sade spoke of the second. Another compromise has been
that of taking the average of the number of "repeats" by the
two parties, alleged Sade speaking of "three or four" and Rose
Keller of "seven or eight".

THE FLAGELLATION OF ROSE KELLER

*Easter Sunday, April 3rd 1768. Nine a.m., Place des
Victoires.*

The Marquis, in grey surcoat with white sleeves, hunting
knife and cane, is leaning against the statue of Louis XIV. A
little distance from him is Rose Keller, accepting alms from a
passer-by. The woman has a German accent and speaks French
badly. She is thirty-six years old, the widow of a pastrycook's
assistant. A cotton-spinner by trade, she has been out of work
for a month. The Marquis signs to her to come over to him
and promises her a crown if she will go with him.

Rose Keller objects, she is an honest woman. Sade reassures
her. She has misunderstood him, he only wants her to do out
his room. Rose accepts, and the Marquis takes her to a room
near the new market. But now he asks her to wait for him. He
has business to see about. It is to his house out in the country
that he proposes to take her. In an hour's time.

After an hour, he reappears, with a cab. Rose Keller gets
into this, and the Marquis sits down beside her and draws the
wooden shutters of the windows. As they drive through the
town he does not say a word to her, but as they draw near the
Enfer Gate he thinks it better to put her mind at rest, and tells
her she will be well fed and treated kindly. After that he says
no more, but sleeps, or pretends to be asleep.

A long drive through the countryside follows. When they
reach Arcueil crossroads and the first houses of the village, the
cab halts at last and they get out. It is about half past twelve.
There is a short walk to the *rue de Lardenay*. At the house, the
Marquis asks Rose Keller to wait a moment, goes in the main
entrance, then from inside opens a little green door, for her to
enter.

Rose is taken upstairs to the first floor, to a rather large room.
The tightly-closed shutters let in a meagre light, by which she
can distinguish two canopied beds, and the Marquis tells her

to wait there while he fetches bread and something to drink, assuring her she has no need to worry. Going out, he double locks the door.

In all probability he now went to see the two girls whom his valet Langlois had brought that morning for him.

An hour later, runs Rose Keller's story, there he is back, with a lighted candle. "Come downstairs, my dear," he says to her, guides her to a small chamber on the ground floor which is no less dark than the first room, and the moment they are inside, tells her to take off all her clothes. She wants to know why and he says it is for a bit of fun. When she protests that she had not come there for such goings on he tells her that if she refuses he will kill her and bury her in the garden.

With this threat, he leaves her. She gets frightened, and undresses. When he comes back and finds her still in her shift, he tells her to take that off too. She says she would rather die. He then strips her himself. Then she is pushed into the neighbouring room. In this there is a divan upholstered with red and white calico. Sade throws the girl face downwards on to this, ties her arms and legs to it with hempen cord and puts a bolster and a lynx muff across her shoulders.

Now he takes off his coat and shirt and puts on a sleeveless waistcoat and ties a handkerchief round his head, takes a switch and gives the girl a severe whipping. She shrieks, but he shows her a knife and swears he will kill her if she does not keep quiet, and for the second time assures her he will bury her with his own hands. She then suppresses her cries and the Marquis whips her five or six times more, turn and turn about with a switch and a cat-o'-nine-tails. Two or three times he pauses, to rub some ointment into the weals, then immediately resumes the beating, as savagely as ever, and when Rose Keller craves mercy and begs him to spare her life, she does not want to die without having made her Easter confession, he tells her that that is of very little consequence, he will confess her himself. While she continues her efforts to soften his heart, the blows become more rapid and frenzied till all at once the Marquis utters "loud, very terrifying cries".

Sade had reached an orgasm and the torture was over.

He unties his victim and takes her to the smaller room to dress. He leaves her alone for a moment, to come back with a towel, a bowl and a jug of water. She washes and dries herself. But as the towel now shows traces of blood he makes her wash it out. After that he brings a small bottle of brandy and persuades her to use this as lotion on her wounds and, so he says, in an hour there won't be any trace.

The girl does as she is told, not without terrible smarting. She completes her toilet, and the Marquis then offers her a dish of boiled beef and a flask of wine and takes her back to the upper room. But before locking her in again, tells her not to go near the window or make any noise and promises to let her go again in the evening. She implores him to let her go early, as she has no notion where she is and, being without money, does not want to spend the night on the road. He assures her she need not worry about that.

Once alone, the prisoner bolts the door on the inside, takes the coverings off the beds and knots them together, then, slashing the felt packing of the shutters apart, she opens one without any difficulty, ties her improvised rope to the cross-bar of the window and lets herself down into the garden, which is at the back of the house. Rushing to the wall, she clambers up the trellis on it and drops down on the other side, grazing her left arm and hand. From the vacant ground on which she finds herself she makes her way to the *rue de la Fontaine*.

The Marquis' valet now comes running after her, shouting to her to come back, his master wants to talk to her. But she refuses. Then Langlois takes out his purse and says he wants to pay her. But in vain, Rose Keller pushes him aside and continues on her way. Her torn hand hurts and her slip is torn and hangs in tatters below her skirt.

She meets a village woman, Marguerite Sixdeniers and sobbing tells her what has happened to her. Two other women, named Pontier and Bajou, come on the scene, and declare the man must be a devil. They are terror-stricken and lament with the victim. They take her into a courtyard and lift her skirts to see her wounds for themselves.

THE MEDICAL AND LEGAL ASPECTS

Comparison of Rose Keller's principal points of evidence and the Marquis de Sade's replies to Councillor Jacques de Chavanne.

1. When he asked her to go with him, the Marquis said it was to "do out his room".	1. He made it clear to her that it was for a bout of libertinage.
2. He threw her down on the bed on her stomach and roped her arms and legs with ropes to the bed and another round her middle.	2. He told her to lie down on the divan but did not tie her to it.
3. Every time he began again with a birch he also hit her with a stick.	3. He whipped her with a cat-o'-nine-tails with knotted cords but used neither birch nor stick.
4. He slashed her with a little knife, perhaps a pocket knife and poured red and white wax into the wounds, after which he started whipping her again, again slashed her and again poured wax in.	4. He used neither penknife nor Spanish wax, but merely "smeared a little white wax ointment here and there, to heal her wounds".
5. All of which ill treatment he repeated seven or eight times.	5. He agreed he whipped her "three or four times more".

OBSERVATIONS

Point 1. Maurice Heine admits that absence of intention on the part of the Marquis might well be pleaded.

> "Whom indeed are we to credit, Rose, out of work, maintaining she only consented to go to the Marquis' house for honest work, or the Marquis, habitual loose-liver, who made out that there could be no question but that the woman readily agreed to do all he wanted? There is nothing in the statements made by either which can tip the balance either way between these two diametrically opposed assertions. And it is moreover clear that with the Royal reprieve which he held Sade risked nothing by being cynically frank, while at the slightest hint of admission that Sade's was the true story, the woman risked incarceration. Yet nothing suggests that she was telling the magistrates a lie, and on the other hand, Sade's own care to hide the woman's presence from the two girls whom

Langlois had brought, who were in another part of the house, prompts us to doubt whether the cotton-spinner was really a whore. At the same time it is still possible to suppose that in her extreme need Keller really did—as an exception—consent to make love with the Marquis. Which leaves us with the problem as insoluble as ever."

Twenty years after, when a prisoner in the Bastille, Sade was to insist that he had had to do with a whore; on the one hand, in his story entitled *Le Président mystifié* he was to complain of having been the victim of *Grand-Chambre* magistrates who were, fantastic to relate, actually "moved to compassion for the whipped backside of a street pick-up"; on the other, in his novel *Aline and Valcour* once again he classed the beggar-woman of the *Place des Victoires* as just as much a prostitute as the girls at Marseilles. "It is only in Paris and London," he wrote, "that these despicable creatures are thus supported. In Rome, Venice, Naples, Warsaw, when they come before the courts on which they depend, they are asked if they were paid or not, and if they were not, the court insists on payment, which is fair. But if they have accepted payment and are merely complaining about ill treatment, they are at once warned that they stand a chance of imprisonment if they insist on plaguing the court with such foul talk. Change your profession, they are told, or if you prefer to stick to it, put up with its drawbacks."

Point 2

Did the Marquis rope Rose Keller to the bed, with one cord round her middle and each limb tied down separately? Anne Blougé Bajou gave evidence that she "saw no traces of rope marks on her limbs or her body". Nor did Surgeon Le Comte see any traces, either on limbs or body, "which he examined". On the other hand, these two pieces of evidence, which support Sade, are in the author's opinion not a complete refutation of Rose Keller's charge, for the ropes need not have been tied very tightly, and so any traces may soon have disappeared. Besides, if we are considering the sexual psychology of it all, why on earth should the Marquis, having once gone so far, have deprived himself of the rich and essentially sadistic experience which the sight of a young woman naked and immobilised by ropes on a bed of flagellation might provide him with?

Points 3 and 4

First a general observation, in which the view adopted by Dr André Javelier and the author coincide : whether the Marquis really did tell Rose Keller what he wanted of her, or whether he cheated her by offering her honest work, does not alter the fact that, possibly with promptings from Marie Louise Jouette, the Registrar's wife, she very soon grasped the advantage she stood to gain from her unfortunate experience. Perhaps Dr Javelier does exaggerate a trifle when he says that in Rose Keller giving evidence to the la Tournelle court it is easy to "perceive the blackmailer who knows how to pitch her yarn". But at the same time he adds in her favour that "her posture made it impossible for her to realise clearly what was being done to her or about her". This led Dr Javelier to conclude that it might be not a matter of "invention", but rather of "erroneous interpretation of the facts, which for her were more tactile than visual".

This means that Rose Keller's position prone on the bed makes it impossible for us to credit all she said, which very largely explains the divergencies between her and Sade on these points. Did he for instance use a birch or a cat-o'-nine-tails? Perhaps he used both. But what is certain is that he used the latter instrument, as we shall see later. Either whipping instrument would fit the Arcueil surgeon's evidence, for in his report made on April 3rd he said that "he found all her buttocks and part of her loins whipped and excoriated with long cuts and bruises down her back ... all of which seemed to have been made with some bruising, cutting instrument".

Two of this doctor's expressions ("excoriation" and "cutting instrument") gave rise to uncertainty what was meant, but they were explained away when he was interrogated on April 23rd, for then he told Councillor Jacques de Chavanne that "by excoriation he meant that the epidermis only was removed in some places ... and that as for the bruising, this was only what arose from the appearance of birch marks; as for the cuts, all he saw was fragments of epidermis removed".

We shall return to the cuts or incisions in a moment. All we need do for the moment is emphasise the great credibility of what the Marquis admitted regarding a cat-o'-nine-tails with knotted cords, together with Surgeon Le Comte's precise term (which he confirmed), adding Dr Javelier's observation that however small it may be, a knot in a length of whipcord is certainly—to use Le Comte's term—a "bruising instrument" (*instrument contondant*).

Now that stick. Who knows? For a moment Sade may have whacked her with the handle of his cat-o'-nine-tails! When Le Comte was asked whether "he observed any injury which might have been caused by blows made with a stick" he replied that he "saw only two marks, slightly above the lumbar region, on the spine, but with no subcutaneous effusion of blood, merely redness".

Between the alleged birch-rod blows (*point 3*) and the incisions (*point 4*) there is a certain connection. We have to decide whether the term *cut* which the surgeon uses really fits the notion of a lesion caused by a penknife, such as Rose Keller alleges having felt. In fact it does not, for when cross-examined the Count specified that "there may have been about a dozen excoriations in the form of cuts ... of the size and shape of a piece of six sous ("a sixpence"), but these did not go deeper than the epidermis".

In short, it was all a matter of excoriation, of grazes, not of cuts in the sense of incisions. Here Dr Javelier's explanation is worth considering. He says that Rose Keller must have been so "distracted by the pain" that she took lashes for incisions. Finally, Maurice Heine's comment brings us back to the positive evidence. "Sade's declaration," he says, "that all he used was a cat-o'-nine-tails with knotted whipcords gives us the exact picture of the lesions which were found, particularly the rounded excoriations".

Finally, we have the burns. Here Le Comte's reply is decisive and definitely excludes giving credence to Rose Keller. The surgeon found "no mark of red wax nor any trace of burning such as might have been caused by Spanish wax dripped on to the grazed places ... all he found were drops of white wax on the girl's back which did not seem to have caused any burning".

Here once again we may allow Maurice Heine to sum up: "Without denying any more than Sade did in his own writings the trend towards cruelty proper to any flagellator, does it not seem likely that when, as the Marquis says, he stopped striking his partner because he noticed an 'inflamed' place, he there and then treated this with a suitable wax ointment?"

Point 5

This is really not very important. Need one emphasise that it was but natural for the victim to tend to exaggerate the number of repetitions and for the flagellator to minimise them? Fixing a mean between them seems likely to bring us nearer the truth.

JUDICIAL PROCEEDINGS

1. Generalities

When one grasps the insubstantial nature of the crime with which the Marquis de Sade was charged and further takes into account his powerful connections of rank and marriage which might have protected him, what first astonishes us is that any fuss at all was made about the matter. What next astonishes is the high level of the court intervention (the criminal Court of La Tournelle), and finally the duration of the preliminary incarceration, which was at least seven months, followed moreover by a period of restricted domicile.

To understand such disproportion between the facts and their consequences, two factors above all must be taken note of. On the one hand there was a persistent clamour of public opinion, on the other there was the prejudice of the Chairman of the Tournelle bench and the active hostility of a still more important judicial figure, the first President of the Court, Maupeou, who was soon to become Chancellor of France.

Regarding the first point, an unpublished letter of Lady de Saint Germain to the Abbé de Sade, dated April 18th 1878, is clear enough :

> "Public hatred against him has become inexpressible. Judge for yourself : it is being said that he carried out this flagellation to mock the scourging of Christ. . . . He is the victim of popular violence; the case of M. de Fronsac and of many another are quoted in the same breath; there is no doubt about it, the frightful things that some members of the Royal Court have done in the past ten years are incredible."

These few lines bear out the following observations which Maurice Heine made :

> "Then why so much fuss about a beating? The reason was that public opinion, with which a weakened central authority was to have to reckon more and more, had for a long time been made indignant by the impunity granted to misdeeds, or even crimes of libertinage, provided they were committed by somebody bearing one of the big names. The indulgence or at least the lenience shown in a high place to certain guilty persons, especially a prince of the Royal blood, Count de Charolais, notorious for his bloodthirsty fancies, demanded some compensation, a sort of sacrificial goat. . . . And did not this particular loose-liver seem deliberately to have chosen for his act of debauchery one of the most respected feasts of Christendom? Was it not his frank purpose in whipping his victim to make mock of the flogging of Christ, just as his suggestion that he would confess her, merely ridiculed the sacrament of penitence?"

Regarding the second point, Heine (whom we cannot but quote on this matter) also says :

> "The libertine could not have made a worse choice of location for his little retreat. . . . Hardy the bookseller indeed remarked that 'since the incident made some stir in the neighbourhood, M. Pinon . . . who was at the time Chairman of the Tournelle bench, and who had a country house there, where he was staying at the time, was most outraged when he heard about it.' Now, although Pinon was not present at the first two sittings of the court (April 15th and 16th 1768), he certainly presided at those of April 19th and 21st, and signed the two court orders dated April 19th and June 10th. Let us further note that the second of the decisions taken on this latter date, namely, the judgment passed by the full bench of the court, bears the signature of First President Maupeou, whose personal hostility to the President of the Taxation Court became still more to be feared when he exercised the high functions of Chancellor at the time of the Marseilles affair."

The consequences of the Arcueil affair include a peculiar feature too outstanding for us not to try to explain it here. Some days after the flogging of Rose Keller, the Marquis de Sade was on Royal orders confined to Saumur Fortress. Further, by Royal decree, he was transferred at the end of April to Pierre Encise Fortress. But on April 19th we find the Tournelle Court ordering Sade's arrest, on May 7th it charges him with ignoring the court order, on May 11th it proclaims his arrest by public crier, and on June 1st it issues a second warrant against him for failing to respond to the first warrant. Was it really feasible that these magistrates did not know where Sade was? That is scarcely likely and would indeed seem to be denied by the following passage in a letter from the Minister of the Royal Household to Lady de Sade, dated April 23rd: "The High Court would not fail to insist on possession of the Marquis if they saw him in the regular company of people who come to the castle."

What happened was probably this. Once, under the pressure of First President Maupeou, who was worried to see a case so well calculated to dishonour the son-in-law of his enemy slip from his hands, the Tournelle Criminal Court had with strange celerity (which did not fail to disturb the arrested man's family) ordered Sade's arrest, it could not but insist—if its authority were not to be reduced to *nil*—on carrying on with every subsequent procedural step, taking no official cognizance of the fact that Sade had already, by extra-judicial procedure, been put under lock and key.

BAIL AT ARCUEIL AND SIMULTANEOUS INCARCERATION AT SAUMUR ON ROYAL ORDERS
1768

April 3rd. Reaching the *rue de la Fontaine* after her escape, at about 4 p.m., Rose Keller met three village women and told them about her mishap. The women took her into a yard, examined her injuries and went with her to the public prosecutor. He took her to the mansion of Charles Lambert, the Registrar. Here Mme Lambert (Marie Louise Jouette) saw her and Rose told her story again. But the lady was so upset that she could not bear to listen. No doubt because of an unconscious sado-masochism of her own (which the lady's own evidence, given later, indeed suggests), she felt obliged to retire.

Meanwhile, as the Arcueil magistrate was away, the Constabulary Brigadier of Bourg la Reine was summoned. He arrived a little before eight, took the victim's statement down and at once had her examined by Surgeon Pierre Paul Le Comte, after which the Registrar's wife asked a neighbour to take Rose Keller in (she did not lodge the woman herself till two days later). Mr Vermouret provided Sade's victim with a straw mattress in his cow byre.

At about six p.m. the Marquis de Sade said goodbye to his gardener and went back to the house in the *rue Neuve du Luxembourg* in Paris.

April 4th. The Arcueil magistrate took down Rose Keller's statement.

April 5th. Installed at Arcueil House, Rose Keller told the lady of the manor (Lambert's spouse) the whole of the story that the latter could not bear to hear two days previously!

Before leaving the house in the *rue Neuve du Luxembourg* "for the country" the Marquis de Sade dismissed his valet and told him he could go wherever he wished.

April 6th. The Arcueil magistrate proceeded to hear six witnesses.

April 7th. First thing in the morning Lady de Sade sent messages to the Abbé Amblet and M. Claude Antoine Sohier, Barrister and Court Prosecutor, to come to see her at the *rue Neuve du Luxembourg*. They came without delay, with only a few minutes gap between them. The *Marquise* received them in Lady Montreuil's apartments, and Lady Montreuil informed them that a charge was being preferred against her son-in-law on the plaint of a prostitute and requested them to lose no time in going to Arcueil to find out if the girl could be prevailed upon to withdraw the charge and pay her the necessary "satisfaction".

Reaching Arcueil, these emissaries applied to the Registrar, who took them to the room where Rose Keller was sleeping. She then alleged that she had been very badly maltreated and was now quite incapable of working. When the lawyer asked if she could consent to withdraw her charge, she said she would not do so even if they gave her a thousand crowns. The lawyer pointed out that this was really a very big sum of money indeed, and even if she went to law and won her case, the court would certainly not grant her so much. Keller would not give way, and the two envoys withdrew for a moment to discuss the situation, after which 1,800 *livres* was suggested.

The woman then came down to 2,000 *livres*. But as this sum was still considered to be too large, the two men decided to go back to Paris and inform Lady Montreuil what Keller wanted. Lady Montreuil told them they were to see the charge was withdrawn, whatever the cost, to put a stop to the rumours which already threatened to spread, and when they got back they found Rose Keller sitting up in bed, in cheerful conversation with a number of women. The lawyer then remarked: "There, you see, you are not as ill as you made out, and I expect you will soon be quite well." Finally the agreement to withdraw the charge was drawn up in Master Lambert's presence, and signed by Rose Keller, and she was paid an agreed sum of 2,400 *livres*, plus seven gold *louis* for dressings and medicaments.

April 8th. The Minister of the Royal Household informed the Commandant of Saumur Castle that he was to accept the Marquis de Sade as his permanent prisoner. It was His Majesty's intention that the captive should be kept "in close confinement" and not under any pretext allowed to leave the castle grounds.

The same day the Minister transmitted the Royal instructions to the Lieutenant of Constabulary, de Sartine, so that Sade might be arrested and taken to Saumur.

April 9th. On Lady de Sade's request, the Abbé Amblet went to the maisonette at Arcueil to settle some bills and fetch "some silver and some prints" as well as "the key of the Paris wardrobe".

April 12th. Having obtained the privilege of not being taken to Saumur under police escort, Sade set out for prison in the charge of the Abbé Amblet. From Joigny he wrote to his uncle the Abbé de Sade at Saumane as follows:

"In the name of this misfortune which harasses me, I
pray you to pardon any wrongs I have done you and,
dear uncle, be inspired in all this rather by a spirit of
peace and not the vengeance I have deserved at your
hands. If the business is gossiped about down there, you
might maintain it is all a tissue of lies and insist that I am
with my regiment."

The Marquis concluded by further leaving all the business
he had entrusted to him "in his good care", in particular his
lawsuit with Lord de Gadagne.

PROCEEDINGS IN THE CRIMINAL COURT OF LA TOURNELLE
(AND SIMULTANEOUS INCARCERATION AT PIERRE-ENCISE BY
ROYAL COMMAND)
1768

April 15th. During a sitting of the Criminal Council of the
High Court of Paris (Chairman Lord de Gourgue) one of the
bench said he felt obliged to inform his colleagues about "a
horrible crime which has just been committed at Arcueil".
After discussion, the Council resolved that the Royal Prosecutor
General should at once be sent for and charged to enquire into
the matter and also into what stage any proceedings had
reached, and to report back to the council the following morning at 8.30 a.m.

April 16th. At the hour fixed, the General Prosecutor reported
back to the Criminal Council, under the same chairman. He
had written by express letter to his deputy at Châtelet, to the
magistrate and registrar of Arcueil, and to the Constabulary
Brigadier of Bourg la Reine, and they had all replied at once
that proceedings had been started and he would be kept informed at every stage, although his deputy had not yet been
informed. When the Council had perused the four replies, it
ordered them to be attached to the reports which would come
in, the whole to be brought before it again on April 19th with
the conclusions of the Prosecutor-General, "so all may be
properly proceeded with".

April 18th. Lady de Saint Germain, a friend of the family,
wrote to the Abbé de Sade at Saumane. She had received a

letter from him on Easter Sunday, "a day for ever fateful for the house of Sade". Had he been informed about his nephew's affair? The Dowager Lady de Sade and Lady Montreuil had engaged her to write to him about it. "But how can I bring myself to it? How tell you all the terrible details of the wrong-doings of that wretched man—though, if we are to believe his own story, he merely committed an act of wild folly, to gratify his desires, but for which he has paid a high price?"

While making that dismal journey to Saumur the Abbé Amblet had written to her to beg her "not to abandon his child". Lady de Saint Germain had already defended the Marquis and would continue to do so as much as she could, but how reply to those who had seen the charge and the evidence of witnesses, several copies of which had been distributed in Paris? "Public hatred of him has gone beyond all bounds . . . people make out that he committed this flagellation to mock the Passion. . . . For the past fortnight it is all people talk about." They had thought the matter ended, "with the civil plaintiff being 'satis-fied' and the Marquis punished by loss of the pennant he would otherwise have acquired and by imprisonment for a year and some days; but then a malevolent councillor had entered a denunciation" and the Prosecutor-General had been obliged to take notice of it. The Marquis, she maintained, was "the vic-tim of public ferocity, he being made to answer for the case of Lord de Fronsac and many others".

April 19th. The President of the Montreuil court wrote to the Abbé de Sade to ask him to come to Paris at this critical moment and plead his nephew's cause in high places. At the same time the Duke de Montpezat wrote to tell the *Marquise* de Villeneuve-Martignan, at Avignon, that her nephew's posi-tion had become more serious since the High Court has taken an interest in the Arcueil proceedings. His correspondent should warn the Abbé de Sade, who if he respected the family wishes could not come to Paris too soon.

The same day the Prosecutor-General let the Council (Pinon still the chairman) read the reports he had received and also his own conclusions. After deliberation the Council gave precise instructions: the court proceedings were to go on, the Marquis de Sade and any others indicated by the Prosecutor-General

were to be held at disposition, the accused was to be "arrested
and made a prisoner of the prisons of Paris" and his property
was to be seized and an inventory of it made, while Rose Keller
was to "be seen and examined by the physician and surgeons of
the Court".

April 20th. "Distraint on Lord de Sade." Griveau, High Court
bailiff, appeared at the Marquis' domicile in the Montreuil
Mansion in the *rue Neuve du Luxembourg*. In the absence of
the accused, who had quit the house about a fortnight previously, he left a copy of the decree of arrest of April 19th with
the porter, together with a summons to appear in a fortnight's
time. As for the seizing of Sade's property, here the bailiff
could do nothing, because the furniture of the apartment occupied by Sade all belonged to his father-in-law!

The same day, Paul Estienne Charles Mayneaud and
Jacques de Chavanne, Councillors of the High Court of Paris,
went to Arceuil to collect evidence concerning the dwellings
which the Marquis had hired there and any other matters
relating to the case.

April 21st. At 7 a.m. there was a "resumption of the case
against the Marquis de Sade". Rose Keller appeared before
Councillor de Chavanne. The following witnesses also
appeared: Anne Croizet Pontier, Marie Louise Jouette
Lambert, Anne Glougné Bajou, Marguerite Duc Six-
deniers, Jean François Vallée, The Fiscal of the Bailiwick of
Arceuil, Claude Antoine Sohier, Court Prosecutor, Charles
Lambert, Notary and Registrar, Pierre Bourgeois, Gardener at
Arceuil Manor, (the property of the Lamberts), Pierre Marin
Lambert, Gardener to the Marquis de Sade, Charles François
Fleurot, wheelwright, Jacques François Amblet, Tonsured
Clerk of the Diocese of Geneva and "sometime tutor to the
Marquis de Sade", Paul Sébire, manservant of the accused
at the Mansion of the President of Montreuil.

The Abbé Amblet stated that he "had known the accused
since childhood, having been in charge of his education", that
he "had found him to be of a fiery temperament which readily
prompted him to a life of pleasure" but had always known him
to be "a kind-hearted man, far removed from the horrors imputed to him in the charge", and that when in college he had

been much liked by his fellow-pupils, as he had been in the various army units in which he had served. "That he had known him to perform acts of benevolence and humanity, among others to a joiner named Moulin who died the year before after a long illness during which the Marquis had assisted him, and that this man had left several children, one of whom the Marquis had undertaken to maintain, and hence he, the Abbé, could not credit all the foul deeds imputed to him."

April 23rd. Cross-examination by Councillor Chavanne of Pierre Paul Le Comte, surgeon at Arcueil, treated as hostile witness.

The same day the Minister of the Royal Household informed de Bory, commandant of the Pierre-Encise Fortress near Lyons, that he would be shortly receiving a new prisoner, the Marquis de Sade. "It is His Majesty's desire," wrote the Minister, "that he should not leave his room or have any contact with the other prisoners." When he needed air he was to be escorted. But as he had an incipient abscess, for which certain treatment had been prescribed, if he needed to see any surgeon of the city of Lyons, would M. de Bory kindly make any arrangements necessary to facilitate this and also take in the valet being sent to him who was used to dressing the fistula night and morning.

In another letter, dated April 23rd, the Minister of the Royal Household wrote to the *Marquise* de Sade concerning the detention of her husband at Pierre-Encise. She had asked if he might have freedom of movement within the fortress. That was impossible, particularly after what had just happened in the High Court, which would not fail to take up the matter if it found the Marquis associating with any visitors to the castle.

Towards May 10th. Inspector Marais reached Pierre-Encise with his prisoner.

April 26th. Lady Montreuil wrote to the Abbé de Sade. This business of his nephew was "an act of madness or libertinage which was beyond excuse, no doubt, but without a hint in it of the horrors with which the charge has been augmented". But unfortunately the decree for arrest which the High Court had "hastily issued against him on the first rumours will none the less still hold till he has been cleared in court".

Further she informed the Abbé that the Duke de Montpezat had very kindly shown the liveliest interest in the Abbé's nephew, and the whole family was most grateful to this lord.

On the blank third page of this letter there is a note in the Abbé de Sade's hand, addressed to an unknown correspondent. It runs:

> "As you see, I was right to insist that my nephew was not capable of the atrocities that public gossip charges him with and all one can reprove him for was an excess of frolicking, an act of mere imprudence. The high court was a little too much in a hurry in issuing its indictment, which now will have to be cleared, a proceeding both unpleasant and expensive. But it's an ill wind—this will be a lesson to him for the future."

Some date just before April 30th. Furnished with the instructions of de Saint Florentin, Minister of the Royal Household, Inspector Marais appeared at Saumur to take the Marquis from that prison to Pierre-Encise prison, to find him enjoying the freedom of the castle and the board of the Commandant. The Marquis felt quite lost, learning that he was to be transferred to Pierre-Encise. On the way there he protested that all he did was to give the wench a whipping—"which he made out to regret," though Inspector Marais thought that at the bottom of his heart "he was completely unchanged".

May 3rd. The Minister of the Royal Household informed the Dowager Countess de Sade that in his view it would be against the prisoner's own interests for His Majesty to be handed her complaints about the way she alleged her son was being treated in Pierre-Encise Fortress, for His Majesty might well decide to hand the Marquis back to the High Court of Paris, which would not be at all to his advantage.

May 7th. It was reported to the Prosecutor-General that the Marquis de Sade had failed to appear in the fortnight given him.

May 11th. Louis François and Claude Louis Ambezac, sworn trumpeters of His Majesty, duly performed on their instruments not only on the grand staircase of the palace and in all the other customary places, but also outside the town mansion of the President of Montreuil, to be followed by Philippe Rouveau, Usher of the Rod and sole sworn public crier of His Majesty, who in loud, clear tones called on "Lord de Sade, absent and fugitive . . . to appear in person a week from today before our Lords of the High Court of *Parlement* sitting in the Chamber of Criminal Justice of *La Tournelle,* and to constitute himself prisoner of the *Conciergerie du Palais* of Paris, to be judged, heard and cross-examined . . . and to take knowledge to wit that failing so to do his trial shall be conducted and completed in default and contempt of court".

May 24th. The Dowager Countess de Sade wrote to de Sartine to protest against an article which has appeared in the *Gazette de Hollande,* presenting the "unhappy affair of her son-in-law" "in the blackest hues".

June 1st. A second cry of default against the Marquis.

June 3rd. Two Royal Orders were forwarded to the Lieutenant General of the Constabulary. 1. The Marquis de Sade, imprisoned at Pierre-Encise, was to be transferred to the *Conciergerie du Palais,* there to have the High Court ratify the Royal Letters of Nullification which he had been granted. 2. This ratification being accomplished, the Marquis was to be taken back to Pierre-Encise.

June 8th. Arriving from Pierre-Encise under the escort of Inspector Marais, the Marquis de Sade was incarcerated in the *Conciergerie du Palais* prison for the night.

June 10th. 10 a.m. The Marquis was cross-examined by Councillor Jacques de Chavanne. The Marquis admitted the principal allegations, but insisted that when she agreed to go with him Rose Keller was not unaware that she was required for a bout of sex play. When at the close of the cross-examination the magistrate asked whether he had obtained letters of annulment, Sade replied that he had and intended to make use of them.

THE HIGH COURT OF PARLIAMENT PROCEEDINGS
THE GRAND-CHAMBER ASSEMBLES
1768

June 10th. The *la Tournelle* criminal court relinquished the Arcueil case in favour of the *Grand-Chambre* court, which alone was able to take cognizance of the Royal Patent of Annulment.

On the same day the High Court of Paris, assembled *in pleno,* definitely ratified the annulment obtained by the Marquis "for the grantee thereof to have advantage of the effect and contents of these same presents", condemning the Marquis at the same time "to refund the sum of one hundred *livres* relative to the board of prisoners in the *Conciergerie du Palais* prison".

SADE REIMPRISONED ON ROYAL ORDERS AT PIERRE-ENCISE

June 11th or 12. The Marquis de Sade was conducted back to Pierre-Encise.

June 13th. A letter of Lady Montreuil to the Abbé de Sade at Saumane. She informed him that the full Assembly of *Parlement* had indeed ratified the Royal Patent of Annulment and remarked that the magistrates conducted the case "with the utmost consideration". But her son-in-law has been immediately returned to Pierre-Encise, where he was to be held "as long as His Majesty finds fit". The reason why she had not written to the Abbé earlier was that for the past two days all her time had been taken up with calls on one and another who had helped in the matter, to thank them. "An indecent matter which is beyond condoning," concluded Lady Montreuil, "could not have been concluded more decently".

June 17th. The Minister of the Royal Household confirmed to Lord de Bory the orders he gave on the first occasion of the Marquis' incarceration at Pierre-Encise. Should His Majesty consider it proper to reduce the rigour of the Marquis' treatment in any way, Lord de Bory would be informed thereof.

June 21st. On this day Councillor de Chavanne cross-examined Jacques André Langlois, detained in Paris and awaiting a decision on his case. Sade's valet insisted that he was not involved in any way in the business at Arceuil. All he recalled was bringing his master a light while he was shut in a room with this Rose Keller, but even so his master did not let him into the room, but came out to the ante chamber to take the light.

July 18th. The Minister of the Royal Household informed de Bory that the *Marquise* de Sade has asked whether her husband might not be allowed to take the air, for health reasons, and he authorised de Bory to allow him to do so subject to all the necessary precautions.

Early August. The *Marquise,* whose husband had asked her to come to Lyons, arrived in that town, but to pay her travelling costs was obliged to sell some diamonds.

August 24th. The Minister of the Royal Household to the *Marquise* de Sade, at Lyons :

"My Lady, I am writing to Lord de Bory ... to tell him he may let you see your husband once or twice more during your stay at Lyons which I trust will not be protracted. I would advise you in the two talks you will be having with him to obtain the fullest possible instructions concerning the settlement of his affairs, for I should not conceal from you that it is not His Majesty's intention to restore his liberty very soon and you should not think you will be able to take him to his estates."*

November 5th. The Minister of the Royal Household on this day authorised de Bory to let the *Marquise* see her husband as much as she pleased, provided she lived in Lyons with extreme circumspection.

November 16th. The Minister of the Royal Household sent de Bory two Royal orders, one instructing him to release the Marquis, the other requiring the latter to retire to La Coste.

*From the letter which the Minister wrote to de Bory on the same day it would seem that out of the "kindness of his heart" the Commander of the Fortress had allowed Lady de Sade to exceed the number of talks with her husband which had been allowed (two or three at most). It was, one may be sure, the favours she had reason to expect from kindly de Bory, plus the hope she had of being able to take her husband to La Coste, that had prompted her to stay in Lyons long enough to annoy the Minister. But, as will be seen, she nevertheless stayed on at Lyons till her husband was released.

At the same time the Minister requested de Bory to impress on Sade that he should conform as strictly as possible to that injunction and not stay on in Lyons or make any long stay in any large town on the way to La Coste.

On the same day, informing the Dowager Countess de Sade of His Majesty's orders, the Minister told her that it would depend directly on her son's further conduct how much liberty he was allowed and the Marquis could not be circumspect enough to wipe out the past.

November 19th. Lady Montreuil to the Abbé de Sade, at Saumane: His Majesty had released the Marquis and was allowing him to withdraw to his estates, together with the *Marquise,* who was now in Lyons.

"She has done too much not now to complete her work by showing him every possible mark of devotion."

And she herself was sure that he must by now have thought seriously enough over it all never again to cause his wife such sorrow or his family such worry. But she nevertheless asked the Abbé, who would not be far away from the couple, to be kind and keep an eye on things. The Sades would very soon reach Provence. The Marquis' health was poor. He was anxious to rest in his Provençal home. But the Royal order had only just been sent and her son-in-law could hardly leave Lyons before the 25th or even the 28th. . . .

"Your grand-nephew is very well," she added in a postscript, "a handsome child indeed, I have been giving him all the care that my affection for his father and his mother inspires in me."

CHAPTER SIX

From Release from Pierre-Encise Fortress
to the Eve of the Marseilles Incident
1768 - 1772

CHRONICLE

THE MARQUIS, as we have seen, was set at liberty by a Royal Order dated November 16th. The moment this order reached Pierre-Encise, he joined his wife who had come to Lyons a month after his reincarceration in that fortress. She still loved him, despite his loose living, and craved to be as near him as she could. From Lady Montreuil's letter of November 19th we see that the young couple had fixed on La Coste as their obligatory residence in the country. Lady Montreuil was indeed delighted at the thought that any day now her daughter would make the acquaintance of the Abbé, who, she said, was to welcome them down there. But when we look into the evidence covering this period it seems that the *Marquise* did not do as her mother hoped. Perhaps her four months' pregnancy played a part in her decision. Or was it that she was obliged to return to Paris to try to patch up her husband's financial position, which by now was desperate? Whatever the reason, she certainly decided, and not without tears, that she must part from him, and after a few days together in Lyons he went to Provence while she went to the capital.

What sort of life did Sade lead at La Coste from now to the end of April 1769, when he returned to Paris? Instead of living quietly, so that the last year's scandal might be forgotten, he gave up all his time to dances and play-acting! And with what sort of actresses, the President's lady lamented! For Lady

Montreuil began to realise that her daughter was better off in Paris. She would have been "worried to death to think of her shut up in a remote chateau with that madcap".

At last, however, on the *Marquise*'s application to Minister Saint Florentin concerning the Marquis' health, which required his presence in Paris for indispensable treatment, the King was gracious enough to allow Sade to settle in "some country house in the immediate neighbourhood of Paris", provided he did not entertain largely but concerned himself solely with medical treatment. And so in May 1769 we find Sade back in Paris.

June 27th 1769. Birth in Paris in the parish of la Madeleine de la Ville l'Évêque of Donatien Claude Armand, *chevalier de Sade*, the Marquis' second son, christening taking place the following day at St Mary Magdalèné's, the godparents being the Lady Montreuil and the Dowager Countess de Sade.

June 29th 1769. Writing to the Abbé de Sade to inform him about the birth of his grand-nephew, Lady Montreuil remarked that since his return to Paris the Marquis had been completely free and it was her hope that he would not misuse his liberty. At the moment he was "being a good father", most attentive to his wife and seeming to enjoy being preoccupied with his first born, who was also present at the christening of his younger brother.

September 25th to October 23rd 1769. Sade travelled in the Low Countries. On September 25th he was in Brussels, on the 28th in Antwerp, on October 2nd in Rotterdam, on the 7th at The Hague, on the 16th in Amsterdam and on the 23rd October back again in Brussels.

March 24th 1770. The Minister of the Royal Household to Lady Montreuil :

"It was my wish to ascertain His Majesty's feelings regarding the Marquis before suggesting to His Majesty that the Marquis might be allowed to reappear at court; I felt that the impressions which His Majesty may have gained of the Marquis from time to time were perhaps too vivid to have been erased, which decided me to take no further step, thinking it would have done no good and that had

> any request been refused, as there was every reason to think, this would have been much to his detriment in his Regiment. It is my view that in the matter we should have complete reliance on the benefits of time."

July 24th 1770. The Marquis informed lawyer Fade of Apt, who was managing his properties in Provence, that he was joining the army and he gave his address as *Captain in the Burgundy Regiment at Fontenay-le-Comte, Poitou.*

Early August 1770. Sade reached Fontenay-le-Comte, but the officer commanding in the absence of the Count de Saignes, Lt-Colonel of the Regiment, at the time at Compiègne, refused to allow Sade to take over his duties. But he refused for bad reasons. What is worse, when Sade protested, he ordered him to consider himself under arrest and forbade the quarter-masters and company suppliers to obey any order of Sade's or pay any heed whatsoever to him.

The Marquis at once wrote a furious letter to de Saignes, who wrote from Compiègne on August 23rd to tell his deputy that he had difficulty in believing that such astonishing things could have taken place and he was at once to send in a full report. He was astonished that his deputy should not have done so before.

Unfortunately, we have insufficient evidence to state exactly what followed, but it would seem that Lord de Saignes' letter was couched in such terms that it decided the deputy at once to mend his ways and allow Sade to assume the duties conferred on him by the King. Anyway, the next we know is that on March 31st 1771 Sade applied to the Minister for War, asking for the rank of Colonel, without stipend, and on March 19th this application was granted.

April 17th 1771. Birth in Paris of Madeleine Laure, daughter of the Marquis de Sade.

May 27th 1771. The Marquis, who had shortly before this arrived in Provence, ordered the public officials of Saumane, of which he was lord of the manor, to pay him homage.

June 1st 1771. Back in Paris, the Marquis was authorised to draw 10,000 *livres* as the fee payable on his cession of the regimental colonelcy to the Count d'Osmont.

September 9th 1771. Release of the Marquis from Fort l'Évêque prison, where he had spent a week for debts. He obtained release by a cash payment of 3,000 *francs* and a promissory note for the remainder dated October 15th. After this little experience he seems to have made haste to La Coste, together with his family.

November 7th 1771. Lady Anne Prospère de Launay, canoness Sade's sister-in-law—to whom we shall devote a whole chapter later—joined the Sades at La Coste.

January 15th 1772. The Marquis invited M. Girard de Lourmain to see a comedy written by himself, to be played on January 20th in the manor theatre.

February 25th 1772. Sade engaged Bourdais, actor, and his wife, to act at La Coste from Easter to November.

May 29th 1772. Lady Montreuil wrote to the Abbé de Sade. She hoped he would give her some news of her children, for she knew nothing, not even where they are, as theatre acting and other entertainments make them "very unfixed". The Marquis must manage his own life, but that should not go so far as to compromise his wife or his sister-in-law. That was an "indignity" which Lady Montreuil intended to put straight. All these festivities were eating up a fortune already greatly diminished. The Marquis was always pressing her to settle this or that debt for him, but she was very tired of being his dupe. One might put oneself out for a decent cause, but not for wild living.

DESCRIPTION OF LA COSTE MANOR

The village of La Coste, two and a half miles from Bonnieux, six and a half miles from Apt and twenty-eight from Avignon, is built at a height of 1,000 feet above sea level on one of the spurs of Mt Lubéron. It was one of the first places to be seized by the Waldensians. In 1545, very soon after the massacres of Cabrières and Mérindol, organised by that sinister character

Meynier d'Oppède, first president of the high court of Aix,* the Catholic troops proposed to set up a garrison there. They began advancing on this fortified village, where all the Waldensians of the region had taken refuge. The lord of the manor— it must have been Balthazar de Simiane, who died in 1552— undertook to mediate. The suggested conditions were the destruction of the ramparts at four points and the execution of a number of individuals. The inhabitants thought the terms agreed, and were about to lay down their arms when, seeing the ramparts unguarded, the Catholics attacked in force. All the men were killed at the point of the sword and all the women and girls herded into an orchard for the soldiery to vent their lust on.

In 1601 François de Simiane, Lord of the Manor of La Coste, married Anne de Simiane-Châteauneuf, by whom he had four sons, Joachim, who succeeded him in the title, Gaspart, Abbé d'Anchin, and two others (who were Knights of Malta) and one daughter, named Diane, who on April 12th 1627 married Jean Baptiste de Sade. Joachim de Simiane La Coste, who married Gabrielle de Brancas, had only one daughter by her (Isabelle, who married Joseph Dominique de Berton de Crillon, Marchal of the Camps and Armies of the King). Joachim dying thus without a male heir, the castle and lands of La Coste passed to the house of Sade, through Jean Baptiste François Joseph, father of the Marquis.

> "The manor-house and lands of La Coste," says P. Bourdin, "were originally a Royal grant, the holder of the fief rendering His Majesty the allegiance that his vassals paid him 'on bended knees'. The lord had the rights of justice, high, intermediate and low, tolls, fowl, fish and hunt,

*Sade could never hear of any act of religious fanaticism without becoming furious with indignation. He particularly loathed those which had devastated his beloved homeland in the sixteenth century. Here is an extract from his *Le President Mystifié* in which he apostrophises a member of that high court of Aix: "The public horror that your execrable deeds at Mérindol awake in my heart still lives on, for did you not then present the most horrible spectacle one could imagine, so that one cannot even think of it without a shudder, the guardians of peace, order and justice tearing through the district like mad things, torch in one hand, dagger in the other, burning, slaughtering, violating, massacring all they came upon, like a horde of mad tigers escaping from the forest—was it seemly for magistrates to behave thus?"

kiln and 'pasture' on the mountain and a quit-rent on the lime-kilns built there, and an oil press in the village to which the inhabitants used to bring their olives and wal-nuts. He was paid one-eighth tithe of grain, vegetables, olives, hemp and acorns, one-tenth of grapes. Three small properties, Lavelan, la Maison Basse and le Petit Moulin, went with the manor: The farmers paid feudal dues, or at least, those still payable—scarcely five or six thousand livres altogether."

In point of fact, La Coste and the other lands were assessed at 5,750 *livres* in 1772, if we are to judge by the distraint made on July 11th of that year on Sade's property, after the Mar-seilles affair.

*   *   *

To drive from Bonnieux to La Coste one needs to take the road which winds round the slopes of Lubéron towards Méner-bes, then at the end of about three-quarters of a mile turn off right on the road which leads straight to Sade's manor house. After two loops on the level of Juliens the road rises and dips alternately as far as the south-west outskirts of La Coste. About half a mile away there is a water-spring on the left and soon after comes a slope dense with evergreen oak, one of which, many times a centenarian, lies beside the road, struck by light-ning, its huge roots in the air.

The short-cut footpath through the vale of Calavon, how-ever, affords a more beautiful approach firstly by a narrow Roman Gaulish road running between half-demolished walls, then on for more than an hour through fields, olive-groves and vineyards. La Coste dominates the whole of this magnificent landscape, growing larger and more precisely outlined as one draws nearer, like a long coveted treasure one is at last about to reach. . . .

The inhabited part of the village rises by steep slopes to the western gateway in the ancient ramparts. After this comes the upper village, now deserted, the ruined houses like a phantom guard of the Marquis' residence. To the right winds an ancient stairway, with gaping rooms of a keep opening off it on either side, a troublesome climb now. Then, all at once, at chest level, there is the whole eastern front, seeming as if on the point of collapsing and burying you under all its stones as the *mistral* beats down on them. . . . The still-room is like a cavern, littered with broken pillars, like so many giant phalluses. Farther on this front, now rent lengthwise by a deep crack, one clambers over crumbling masonry to an enormous vaulted room on the first floor. When the author was last there, in May 1948, that mass of ruins had by an exceptionally rainy season been transformed into a mat of poppies!

Above the north-west tower a glazed door set in a sixteenth century frame opens onto a tiled terrace, and between the dilapidated tower and what remains of the north front—like a stone giant buried head down, only his parted legs above ground —is a mass of debris covered with verdure over which one climbs into the Marquis' one-time park. "My poor park," Sade wrote at the end of 1813, "is there any more trace of me in it?"

Now all one can distinguish are clumps of shrubbery, a few miserable peach-trees and some wild almonds thrusting out of an undergrowth of lavender, with the hint of a central alley running from the ruined house to the St Hilaire road, Ménerbes way. In all probability it was at the end of this that the main gates of the *château* once stood. The broad expanse of the La Coste plateau, which runs from the west front, still stretches very far beyond the ancient limits of the park. On the right are deep quarries which have not been worked these fifty years.

All that remains of the west front are half-ruined stretches of wall. Only the south-east tower still stands. On the ground level of this tower is the main hall, opening on to the park, not far from a delightful sixteenth century well. It is almost square, and there are two joists to be seen, covered with moulded plaster, dividing the ceiling into three parts, each with Louis XV style mouldings and stucco shell work. The floor consists of hexagonal tiles. The mullioned east window is partly blind. The walls here still show traces of yellow wash, the ceiling of a red wash. On the right as one enters are the remains of a fireplace. And beyond the park and the plateau is spread out one of the loveliest of Mediterranean landscapes, the plain of Calavon, rich in all the austere splendour of southern flora, with lovely Mt Lubéron, its sides overgrown with thyme, myrtle and lavender, like a slumbering goddess silhouetted against a sky of impeccable blueness. . . .

* * *

The vicissitudes of this ancient manor house of La Coste will landmark our pages from now on, from the first hints of dilapidation which followed when the Marquis and his wife left their estate at the end of January 1777, never to see it again, to the act of sale of October 13th 1796, which after the shameful revolutionary devastation of September 17th and 21st 1792 was to transfer the ancestral house of the Simianes to J. S. Rovère, a representative of the people.

LADY ANNE PROSPÈRE DE LAUNAY

There is little documentary information on Lady Anne Prospère de Launay, who after the passionate love he bore for the de Lauris girl and Mlle Colet of the Italian Theatre was one of the great passions of Sade's younger years. Most regrettably, not a page of the correspondence between her and her brother-in-law has come down to us. All those letters were without doubt meticulously destroyed by Lady Montreuil, who was not going to leave in existence any evidence whatsoever of a union which so besmirched the honour of her family. Yet in a brief outline of his love-life, which leaves much that is indeterminate, it is not far from the truth to say that the Marquis' love for Lady Anne was perhaps the most important event in his life. For those alleged crimes at Marseilles would never have earned him thirteen years imprisonment in Vincennes prison and the Bastille, had Lady Montreuil not been instrumental in securing his arrest for the second time in February 1777 and his incarceration by *lettre de cachet* despite the indemnification of 1772. Without wishing to omit a number of other motives, both in Lady Montreuil and the Ministers concerned, we have to observe that it was solely the incarceration for life of her son-in-law in his incestuous role that offered any hope of clearing Lady Anne's good name.

We do not even know when Lady Anne was born, and there is no hope of finding out even that detail, since the registers of the parish of Saint Sulpice, in which her parents' domicile lay,

perished when the Seine prefecture archives were burned under
the Commune. All we know is that Sade's wife, Renée Pélagie,
was several years her sister Anne's senior. So we may assume
Anne was born between 1743 and 1745. The first evidence
we have of her existence is her signature on the Marquis' marriage contract (dated May 16th 1763).

The Marquis' thwarted love for Lady de Lauris at the time
of the marriage is of itself sufficient to invalidate an invention
which all Sade's biographers from Lacroix to Desbordes have
copied one from another, without the slightest attempt at veri-
fication. Sade is supposed to have fallen in love with Anne the
very first time he called at the house in the *rue Neuve du
Luxembourg* and in vain implored Lady Montreuil to let
him marry that daughter, Lady Montreuil being set on finding
a match for the eldest one first! We have far too much
evidence to handle in the present work to waste the least space
on the ridiculous story which Paul Lecroix said he had from
a certain Lefebure, a contemporary of the Marquis. Maurice
Heine has already dealt with this romantic tissue of lies, so back
to our story.

In November 1771 we find Lady Anne already living at La
Coste, where she seems recently to have joined her sister and
brother-in-law. On November 7th she wrote thence to the
Abbé de Sade to thank him for a little hack he had just sent
her; on December 1st we find her listing her brother-in-law's
lace and linen; while on February 4th 1772 she is visited by
Dr Terris of Bonnieux, because she has a chill, and on March
11th, 13th, 15th and 21st and also on May 14th the same
physician further attends her, for ailments not specified in his
diary.

There is also a bill of Master Silvestre, shoemaker in the
village of Ménerbes, which dates from sometime between the
end of 1771 and June 1772. It mentions a pair of pink silk
drugget shoes made for Lady de Launay and a trifling debt of
13 *sous* contracted by that young lady when out for a walk in
the village.

Nevertheless, before we go on with the scanty facts the date
of which we can check in Lady de Launay's life, we have to
put the following question : When exactly was it that she
became her brother-in-law's mistress? There is reason to guess

that it was only when the two lovers went off on their Italian escapade that the scandal became common knowledge. But though Sade's wife may have been aware of it some time before the Italian journey, it would seem that Sade's mother-in-law was quite uninformed, for in a letter written on May 27th 1772 all she complained of was the "unseemliness" of the performances in which the Marquis made his wife and his sister-in-law play a part, in and around La Coste.

On the *Marquise*'s own admission there was a sentimental bond, if not actual sexual intimacy, between the Marquis and Anne even before the latter came to La Coste at the end of October 1771, for in her Application of 1774 the *Marquise* said that she was "joined by Lady Anne her sister, *under the pretext* (we may underline these words) of being her companion and of enjoying the purer air of La Coste". She added that her "husband's urgency was not such as to make her imagine that a fateful love affair was soon to be the cause of a chain of misfortunes and ill luck". In the same document Lady de Sade said that when she heard of the Marseilles indictment and wanted to "ease her own mind" and "to calm her fears" she turned to her sister, but "the anxiety she read in her heart and the evasiveness of her answers merely upset her all the more".

Further, is not a trace of Lady Anne's jealousy about her lover, now guilty of deceiving her with some Marseilles prostitutes, to be read into another passage in Lady de Sade's petition? "Everybody, and that not excluding Lady Anne, joins in rousing her indignation" (Lady Montreuil's).

Whatever the truth of this, it remains a fact that somewhere about July 3rd 1772, a week before the proposed arrest of the Marquis, Lady Anne followed her brother-in-law in his flight, and the two lovers travelled the length and breadth of Italy till the end of September, halting in the principal towns, notably Genoa and Venice. Sade passed his sister-in-law off as his wife and, to use the language of the Count de la Tour, allowed himself "all the privileges appertaining thereto".

And now that we have reached the flight to Italy after the Marseilles business, we must quote Maurice Heine, who made an excellent examination of the episode and commented on it in terms which cannot be ignored :

"It was decided that the *Marquise* should ostensibly stay at La Coste, to draw the search that way, while the Marquis reached Italy, but that, either to put the *Marquise*'s mind still more at rest, or to give the flight the semblance of an innocent tour, the Lady Anne should accompany her brother-in-law to the frontier. However, Lady Anne did not restrict herself to that, but thought she should extend her protective mission beyond the limits of prudence. So seriously did she thus compromise herself in that unedifying company that society came to the conclusion she had been abducted by force.

There is no foundation for that romantic version, which is entirely the work of pressmen. But now she had become the prey of inventive minds, she certainly provided them with enough supporting material. In their passionate, incredible stories we find a wild freedom just like that which enabled authors to describe the Marseilles orgies in defiance of any probability. We find the same crude, common dramatics and the same tragi-comic details in them both.

They even go so far as to suggest that the Marquis stage-set the Marseilles business merely to seduce a fractious little schoolgirl. Donatien had no need of such additional fame to win Anne's love. Had he not already all the prestige of a great libertine in the eyes of a girl who, if so far innocent, was inquisitive and very likely highly sexed and possibly also stimulated by the intimacy of living under the same roof as the husband of a sister who may well have been jealous of her. She was unquestionably a perfect product of an education which was half worldly and half religious in the style of the age—and what effect can the stern principles at the base of such schooling have had in the eighteenth century? Here as in any other field of life all one had was a more or less skilfully masked façade which only too easily gave way to any rebellious personality."

Heine's picture of a girl who was at once daring, dreamy and dissembling matches what Sade himself wrote in his *Portrait of Lady Anne de Launay*. "She was well aware that to turn the sweetest impulses of the heart and the sweetest inclinations of the temperament into crimes was to blot out her reason and cloud her mind." And here is the lovely canoness as the future painter of the Duchess de Blagis and Adélaïde Durcet heroine of the *120 Days of Sodom,* depicted her—let so much satisfy us till the miniature of her is discovered which is mentioned in the *Post-mortem Inventory* of the Marquis' effects.

"Julie is at that happy age where a girl begins to feel that her heart is made for loving. The gentlest light of love's enjoyment shining in her fair eyes tells us so much, her engaging pallor is the very image of desire and if love does occasionally enliven her complexion it is only love's most delicate warmth rising within her. Her mouth is small and pleasant; the gentle breath of the zephyr is less pure than her breath; her smile is a very rose expanding to the touch of the sun.

Julie is tall; her form is lissom and elegant, her bearing noble, her walk easy and full of grace, as is all that she does. But what grace! And how rare it is! It is that natural, moving grace which is so seductive to any heart, that grace where artifice counts for nothing. Artifice? Heavens! What can artifice do where Nature itself has been drained dry? . . .

To all the lovely naturalness of the spirit of her age Julie adds all the amiability and subtlety of the most charming and developed of women. She goes further: not content with having a mind which is generous, she would have it well furnished too. From early on she learned how to let her intelligence speak, and with reasoning mind enlivening the prejudices of education and childhood she learned to know things and judge of them at an age at which others hardly thought at all.

With such subtle sense of things, what discoveries Julie made! She was well aware that to turn the sweetest impulses of the heart into crimes was to blot out her reason and cloud her mind. What happened? Seeing that the world wanted to cheat her heart, Julie let it speak out, and it very soon had its revenge for the insult. . . . The bandage dropping from her eyes, Julie saw everything in a new light and all the powers of her heart acquired new strength. Everything, even her countenance, gained thereby. Julie became the lovelier for it. What chill enwrapt her former delights, and what warmth her new ideas! She was no longer touched by the same things. The precious pet bird which had been all her love was now loved merely as a bird. There was an emptiness in the affection she had for her companion. . . . In a word, it was clear that something was lacking. And did Julie find it? May I flatter myself? . . . Forgive me, I am venturing on the story of your soul when all I wanted to do was to depict it. Oh, how I fear you will see a touch of vanity where I should only have given the truth! Forgive me, loveliest Julie, I have ventured to mention my love when I should have spoken solely of you!"

This portrait was no doubt written in the first dawn of the love between Sade and Lady Anne. But after three months spent in Venice and other Italian towns, when the Marquis and his sister-in-law were able to indulge in their mutual passion without any constraint, the time for this adulterous couple to separate was not far off. On October 2nd 1772 we find Lady Anne back at La Coste, though papers which have recently come to light inform us that very soon after this she joined her brother-in-law again, probably at Nice, and together with him came to Chambéry in Savoy on October 27th, though they only stayed in that town a few days.

The Marquis thought he had found sanctuary in the Duchy of Savoy. But his mother-in-law had quite different ideas. The scandal of his cohabitation with his sister-in-law was too brazen. Newspapers and broadsheets were commenting on it and spreading the news, and on December 9th 1772, the Marquis was suddenly arrested and taken to Miolans Fortress *by order of His Majesty the King of Sardinia, acting on the request of Milady of Montreuil!*

Fear of providing written evidence of her youngest daughter's incest spurred the President's lady relentlessly to the most detailed precautions. The moment her son-in-law was under arrest she requested the Count Sallier de La Tour, Governor of Chambéry, to have sent her "a little box, a wooden casket, probably mahogany, brass bound" before the Marquis could forestall her and extract any papers. And when she heard of Sade's escape on April 30th 1773 her first care was to make sure of any letters that the fugitive might have left in Miolans Fortress. "She assures me," wrote Count Sallier de la Tour on July 21st, "that she has pressing interest in their contents not being made public, as there is mention in them of her youngest daughter, who was seduced by her brother-in-law, this same Count de Sade. . . ."

Writing to the Count de la Tour from prison in March 1773, Sade stated that he was doing everything possible to break off any connection with Lady Anne, and that he would return to this young lady the letters she wrote him. If those who imprisoned him

> "allege that their sole reason for his imprisonment is their wish to break off a love-affair which is unseemly and troublesome, they press their annoyance too far, for I have very solemnly declared that I give it all up, and never cease saying so, as I do most expressly in the letter to Paris which I enclose herewith. . . . Then please tell me what I am to do to be believed; I crave your counsel. I give up all contact; I offer to give back all her letters; I swear not to go within a hundred leagues of Paris as long as they want, to forget everything; I ask for nothing; I make no suggestion calculated to harm or hinder a settlement of the matter which perhaps I desire more than they do. They still will not give me credit, so whatever am I to do? My position is indubitably extremely hard, but unfortunately I am the only one to feel it so."

Was there already talk of Lady Anne's marrying Lord de Beaumont, to whom one may assume the *Marquise* referred in her letter to Gaufridy of July 29th 1774, when she said: "Le Beaumont and his family will not agree to the marriage unless he (that is, Sade) is imprisoned for life and they want the minister's word on that."

It seems that in her inexhaustible kindness Lady de Sade found it easy to forgive those two who were dear to her, for in the same letter to Gaufridy she even refers to her husband and sister's union with a sort of playfulness.

"That part of the plaint which concerns my sister they
did not understand (i.e., the magistrates did not) and he
(his lawyer) had to explain it to them. He was the more
surprised at this, seeing that they were quite intelligent
men of the world. For his part he had at once grasped
what was afoot and the reasons for hushing up the
business."

On July 14th 1774, Lady Anne, whom we find back at La
Coste (since when, we have no evidence), wrote to the Abbé
de Sade to tell him she is suddenly leaving for Paris with her
sister the *Marquise*. Perhaps their mother had urgently sent
for her younger daughter, in connection with those negotiations with the de Beaumont family—for a marriage which,
we must not forget, never took place!

The following November 17th, the Marquis and his spouse
being at La Coste, we find Lady Anne complaining to the
Abbé that she has no news of them.

There now comes the upper half of a letter (in the possession
of the author) written personally by that delightful young lady,
and the exquisite spirit which stole the Marquis' heart is revealed as much in the exquisite handwriting as in the wistful
charm of the language. Lady Anne envies the Abbé his isolation. "There is none worse than one's own," she says, and certainly Lady Montreuil cannot have been sparing either of insulting reproof or ill treatment. Lady Anne withdraws to her room
as much as she can, she says. Only study provides relief from
the trials of life.

Are we to understand from the fragmentary evidence of this
letter that Lady Anne still loved Sade and that the "change"
she mentions as "in everybody's interest" is really that of the
liberation of the prisoner of Vincennes?

"You are always gracious, dear uncle, but can I trust
you? Is what you write just gallantrie? (her spelling is
fitful!) In truth I knowe not what to think of it, but as
my heart likes to soothe itself with its cravinge it is very
sensitive to the remembrance and sentiments you sweare
to. I am not less so regarding the interest you are so kynd
as to take in me and it is with grattitude that I impart
this, in generall I have not ... [here the bottom half is

missing]. . . . There is none worse than one's own. (You know as well as I do, *Monsieur l'Abbé*, that often those nearest to us are not our best friends.)

You are very lucky, Uncle, to be in isolation with only Yourself to contend with, when for myself that is all I would desire, Paris wearries me, society I find burdensome, my only happy hours those I spend alone in my room where I withdraw as often as possible, and studdy alone provides relief from the trials of my life. I must hope that time will bring a change, it is in everybody's interest and to secure it nobody should neglect anything. . . . " [the bottom of page two is missing].

It seems that as soon as Lady Anne went to Provence, some time in mid-October 1771, a genuine friendship sprang up between the Abbé and his delightful niece, a friendship with possibly a hint on the young lady's side of making up to him and of scarcely hidden desire on the part of the Abbé. It is indeed unlikely that this worldly sort of clerical gentleman, steeped as he was in the emotional romantic love moods of Petrarch, and in any case a man of amorous complexion, would have remained unmoved by the physical and mental charms of Lady Anne; some aspirations of love, which were certainly fanned by his niece's "playful ways" and such announcements as: "Oh, my dear uncle, how fond I am of you, since I met you I cannot get you out of my mind!", must surely have stirred in his bosom.

In this connection there is a very striking letter from the Abbé to his niece. Unfortunately it is not dated and we know so little about the young lady's movements that we cannot date it with any precision, but it would seem from internal evidence that when in some convent at Clermont or thereabouts, Lady Anne implored her uncle to cease writing her letters which in their flowery Provençal style were too compromising by far and might have been fatal for her good name, her honour, even perhaps her life.

In the Marquis' reply there is a phrase which certainly strikes a familiar note. "That is not the way we can control the impulses of our hearts; their vigour comes from the circulation of our blood, which we can never control. . . ." Might one not think that was written by Sade himself? In *Justine* Sade wrote: "When the science of anatomy is perfected it will be easy by its means to show the relationship between man's inner organisation and the urges which move him." No doubt about it, the five early years which Sade spent living with his philosopher uncle certainly helped to bring out that obsession with love of which nature had already planted the seeds in Donatien Alphonse François' heart.

"No, my dear niece," wrote the Abbé to Lady Anne, "your uncle will never refuse you anything in his power, so however could he refuse you an act of mercy on which 'your good name, your honour, perhaps even your life' depend? ... I feel the deepest affection for you, but it is at the same time the purest possible and the freest of anything you could call unworthy. So much for the essentials; you ought to be satisfied with us it is just a matter of 'form'. Our emotions take the shape of the head which contains them; friendship is more or less exciting according to the character of the person who feels it and the attractions of the woman who inspires it. I know nothing so delightful as yourself and I am a child of a warm climate; from the combination of these two things you cannot but have a very warm affection, and such I have for you. You want me *to sacrifice it* and *substitute a calmer emotion;* I am quite resolved to do whatever you wish me to do; the only question which remains open is whether I can.

You want a man of Provence to love like a man of the Auvergne. Suggest he should dance a *bourrée* and he will do so at once, though more used to dancing the *rigaudon,* because your request is all that is needed to make his body move differently and follow another beat. But that is not the way we can control the impulses of our hearts, their vigour comes from the circulation of our blood, which we can never control. The sun whips up the blood of a man of Provence, the snows slow down that of a man of the Auvergne. Thence arises the difference in the way they love, which is such that it is not at all surprising that the friendship of a man of Provence should be taken as

passionate love by a woman who has spent her life in the
Auvergne. . . .

I would like to spend my whole life with you: but I
shall see nothing of you. I am burning to go to Clermont:
I shall not go. Were I to follow the promptings of my
heart, I would write to you every day, and my letters
would be full of affection and warmth: to please you I
shall write, at long intervals, cold epistles, in which I shall
try to imitate the style of Auvergne. I think I can flatter
myself that protected by that mask your honour and your
life will be safe.

If you want anything else of me that is in my power,
you have but to say so, but if you want me to keep my
word, take care not to exceed the limits which you yourself have drawn. *Oh my dear uncle, how fond I am of
you; since I met you I cannot get you out of my mind.*
Now, niece, is that the style of friendship of the Auvergne?
I assure you, I look upon that declaration as an intrusion
into my province. If you go on like that, I shall no longer
be master of myself: I shall gather up all my warmth and
come and melt all your snows and so make a torrent which
will sweep you right away. . . ."

In his letter of February 17th 1779 containing the moving
account of his dream about his ancestress Laura, the Marquis,
still haunted by that apparition, enquires of his wife about
some marriage proposal, or some broken engagement, of which
she has written to him and which must have concerned him
closely. The prisoner of Vincennes goes so far as to underline,
not without a certain mocking bitterness, the grammatical am-
biguity of the actual wording of his wife's letter:

"Lady de Launay, you say, is certainly not married *and
I shall certainly not attend her wedding.* Since you do not
propose to attend the wedding, she is obviously going to
marry! Hence Marais was not lying to me so much as
you make out."

There is no question but that at this time Sade more than
once asked his wife for news of her sister. He put insistent questions which were embarrassing to the *Marquise.* She was loth

to give her husband information which might make him draw a dangerous conclusion and would have made him lose all hope of being set at liberty. But could Sade possibly have forgotten that lovely young woman, who had been the source of so much pleasure to him and was now quite unwittingly the cause of his irksome captivity?

After a very understandable silence the *Marquise* could no longer remain deaf to the prisoner's appeals. So she decided to satisfy him, but still without revealing where Lady Anne was.

"My self-imposed determination to say nothing about my sister was very sensible. Since breaking my resolution, out of a desire to satisfy you, can only serve to make you draw false conclusions, this is the last time I shall mention her. You want an answer to your questions, swearing you will not mention her again and will be calm afterwards. Well, I am now writing so as to calm you.

Why did she leave our mother's roof?—For no reason that concerns you or dishonours her.

Is she my enemy?—No.

What sort of home has she now?—I can tell you neither street nor district. Whatever it is, it cannot harm you. There is no sense in answering that question."

But the Lady Anne, alas, departed this life on May 13th 1781 at one p.m., after three days' illness, the victim either of small-pox or of a peritonitis which developed simultaneously. When Mlle de Rousset sent the sad news to Gaufridy she added that "an inflammation of the lower bowel" had complicated Lady Anne's complaint (small-pox). This phrase most probably meant peritonitis, for it would be surprising if this inflammation of the lower bowel which Mlle de Rousset so clearly indicates could even in the eighteenth-century have been confused with the acute gastro-enteritis which often accompanies small-pox. If our supposition is correct, it was then peritonitis which carried Lady Anne away, as the effect of this is so much more dramatic than the average small-pox. It is therefore almost pointless to regret that at a date when empirical vaccination already had many followers in France the de Launays did not follow the example of the Duke of Orleans, who as early as

1748 had all his family inoculated by the famous Dr Tronchin. Here is Mlle de Rousset's letter in full:

> "*Monsieur,* Lady de Sade informs you of the illness and death of her sister Lady Anne de Launay, which she has just learned of. This so sudden death is very likely to effect the revolution she wishes. She is grief-strick and weeps. As Nature has its rights, I let it take its course. Friday evening, on the tenth instant, small-pox appeared; an inflammation of the lower bowel followed as a complication of the illness. Death took her from her affectionate family on the thirteenth, at one of the afternoon. Lady Montreuil is said to be inconsolable. Milady fears lest she makes herself ill. Tomorrow she is to go to that house of sorrow to join her tears to those of the family. She will write to the Lord Commandant and to her aunts this afternoon."

It is all wrong for the delectable wraith of Lady Anne Prospère de Launay to be thus destroyed by sickness and death. So let us end this chapter with the following words of the Marquis de Sade referring to the finest passion of his life, lines which in their incoherency seem to be broken by the profound sighs of passion itself:

> "Love, will you then let me for a moment raise the shroud which hides from mortal eye the delights you once permitted me to set eyes upon? May I depict both thy temple and its setting? Never was any woman more wantonly beautiful. . . . But you blush, Julie darling, your sensitivity is hurt by the boldness of my brush. . . . Love, love, you distracted me . . .* stay for ever in my heart, divine delight filling it to the full; for you alone love created these features and to reveal them is an outrage. . . ."

*A passage is crossed out.

CHAPTER SEVEN

The Marseilles Affair

1772

JUNE 27TH

TOWARDS MID-JUNE 1772 the Marquis de Sade said goodbye to his wife, children and sister-in-law and left La Coste manor with his manservant Armand, known as Latour, to go to Marseilles to collect some money due him. He put up at the *Hôtel des Treize Cantons*. What he did up to June 25th we do not know, except that he paid a number of visits to a nineteen-year-old girl named Jeanne Nicou, a native of Lyons, who lived in the *rue Saint Ferréol le Vieux*. He had originally asked her to come to him in his hotel, but this she had refused to do.

On Friday June 25th Latour accosted Marianne Laverne in the street. She was eighteen, and he told her that his master had come to Marseilles solely to have a good time with some girls and that he wanted some who were "quite young". He told her that an appointment was hardly feasible that evening as his master was to dine with some actors, but tomorrow at eleven p.m. he would bring his party round.

However, the next day Marianne went boating. Had she forgotten the appointment? Anyway, when the two men called at her dwelling (she was an inmate of a house kept by one Nicolas, *rue d'Aubagne*), they were told she had gone away. The very next morning, there was Latour up at her rooms to see her, and to find her back. He made another appointment, but said it must be somewhere else; her house was not secluded enough for his master, so would Marianne come at ten to

Mariette Borelly's place at the corner of the *rue des Capucins*? (The day before Latour had agreed the same *rendezvous* with Mariannette Laugier and Rose Coste, two other inmates of the same house. He had also asked Jeanne Nicou, but she had refused).

At the appointed hour, accompanied by Latour, Sade—height medium, hair fair, "handsome and full-faced", dressed in grey surcoat lined with blue, with waistcoat and breeches of marigold silk, plumed hat, sword and gold-knobbed cane—entered a third-floor flat of a house which is now *15bis* in the *rue d'Aubagne*. Latour was taller than his master. He wore his hair hanging loose and long and his face was pock-marked. He wore a mariner's blue and yellow striped tunic.

There were four girls for the Marquis to handle: Mariette Borelly, mistress of the apartment, born at Valensole, aged twenty-three; Marianne Laverne of Lyons, eighteen; Mariannette Laugier of Aix-en-Provence, twenty; and Rose Coste of the same age, a native of Mérasset in the Rouergue.

The moment he came in Sade produced a handful of crowns and said that the girl who guessed how many there were would have first turn. Marianne won. Sade sent the others away, except for his man, and locked the door. He had Latour and Marianne lie on the bed. With one hand he whipped Marianne while with the other he "worked up" his servant, addressing him as *Monsieur le Marquis*. Then Latour was asked to leave the room. Sade offered the girl a bonbon-casket of cut-glass bound in gold in which there were some aniseed sweets the sugar of which was soaked with Spanish fly extract, or cantharides. He told her to eat a lot, it would give her the wind. She took seven or eight. Then he asked her to let him or his man commit sodomy with her, for which he promised a *louis*. She refused, or rather, that is what she told the Lieutenant-General of the Seneschal's Court she did.

It is worth noting that of the six Marseilles prostitutes who gave evidence against Sade, five stated that he wanted "to take his pleasure of them by the back passage", but that they would not hear of it. These refusals, which could not have failed to cool off their client's liberality, seem most improbable in such girls. On the other hand, that they should have given such evidence need not astonish us at all, for to admit sodomy, whether passive or active, was to admit a mortal crime in the eighteenth century. We find Muyart de Vouglans, a lawyer, writing in a handbook: "The law *cum vir* 31 in the Code *de adult,* lays down that whoever sinks to this Crime shall be punished by 'living fire'. This punishment, which our Jurisprudence has adopted, applies equally to Women as to Men." We shall therefore assume that not one of the girls who was asked to supply this pleasure failed to consent, whatever she may have declared in evidence. Though this is mere conjecture, it is a conjection which may be taken as certainty. We might add that the Marquis de Sade was not the sort of man to suffer lightly constant frustration of his sexual whim, and we note that he had insisted on girls who were "quite young" (he said this a number of times) no doubt because the elasticity of young flesh favours such practices.

But to return to the story. From his pocket Sade produced a cat-o'-nine-tails, made of parchment studded with bent pins, "which was blood-stained" and asked Marianne to whip him with it. She was able to give him only three blows. Her heart failed her, and as he wanted her to go on and she refused, he asked her to go out and buy a heather broom. She left the room for a few moments to get the maid, Jeanne Françoise Lemaire, who was in the kitchen, to run the errand for her. A few minutes later the woman returned with the broom, which cost one *sou.* She gave it to Marianne who went straight back to the room and, less frightened by this than the cat-o'-nine-tails, consented to apply it to her client's behind, Sade urging her to strike hard. Suddenly she asked to leave the room as her stomach ached. She went groaning to the kitchen and the maid gave her a glass of water.

Now came Mariette's turn. She came in with the footman. Sade made her strip and bend over the bottom of the bed, when he beat her with the besom. After he had dealt her a number of severe blows, he asked her to beat him in turn, and while Mariette flogged him he took his penknife and made cuts in the mantelshelf. (Later the police found a column of figures, which must surely have included the blows he dealt the girls, for they were 215, 179, 225 and 240.) Then he put the girl on her back on the bed and took his pleasure of her, at the same time working up his man and allowing him to bugger him at the same time.

Mariette was followed by Rose Coste. She was asked to strip and lie down beside Latour. Latour caressed her and had normal connection with her. Then Sade whipped Rose, at the same time, just as when whipping Marianne Laverne, working up his man. After the beating he requested his victim, for the fee of one *louis,* to allow his man to commit sodomy with her.

After Rose Coste came Mariannette. The Marquis caressed her, then got ready to whip her, saying he still had twenty-five blows to administer, but Mariannette caught sight of the blood-stained cat on the bed, took fright and tried to escape. Sade kept her in the room and sent for Marianne who had been suffering from the dose of Spanish fly and had been obliged to send the servant out for a cup of coffee. The door was locked again. There were now Marianne, Mariannette and Latour in the room with Sade, whom Latour addressed as *Lafleur.*

Sade offered sweets to the girls. Marianne Laverne declined; she had already had too many, but Mariannette took some, but spat them out at once without eating them. (The police found two or three on the tiled floor.) Marianne was now suddenly flung on to the bed and her petticoats raised. Sade sniffed at her bottom, hoping to detect some appreciable effects of the aniseed, after which, proceeding to give her a whipping, he told Mariannette to stand at the head of the bed and watch what he did.

He then undressed and sodomised his victim. In their evidence to the Lieutenant-General of the Seneschal's Court the two girls both declared that at the same time Latour buggered his master. Mariannette, indeed, avowed that the sight "so disgusted her" that, seeing she could not leave the room, she had to go to the window, not to see. By now the little Laverne girl had been sodomised and the Marquis then requested Marianne to provide Latour with the same pleasure. She refused and tried to get away. The other girl by now was in tears. Sade threatened them, but in the end let them go, giving each of them a six-*livre* crown, promising them ten more if they would go boating with him that evening.

Thus this Cytherean morning ended. Towards the end of the afternoon Latour called at the *rue d'Aubagne,* to fetch the two girls for the boating excursion, but they would not go with him. A little before nine in the evening Latour, scouting for the Marquis, who was to leave Marseilles the next day and had no intention of wasting his last hours of freedom, accosted a whore in the *rue Saint Ferréol le Vieux,* who was standing at her door. He requested her to go up with him for a moment as he had something to tell her. This was Marguerite Coste, aged twenty-five, a native of Montpellier. He fixed an appointment with her for his master; would she please be ready to receive him at once. He gave her a handkerchief as gage, but meanwhile the Marquis, who had been at his tailor's, had been visited by the actor Des Rosières and had retained him to sup with him. However, that repast was soon over and the guest despatched likewise, for Latour had come in and whispered in his master's ear.

The two men went forthwith to Marguerite Coste's. Latour merely showed his master where she lived, himself retiring at once. Sade took off his sword and lay his gold-knobbed stick beside it and sat down on the bed. Marguerite sat down in a chair. She was immediately offered the cut-glass sweet-casket and sucked a number of sweets, with Sade pressing them on her, when she declined assuring her he always treated his girls to sweets. He managed to get her to consume a considerable number, then asked her if she felt nothing in her stomach or her bowels. Then he said he would like "to take his pleasure of her by the back passage and in a number of other ways which were most disgusting". If we are to believe her, Marguerite persistently refused and only allowed him to take her "as God ordained". Finally Sade left the girl, leaving six *francs* on the table.

When the next morning at cock-crow the Marquis set out on the Aix road in a two-wheeler drawn by three horses, intending to go to La Coste, he was far indeed from suspecting that the last girl he had taken his pleasure with was going to be the principal witness in a criminal trial which was to be instituted against him against all justice or sense and to lead to a sentence which would be a unique example of disproportion between crime and punishment.

*   *   *

In the sphere of psycho-sexual morbidity everything that the Marquis did that June day in 1772 is so clear and definite and at the same time presents such an attractive variety that one might even present it as a demonstration piece of his debauchery. Indeed, had Sade, pending that transcendental handbook of the *120 Days of Sodom,* wished to present us with a beginner's lesson in experimental sexual psycho-pathology, he could not have done better.

Sado-masochism

Whereas on that Easter Day of 1768 the only sadism was that of the Marquis, on June 27th 1772 we see that urge combined with its invariable counterpart, masochism. If the Marquis makes a point of whipping Marianne Laverne and Mariette Borelly, he is also prompt in requesting these young ladies to whip him in turn. (If in the case of Rose Coste she was not also requested to handle the cat after receiving a few cuts herself, that was no doubt because she did not look to Sade the right sort of girl for the sadistic role.)

Secondly, despite the girls' denials, it seems that after whipping them Sade did not omit to have connection by the back passage. Now this choice of sodomy, which makes the act more violent than when performed normally, is precisely evidence of sadism (In *Justine* the Benedictine monks of *Sainte Marie des Bois* make a regular practice of first possessing in this way the girls they take from their homes.)

Thirdly, we must note that in the active form of *algolagnia* we have Sade first sodomising Marianne Laverne, then ordering Mariannette Laugier to engage Latour in the same way. Is it not clear that when a woman is tyrannically ordered to let a man do this to her it becomes a debasing act for her.

Coprophily

Coprophily (which occupies so important a place in the *120 Days of Sodom*—perhaps too much space, proportionately, since this is out of all proportion to the infrequency of such substitute satisfaction pushed to the limit)—coprophily considered in a general sense as a form of masochism only appeared during these scenes in Mariette's room in one of its most rudimentary forms. The only comment to make here is that which Maurice Heine has already put well—that when Sade made his maidens take "double action" sweets, with both Spanish fly and aniseed in them, one of his aims was to establish the carminative effects of this latter plant.

Exhibitionism and VOYEUR-ISM

We find equal evidence in the Marquis of this contrasted pair of perversions. When he asks the girls to let Latour take them by the back passage, he does so in order himself to watch the act, and we also know that Latour had normal commerce with Rose Coste with his master looking on. Sade's exhibitionism, on the other hand, we see in the almost constant presence of Latour while the debauchery is going on and also in the fact that first Marianne and Mariannette, then Mariannette and Rose Coste, are required to be there together. Finally, let us recall that when Sade prepares to whip Marianne he insists on Mariannette standing by to watch the torture.

Here in brief we have the principal aspects of the Marseilles debauch. But we should also not lose sight of the subversive impulse which Sade's exploits clearly contained. Maurice Heine noted in him a definite "intention of repudiating and defying every moral convention".

One more point : some readers may be astonished that nothing is said here about inversion. Let it be said at once that the omission is deliberate. Neither inversion nor bi-sexuality can be treated as pathological conditions of the love impulse, for these are merely a sort of constitutional expression of it. For instance, one cannot class together on one plane what one might call a "normal" case of inversion and, say, a necrophilous or fetishist inversion, let alone an individual with bi-sexual tendency but no other special features and one of the same sort who is also a sado-masochist or an exhibitionist. This is why we have purposely kept the homosexual point of view out of our psychopathological argument, reserving the right to investigate later on the degree it reached in Sade's case, or even whether Sade's acts, which seem to be classifiable as hermaphroditic, are not to be considered as undefinable or part of a complex in which inversion is so tangled up with blasphemy and mystification that there is no possibility of treating it separately from these.

THE LEGAL PROCEEDINGS

June 30th. M. de Mende, Royal Prosecutor attached to the Seneschal's Court of Marseilles, was informed that after consuming an excessive number of sweets given her by a stranger, Marguerite Coste was racked for some days by intestinal pains, accompanied by continuous vomiting of black, blood-stained matter. He ordered cross-examination of the girl and the Lt-General for criminal matters, Chomel, took down Marguerite Coste's allegations. A doctor was appointed to examine her and a chemist was to be summoned to analyse in the presence of a magistrate the matter vomited.

July 1st. Mariette Borelly made a statement to the Lt-General and the Royal Prosecutor. Three other whores of the *rue d'Aubagne* and seven witnesses also gave evidence to the Lt-General. Marianne alleged digestive trouble which she ascribed to the Marquis' aniseed and like her fellow prostitutes pretended to have been outraged by what she calls the homosexual sodomy of her clients.

July 4th. Medical reports on Marguerite Coste and Marianne Laverne were ready. The Lt-General signed the submission to the Royal Prosecutor of the ten statements made without that person's being present, and the Prosecutor decreed the arrest of Sade and Latour.

It was about this date that, being semi-officially informed of the proposed curtailment of his liberty, the Marquis took flight from La Coste manor, accompanied by Latour and his sister-in-law Anne.

July 5th. Two chemists who had analysed the matter thrown up by Marguerite Coste and the aniseed sweets found on July 1st in Mariette Borelly's room stated that they had found neither arsenic nor corrosive sublimate in the specimens.

July 11th. A bailiff of the Royal judicature of Apt, together with three mounted men and a brigadier of the Marshalsy, went to La Coste to execute the warrant of arrest of July 4th. They were told that Sade and Latour had left a week before this. Three warrants were then issued against the defaulters:

search orders were signed, the possessions of the two wanted men were impounded and listed and they were required to appear a fortnight from that date.

About the same date the *Marquise* went to Marseilles to appeal to the magistrates in her husband's favour and "observed that the minds of them all are prejudiced in the extreme".

August 2nd. The fourth stage in the proceedings was the public crying of the wanted men outside La Coste Manor House and at all other recognised places in the village, requiring them to appear a week hence.

August 8th and 17th. Marguerite Coste and Marianne Laverne appeared before Maître de Carmis, a Marseilles lawyer, and withdrew their charges.

August 24th. The fifth stage : the papers were passed to the Royal Prosecutor.

August 26th. The sixth stage : the Royal Prosecutor ordered special proceedings against the accused and insisted that the re-examination of witnesses would require confrontation.

August 27th. The seventh stage : the re-examination was formally recorded.

August 29th. Lady Montreuil joined her daughter at La Coste.

September 2nd. The eighth stage : final conclusions of the Royal Prosecutor.

September 3rd. Conclusion of the eighth stage and ninth stage. Presentation of the Prosecutor's conclusions in his statement to the Council Chamber, and final judgment in favour of the Royal Prosecutor : "The Marquis de Sade to be punished for poisoning and sodomy !" Sade and his man were required to expiate their crimes at the cathedral porch before being taken to the *Place Saint Louis* "for the said de Sade to be decapitated on a scaffold . . . and the said Latour, on a gallows, to be hanged by the neck and strangled . . . then the body of the said de Sade and that of the said Latour to be burned and their ashes thrown to the wind".

September 11th. In pursuance of the ninth stage : the sentence was laid at the bar of the High court of Provence at Aix (Second Chamber of the Court of Accounts summoned during vacation under the presidency of de Mazenod) which confirmed the sentence obtained by the Royal Prosecutor at Marseilles and rendered this executive.

September 12th. Effigies of Sade and Latour were executed and burned in the *Place des Prêcheurs* at Aix. Then followed the tenth and final stage of the criminal proceedings, the attachment to the sentence of record of the execution "in effigy".

October 2nd. Having travelled the length and breadth of Italy with the Marquis, who gave her out to be his wife and allowed himself "all the privacies due to that status", Lady Anne de Launay rejoined her sister the *Marquise* at La Coste.

Mid-October. Lady Anne de Launay again left La Coste to join her brother-in-law.

COMMENTARY FROM THE STANDPOINT OF MEDICAL JURISPRUDENCE

The only one of the four girls of the *rue d'Aubagne* who actually consumed the Marquis' sweets doctored with Spanish fly was Marianne Laverne. An early symptom as of poisoning rapidly showed. Leaving the room in which the debauch took place, Marianne felt ill and took refuge in the kitchen, where Jeanne Françoise Lemaire gave her a glass of water, after which, still feeling ill, Marianne sent the woman out for a cup of coffee. But Marguerite Coste, the evening whore, consumed all that the sweet-casket held, and "he had hardly left when she felt her stomach on fire and vomited copiously, the matter being of various colours but mainly blackish".

Here let Dr André Javelier speak. He is more qualified than the author to give a clinical explanation of the two girls' allegations and the medical reports.

> "In Marguerite Coste the poisoning began violently, a quarter of an hour after ingestion, taking the form of acute gastric trouble with abundant vomiting of dark matter. Marianne merely showed initial lipothymia—

before Mariette appeared on the scene—and it was only in the evening, after looseness of the bowels, that gastric intolerance showed. The course, apart from the intensity, was the same in the two cases, gastric trouble reaching a peak with profuse vomiting of dark matter stained with blood and evil-odoured (Marguerite Coste's evidence) compared by the experts with scouring. Gastric pains were intense, increasing on palpation and accompanied by a sense of burning at the oesophagus, the tongue coated and the general condition weak. Of particular interest were signs suggestive of localisation of the poisoning in the urinary tract, with hint of the cause—there was lumbar pain caused by Spanish fly nephritis (medical reports on Marguerite Coste) and dysuria accompanied by cysto-urethritis (medical reports on Marianne Laverne). Rose Coste was most affected, which was logical enough, since she had consumed a whole box-ful of the sweets, whereas Marianne had taken only seven or eight. Thus the clinical picture was that of acute toxic gastritis due to a corrosive agent with symptoms of urinary irritation."

We should however not forget that Spanish fly was not once in question at all in the Marseilles proceedings! The chemists' reports made no mention of it. It was only mentioned as a possibility in the letter which de Montyon wrote to the Duke de Lavrillière on July 22nd 1772, then again much later when quashing of the judgment was in question in the private correspondence between the Marquis and his family.

Defending himself against the charge of having used Spanish fly, Sade in a letter of April 21st 1777 avowed that the stomach troubles were all due to the girls' over-eating, while in his story *Le Président Mystifié* he makes a point of reasserting this hypothesis. "At Marseilles or Aix," he wrote, "a little looseness of the bowels is a trouble to be reckoned with, and since we have seen a band of rascals, consider some whores who had colic to have been poisoned, one should not be surprised to find any Provençal magistrate taking colics seriously!"

Even if we hold that the Marquis' denial is only to be expected, it remains none the less true that the actual symptoms which Marianne Laverne and Marguerite Coste showed are not enough for us today to assert that there was any Spanish fly in the Marquis de Sade's alarming sweets. Besides, it is plain how prejudiced the bench was if we reflect on the one hand that they were ignorant of any precise aphrodisiac ingredients in the sweets and on the other that the vomit showed no hint of any of the substances likely at the time to have been flowers of yellow sulphur or red arsenic.

Need we add the plea that there was no criminal intent? Lady Montreuil most wisely put it that there was "No motive, no gain to be had from giving poison to strange girls, whose profession was unlikely to inspire either love or jealousy in a man of so markedly different a class from theirs." In short, if the girls were intended to suffer any toxic effects of Spanish fly, there was no intent actually to poison them; this was accidental and only to be imputed to the clumsiness of our libertine as to dosage.

"The Marquis' double-action formula," Maurice Heine explains, "offered the danger in practice of combining two substances, one of them very active (the Spanish fly) the other an anodyne. The need to use a heavy dosage of the latter to get any effect at all from it matched up ill with the need to use the other in a very cautious dosage. The effect was bound to cheat the inventor of the result he wanted, while at the same time the seriousness of that effect was such as to deceive him in quite another way."

Here we should also point out that Spanish fly preparations had been in use in France since the sixteenth century, and thanks to Cardinal Richelieu were now in much greater vogue than ever before. Was it likely that the Marquis de Sade would feel himself a criminal for offering some Marseilles whores aphrodisiac sweets such as one of the victors of Fontenoy used to use quite openly, and in quantity too, so that they were actually named after him?

JURIDICAL COMMENT — *by Maurice Heine*

"The dominant impression that perusal of this record leaves seems to us to be that of a clear disproportion between the verifiable facts and on the one hand the judicial sanctions imposed and on the other their consequences in public opinion.

Regarding the first contrast, can we find any other reason but the savagery of a code of law still in force at the time, hence properly applicable to the case? In other words, can we approach the tragi-comedy of that *auto-da-fé* of 1772 with our less savage notions of crime and punishment without falling into anachronistic thinking?

Here the texts are our justification. Jurists of the time clearly feel an uneasiness about those laws, which is to their credit. Only four years later we find the first magistrate of Provence admitting that 'the sentence was excessive' and that public opinion has it that 'such crimes should either be hushed up altogether or when they cannot be so treated, punished solely by penalties fitting the case, by deprivation of the benefits that society has connected with purity of morals'. That Mosaic concepts of justice are no longer fitting could not be better put.

No doubt the Marseilles magistrates were only so rigorous because the culprits had decamped. But, the counsel of these can reply, 'is mere absence in itself a proof of guilt? Or is it a crime in itself? It is to this mistake that we owe so many decisions which make justice itself groan'. Reasons for the nullity of the proceedings are also given. 'In this case the very fundamentals of judicial order, as of special prescriptions of the Parliament of Provence, were abandoned.' In short, the Seneschal's Court 'ordered proceedings without any application from anybody; the edifice of legal proceedings was built up without the essential foundation stone'. Worse, in flagrant disregard of the decree of April 18th 1766 witnesses were allowed to give evidence 'on facts not relative to the plaint', facts emanating from the magistrates themselves, who had no legal foundation for building a case of sodomy on an allegation of poisoning. These were the principal juridical reasons put forward against the Marseilles sentence.

What follows seems to be of a different order of gravity. 'This sentence was sent one week later to the bench of the Chamber of Accounts at Aix, then in assembly, and was confirmed by the Chamber of Vacations with a celerity so strange that one cannot but suspect it was provoked by somebody.' Let us indeed note that those magistrates who on September 11th 1772 signed the Marseilles sentence and made it executive normally sat in the Provençal Court of Accounts and only appeared in the High Court (*parlement*) as creatures of Chancellor Maupeou, who in an absolutist manner suspended legality in so doing. Is it then mere chance that we find here the hand of one who four years earlier, as first President of the Paris High Court, handled the debates in the main chamber when this was assembled to try the libertine of Arcueil and himself signed the sentence on that occasion? This was the same de Maupeou, sworn enemy of the Malesherbes and of the Board of Excise over which Lord de Montreuil presided. It was so easy to strike at Montreuil by striking at his son-in-law.

This seems the more clear to us since no step taken by the family, not even the withdrawal of their charge by the two girls in the case, made before Master de Carmis, lawyer of Marseilles, on August 8th and 17th 1772 had any effect at all upon the course of the proceedings. On the other hand, the ultimate fall of the chancellor with the re-call of the High Court by Royal decree, greatly aided the legal advisers who in agreement with Lady Montreuil prepared the way for a revision of the case."

CHAPTER EIGHT

Detention in Fort Miolans

1772 - 1773

WHAT EXACTLY took place on the eve of the arrest of the Marquis and his imprisonment in Fort Miolans? Here is Maurice Heine's brief account—as an introduction to the chronicle that follows it could not be bettered.

"Lady Montreuil would more readily have forgiven her son-in-law his alleged guilt in the Marseilles business, of which she knew more than anybody, than his conduct with her younger daughter, who had been obliged in the end to admit in whispers what the gossip of scandal already proclaimed out loud. With the Marquis de Sade as son-in-law it was no longer mere adultery that was introduced to the family, but also seduction and incest. And all that was now public, hawked round by the news-sellers. The honour of the family was definitely and irreparably besmirched, whereas by this union with the higher nobility Lady Montreuil had had every reason to imagine she was giving it a new brilliance.

And what did it all amount to? The Marquis himself was cut right out of society, his property had been seized and sequestered, including the income from his office, of which at any moment he might be deprived. His wife and three children were entirely dependent on the Montreuils and, what was worst of all, those poor children bore a name which to the general public immediately suggested vice and crime.

This was the balance of the situation. Lady Montreuil may not have been the woman to seek a sterile revenge, but she was going to stop at nothing to give satisfaction both to her indignation and to the moral and material interests of those now in her care. Getting the fugitive in a secure place of detention seemed to her to be the best way of satisfying both these aims of hers, so she proceeded with utter relentlessness to pursue that way out, using every possible influence she could bring to bear to achieve it. As the Marquis' injudicious talk had told her where he was hiding, she lost no time taking action at court and got the minister there to intervene diplomatically with the Sardinian minister in Paris, Count Ferrero de la Marmora. He got into touch with the Turin court concerning the undesirable visitor whom His Majesty was now harbouring in his Savoyard lands and it was suggested that the family was greatly concerned to have the condemned man under control because though innocent he would none the less, if set at liberty, be put in a position to commit grievous acts of imprudence or to vanish just when he was needed to counter the charge of contumacy, and in any case it was essential to prevent his disseminating frightful gossip and loathsome writings against his relatives and his judges."

ARREST

October 27th. Leaving his trunks at Nice, the Marquis reached Chambéry. He travelled as the Count de Mazan and with him was Lady Anne, whom he gave out to be now his wife, now his sister-in-law. With him he also had two footmen, d'Armand, known as Latour, who had been his assistant in the Marseilles incidents, and Carteron, known as La Jeunesse. He put up at the *Pomme d'Or,* then, some days later, rented a country house outside the city gates for six months. He did not go out at all or make any acquaintances, except a Frenchman staying in the same hotel, a certain Lord de Vaulx, with whom he struck up a sudden friendship and who was soon to take up Sade's cause in the dispute between him and his in-laws.

Early November. Acting on the request of Lady de Montreuil, the Duke d'Aiguillon asked Count Ferrero de la Marmora, Ambassador of the King of Sardinia, to ask the court to issue a royal order "for the arrest and imprisonment in a fortress in Savoy of the Count de Mazan, a French nobleman in retreat at Chambéry".

November 20th. From this day to the 30th November the Marquis de Sade was under treatment by a surgeon named Thonin. About the same time Latour, who had left Chambéry at the beginning of the month, was asked to return to take the place at Sade's bedside of the valet named Carteron, because Carteron was on the point of leaving for Paris on a mission for his master.

November 28th. Count Lascaris, Minister of Foreign Affairs of Sardinia, informed Count Ferrero de la Marmora that "the King has been pleased to accede to the request of My Lord the Duke d'Aiguillon to have the Count de Sade arrested in Savoy and imprisoned in Fort Miolans".

December 5th. Count Lascaris informs Count Ferrero de la Marmora that he has just written to the Count de la Tour, Governor of the Duchy of Savoy, to request him to secure the body of the Marquis de Sade and conduct that person to Fort Miolans.

December 8th. At 9 p.m. Major de Chavanne, with two adjutants, having surrounded the house, which stood alone, by soldiery, entered Sade's room, finding him alone with his man Latour, and intimated to him the King of Sardinia's decision. After securing the Marquis' two pistols and sword, and searching his clothing, in which he found "neither letters nor any other papers of any significance", the Major withdrew, leaving Lady Montreuil's son-in-law "as surprised as he was upset", under the watch of the two adjutants, who did not take their eyes off him all night.

December 9th. At seven a.m., escorted by four cavalrymen, Adjutant Bouchet and the Marquis drove by post chaise to Fort Miolans, where Latour soon after joined his master as voluntary prisoner. The day before, the Governor had informed

the Commander of the Fort (de Launay) that he was to receive a new inmate in the near future, and gave him definite
instructions about the prisoner : de Launay was to take whatever precautions his good sense indicated to make sure that
Sade had no chance of escaping. The Marquis would be kept
in confinement, his only freedom being permission for a daily
walk in the inner courtyard under the supervision of a disabled
non-commissioned officer. He would be able to receive no
strangers and in addition would not be allowed to correspond
with anyone. Latour would be allowed to sleep in his room,
but would not be allowed to leave the inner fort. This was
"lest he aid his master to escape". It would be for the Marquis
himself to arrange with the canteen what food he wished to
eat and he would be required to provide his own bed and any
other furniture. At the same time the Count de la Tour urged
the Commander of the Fortress to show the prisoner
"courtesies" in order to modify the bitterness of his detention.

*   *   *

The Castle or Fortress of Miolans, the Bastille of the Dukes
of Savoy, rears its proud silhouette of twelfth century towers
above Saint Pierre d'Albigny, twelve miles from Chambéry.
Perched on a precipitous outcrop of rock, this eyrie dominates
the Isère vale, eight hundred feet below it. Charles III, Duke
of Savoy, took possession of it on December 9th 1523. It was
lost again during the war with François I, but won back again
in 1559 by Duke Emmanuel Philibert. It was made a close
prison about 1564.

The walls are triple, with a double ring of moats. Distinction
is made between the Fort proper, which includes the keep and
the St Pierre Tower, and the Lower Fort. The keep is square,
with six floors, the rooms serving both as prison and as quarters
for the Commander. At the bottom is "Hell", a prison "in a
bad state and most murderous". Above is the prison known as
"Purgatory" and above that the "Treasure", which has two
cells, one of them having a south window and a fireplace. The
Commandant's quarters are on the upper floor. Above are two
more cells, on the north that known as "Little Hope", and that
on the south side known as "Great Hope". It was this cell,

from which one has an unparalleled view of the valley of the Isère and the Alps, that was assigned to the Marquis. The uppermost floor of all, 107 steps up, is known as "Paradise".

The St Pierre Tower, which is square, with loopholes and machicolations, had three floors and could accommodate three prisoners. There were altogether twelve dungeon cells, a chapel, a cistern, an armoury and a kitchen with a giant hearth, an oven and a stove, a wood-store and a kitchen garden. There were no concealed cells. The lower fortress included the church, the canteen, the powder-room, a storeroom, quarters for the garrison, the staff gardens and finally "a room where prisoners are not in close confinement", whence they could go to the canteen to eat. (P. Sérieux).

DETENTION

1772

December 10. The Marquis de Sade implored Count de la Tour to obtain for him that liberty which he had never deserved to lose. While awaiting release he hoped the Governor would be so kind as to allow him to write and receive letters and also grant his valet Latour freedom of egress and ingress, so that he might execute outside the fortress those little errands which arose from day to day. Signing, the prisoner indicated his rank : *Cavalry Colonel.*

December 16th. De Mouroux, Minister of the State Home Office at Turin informed the Governor of Savoy, who had passed Sade's request to him, that from now on the Marquis might both send and receive letters, though subject to Commandant de Launay's inspection of the correspondence, to assure that it was suitable for him to receive or to send. Regarding the Marquis' valet, yes, he might let him leave the fortress occasionally, though not without observing all the usual precautions.

December 18th. A family Council met at Avignon and declared before a notary public that they were agreed that during the absence of the Marquis the education of his children, as minors, and the administration of their property, should be confided to the *Marquise,* and that to this end she should be appointed their guardian *ad hoc,* to act in any matter which might affect their interests.

December 19th. Returning from Paris towards December 15th, Carteron called on the Count de la Tour to seek his authorisation to visit the prisoner and was granted that favour. The Governor took advantage of the situation to cross-examine Carteron a little when he handed him his pass, and Carteron revealed a number of details concerning the Marquis' sojourn in Italy, also indicating the purpose of the journey. He also said that he had gone to Paris to carry some important letters from his master. They were addressed to some friends and to his wife, who had remained with her young children.

December 20th. Having reported to the Marquis the day before, Carteron left again to go to Nice by the mountain road, intending to bring the "vehicles and clothes" which the Marquis had left there.

December 21st. Count Ferrero de la Marmora sent Count de la Tour a memorandum which Lady Montreuil had just sent him. The principal points were : (a) the family of the Marquis de Sade implored the Governor of the Duchy of Savoy "kindly to give instructions that this gentleman . . . should be treated with some consideration and afforded all the possible comforts that a man of his standing might wish for in everything which would not . . . facilitate his escape, were he to wish to attempt this"; (b) the family asked that whatever effects Sade might have had with him, either for personal use or for the entertainment essential to so lively a mind as his, should be returned to him, with the exception of his papers, manuscripts, and letters, of whatever nature they be, which the family asked to be sent to them, together with a small wooden box or coffer believed to be of mahogany, brass-bound, also containing papers. If the Marquis had brought this with him to Fort Miolans, the Commandant was to try to get hold of it without Sade's knowing and to remove the papers it contained.

December 28th. Commandant de Launay reported to the Governor on the precautions which had been taken regarding the Marquis.

"Whenever he walks in the lower fort, the sentry cautions
the sergeant of the guard to keep him in sight till he goes
back indoors, while whenever he walks in the Keep, it is
the sentry who keeps him in sight, and the iron gate is
kept closed . . . and his apartment is locked by night."

On the same day Sade complained to the Count de la Tour
against de Launay's treatment of him. The Commandant had
refused to let his valet Latour go out, to take an important
letter from his master to the Governor. "The Commandant,"
wrote Sade, "persisted in this refusal with a tone and manner
that my birth and military rank hardly allow me to suffer."
In a note attached to his letter Sade further requested the
Governor to issue him a letter certifying that from his arrival
at Chambéry on October 27th to December 8th, when he was
arrested, "he had behaved in an irreproachable manner in that
town and this in every sense." He added that he required this
certificate for his family.

Towards December 30th. Replying to the memorandum of
Lady Montreuil, the Governor of Savoy reported on Sade's
state of health and the régime to which the captive was submitted, then among other matters touched on the expenses incurred at Fort Miolans and enquired how these were going
to be met. The Count also stated that when Carteron got
back from Nice with his master's luggage, this would be
painstakingly searched and all the papers of any significance
extracted therefrom. "All this," he added, "will be sealed
and kept . . . at the disposition of the relatives of the Marquis, whom he will not omit to inform in due course."

The Count concluded his reply by remarking that the only
clothing the prisoner had was a "poor surcoat" but that since,
as he supposed, the trunks that the valet has gone to Nice to
bring were "full of suits and other clothes of some consequence"
in all probability the relatives would not be obliged to have
new clothes made for the Marquis.

December 31st. The Marquis informed the Governor that he
would submit to him certain memoirs which the lack of
consideration for him of his family, who insisted against all the
evidence that they were not responsible for his incarceration,
had obliged him to draw up to clear himself. These memoirs

were intended for his friends and those who took his part and he requested the Count de la Tour to be so kind as to forward them and also support them.

He also asked the Count to write to the Count Ferrero de la Marmora to ask the *Marquise* to forward to him one hundred *louis*.

1773

January 1st. In a letter to the Governor of Savoy, Commandant de Launay gave his opinion of the Marquis and also indicated the fears that the custody of this prisoner aroused in him.

> "I can assure Your Excellency that this Lord is very dangerous, as unreliable as he is hot-tempered and inconsequent, quite capable of making me his victim by bribing somebody to help him escape (as he has already frivolously suggested to me) for which reason it would be most convenient for the family to request his withdrawal to some place in France. For there is no reckoning with so wild a head and I cannot . . . be responsible for a prisoner who is allowed the daily run of the fortress, which is not one of the most secure; I even believe him capable of some desperate action. Will you kindly inform the Minister, so that he provides some protection for me. . . ." He adds later : "This lord's letters are so badly written that I cannot make half of them out, and my memory is not good enough to be able to understand what they are all about. As I am not aware why he is retained here I am not in a position to hold up any letters."

January 2nd. The Governor of Savoy informed Count Ferrero de la Marmora that after the prudent steps he had taken to remove any possibility of escape he could reassure the Marquis de Sade's family. He also wrote that although the Marquis did behave honourably and irreproachably during the two months he spent at Chambéry, he would make so bold as not to offer him any certificate, since he did not know what use this Lord might make of it.

January 8th. Commandant de Launay informed the Governor that the "hot temperament" of the Marquis and the "extreme state of agitation" he was in had somewhat upset his health and he requested a doctor to be sent to the fortress to forestall any unfortunate turn, seeing that for some days the Lord had been "suffering from head and chest pains which caused him great loss of sleep".

January 10th. Thanking the Count Ferrero de la Marmora for "all his kindnesses", Lady Montreuil beseeched the ambassador to take care that the memoirs of self-justification which the Count de Mazan had written, which were to be sent both to the Minister of the Court at Turin and the Ministers of France and other outstanding personalities to whose circles the Marquis himself had the honour to belong, should not get through without being seen by His Excellency the Count de la Tour.

"If all they consist of is appeals to those whom he addresses to solicit the kindness and good faith of the King of France and try to make himself out innocent in this recent business, there is nothing against letting them through, but if they contain any falsehoods or injurious matter concerning his wife's family, from whom he has never known aught but kindness, it would be cruel to fan gossip by such imprudent tales and still more awful were he to have a memoir printed in Geneva, as he has threatened his mother-in-law." Lady Montreuil could think only of Lord de Vaulx as possible holder of her son-in-law's writings, unless it was Latour the valet, "a very bad type whom it would be prudent to keep a very close eye on". The man should never be let out without being carefully searched, for he was capable of hiding papers anywhere he could. "Nothing is of such importance to the family as this, for the reasons I have already told Your Excellency," she wrote, no doubt referring to her having told the Ambassador in confidence all about the love affair between Sade and her younger daughter. Lady Montreuil then goes on to ask the Marquis in future to be allowed to write to the Governor of Savoy without his letters being opened by de Launay and she also asked the Ambassador to throw more light on "the occurrence of November 20th" which obliged the Marquis to consult Surgeon Thonin. Apparently her son-in-law had refused to tell her anything about it, "but, *Monsieur*, it is of great interest to the family to know what it was all about".

January 11th. Count Ferrero de la Marmora wrote to the Governor of Savoy to explain that what made him ignore the request for a hundred *louis* which the Marquis had made was that he had felt that the Marquis' family themselves would not have paid any attention to it, being with reason sure that the prisoner could only use it for some bad purpose. He reminded the Count de la Tour that although because of his ill conduct the Marquis de Sade deserved more rigorous treatment than he was getting, it nevertheless behoved them to respect the wishes of the family and ease the condition of the unfortunate nobleman who was only being deprived of liberty in his own interest.

January 13th. Lord de la Tour informed de Mouroux about Sade's illness. The moment he had heard about it the Governor had sent one of the best physicians in the town out to Fort Miolans with instructions to stay with the sick man as long as he thought necessary. But as the bad state of health of the Marquis had improved rapidly after administration of a light purgative the doctor had at once returned to Chambéry.

The Count ended by telling de Mouroux that once again he had advised de Launay not to make any departure from the precautions he had decided upon, but at the same time to see that he modified the security with which he held the Marquis by the facilities and relaxations which were to be granted.

January 14th. De Launay informed the Governor of a violent attack made on himself by the Marquis. "When my intention of obliging this Lord had prompted me to hasten to tell him your kind purpose of securing him an early release, he took the liberty of covering me with the most atrocious vituperation in the presence of Lieutenant Duclos and Ansard the upholsterer, who were in the room, stating I was to blame for the keep door being locked and the orders were that he might take exercise in the lower fort. I withdrew at once, to avoid a worse scene. . ."

De Launay thought he could explain the main reason why the Marquis hated him. He had not wanted to put in a word in favour of his being restored to liberty, but had remained unmoved by a present of wine, coffee and chocolate which the Marquis had had the kitchen take him but which was at once returned to the said Lord. The Commandant, however, had misgivings—there might be others less incorruptible than himself who would give way. He therefore asked the Governor for authorisation to lock the Marquis in. In view of his apprehensions he had already forbidden his officers to have any dealings whatsoever with the Marquis.

January 14th or 15th. The prisoner too complained to the Governor. He told his version of the "violent altercation" he had had with de Launay.

"I am not used," he said, "to being spoken to in language all f—— and b—— and M. de Launay's thus addressing me prompted me to answer him back with some heat." For this reason he asked to be put under the control of the Major, de la Balme, "a man of great correctness and courtesy", for there must always be "real danger in placing a man of honour, who has received an education, under the orders of a de Launay".

January 15th. Lady Montreuil sent a brief note to Count Ferrero de la Marmora to specify the objects which should be in the trunks expected from Nice and which were of a sort that they should be extracted and sent to Paris "well sealed", namely in the first place, "all manuscripts, letters and other papers"; secondly, the crockery, because of the abuse the prisoner might make of it in his situation; thirdly and finally, the suits and linen which were not suitable for him and should be sent to Lady de Sade.

January 21st. The *Marquise* wrote reproachfully to Commandant de Launay. Not only had he not carried out the orders to relax the treatment meted out to the Marquis; he had also failed in the respect and attentions he had been advised to show the Marquis and which were due Lady de Sade's husband on all possible grounds. She wound up with the assurance that all this would be reported to the Sardinian Ambassador.

January 24th. The Commandant informed the Governor that the Marquis had "latterly become much quieter". He was endeavouring to keep the prisoner "between fear and gratitude". He afforded him all possible comforts and accompanied him whenever he wished to walk in the lower fort.

January 27th. The Marquis on this day paid Bailly, who ran the canteen, 240 *livres, 3 sous,* being his expenses from December 24th 1772 to date. The bill included the cost of meals given to Lt Duclos (nine times) and another detainee, Baron de l'Allée de Songy (four times). There were also sums given to a "messenger" or "commissioner", almost certainly young Joseph Violon, of Émieux, who three months later was persuaded to play a leading role in the escape of the Marquis and Baron de l'Allée.

Every week Joseph now went to the *Pomme d'Or* to call on Lord de Vaulx and collect any letters which that French Lord might have received for the Marquis—or to take him the Marquis' replies.

February 4th. In reply to the letter which Lady de Sade wrote him on January 21st, the Commandant, "somewhat disturbed" by the terms in which the letter was couched, tried to convince her how unjust her charges against him were. However rude the Marquis may have made him out to have been, he had never used his authority to punish the Marquis, but on the contrary, had procured every possible mitigation for him. The Commandant however said he would use Lady de Sade's letter to clear himself at the Court of Turin concerning his conduct regarding a prisoner whom he had always looked upon as a man "of the first distinction and one who should not have deserved having been held in so austere a place as this".

February 5th. De Launay sent the Governor of Savoy news about the Marquis. "I have sounded this gentleman and secretly had him examined; I find no reliability in him at all and am sure all his moves have had the sole aim of effecting his escape, since apart from the suggestions he has made to me he has had all his Piedmontese money changed into French and ... has been inquiring whether there is a bridge over the Isère which is well away from France."

The Commandant added that he could not answer for a prisoner "who has the run of the fortress and could clamber up the walls in an instant, despite all my precautions" and he begged the Governor to inform the Count de la Marmora of this, "so that he may graciously engage the family of the Marquis to take him away from here without delay". He ended his letter by saying : "That would be a superb act of kindness for which I would be obliged for the rest of my life."

February 7th. The Count de la Tour sent de Mouroux the letter which the *Marquise* had sent the Commandant, who certainly had good reason to complain about the contents. The Governor also informed his correspondent of the news he had received on the fifth, namely, that the Marquis de Sade's mind was constantly preoccupied with how to escape, and that in any case he was "of a vainglorious, overbearing turn of mind and in no wise disposed to suffer the least restriction". "And so," the Count concluded, "de Launay feels authorised to hope he will be relieved of the man."

February 8th. The Marquis informed the Count de la Tour that a plea which he had written to Turin was in the hands of Lord de Vaulx. He implored His Excellency to ask that gentleman to let him see it and judge for himself, since the Governor of Savoy had been given the very false notion that such an application was insulting both to the Court of France and to the *Marquise* de Sade. At the same time he asked his correspondent to have a packet containing a letter for his wife and another for his mother-in-law handed to Lord de Vaulx.

February 13th. The Governor informed de Mouroux that when he reminded de Launay that he should keep a closer watch on the Marquis de Sade's movements and his contacts with the outer world he did not authorise the Commandant to limit the prisoner's consolation of walking about within the walls of Fort Miolans "from fear lest by keeping the Marquis in close confinement he should feel more and more provoked".

On this same day the Marquis sent a peasant to the Count de la Tour with a letter in which he asked the Governor kindly to hand the messenger twelve *louis d'or,* being the price of a watch which he had just acquired and wished to pay for at once.

February 14th. The Count de la Tour informed Commandant de Launay about this request for twelve *louis d'or* which the Marquis wished him to provide. This request, which the Governor did not feel obliged to grant, since in any case he held no funds whatsoever belonging to the Marquis, had made the Governor begin to think. By cross-examining the messenger he had found out that it was Lieutenant Duclos that had handed him the Marquis' letter. Now, by doing this the officer in question had infringed the orders given him not to aid any correspondence between the prisoner and the outside world without Commandant de Launay's approval.

"I gravely suspect," wrote the Governor, "that it was by rendering de Sade services for some advantage that Duclos persuaded the Marquis to buy this watch from him, as the pretext for getting these twelve *louis* out of him, the more so since the Marquis had one *louis d'or* on him when arrested. . . . Whence I conclude . . . that M. Duclos sells his services, and it is to be feared that if he had the means he might try to secure de Sade's escape." He enjoined the Commandant to take this as a hint to keep as careful a watch on the officer as on his prisoner, not to forbid contact between Duclos and Sade, but to try to find any excuse to make the visits less frequent.

The same day the Marquis de Sade requested the Count de la Tour to forward to the King of Sardinia, and also himself to support to that sovereign, a plea which he had just drawn up. In this the prisoner outlined Lady Montreuil's manoeuvres to His Sardinian Majesty. "My mother-in-law aims at nothing less than my total ruination and she profits by my misfortunes to call down all the rigour of the law on me . . . and so force me to perpetual absence, suspecting that my intention was to face my judges in court for the sole purpose, so—not, after all, unreasonable—of clearing myself of the charges of that Marseilles affair, which have been so much exaggerated and fortified by my absence."

The Marquis dared think that "the most just, the most sympathetic of kings" would refuse to go on aiding "persecution and injustice or giving his support to avarice and self-seeking. . . . Sire," he cries, "if this woman who is out to ruin me were not afraid of my complaints, why should she seek such a roundabout way to achieve the punishment she thinks I deserve? Why would she not have me imprisoned in my own country?" And he implored the King graciously to enquire into the truth of the matter. When His Majesty came to know "the falsehoods by which certain persons have attempted to deceive Him he would not delay in rendering him (the Marquis) "a freedom which he only desires so that he can shake off the yoke of that woman and clear himself of the frightful things she makes him responsible for . . . and repeats daily with the sole intention of blotting him out for ever".

February 19th. De Launay reported to the Governor that about the 8th of the month a Miolans peasant (the same one that brought him the letter?—for all his enquiries in the village the Commandant never could find out who that had been!) brought a message given him by Lt. Duclos which had been meant for "a gentleman putting up at the *Pomme d'Or*". (This would be de Vaulx.) As for the Marquis de Sade, he seemed calm enough, and often took a walk on the upper or the lower ramparts, and considering the way he was guarded night and day there would seem to be no possibility of his escaping, not even by night, unless he had outside assistance, as a watchman was placed at the door of his room . . . "but I cannot be answerable for his getting out of the windows, which is fairly easy, though I remind the Keep sentries daily not to relax their watch on that side".

"But what most worries me," the Commandant added, "is that M. Duclos has struck up a friendship with him; they take supper together every evening. . . . In any case, it is always very risky, having a spirit like de Sade, which does not in the least match his birth, in a fortress in which there are state prisoners."

The same day, the ambassador of the King of Sardinia in Paris intimated to the Count de la Tour that the attitude of the Montreuil family towards Sade's imprisonment was well enough known for Commandant de Launay, without the least difficulty or risk of reproof, to be at liberty to limit any amenities or relaxations of rule if he thought any of them endangered security or that by reason of his outbursts and evil temper Sade did not deserve them.

February 20th. Charles Emmanual III, King of Sardinia, died at Turin, and his son Victor Amedeus III succeeded him.

February 26th. De Launay informed the Governor that despite every precaution the Marquis de Sade continued both to send and receive clandestine letters. Under such conditions the Commandant felt obliged once again to state that it was difficult to be responsible for the prisoner.

The same day the Governor was informed by Count Ferrero de la Marmora that the *Marquise* de Sade had left Paris by post chaise* to return, so she said, to Provence, but that there was every reason to fear that she had gone to Savoy to try to see her husband. As it was of the greatest importance that she should not be granted such a privilege the Ambassador had, he said, been asked to request the Count de la Tour kindly to prevent any contact between the lady and the prisoner, since troublesome consequences were all that could be expected from any such meeting.

February 27th. On this day the Marquis de Sade admitted to the Count de la Tour that time was so heavy on his hands that he had been reduced to playing *faro* with Lord de l'Allée de Songy** and had lost twelve *louis*. The Baron had made some unpleasant remarks and even threatened him, insisting he must be paid "at once", and the Marquis now assured the Governor that this was the real reason why he had asked His Excellency

---

*The most expensive "express"-mode of travel.

**François de Songy, Baron de l'Allée, born at Annecy, was imprisoned at Fort Miolans on February 22nd 1772. On December 4th 1770 a little before 8 p.m. he had entered the Royal prison of Bonneville with four men, to free a friend, Benoît Bizelon, held for debt. He pretended he was on a personal visit, and he and his company stayed wining and dining till 10.30, when, dressing the prisoner in his own clothes and the wig of one of his companions, he enabled Bizelon to get out. The Baron was also charged with the attempted murder of a soldier in the following circumstances: in the evening of December 25th, a few days after the Bonneville affair, he made a fracas outside the Chêne guardhouse and when a soldier came out to ask what it was all about, drew a sword from under the long cloak he was wearing and thrust at the man's right nipple, piercing his bandolier and coat, but then striking a brass button, which saved the man from injury or possibly death.

After this exploit the Baron took refuge in Geneva. When he had escaped from Fort Miolans with Sade, on May 1st 1773, the Baron took refuge in Paris, where he was arrested in August 1774, again to be imprisoned at Fort Miolans. He was not to leave the Fortress again till March 17th 1778, when his mother obtained a Royal pardon from Victor Amedeus III. Some time after this the Baron married, but new follies—the theft of some cattle—brought him back yet again to Fort Miolans in 1786. Of this person, who has become historic because of his being co-prisoner with Sade, the police record ran: "Very dangerous in his cups, a disturber of public order of murderous disposition; everybody keeps out of his way."

for 12 *louis,* under the pretext of wanting to buy a watch. Sade also complained to the Governor that the same de l'Allée had "inveigled" his servant d'Armand, known as Latour, "a young man of good family . . . who may be well off some day" and in two days had won two hundred gold *louis* from him. The Marquis mentioned "the queerness" that such incredible luck at cards must suggest; luck would seem to have been on de l'Allée's side too persistently by far for there to be much doubt about de l'Allée's knowing how to control it. In this matter, the Marquis went on, he had no hesitation in making the Commandant in part responsible for not putting a stop to this gambling, since it was almost beyond question that the game was "rigged". As far as he himself went, the Marquis was quite agreeable to losing the twelve *louis,* but he begged the Governor to insist on his young valet's being returned the promissory note for one hundred *livres* payable in three years which de l'Allee had extorted from the young man, for even with the legacy he had reason to expect some day, Latour would never be able to pay this sum without ruining his family. Further, the prisoner implored His Excellency not to entertain any fears about the plans of escape of which he himself was suspected; he was incapable of breaking the word of honour which he had signed when he arrived at Fort Miolans. He then asked the Count very kindly to keep this letter confidential, for if its contents were revealed he "would be exposed to new scenes with the Commandant and insults from the Baron".

March 1st. Count Ferrero de la Marmora reported to the Governor of Savoy a conversation he had had the day before with the Duke d'Avignon about the detention of the Marquis de Sade. The French Minister had told him that he strongly disapproved of the letter which the *Marquise* wrote to de Launay, who certainly did not deserve such an attack. De Launay could hardly take offence "at the hasty words of a lady who has been misinformed and who is also led astray by the credit which unfortunately the husband she still loves had with her". But what was most important was that "Lord de Mazan is still detained . . . and everything else being merely secondary to this, must be made to depend on that circumstance".

It was indispensable that de Launay should not let himself

fall under any influence whatsoever. He should not hesitate, should he think it necessary, to send the Marquis' valet packing and withdraw any relaxation from the former which he could not take the trouble to earn or which there seemed reason to fear he might make ill use of. It would even be very desirable, and would correspond to the wishes of the prisoner's family, if all contact with the outer world, including any correspondence, were forbidden him. In that respect it would be sufficient were the Count de la Tour to undertake from time to time to pass on news of the prisoner to the Sardinian Embassy.

Further, Count Ferrero de la Marmora informed his correspondent that he was that same day going to give the Marquis de Sade's family news of him, so that some correspondent might without delay be found at Chambéry who would be responsible for providing the necessary funds for his board. "The threat I shall make of setting him at liberty if this is not done will be sure to persuade them not to delay doing it."

March 6th. Having left Paris February 25th or 26th, the *Marquise* arrived by post chaise that evening at Chambéry by the Lyons road. She was dressed in male clothing, a confidential friend, Albaret by name, accompanying her. The two travellers put up at the inn under the name of *Dumonts, brothers, en route to Piedmont*.

March 7th. Declaring their intention of continuing towards Piedmont, Lady de Sade and Albaret left Chambéry at midday in the same post chaise. But they soon halted at Montmélian "ostensibly by some slight mishap", staying there till March 14th. As soon as she reached this village, in which there was only one very wretched inn, Lady de Sade sent her confidence man to nearby Miolans. Albaret duly called on the Commandant one hour before nightfall and handed him a letter from the *Marquise*. It was written *as from Barraux* and in it she "entreated that the man who bore the letter be allowed to see her husband and have quarter of an hour alone with him, to bring him news".

De Launay, however, had earlier in the month been tipped off by the Count de la Tour that the *Marquise* would probably put in an appearance. He was not to allow her to see the Marquis, so he felt obliged to extend the prohibition to any man sent by the *Marquise*.* Albaret returned to Montmélian without seeing the prisoner.

March 8th. This very morning the Governor of Savoy received a report (de Launay sent an express letter) about the previous day's suspicious visitor. The very same afternoon the same messenger, giving himself out to be one Dumont, handed the Count a letter from Lady de Sade dated March 5th, also written as if from Barraux. In this letter the *Marquise* wrote that, having left Paris to go down to her Provençal estates, she had taken the Grenoble road, thinking to see her husband, but an acute chill had detained her at Barraux. She however found solace in the confidence she felt that the Governor would allow a personal friend of hers to go to Fort Miolans and see her husband, to discuss his affairs with him.

The Count informed the messenger that this would not be possible, because the King, his master, had sent contrary instructions on the matter, so he was obliged to insist on refusing Lady de Sade this privilege, while most courteously tending her his profound regrets. However, he would go so far as to transmit to the prisoner any letter she cared to write and would also transmit to her any reply he wrote to this. However, she might set her mind at rest about his state of health; he could not be better and was being treated with the same relaxations and concern as hitherto.

The same day, Lady de Sade applied to the Office of Internal Affairs at Turin, requesting of the Minister the permission which the Count de la Tour had refused her. At the same time she complained that her husband was constantly refused the consolation of visits in prison from friends he had made in Chambéry.

The very same day Count Ferrero de la Marmora informed Count de la Tour that a correspondent at Chambéry respon-

*It is far from impossible that when she set out on this ostensible journey to Piedmont in masculine disguise, Lady de Sade intended working for the prisoner's escape. It is also probable that Lady Montreuil got wind of it and informed Count Ferrero de la Marmora, speaking of "fatal consequences" if Lady de Sade did see her husband. Yet there is no single piece of supporting documentary evidence of this. Count de la Tour indeed found the warning "enigmatic" and "without motive" when without further explanation the Sardinian ambassador passed it all on to him.

sible for monthly payment of the Marquis de Sade's board was to be appointed without delay. He reminded the Governor to make sure that nothing whatsoever put into writing by the prisoner was allowed to leave the precincts of the Fortress, "since he smothers us with rhapsodies and *memoranda* the facts of which are as false as they are artfully set forth".

March 9th. Albaret called on the Count de la Tour a second time. He bore a letter from Lady de Sade, unsealed, addressed to her husband, which the Governor immediately had taken to Fort Miolans. But at the same time this emissary urged his plea to be allowed to have conversation with the prisoner. This the Count refused just as he had done the day before. Albaret woefully informed him that though Lady de Sade, being very poorly, had been obliged so long to delay her journey to Provence, she had nevertheless now postponed departure till Sunday, in the hope of persuading the Count to allow her the privilege. But the Governor requested the messenger to express to the lady in question all the regret that her indisposition occasioned him, but at the same time to tell her that he would never depart in any way from the legal obligations imposed on him and it was his counsel to her to remove herself from the wretched abode she had chosen to shelter in.

The same day too Lieutenant Duclos paid a visit to Montmélian. . . .

March 12th. Informed now by Count de la Tour about the dispute which had arisen at the end of February between Baron de l'Allée and the Marquis de Sade, and also of the sort of denunciation of which by the latter's action he had been the victim, de Launay protested to the Governor that he had known nothing whatsoever about these two gentlemen's gambling. "By this detail," wrote the Commandant, "and all those of which I have had the honour of informing him, Your Excellency will be able to see for himself that Lord de Sade is a very unreliable character, which makes one constantly wary of him, particularly since he established a liaison with Lieutenant Duclos, whereas, had he but had confidence in me and followed various little pieces of advice I have given him, he and I could have worked together and put certain things before his family. Even if we had not succeeded in speeding up the termination of his case, at least we might have obtained from the King the sanctuary he might graciously have afforded him; but on the contrary the Marquis was invariably hostile towards me. . . ."

At the same time de Launay reported the piece of gossip which Sade freely let go the rounds, according to which the young man he had with him as valet was nothing less than a bastard son of the Duke of Bavaria.

The Commandant then wound up his letter by reasserting to the Governor how uneasy he was about the Marquis de Sade, for whom it was almost impossible to answer, especially if Lieutenant Duclos, "who has always been edgy in his relations with his superiors", is kept at Miolans; apropos of this de Launay added that if the Count could find no reason for removing that officer, he would himself be obliged to relinquish his post and ask leave to retire !

March 14th. Losing all hope of seeing her husband, or even of her companion Albaret's being allowed to see him, Lady de Sade gave up and continued by post chaise to Lyons, without halting at Chambéry.

Towards March 15th. Lord de Vaulx was expelled from Chambéry, for having been accomplice in the "loss" of the letters and notes of the Marquis de Sade.

March 17th. The Governor of Savoy informed de Mouroux about the Spanish fly sweets of Marseilles and the trial which followed and also about the incestuous love affair of the Marquis de Sade and his sister-in-law Anne de Launay. The Marquis, he said, was "a mad-cap, an irreligious, immoral man, prepared to go to any extreme". The Governor also told de Mouroux about de Launay's misgivings. Not merely was this officer afraid lest the Marquis succeeded in seducing one of his garrison, and got him to offer assistance in escaping; it was also not out of the question that Sade might take advantage of the liberty of free movement in the fort precincts which he had been enjoying, to fling himself down from the ramparts.

March 18th. Back at La Coste, the *Marquise* de Sade wrote to Count de la Tour. Her recent indisposition had brought her so low that she had been unable herself to call on him to plead those kindnesses by which she had hoped he would alleviate the days of imprisonment of her husband who, never having failed his King or his country, did not deserve to be treated with the rigour he was now subjected to.

The same day she applied to the King of Sardinia, imploring him to set her husband at liberty. "My husband is not to be classed with the rogues of whom the universe should be purged. An excess of fantasy, Sire, resulted in a sort of misdemeanour; bias against him has turned that into a crime and justice then made its thunder resound—and because of what? because of a youthful folly which endangered no life or honour or the reputation of any citizen. . . ."

The same day a mule-driver delivered one of the Marquis's trunks, brought from Nice by Carteron, at Fort Miolans. Sade had it brought up to his room and went through the contents.

March 19th. De Launay reported to the Governor that on March 7th, expecting to be let out, Sade packed his baggage. Now, having been disappointed, he seemed most astonished, and yet calmer. For his after-dinner walk he had chosen the far end of a garden in the lower fortress, whence it would be most difficult for him to escape. "I am as courteous as I can be to him," the Commandant added, "for all that he never sets foot in my apartments, though were he to choose to have confidence in me I would try to afford him every possible consolation short of infringing my orders, and would suggest to him certain applications he might make to his family and the Minister in France. He never speaks to anyone, even his valet. . . ."

The Commandant also reported to the Count that when according to the Count's instructions he had spoken to Baron de l'Allée, the Baron had replied that he did not mean to make any demands on the Marquis de Sade's valet, he would even send him his promissory note back or give it to His Excellency when he was released; he had only insisted on it against the chance of the young man's having a stroke of good luck.

The same day the Marquis wrote the Governor a letter in which he apparently paid heed to the "requests" which de Launay had several times counselled him to make, to obtain his freedom. First, the Marquis undertook not to conduct "any correspondence that the whole land might not read". Secondly, he was anxious to get him to understand that whereas those who had had him imprisoned "allege that their sole justification is their desire to break off an unseemly and distressing love affair, they are going too far in their animosity", for, he added "I have stated very positively that I have given it up and never stop so saying, as I do now again in the most explicit terms in the enclosed letter for Paris which I beg Your Excellency kindly to have despatched by Monday's mail. But do please instruct me what I am to do to be believed. . . . I break off all relations, I offer to hand over all letters, I swear not to come within one hundred leagues of Paris for as long as they insist, and to stop every memorandum, every application, or any insulting word likely to harm or hinder a settlement which they fear I may endanger but which I perhaps desire more than they do".

This very same day it came to strong words between the Marquis and Baron de l'Allée de Songy. Here is the tale as told by de Launay in his report to the Governor:

"Going outside after lunching with M. Pignier (they only drank two bottles of white wine which I had sent them) Lord de l'Allée went outside the chapel, where the Marquis de Sade and Lord de Battines were playing cards to pass the time. De l'Allée told the latter he ought not play with people who complained whenever they lost, to which Milord de Sade remarked that this was a very unseemly remark to make, whereupon Milord de l'Allée replied that he could prove it to them in person. The Marquis then called on me in my room in a rage and cried : '*Monsieur*, I come to lay complaint against Lord de l'Allée who has insulted me, and if you do not render me justice I shall complain about it to Count de la Tour.' I at once went out to find de l'Allée and in a friendly way said he was to withdraw to his room, which I thought he had done, as I did not want there to be a second clash, but when I got back I found him in my room, when he said he ought not be punished because of de Sade's complaints. I tried to convince him that this was not the reason and that I had orders from Your Excellency not to grant him any more relaxations. This incensed him still more, and he assured me he would commit suicide, since everybody had abandoned him.

At last he left my room to retire, then came back still more enraged and evidently with a knife. He went over to the window and then suddenly flung the knife down. Seeing blood on his shirt I was terrified. We forced him to lie down on a bed and I at once sent for the surgeon, who indeed did find several knife-pricks in his stomach, the deepest of which was not more than quarter of an inch. I made a point of having him bled and taken to his room. Even the next day he insisted he would rather die than go on living."

March 22nd. In the columns of two statements of account from Bailly, who kept the canteen, which Sade sent to the Governor, we see that between January 28th and March 21st he dined on more than thirty occasions with Lt Duclos and three times with Baron de l'Allée, who for his part took a meal or drank with Latour on six occasions.

March 26th. Count Ferrero de la Marmora forwarded to Count de la Tour the gratitude of the Duke d'Aiguillon and the Montreuil family for having contrived to foil all Lady de Sade's attempts to see her husband at Miolans and also for the attitude of "rigour and courtesy combined which he had shown that lady". He requested the Governor to make sure that Sade "did not shower his frightful writings and memoranda on the public, for they merely serve to aggravate his misdemeanours in the eyes of persons of sensitivity". He was also "to put some restraint on Lord de Vaulx, a Frenchman without occupation at present domiciled at Chambéry who assumes the role of Sade's champion and must have facilitated the beginning of these writings and letters, up to the point at which you found it fitting to arrest him".

To this letter of the Sardinian ambassador was attached a message from Lady Montreuil to de Launay. The disgrace incurred by Lieutenant Duclos because of services rendered the Marquis de Sade had come to her knowledge and she hastened to take the part of this officer.

"*Monsieur,*" she wrote to the Commandant, "I would be most aggrieved were an officer to lose his position because of me and my family. If you have nothing else to reproach him with, I implore you to keep him, being sure that if better informed concerning the wrongness of the cause he has taken up and the abuse made of his confidence M. Duclos would in future keep his conduct within the limits prescribed by your orders." At the same time Lady Montreuil begged an old officer very kindly to forget any wrongs which the Marquis might have done him and implored him to take account of the natural violence of Lord de Sade's temperament, as well as of the horror of his present position, which was indeed frightful, and on which they should have pity till such time as it proved possible to relax it or change it without untoward consequences.

The same day the Commandant informed the Governor that de Sade was beginning to become quite amenable and had agreed with him that this excessive writing of his and his refusal to submit to his family had delayed his release. As for Lord de l'Allée de Songy, he now never ceased lamenting his follies, which were without doubt going to cost him two years' prison, but he (de Launay) hoped this punishment would improve him, for the Baron had been given a very bad education by his father, who had made use of him "as his bully when he was young", adding liquor "to crown the work, by reason of which de l'Allée is going to find it difficult to reform". Lord de Battines' behaviour at Miolans, on the other hand, was excellent. He did not care to have any contact with the Marquis, but the Commandant had asked him to undertake to reconcile the Marquis and Baron de l'Allée, and this he would certainly do in course of the next few days.

April 1st. The Marquis de Sade told the Count de la Tour that he was indeed astonished that his misfortunes should be so prolonged, despite all the precise accommodations he had given his relations in the letter which he had asked his correspondent kindly to forward to them. He requested the Governor of Savoy to take the matter up with Count de la Marmora and Baron de Mouroux and to secure his early release, since he felt his health to be declining daily in this fortress, "so that it is quite impossible for me to stay much longer here without risking certain illness, made all the worse by my terrible anxieties". At the same time Sade requested news of Lord de Vaulx, about whom he was much concerned.

The same day, Commandant de Launay wrote to the Governor to tell him that every day now the Marquis de Sade "showed greater confidence in him, though was most concerned and depressed by his detention".

April 14th. Count de la Tour to Baron de Mouroux : "The Marquis de Sade has thought fit to threaten to lodge complaints against me at the Throne, in addition accusing me of having gone beyond the orders given me when he was arrested, by having him taken to Fort Miolans. . . . I spurn charges so falsely made, though I must frankly confess to Your Excellency that I would be greatly relieved were His Majesty to relieve me of a person of Sade's mentality."

April 15th. The Marquis de Sade informed the Count de la Tour that he had made his peace with the Baron and, not without the approval of Commandant de Launay, most pressingly begged the concession of allowing Baron de l'Allée to mess with him, it being "so much in my heart to make manifest to the Baron that my reconciliation with him is genuine".

April 16th. We find Commandant de Launay writing to Count de la Tour and assuming the role of advocate of the Marquis regarding his domestic budgeting. When the Commandant fixed the cost of board and maintenance for the Marquis and his valet he gave no thought to clothing or to the cost of messengers, let alone the considerable generosity and charity the Marquis had thought fit to show in the fortress. He also remarked that he had now gained the confidence of his prisoner more, and Sade was proving "more docile in temperament now he is no longer worked upon by gossip" about the Commandant's person, that is, since the departure of Lieutenant Duclos. De Launay also informed the Count about the reconciliation between the Baron and the Marquis, "a most handsome reconciliation". He had even allowed them to stroll together for a few hours a day within the precincts, but had taken a firm stand against any card-playing for money between them, or with valet Latour.

April 17th. The Governor of Savoy reported to de Mouroux that he had just been informed by Commandant de Launay "in gladness of heart that Milord the Marquis de Sade . . . after performing his duty as a Christian at this season of Easter, has suddenly undergone a total change of heart and conduct and not merely has begged forgiveness for all he has written or said against me which was most out of place, but had asked if he might without delay make a sort of apology to certain officers and non-commissioned officers of the garrison who had at times been alarmed by outbursts of temper on his part". The Count considered that this "happy change" was to be regarded as "the effect of the grace of the sacrament".

1773

ESCAPE

Between April 15th and (?) *20th.* When he had obtained permission to take his meals in the company of Baron de l'Allée, the Marquis de Sade made out to Commandant de Launay that the food prepared in the kitchen often reached his room cold. For this reason he begged the favour of being allowed to take his meals somewhere in the canteen messrooms. The Commandant kindly granted this new request and as dining-room for the two prisoners set apart a room which had become vacant when Lieutenant Duclos left, adjoining the main messroom. This room was part of an apartment recently built on, and it consisted of two rooms leading one out of the other. The first was now placed at the disposal of the prisoners, the second was almost invariably kept locked. It served the canteen cook as a store-room. In a corner of this store-room there was a partitioned-off closet. One wonders whether when he used to visit Duclos the Marquis had not noted the special features of this closet, so that his request about meals concealed a plan. Or did he only come to notice what we shall now learn when he began to take his meals there?

We do not know, but however the matter stood, here is what he at some time or other noticed in the closet—the window was the only window of its kind among all the windows of the fort over a certain size, *in that it had no iron bars.* Secondly, it looked large enough to allow even a rather portly figure to squeeze through it. Thirdly, giving on to the rear of the fortress, on the mountain side, it was no more than about thirteen feet above the ground level. . . .

April 29th. Messenger Joseph Violon, who since some time had been prohibited entry to the fortress, haunted the lower ramparts, on the gardens side, and succeeded in having secret talk with the Marquis.

April 30th. Knowing that he would have to be up all night, Joseph Violon entered a public house in Saint Pierre d'Albigny and slept till four p.m.

At seven p.m. Lords de Sade and de l'Allée entered the messroom to sup. Apparently Latour, who brought their meal in, waited till the cook and her staff were taking their own meal, and contrived to steal the key of the little room. The valet then went up to his master's cell and, lighting the candles, placed on the table two letters to the Commandant.

At 8.30 the three men clambered out of the closet window. Standing at guard underneath, Joseph Violon helped them down, either by reaching up to them, or by means of a small ladder. Guided by the young farmer, the fugitives then made off rapidly in the darkness towards the French frontier.

It was a little before nine o'clock that watchman Jacquet finished his supper and, coming back on duty, noticed a light in Sade's room, which was next to his, but concluded that the Marquis was playing draughts with Baron de l'Allée. With the idea of letting them have a little more time to themselves, he lay down dressed, till the time should come when he would have to separate them and escort the Baron back to his cell. But, being tired, Jacquet fell asleep almost at once.

May 1st. Waking a little before three in the morning, Jacquet noticed the light still burning in the Marquis' room. This made him suspicious and he hastened to inform the Commandant. The Commandant rose at once to come to see for himself. Assuring himself that the door was locked, he had it forced, to find no prisoner, only two guttering candles and the two letters addressed to him, one from the Marquis, the other from Baron de l'Allée.

"If there is anything that mars the delight with which I fling off my chains," the Marquis began, "it is my fear of making you responsible for my escape. After all your decency and courtesies, I cannot conceal the fact that the thought does trouble me. . . ." Later on he counselled the Commandant not to try to pursue him. "Fifteen well mounted and well armed men await me under the Castle wall . . . all determined to give their lives rather than let me be recaptured."* After some more in this style he said : "I have a wife and children who would avenge my death to your last breath." He ended by thanking the Commandant once again for his kindness. "I shall be grateful to you all my life and crave but the opportunity to prove it. I trust the day will come when I may be able to give public testimony of the feelings of gratitude you have inspired in me. . . ."

Sade also left a list of his effects and requested they be sent to his wife at La Coste, especially the six geographical maps which furnished his room, the "quite new blue frock coat" which he left at the point of his escape, as well as "two little recumbent china dogs, one all black, the other black with white patches, to which I am very attached".

Meanwhile, tramping all night, the fugitives and their guide reached the village of Chapareillant by the time the sun was fully up. Here Sade paused to write a note to the Governor of Savoy. The horror of his situation (he wrote) had made him forgetful of the kindness his correspondent had shown him, but "the hotness of his blood rebelled against such a form of punishment, and was so ill suited to his nature that he would rather suffer death than loss of liberty".

During the morning a posse sent out by Commandant de Launay reached the French frontier, but long since, they were forced to admit, the four fugitives were away on the Grenoble highroad.

*The Marquis hoped this threat would discourage pursuit, for of course there was no truth in it all. We need only glance at the letter which the Count de la Tour wrote on May 5th to de Mouroux to see that on Saturday at daybreak the two fugitives were seen in the village of Barraux, where they had arrived on foot. There is no question in any case but that fifteen armed mounted men would have been noticed. "When we note how wary the Savoyan police were," writes Georges Daumas, before Count de la Tour's letter was found in the archives of Turin, "how could anybody ever have credited that story of Sade's commanding a troop of armed men for several days in the countryside?" And he added: "What after reading Joseph Violon's application to the King of Sardinia in 1788 are we to think of the romantic yarn which Sade served on Commandant de Launay, since then so often repeated that these fifteen men ready for anything were recruited and armed by the *Marquise*—better still, were under her command, an improvement due to biographers—and assisted Sade to escape. Is not Joseph Violon's plea sufficient indication of the essential part that this young man played in the escape of 1773?"

AFTER THE ESCAPE

May 5th. The Governor of Savoy wrote to inform de Mouroux about an event which would upset him considerably : the Marquis de Sade and Baron de l'Allée had got away ! He was forwarding the detailed report despatched yesterday by Commandant de Launay, and implored the minister's indulgence and support for this veteran officer, whose devotion, honesty and zeal were so well known.

May 8th. De Mouroux to the Count de la Tour : His Majesty had "learned of the escape of the Marquis de Sade with extreme displeasure". And although His Majesty had had great esteem for Commandant de Launay, he could not but observe that there had been negligence on the Commandant's part. "His Majesty desires a full enquiry into the matter and anything that may have any bearing upon it."

The same day, the Marquis d'Aigblanche, Minister of Foreign Affairs since April 22nd, sent a note of reproof to the Governor for not considering it necessary to report Sade's escape *to him.*

"If," the Minister said, "if His Majesty had not deigned to inform me himself, the event would still be unknown to me."

May 10th. Lady de Sade intimated to Count de la Tour that in the near future she would send an emissary to fetch her husband's effects from Miolans Fortress.

May 12th. M. Chiaravina, *Knight,* in charge of the Department of War at Turin, transmitted to the Governor of Savoy the decisions taken by His Majesty following reports which reached him concerning the escape of the Marquis de Sade and Baron de l'Allée : warder Jacquet to be imprisoned and kept *incommunicado,* Commandant de Launay to be placed under arrest at Chambéry till otherwise ordered.* In his absence the Fort Miolans would be commanded by Major de la Balma.

---

*Young Joseph Violon, the real culprit, was not arrested till two years later (March 2nd 1775), on July 24th to be condemned to life banishment from the realms of the King of Sardinia.

May 14th. The Ambassador of Sardinia in Paris informed Count de la Tour that he had informed Lady Montreuil of the escape of the Marquis de Sade and he could leave it to his correspondent's imagination how aggrieved that lady had been when she heard the news.

May 20th. The Marquis' mother-in-law informed the Governor of Savoy how distressed she was to see that His Excellency's great favours to the Marquis de Sade's family "had not been effective so long as she would have desired". None the less the Marquis' family and she herself were grateful to the Count de la Tour for the attention he had shown them and begged him to accept their sincere thanks.

May 26th. Count de la Tour informed de Mouroux that Commandant de Launay reported at Chambéry for detention the moment he received the order. The sad lot of that excellent officer seemed to him worthy of pity.

"This escape ... should not be laid at his door but rather at that of the officers to whom he entrusted watch over the prisoners. I venture to hope that, convinced of his innocence, Your Excellency will press the matter with His Majesty in his favour."

June 10th. In response to the Count de la Tour's advocacy in favour of de Launay, Minister Chiaravina informed him that His Majesty did bear in mind "that this officer has served well and on great occasions", and would "take this into consideration. But as for his responsibility in this matter, His Majesty desires justice to take its course", the more so since de Launay might also be to blame for the tardiness with which the Count de la Tour had reported the matter to Turin, the Home Office not being informed till the fifth day after the escape.

July 21st. The Governor of Savoy informed Chiaravina that for some time now Lady Montreuil had been requesting him "to obtain all the letters that her daughter and she herself had written to the prisoner and which, being in the trunks left by him at Miolans, were impounded by the Auditor-General of War as possibly bearing on the escape of the Marquis. At the same time she insists that she is much interested in their contents not being made public, since there is mention in them of her younger daughter, who was seduced by the Count de Sade, her brother-in-law."*

*What exactly did happen to those trunks and those letters? On May 22nd 1772, Lady de Sade wrote to the Count not to have the trunks sent her, but to deposit them in some safe place. Two months later she came to Miolans herself to fetch them and to her intense indignation was refused them. It was not till February 17th 1774 that Lady de Montreuil was able to thank the Governor of Savoy for kindly getting the Court of Turin to issue orders for the return of the trunks left by her son-in-law. However, she implored His Excellency to keep the letters till the matter was cleared up.

CHAPTER NINE

The Libertine of La Coste
1773 - 1777

DEFAULTER INVIOLATE

April 30-December 16 1773. All we know of the fugitive Marquis during the eight months from May 1st 1773 when he reached Grenoble to early January 1774 is that he withdrew to his *château,* La Coste, joining his wife there (though taking precautions, it would seem, to ensure a safe retreat somewhere in the neighbourhood at the least alarm) and that both husband and wife made every possible effort both to calm Lady Montreuil's rage and to forestall any consequences of this and also, without endangering the Marquis' liberty, to have the 1772 Court of Aix sentence passed in contumacy quashed, for it meant civic death.* But when we come to look at the terms of Lady de Sade's application we see that her mother "looked with real alarm upon any proceedings intended to justify or establish the liberty of her son-in-law". What is more, on December 16th 1773 that lady actually succeeding in obtaining two Royal orders to de Sartine, one to seize and sequester all the Marquis' papers and the other to seize his body and incarcerate him in Pierre-Encise Fortress. As we shall now see, it proved possible to put into effect solely the first of these.

January 6th 1774. Equipped with those Royal orders of December 16th, Inspector Goupil of the Paris police, with four

---

*It seems beyond question that Sade was not so foolhardy as to go to his estate at once, but where he hid for a time is not known.

bowmen and a posse of cavalry of the Seneschalty of Marseilles, forced an entry into La Coste manor in the middle of the night, to find only Lady de Sade there. He searched the place from top to bottom, pillaging the Marquis' study and burning or impounding papers, then withdrew, uttering threats. The Marquis had been informed in time to escape.

It was several weeks before Sade returned to La Coste. No doubt he was put up by friends in the area, changing from one house to another frequently, to escape search-parties. Inspector Goupil's "statement of costs, fees and petty expenses", reaching the enormous sum of 8,235 *livres,* 12 *sols* (upwards of £1,000 in present-day values) gives us some idea of the extent of the preparations for the abortive police coup of January 6th. We find all the details of a well worked out police action, down to the purchase of two complete peasant outfits "as agreed with Lady de Montreuil". And if we had any doubt that all this little tragic farce was the work of the Taxation Court ex-President's lady, there is a diary note of Inspector Goupil's to clinch the matter. The good lady had ten different meetings with the inspector, to hold council before and after the expedition—this we even see from cab charges. There are also other fascinating details,—for instance, the way the police assembled in the village of Bonnieux before the attack was made. To crown all, however, we find proof of dastardly treachery on the part of the Abbé de Sade and of Elzéar Fage the lawyer, of Apt. Both of these without any hesitation offered Goupil their assistance.

* * *

It was about a month after these events that the Marquis and his wife decided to take the management of their affairs out of the hands of *Maître* Fage, and another legal adviser was found. This was *Maître* Gaspard François Xavier Gaufridy, also of Apt, where he was both notary public and solicitor. On May 18th, as administrator of the estate of a husband all of whose rights as a citizen were annulled, Lady de Sade confirmed to Ripert that Fage no longer enjoyed her confidence and Gaufridy was going to take over.

As Gaufridy was to administer the Sade estates in Provence

throughout the last quarter of the eighteenth century, let us borrow Paul Bourdin's lively portrait of this man :

"Gaufridy was no stranger to Sade. His father had managed the affairs of Sade's father, the Count, for a long time. The lawyer was of the same age as Sade; as boys they had played together, and they had never lost contact with one another. Gaufridy managed Sade's affairs for twenty-six years, and the local bailiffs at Mazan, Saumane and Arles were under his instructions. He was known as "Lawyer Gaufridy" though he really had no right at all to the title, just as that of solicitor was really not his. He soon had the confidence of the whole family and everybody felt sure he had first place in his heart and ran to him the moment he had any trouble. He supplied the nun sisters with game and fresh vegetables, he advised the Abbé de Saumane on his lawsuits, he conducted the business of the lords of the manor and supplied the *château* with comestibles. He was a very subtle and seems also to have been a jovial man, despite a tendency to be heavy and pompous in language. He was highly esteemed by everybody, a good business man and a wise counsellor. His caution almost amounted to wiliness, his elasticity to double-dealing, his tact to easy-going, his carelessness to extreme indolence, and this latter trait increased steadily with the years. After the Marquis was freed and during the four or five years which preceded the break between them, Gaufridy's one thought was to protect his own peace from the Marquis. . . Without a word he bore with the grousing and the insults which soon enough that outrageous client showered on him, he ceased replying to his letters, he no longer even read them, he was afraid for his own security without daring to break off relations with that embarrassing debased noble, yet his professional conscience remained ever alert and it was only if suspected of having neglected his duties that he emerged from his state of apathy. . . .

For the rest, Gaufridy was as honest as a man should be occupying that position, in that profession. . . . He was the open depositary of all secrets, but every one had its file and there was no intercommunication between the covers. Working like that a man becomes pigeon-holed himself and even ceases to be curious about the confidences reposing in the various corners of his memory. This explains how it was that he was so quick to serve Lady Montreuil too and become, if not her spy, at least her best agent. . . . For that matter, Gaufridy had no thought of betraying anybody. He served Lady Montreuil's ends, but for good. He was full of pity for Lady de Sade and most attached to her, but if he nevertheless worked with her mother to counter the *Marquise*'s intentions, this was merely the better to wrest her daughter from her blind infatuation for the Marquis. . . . Thus Gaufridy heard them all and satisfied everybody . . . seeking justification for his double-dealing in the opinion he had come to form of the moral value of those who employed him and the rightness or wrongness of the various aims they pursued. When in a tight corner he extracted himself by means of his inertia, and time came to his aid."

March 1774. In Lady de Sade's name Gaufridy drew up an application against her mother. Sade had returned to La Coste some little time before this, but was on the point of leaving again. He had the application sent urgently to Chapote, who was a solicitor at le Châtelet (Paris).

On the 25th of the month the Minister of the Royal Household, now the Duke de la Vrillière, sent M. Sénac de Meilhan, Governor of Provence, Royal instructions to have Sade interned at Pierre-Encise—the instructions which failed when Inspector Goupil arrived too late.

April-May 1774. Early in April Sade was no longer at La Coste, which we see from the Governor of Provence's reply to the Duke de la Vrillière (dated April 12th). It would seem that the Marquis had gone to Bordeaux, after which he stayed in Grenoble for a time.

By now funds began to run out at La Coste. "The late Count left many debts and his lands are heavily encumbered." Threatened by creditors, Lady de Sade pleaded her cause at Avignon and Aix, and also wrote to the Abbé de Sade, trying to get him to take up his nephew's cause, but the Abbé thought his nephew's duty was to give himself up, to which the

Marquise refused to consent, even if it would have suited her finances for her husband to have done so.

June 1774. The Marquis was back at La Coste, urging Lady de Sade to go to Paris, for there were two pieces of business that required her presence in the capital. First, there had been no response to the application to the Châtelet court, not even word whether the application had been filed, and this after four months. Above all, nothing had been done to quash the decision of the High Court of Aix. Sade, who had drawn up a statement defending himself, held that publicity was essential, especially in his in-laws' family, so the passivity of Lady Montreuil astonished him and made him indignant. "I am sure you will agree with me, *Monsieur*," he wrote to Gaufridy, "that Lady Montreuil's passion for leaving everything in the air is most extraordinary. For after all, what does she gain by it? It merely perpetuates the disgrace of this wretched business, and of her daughter and her grandchildren, putting frightful disorder into my business affairs and compelling me to lead the most wretched and dismal existence."

It was up to the *Marquise* while in Paris to put this so distressing situation right. "Have a care!" the Marquis continued, "do make a point of encouraging Lady Montreuil, give her some good advice, and let her do the impossible to put an end to it all in the four months I give her for it. But in Heaven's name let her see that I am not obliged to go on leading this roaming, unsettled life. I don't feel cut out for an adventurer, and being forced like this to play the part is one of the greatest trials of my situation."

July 1774. On July 14th Lady de Sade left La Coste for Paris with her sister (how long Lady Anne had been at La Coste and what the relationship now was between her and Sade we do not know). Lady de Sade apparently reached the outskirts of Paris on July 26th. With her husband's exhortations still ringing in her ears, she set to work immediately, and by the 29th was able to report to Provence on her first steps, which were the motion against Lady Montreuil.

"I presume," she wrote to Gaufridy, "that the Attorney-Royal might well intervene in the matter, for all that he has found it necessary to tell everybody that I am out of my mind."

This was a compliment which she was now told she would often hear. The Châtelet magistrates failed to understand the reference in the application to Lady Anne. Attorney Chapote ("gentle, decent young fellow, very intelligent") had to explain. He had "at once grasped what it was about and the reasons for hushing up this matter".

Lady de Sade did not call on her mother, but somebody revealed to her that Lady Montreuil "was madly fond of the Marquis" and much more enraged with her daughter than her son-in-law. To which Lady de Sade replied that that was good news. Gaufridy she informed that she had put up at the *Bourgogne* hotel in the *rue Taranne* out at Saint Germain* but begged him not to address mail to her otherwise than through a tailor named Carlier in the *rue Saint Niçaise,* as hotel rooms were not safe, "telling the police everything".

August 1774. Lady de Sade was now of the belief that provided the marks of courtesy and interest which the Châtelet magistrates had shown her were genuine, her affairs would soon take a happy turning. It was her impression that the best way to secure a quashing of the Aix judgment was going to be to enter a flat denial of any act of sodomy. Lady Montreuil was "like a lioness" but it was Lady de Sade's impression that the plea submitted to the Châtelet bench worried her and might well persuade her to use her influence in favour of "the main matter". She also requested her lawyer to persuade the Abbé de Sade in his applications to stop writing out "in full" that his nephew was civically dead. "They were outraged by this both at Aix and in Paris."

September 1774. On the 3rd September Lady de Sade wrote to Gaufridy that she had had a definite promise that the plea for quashing would be submitted to the old assembly** in six weeks time, as this was to re-assemble. But the Minister did not want to request the cancellation of the *lettre de cachet* which the late King signed till after the quashing of the court finding. To tell the truth, the "turning of the tables" which had just occurred—that is, Maupeou's fall from favour—had resulted in

---

*Shortly after this Lady de Sade stayed with the Dowager Countess de Sade in the Carmelite Convent in the *rue d' Enfer* in Paris.
**The traditional *parlements,* assemblies of nobles.

everybody's attention being directed to affairs of state. The appeal to the Châtelet bench was still in the hands of the Royal Attorney, "a man of great intelligence but very changeable and all sophistry". Lady de Sade hoped the Marquis had followed her advice and returned to La Coste, rather than stay with others, where he had to disburse so much money.

November-December 1774. Towards mid-November Lady de Sade returned to La Coste. The records, as Paul Bourdin points out, do not show whether the Marquis preceded or followed her. He may even have travelled with her. One thing, however, is certain, the couple were together at Lyons, for here they engaged a young maid named Nanon, five other girls of about fifteen and a secretary who was little older, concealing from the young man's parents that his master-to-be was the hero of the Marseilles scandal. As the secretary's parents intended to go to see Gaufridy, the latter told them, on the *Marquise*'s instructions, not to be alarmed by the name *Sade*; there were several branches of the family—there were the Eyguières, the Saumane and the Tarascon branches.

At this point, although they did not hesitate to take on seven new servants, the Sades were in an alarming financial position. The Marquis' revenues were under sequester and the couple had involved themselves in great expense to complete the walls round the *château*. In vain Lady de Sade tried to persuade her mother to accept a bill of exchange for eighteen hundred *livres,* alleging she had pawned her silver to some Jews in Mazan and wanted to get it back.

The Sades now continued to lead a very secluded existence on their estate, seeing only very few people all the winter through. They dined at three. The Marquis then spent the evening in his study, while in the adjoining room "Milady and her girls busied themselves till bedtime. As soon as it was dusk the house was without fail completely shuttered up, without a single light showing." But yet those winter evenings were sweet in the arms of five young maids, while the giant *mistral* whirled round the outer walls. . . . Was it solely to appease some Goddess of Chastity that this winter the Marquis refused to allow some wandering players to come to La Coste and show the *Husband Deceived, Beaten, and Content* and ordered his servants to tear down their posters as "giving rise to scandal and offensive to the freedoms of the Church"?

THE AFFAIR OF THE FIVE GIRLS AND THE
ITALIAN EXCURSION

December-January 1775. The "young girls scandal", enacted at La Coste in December 1774 and January 1775, is one of the least known episodes in Sade's life. The little we have been able to ascertain is to be found in Paul Bourdin's collection of documents, in Maurice Heine's *Chronique Sadiste,* in an unpublished letter of Lady de Sade's and in a "long letter" of the Marquis himself. There is no trace in the archives of Lyons of the criminal proceedings instituted in that city. All the records of persons detained by *lettre de cachet* (1720-1790) perished when the police Prefecture there was destroyed by fire, in 1871. Was Mlle de Rousset referring to the Sade file in her letter to Gaufridy of October 21st 1780 and were the facts so grave as to justify Paul Bourdin in saying "it was not the too well known affairs of Keller and Marseilles, but the excesses committed by Sade in his country home that we must look to as explanation of an imprisonment which was to last fourteen years and begin just when Sade instituted his successful suit for the judicial quashing of the earlier scandals"? Such a theory seems hard to justify. If we think of the extent of the scandal caused by the simple episodes of Arceuil and Marseilles and the frightful stories to which those incidents gave rise, it is difficult to believe that any real crimes could have been committed at La Coste and leave no echo in the legends about the Marquis.

What facts we can get at or assume boil down to very little indeed. Either at Lyons or Vienne Sade certainly engaged five young girls, perhaps without their parents' knowledge. To diminish his own responsibility he was later to insist that it was Nanon, who had been a professional procuress in Lyons, who found them for him. Nanon herself and a young secretary were also new engagements. The Marquis took them all down to La Coste. He made no bones about admitting that he "made use of the five girls". Not without reason Paul Bourdin described evenings at La Coste as "a frenzied witches' Sabbath with the aid of the servants' kitchen. Gothon* probably had her turn,

*Lady de Sade's maid.

without always taking a general part. But Nanon's partici-
pation certainly left her somewhat gravid, the *Marquise*'s little
sempstresses had their backsides well buttonholed with the
young secretary no doubt serving as assistant".

This sly reference to buttonholing was sheer fantasy on Bourdin's part. It was based on the false charge of Sade's having
slashed Rose Keller at Arceuil. In its place we should probably
do well to substitute the Marquis' never-failing delights—the
birch and the cat-o'-nine-tails. Further, in the author's opinion
it is quite possible that Lady de Sade, whose complete subser-
vience to her husband seems beyond question, herself took part
in the orgies. "What frightful things can this wench say about
me?" she was to write to the Abbé de Sade of the girl who took
refuge at Saumane. And we shall also see that the "children"
—i.e., the young girls—indicated the *Marquise* as the "first
victim of a fury which can only be described as madness".

By now some of the parents, namely, a man named Berh, a
woman named Desgranges or Lagrange and another named
Abadie laid a complaint, and criminal proceedings were begun
at Lyons. Lady de Sade went there and tried in vain to hush
the new scandal up. "One of the girls, the one who had suffered
most, was secretly taken to Saumane, to the Abbé de Sade, who
was most embarrassed by his ward, and on the allegations of
the little victim roundly accused his nephew." Another girl,
Marie Tussin, from the hamlet of Villeneuve-de-Marc, was
placed in a nunnery at Caderousse, whence she escaped some
months later.

January 21st 1775. Sade prepared a formal refutation of the
statements of the girl now with his uncle and also of the accusations which his uncle now made.

February 11th 1775. Lady Montreuil, to whom Lady de
Sade had written for her advice about this new affair, sent
Gaufridy the first of a long string of letters. This might become a
very serious matter. She did not think the Marquis's good conduct certificate would be sufficient to exculpate him. It was
essential "to take the girls to their families, obtaining valid
clearance papers, sufficient to ensure never being worried
about the matter again, even perhaps to deliver the girls to
their families in the presence of the Attorney Royal to whom

the parents had complained that the girls had been taken or inveigled away without their knowledge, or even with the priests present who had written to Lady de Sade to ask for the girls back. The girls should further give their formal withdrawal of the charges in the presence of these, seeing that the girls had been given what they had asked and there had never been any thought of retaining them against their wishes". The day before, Lady Montreuil had written a letter to the Attorney at Lyons stating that Lady de Sade "certainly had no thought whatsoever of retaining these girls against their wishes, since she had only taken them on as a charity, but she did insist on having proper proof of handing them back and their statement that she had done them no injury".

But this should be accomplished without delay. Gaufridy should at once assume responsibility for giving these young girls back subject to the guarantees here mentioned. She had news from Lyons "only yesterday". The case was already the subject of much comment there. And Lady de Sade had made most compromising replies to the questions of the Royal Attorney and the priests. She had "tergiversated, spoken of entering a nunnery, said she would not give up the girls till she was refunded their keep. . . ." All this had worsened matters, seemed most suspicious, and altogether made a very bad impression.

March 1775. Records do not tell us whether Gaufridy himself went to Lyons and Vienne to get the new quittances, a copy of which he sent Lady Montreuil, but he certainly did not take the girls back. Mrs Lagrange came to La Coste herself to get her daughter. Gaufridy had taken the girl to his own house, "and she was there worked on, got round with fine words and some rags of clothing". But now apparently proceedings were indeed on the point of being stopped, thanks to the all-powerful intervention of Lady Montreuil, who got into direct touch with the Royal Attorney at Lyons.

The girl now at Saumane was the one who worried Lady Montreuil most, "because of her long tongue". "A nunnery for her would be the best as soon as she can be handed over to one with safety, if only she did not babble so." Does this mean "as soon as she heals up after the Marquis' erotic cruelties"? They must din it into the girl's head that she was the first person in whose interest it was advisable to keep quiet for anything she said would be much to her disadvantage and do her a deal of harm in years to come.

March 14th 1775. Lady Montreuil was now furious with the Marquis' uncle because he "maintained that stoical calm of his" and still, despite her direct request, had not consented to make the trip to Aix.*

March 28th 1775. The Abbé de Sade begged Gaufridy to do all he possibly could to unburden him of the girl, who was still in his house at Saumane "from his own excessive kindness towards folk who merited none" and with whom he wanted to have no dealings whatsoever.

End of March 1775. Sade succeeded in persuading his uncle to continue to house the girl.

April 8th 1775. A letter from Lady Montreuil to Gaufridy tells us that she had received the papers he had sent her about "the people at Lyons". They were well drawn, excellent in form and would make a very good defence line later in this business. With these papers she had consulted some legal authorities and thought their minds might be at rest now. True, Behr had lodged a second charge, but it was not enough to lay charges, one had to prove them. True, again, the woman had made out that the proofs were to be found on the girls' bodies and bore out what they said. Gaufridy no doubt knew what that was worth. But was this not all so much talk just to extract more money? Against Lady de Sade, the girls made no complaint. On the contrary, they spoke of her as being "the first victim of a fury which can only be described as madness". But they made fierce charges against the other woman. "Could a mother's mind be at rest, knowing her daughter to be under the same roof?" Every letter that she opened made Lady Montreuil shudder. "If all that is said is true, whatever may one expect next?"

But though her husband made her submit to all this, the *Marquise* would not say a word. "She would let herself be

*In pursuit of the application for quashing of the 1772 decision.

chopped into mincemeat rather than agree to anything that might harm him."

*   *   *

In her letter of April 29th to Gaufridy, Lady Montreuil wrote of the case of the girls of Lyons and Vienne as "all over". As a matter of fact three other girls had stayed at La Coste for several weeks, either before or after the events we have just been discussing—a dancer named Du Plan, a girl called Rosette and a girl called Adélaîde, to whom later a number of scullery maids and Nanon's niece may be added.

To ballet-dancer Du Plan's name is attached a psychotic sexual confession going all the way to necrophily, or, to be more precise, to necrophilic fetishism, which fits perfectly with all we already know about Sade. In this story we find Sade declaring he did not really commit the murder imputed to him when some human bones were found in his garden :

> "They were brought in by the girl named Du Plan; she is full of life, cross-examine her; the joke—seemly or otherwise—was played on her of decorating a closet with them; the bones were indeed used for this purpose and returned to the garden when the feeble joke was over. Let the number of bones found there be counted and compare it with what I have in Du Plan's handwriting about the number and sort of bones which she brought to Marseilles, and see if there is a single one more."

There is no doubt but that this "joke" at La Coste inspired a passage in Sade's novel *Juliette,* namely, the scene in Durand's garden with skeletons stuck up everywhere : here Juliette and Lady Clairwil used human femurs to masturbate with, a macabre form of indulgence in all conscience!

April 29th 1775. Lady Montreuil to Gaufridy. What difficulties there were in the way of securing a quashing of the Aix sentence! Though the good will of the magistrates of that city seems to her to be won, these gentlemen still would like to have direct Royal orders, to feel authorised to act. In Paris she has found equally good will in the new Guardian of the Seals, Hue de Miromesnil. "But a Chief Justice still scarcely established in his post is chary of compromising himself in any case in which he cannot find the step to be authorised by the laws." At the same time, neither the Ministers nor she herself felt it a propitious moment to have recourse to the full authority of the King sitting in the Council of Despatches. It would not be seemly "to befoul the imagination of a young King with the detailed story of this case. Besides, that would be only too likely to turn His Majesty against the person concerned."

May 11th 1775. Anna Sablonnière, known as Nanon, aged twenty-four, daughter of a labourer of the Thiers district in Auvergne and chambermaid at La Coste manor, gave birth at Courthézon to a baby girl, Anne Élizabeth, the act of baptism attributing paternity to her husband Barthélemy Fayère, "but some people maintain it was conceived by the work of the Lord of the Manor".

May 18th 1775. The Abbé de Sade requested the capture and incarceration of his nephew, as a madman.

Towards June 15th 1775. Gaufridy handed Lady de Sade a secret missive from Lady Montreuil regarding Nanon. His orders had been to deliver the note during a stroll, for in a room of the *château* he might think himself alone with the *Marquise,* but the Marquis be listening hidden behind a curtain. Lady Montreuil vouched that she had "commonly seen him so do".

It was at about this time that Rosette, the girl from Montpellier, who had been living hidden at La Coste for the past two months approximately, left the Marquis.

June 10th 1775. After a quarrel with the *Marquise* Nanon "made off from the *château* like a mad thing" showering "a million impertinences" on Lady de Sade. Lady de Sade immediately charged the girl with an alleged theft of silver. This was merely to gain time and make it impossible for Nanon to do any harm before the arrival of a Royal *lettre de cachet* to imprison her which Lady Montreuil said would be coming. The fact was, her employers now considered Nanon a dangerous wench. She was responsible for all the trouble about those other girls, and the Sades were apprehensive lest she should go to Lyons to start the whole business up again.

June 22nd 1775. Alexandre de Nerclos, Prior of Jumiège Convent, from whom Nanon had requested sanctuary and who had protected her from three of the Marquis' servants who had come to seize her, wrote to the Abbé de Sade to tell him that his nephew would have to be shut up for the rest of his life. The Prior was "convinced that Lady de Sade is no better than her husband, for to his knowledge nobody in that house went to confession at Easter and Lady de Sade allows her young maids to have dealings with a married Lutheran woman".

End of June 1775. Lady de Sade went to Aix with the Marquis' little secretary, to return him to his mother who had without warning appeared in Lyons to "make the hell of a row" before the magistrates, asking for her "child" back, as if anybody had ever refused him.

The Marquis interpreted this step as a manoeuvre of the Royal Attorney of Lyons, who was anxious to swell out his files with all the "new cock-and-bull stories" the young fellow might be persuaded to tell.

July 5th 1775. The Minister of the Royal Household informed Lady Montreuil that he had issued the necessary orders for Nanon to be shut up in the house of constraint of Arles which Lady Montreuil had herself suggested.

July 26th 1775. Finding himself shadowed, the Marquis took flight in the direction of Italy, accompanied by his valet Carteron, leaving instructions that letters were to be passed to him through Gaufridy and Reinaud, a lawyer of Aix. Lady Montreuil informed Gaufridy that she had had nothing to do with the orders issued against her son-in-law. "These constant recurrences of the same misdeeds are the sole cause of these orders. However, they are not such orders as will be likely to delay the effect of the care she had taken to make the gentlemen at Aix make up their minds." For the moment she did not think this business would have any other consequence. The Marquis would get right away or go into hiding, as he has already done before, and if he kept quiet and his wife ceased compromising herself and granting him facilities unworthy of them both, in due course it would all be forgotten. But, Lady

Montreuil added, it is "his poor boys who are here under my eyes that lacerate my heart, but when their father and mother always destroy all I do when just on the point of success, I cannot do the impossible".

July 30th 1775. With Nanon in the Arles house of constraint since July 5th, her little girl, Anne Elizabeth, aged six weeks, died at La Coste because the wet-nurse, being pregnant, had no more milk.

August 1775. Travelling incognito in Italy under the name of the Count de Mazan, the Marquis de Sade was now at Florence. Here "not a soul speaks French" and he "is far from speaking Italian". However, he is "working devilish hard" at it, but du Donis, the father of Lady de Valette of Mazan, has assured him that he will never succeed without an Italian mistress.

In the fourth part of *Juliette* the reflexions which Sade lends his heroine visiting the Grand-Duke's gallery without doubt reflect his own impressions of Florence. They should in the author's opinion be inserted under the heading *August 1775,* always bearing in mind that it is not out of the question that when in Florence three years previously with Lady Anne he had already visited the mansion.

Whereas his horror, as he called it, of anything pertaining to religion prevented his visiting the churches of Florence, Sade spent a long time in the Grand-Duke's "superb gallery". His enthusiasm reached the height of heights when surrounded by that "infinity" of masterpieces, from Veronese and Guido to Titian, but it was above all d'Urbini's *Venus* that "delighted the senses" and he never tired of examining all the details of the beauty of that "sublime picture".

In the realm of sculpture the Marquis could not help "being most moved" by the "divine forms of every limb and the graceful rotundities of bosom and buttocks" of the Venus de Medici. From this work his glance next went to the Hermaphrodite statue, though he greatly regretted that by crossing that "delectable" freak's legs the sculptor had chosen to conceal "what charactises double sexuality", but he was nevertheless all enthusiasm about "the voluptuous backside" which he was able to contemplate. Nor was the Marquis indifferent to the marble of *Caligula caressing His Sister* or the "celebrated effigy of Priapus", the dimensions of which made it easy for him to understand why maidens who went up to it "out of piety" could not help rubbing "those lips of theirs which are hidden" on it.

September 29th 1775. The Marquis reached Rome.

October 6th 1775. Lions, tax collector of the Maltese Order at Arles and bailiff of Cabanes Farm, a piece of property of the Marquis', was charged to visit Nanon Sablonniére. He went to the house of constraint, when the prisoner told him "a thousand horrors" and said that if she were not set at liberty she would put an end to herself so everybody should know the whole truth and punish the nuns who refused to let her write to her parents.

October 17th 1775. Lady de Sade thanked the Abbé for persuading the Isle-sur-la-Sorgue hospital to take in the girl whom he was taking care of. She would pay the costs but requested that the girl should not be allowed to talk to anybody.

October 1775. Extract from a letter from Sade to Gaufridy in which he made Lady Montreuil responsible for his position :

> "There is no doubt about it, Lady Montreuil really aims at my ruin and that of my children and I find it very saddening not to be able to find anybody with enough character to make her realise it. I counted on you to do so, but by her charm (which she owes to Satan, to whom I am sure she has willed her soul) that wretched woman ... sweeps away all she comes into contact with and as soon as her magic signs have struck anybody's sight, I am abandoned and fit only to feed to the dogs.... I can hear you saying '*Monsieur*, new misdemeanours have prolonged your misfortunes'. But you must also hear my reply to that: '*Monsieur*, it is my misfortunes, my discredit, my present position that prolong my

misdemeanours and so long as I am not rehabilitated there won't be a cat whipped in the whole province without it being said : *That's the Marquis de Sade!* ' "

Early November 1775. The wet-nurse whose lack of milk had caused the death from starvation of Nanon's baby girl the previous July 30th, had just been confined. Lady de Sade wrote to Gaufridy to tell him that the priest and her sister had tried by dint of much cross-examination to get the woman to admit that both she and those who gave her the baby had known she was pregnant when she took the babe, but the woman insisted that she had not known she was pregnant, but thought her milk had failed her because she had to work so hard with those silk-worms.*

November 10th 1775. The Abbé de Sade reported to Gaufridy that the girl was completely well again and he was going to take her out of the l'Isle-sur-la-Sorgue hospital and give her in the care of Ripert, who farmed for the Marquis at Mazan, where she would be better off than at Saumane and less in a position to talk to strangers. He did not think it suitable for Lady de Sade to go to Aix to press the application on "the main matter". "The lady would make a bad impression in a town in which she is known to have been her husband's accomplice in his latest debauchery."

None the less, a few days later the *Marquise* did travel to Aix, with La Jeunesse, who had returned from Italy in mid-August "with a bull-dog as swart as himself". For the occasion she had had a peach coloured suit made for La Jeunesse, with grey ratteen frock coat and black breeches.

December 13th 1775. The Abbé de Sade to Gaufridy. It was his opinion, as he had maintained the year before, that his nephew should give himself up and himself apply for quashing of the decision of 1772. De Castillon and Siméon both thought as he did that the proceedings contained much that was *ultra vires* and the sentence and decision were counter to justice, but it was illegal to oppose the sentence.

End of January and February 1776. The Marquis was at Naples, where the French *Chargé d'Affaires,* M. Béranger,

*One of La Coste's industries.

took him for a certain Mr Tessier, cashier of the Lyons Salt Store, who had decamped with eighty thousand *livres*. Travelling as the Count de Mazan, Sade was chary about giving his real identity, but since he had stated that he was a Colonel, and a Lord de la Bourdonnaye, himself a French officer, had insisted that there was no such Colonel as a Lord de Mazan, Sade found himself obliged to admit his real name. Further to confirm this declaration, he was obliged to write to Provence for supporting documents! While waiting for these, he was subjected to the "degrading suspicions" of M. Béranger, who had him shadowed by the Royal Neapolitan police. A letter containing his portrait, which he sent to the *Marquise*, never reached her. He suspected the *Chargé d'Affaires* of having diverted it, to send the portrait to Lyons to enquire if this were not Tessier.

To make the position quite clear, Sade in the end found himself obliged to agree to being presented at court in his Colonel's uniform. He "died of fear" of having to endure some insult because of his ill reputation, and, writing to both his wife and Gaufridy, asked whatever he was going to do if recognised and attacked?

What actually happened at that court reception—indeed, whether it ever took place at all—we do not know.

March 15th 1776. The *Marquise* now learned that one of the girls involved had left Caderousse Nunnery for Lyons with two young men who had come for her, one declaring himself her godfather. It was at about this time that the Marquis wrote to tell his wife that he was beginning to find time long in Italy and would give anything to be back at La Coste. He thought of coming *via* Marseilles. In terror Lady de Sade at once despatched La Jeunesse to Naples to dissuade him from so risky an undertaking.

May 4th 1776. Sade left Naples for France. In advance he sent two huge chests full of antiques and curiosities.

June 1st to 18th 1776. Sade reached Rome on June 1st, Bologna on June 13th, Turin on June 18th.

End of June 1776. Sade reached Grenoble, where he found letters of recommendation sent by Reinaud, who was afraid that Sade was "flitting about too much".

Writing from Grenoble, Sade asked Gaufridy to get him a copy of Martial and sent La Jeunesse on to La Coste with instructions for them to expect him by mid-July.

*   *   *

Letters and packages continued to come in from Rome and Tuscany. For a long time Sade kept up a correspondence with Florence, where he had made friends, among them real collaborators, such as Dr Mesny, physician to the Grand Duke. Even when Sade was imprisoned at Vincennes this Italian correspondence continued, and these were the only letters he was allowed to receive directly. He was working on a book which, in spite of the wealth of material that he had collected, he was never to complete. It was to be entitled *A Critical and Philosophical Description of Rome, Florence and other Cities*. Not only Dr Mesny but also another Italian physician, Sade's "little Roman doctor", were aiding him in this. The Roman friend was Dr Giuseppe Iberti, whom Sade praised in *Juliette* and mentioned in the "long letter" of February 20th 1781. There was one most entertaining epistle from Iberti to the "Count de Mazan", from which we see that Sade had not only ordered sober descriptions of the Vatican, but had also engaged his correspondent to send him striking instances of wild living, whether taken from ancient authors or contemporary Rome. But unfortunately a compromising letter from Sade happened to fall into the hands of the Inquisition. The bowmen of the Holy See suddenly appeared in the "little doctor's" apartment just when he was setting down some of the scandalous stories his friend had asked of him. And so Giuseppe Iberti paid a high price, twenty years before the time, for his striking appearance in *Juliette*.

Early July 1776. Sade was still in Grenoble. Here he had incurred some debts and engaged a secretary named Reillane.

July 26th 1776. Rumour in the La Coste country, Sade now having reached home, had it that the Marquis had turned religious. Lady de Sade made no bones about accepting this story and even assured anybody who cared to swallow it that her husband had been in audience with the Pope.

Meanwhile, the girl placed in Ripert's care had flown. But before going back to Vienne she spent a week at Orange, letting her tongue run and making a statement to the local magistrate.

July 13th to August 27th 1776. One of the girls—from Lyons or Vienne—scullery-maid Marie, who had stayed on in Lady de Sade's service, fell ill of "malignant fever" (measles). Between August 13th and 27th Dr Terris junior of Bonnieux visited La Coste eleven times, and despite her tears the girl was taken away from the manor-house.

August 30th 1776. Reaching La Coste to attend Marie and Vincent, the estate keeper, who was also ill, Dr Terris found Marie dead.

THE TRILLET AFFAIR

Some time just before October 15th 1776. Sade left La Coste to go to Montpellier, where he intended to stay till All Saints' Day.

Between October 15th and 31st 1776. At Montpellier Sade came upon Rosette again—Rosette who had left La Coste in June 1775, after two months' service there. Not merely did she now let her former master have all he wanted, she also established contact with a woman named Adélaîde, assuring her that if she agreed to work at La Coste, she might find it a bit lonely but all she would have to do would be to lend herself to the Marquis' little ways. The deal was concluded at once.

Towards the end of October 1776. Father Durant, Recollect Monk, charged by the Marquis to find a cook for La Coste, approached two sisters named Besson and they suggested "very pretty" Catherine Trillet or Treillet, aged twenty-two, whose father was a coverlet weaver. All three came round to the *Hôtel du Chapeau Rouge,* where the Marquis was staying. Catherine was earning forty *crowns* in Montpellier and asked Sade to pay fifty. He promised he would pay this, even more if he was satisfied with her service. The monk vouched to Catherine's father for the standing of La Coste, and assured him that as far as morals went, it was like a nunnery. So the weaver consented and Father Durand took Catherine to La Coste in a vehicle driven by a carter named Bataillet. When they got back to Montpellier they said that the young cook had been a little upset when she reached the *château*, but the *Marquise* had soon eased her mind.

November 4th 1776. Sade was back at La Coste.

Early November 1776. For a long time now money had been short at the *château*. Lady de Sade had almost reached the point of being unable to manage even kitchen supplies. She was short of wood and there were panes missing in her bedroom windows. Poorly dressed for this time of the year, she caught cold and had to take to her bed. The Marquis was indeed in difficulties. The forty thousand *livres* income due to him as Lt-General of Bresse were under sequester. But financial worries still did not destroy Sade's love of fine things or prevent his ordering some framings and some book-bindings at Apt.

November 19th 1776. Solicited by her daughter, who painted a grim picture of the straits she was in, Lady Montreuil sent twelve hundred *livres* to Gaufridy with orders that this money was only to be spent on domestic needs as and when necessary.

November 27th 1776. Lady de Sade was annoyed by her mother's not sending the 1,200 *livres* straight to her. She enjoined Gaufridy to keep back as little as possible, for nothing less than a thousand *crowns* would see her through the winter. She was also much concerned about what that girl who had escaped from Mazan might be up to. It must surely be Ripert and Jean who had prompted her to make a statement at Orange. But what might she not have done at Vienne since then? Gaufridy should lose no time telling Lady Montreuil about it.

Mid-December 1776. Of the strange events which took place at La Coste manor while Mount Lubéron slumbered, between dusk and dawn a day or two before December 15th 1776, there are two accounts, that of the unpublished statement made by the girl named Trillet and that which the Marquis de Sade made when he answered the girl's allegations point by point.

First the story of it, based on what Trillet said.

The Marquis had written to Father Durand to engage four

servants and bring them to La Coste. Soon enough, escorted
by the monk, Bataillet's vehicle arrived, bringing a secretary
named Rolland, a wigmaker who was a native of Paris and
brother to a valet of the Count de Périgord, a chambermaid
named Cavanis, and a kitchen-maid of "foreign origin". After
supper the Marquis locked each of them in a separate room.
But during the night he went in to those rooms and asked them
to let him have his pleasure of them, not without trying to overcome their sense of shame by the bait of his purse.

The very next morning, the alarmed servants (with the exception of the kitchen maid, who agreed to stay on), returned
with Father Durand in the vehicle in which they had come.
Back at Montpellier, they informed Mr Trillet of what had
happened. Trillet was worried about his daughter Catherine,
who (on the monk's recommendation) had been in the Marquis's service since All Saints' Day, and he told Father Durand
in no uncertain terms what he thought of him. The monk said
that it was quite true, he had heard about Sade's perverse ways
in previous years, but for some time had thought the Marquis
quite cured of all that. So he tried to dissuade Trillet from
bringing Catherine home but as Trillet insisted he undertook
to write to Sade about it. Trillet gave the letter to the monk's
Superior, but the Superior thought it was not good enough
and ordered Father Durand to write another. After that he
expelled him from his monastery.

The Marquis said he could only reply to Trillet's story by
the most categorical denial. It was quite untrue that he had
written to Father Durand to engage servants for him. Trillet
was illiterate and could know nothing of any such letter and
the only possible source of his story was lying tittle-tattle. "Besides, even supposing I had found these persons (who were
frightfully unprepossessing) even supposing, I say, I had found
them fit to satisfy any desires, it is probable that if they offered
their services to me I would have kept them, and having decided to keep them would not have tried to break down their
modesty that night, but would have had time to do so later,
while they lived at La Coste. So if . . . I decided to send them
back the same night, it is more than probable that I would not
have laid myself open to being insulted by persons who I knew
very well would be leaving the very next morning and whom I

would thus have put in a position to lay a charge against me. Would I not have counted on their being piqued by having travelled all that way in vain? Would I have been likely to aggravate their annoyance by outraging them during the night? I would have had to be an arch-idiot to do anything so stupid. . . . As for the purse, nobody knows better than M. Gaufridy that at this time I had not got a *sou* of ready cash. The whole thing is a pack of irresponsible lies and charges."

The absence of the least proof one way or the other makes it difficult indeed to decide between statements so contradictory. But let us most tentatively try to weigh up the *pros* and *cons*.

The credibility of Sade's explanation would leave only a shadow of uncertainty, were it to concern anybody less rash than he was when in search of sexual satisfaction. It hardly looks probable that Father Durand would have gone to the trouble to engage four servants and take them from Montpellier to La Coste at considerable expense, if the Marquis had not indeed asked him to do so. It is of course always possible that the monk was merely acting on some quite vague statement that Sade had made while at Montpellier, or even on some much earlier letter, which Sade had never confirmed later. If the Marquis had intended to keep the servants, his lustful impatience would not surprise us at all, for it does seem much more like his nature. And even if when they arrived he really did say they would have to go back the next day, his rashness during the night would still not surprise us, for there are many occasions when we see Sade so swept away by the frenzy of his lust that he took no consideration whatsoever of the fatal consequences to which his self-satisfaction was likely to expose him. Further, it is not out of the question that it was the servants' refusal to let him have what he wanted that made him decide to send them back, since at the same time he did not deny that the kitchen-maid (no doubt the only one that did not reject him) stayed on at La Coste, however little need he said he had of her services. The only argument that might seem unanswerable, is the one about his lack of ready cash, though, who knows, the purse which he showed them, hoping to win them over, may have been empty! As for their unprepossessing nature, here no doubt Sade purposely exaggerated. But even if they had been quite ugly that would not have been any certain protection against his lust, which required ever new material to work on.*

The last days of December 1776. An anonymous note arrived, to warn Gaufridy that a police officer and ten horsemen had been ordered to go to St Clair fair at Apt on January 2nd to arrest the Marquis. This plan had no connection whatever with the four servants case. But even if Sade left La Coste at all he does not seem to have taken refuge far away, for on January 17th he was back home again, ready victim for Trillet's murderous intentions.

January 14th 1777. Marie Eléonore de Maillé de Carman, Dowager Countess de Sade, died at the Carmelites Nunnery in the *rue Enfer* in Paris, aged sixty-five. (The Marquis and his wife only heard the news three weeks later, when they reached Paris.)

January 15th 1777. The Countess de Sade was buried in the parish of Saint Jacques du Haut Pas.

January 17th 1777. This Friday, between midday and one o'clock, Mr Trillet came to demand his daughter Catherine (known at La Coste as "Justine"). During an argument with the Marquis he fired a pistol point blank at him, but missed. He took to his heels. Later he went about La Coste township, shouting his head off about it all. A little before five o'clock Catherine sent somebody out to find her father, as she was anxious to calm him down and make him see reason. Trillet then came back, accompanied by four men of La Coste, but he was still in a rage and fired a second shot into a courtyard where he thought he saw Sade moving about. Instead of seizing

---

*Indeed, their very ugliness may well have been most attractive to him if he ever showed the strange quality of his heroes in 120 *Days of Sodom.* "It is beauty that is ordinary, ugliness outstanding, and any hot imagination unquestionably always prefers the outstanding in matters of lubricity to the ordinary. Beauty and freshness are only striking in a simple way; ugliness and degradation offer something much more reliable, the excitement is so much the greater, more intense. This being so, one should not be surprised that very many people get more sexual satisfaction out of an old woman, an ugly one and even a stinky one than from a fresh, pretty young girl, any more, I insist, than one is surprised when a man prefers the arid, rocky ground of mountain country for his walks to the monotonous footpaths of level country."

him, the four men who had come with him then ran away, while he himself took refuge in a tavern, where Registrar Jouve and other dignitaries now came. But they failed to arrest the culprit, although by not doing so they were risking another attempt on the life of their lord.

January 18th 1777. Viguier, junior magistrate at La Coste, learning of the attempted murder of the previous day, began to hear witnesses.

January 20th 1777. At dawn Trillet left La Coste after assuring Messrs Paulet and Vidal that he felt "the sincerest emotions of friendship and attachment for the Marquis".

After January 20th 1777. Sade asked Gaufridy to go at once to Aix to see lawyer Mouret and find out from him if Trillet had lodged any charge so that if he had done so the true facts might be put before the Attorney General de Castillon and his counsel and support sought. But Gaufridy thought it better not to do as his client instructed him. Alarmed at this indolence, Sade reproved Gaufridy in strong terms.

Alas, Sade's fears were only too well grounded. Trillet had stolen a march on him by entering a charge at Aix backed by a statement detailing what had happened a month earlier at La Coste and stating that Sade had refused to give up Catherine —all this without saying a word about his own attempt to murder the Marquis.

Writing to Gaufridy, Sade replied point by point to the first part of Trillet's statement, and accused the man of lying. As for the two pistol shots which Trillet had omitted to mention, the record of the assistant magistrate's enquiry would establish that all right, while Catherine had signed a statement that she "was happy enough and had nothing to complain about". Finally, Sade requested that Trillet be placed under arrest, "otherwise you will prove to me that people here want to finish me off".

A few days later, in another letter to Gaufridy, Sade again reproved him for not having forestalled Trillet by informing the Attorney of the circumstances of the attempt at murder on January 17th. This was especially necessary if because of old scandals the magistrate was inclined, however slightly, to think that the weaver's yarn was based on real facts. What did it matter if de Castillon did think that despite her ugliness Catherine was at La Coste for purposes "remote from culinary"? That he had slept with Catherine would not be a very grave charge. The girl was of age and her father had found her alive and well.

In fact, Sade complained of having had the worst of the business all round. All the people of Coste were "rogues fit for the wheel" and "were they to be roasted one after the other" he was prepared "to pile on the faggots without batting an eyelid". And Gaufridy might as well admit outright that having (like every Tom, Dick and Harry) got used to thinking the worst of the Marquis because he was an unfortunate, he had now concluded that he was not innocent enough this time for him to take his part openly.

January 30th 1777. The Aix lawyer Mouret communicated to Gaufridy, who had at last been brought round to following Sade's instructions, the opinion of the Attorney General about the Trillet business. That legal dignitary considered Sade's conduct disgusting in every way. Sade should make no more delay about sending Catherine back to her father. Coming so soon after so many other cases which had not been completely hushed up, and having regard to the stir that was being created, the consequences might become very serious.

DEPARTURE FOR PARIS AND ARREST

January 1777. Lady Montreuil, who had received "ten pages of threats and invective" from her daughter, all apparently dictated by the Marquis and "such that only if read could they be believed", was at the end of her tether because of so much "injustice and infamy", and wrote to lawyer Gaufridy that she was going to wash her hands of them all. Their interests would suffer at once, for Lady Montreuil had been proposing to enter a plea to His Majesty "against proceedings which were made unassailable by Sade's contumacy" and now she was not going to do anything at all; she would let the Marquis de Sade defend his head and his honour all by himself.

Whether with the aim of getting back into Lady Montreuil's good books, or because they had just received alarming news from that lady about the state of health of the Dowager Countess, the Sades now decided to go to Paris. But though there can be no doubt but that Lady Montreuil was responsible for Sade's arrest on February 13th, there is no proof at all that she actually set them a "trap", despite Reinaud's opinion, for having no knowledge on February 8th of the Countess's death, he was inclined to think the announcement that she was unwell was lying news, a decoy to bring the Marquis to Paris. On the other hand, there is no gainsaying that, Sade's coming to Paris played perfectly into Lady Montreuil's hands, if we merely judge by what she said in that letter to Gaufridy from which we have just quoted. "If I am attacked, as they threaten, I have my answer ready, and have no fears about what that public answer will be. All the worse for anybody who forces all the explanations and *proofs* which will follow."

There was no doubt about it, to all Sade's supporters in Provence it seemed clear that he was risking his liberty if he went to Paris. Even the maid Gothon later insisted that he had willed his own misfortune by going there against all the advice given him.

February 1st 1777. Sade reached Tain, near Valence, *en route* for Paris, travelling with La Jeunesse, while the *Marquise* travelled with Catherine Trillet (*Justine*) who had begged to be taken too, for despite her father's urging her, she did not mean to go back to Montpellier at all.

February 8th 1777. Greatly fatigued, for the roads were frightful and obliged them to have their carriage repaired again and again, the Sades reached Paris in the evening of February 8th, to learn of the death of the Dowager Countess three weeks before. The Marquis had been in great spirits all the way, and "the blow was all the harder therefore". He put up at the house of the Abbé Amblet, *rue des Fossés Monsieur le Prince,* "opposite the wheelwright's". His old tutor gave him a warm reception and showed him "every imaginable attention".

Between February 8th and 13th 1777. Though in deep mourning, Sade wrote a strange letter to an *abbé* of Paris, who had formerly been his companion in debauch. The death of his mother compelled him to be very careful about appearances, but he was burning to see his old friend again and tell him his "triumphs" and hear his too—and make some more together. Could they meet to go chasing skirts a little?

February 10th 1777. Lady de Sade thought the moment had come to tell her mother that her husband was in Paris. She had not done so earlier because at Shrovetide Lady de Montreuil had so many visitors and they might have given her bad advice.

February 13th 1777. The Marquis de Sade was arrested by Inspector Marais at Danemark Hôtel, *rue Jacob,* and taken to Vincennes Fortress, where at about half past nine that evening he was entered as a prisoner.

CHAPTER TEN

Sixteen Months in Vincennes Prison
The 1772 Decision Quashed
The Valence Escape

1777 - 1778

SIXTEEN MONTHS IN VINCENNES PRISON

February 15th 1777. Arrested on February 13th by *lettre de cachet* and immediately taken to Vincennes Fortress,* the Marquis de Sade was installed in Cell No. 11 on the morning of the 15th.**

February 23rd 1777. Scarcely recovered from a serious influenza, the Abbé de Sade received news which ought to give him a new lease of life (so Lady de Sade remarked!) for another twenty years: he heard that his nephew had been arrested. The Abbé informed Gaufridy in the following terms: "The fellow has been arrested at last and shut up in a fortress near Paris. Now my mind is at rest, and I think everybody else will be pleased."

February 25th 1777. "Aghast" at the blow which has befallen her, Lady de Sade told Gaufridy that "without anger or show of emotion", Lady Montreuil asserted that it was not she who had had her son-in-law arrested; she was incapable of such treachery. The Keeper of the Seals indeed considered that the new situation favoured what they called "the main matter", namely, the quashing of the 1772 sentence. "For the moment I can do nothing," he had said. "But I shall!"

Lady de Sade did not know in which fortress her husband

---

*For a description of this prison, see note to page 210.
**Room 11 had a view being above the enclosing wall.

had been incarcerated. She suspected it was the Bastille, but unfortunately the drawbridges were always up and the sentries would allow nobody to linger near and watch. Her only news of her husband was through the Minister. She was assured that he was well and had "all he could desire".

End of February 1777. Sade wrote his wife his first letter as prisoner : "I feel it quite impossible to endure for long a condition so cruel. I am overcome with despair. There are moments when I am quite beside myself. My blood is too hot to endure such frightful restriction. I mean to turn my resulting rage on myself. If I am not out in four days, nothing is more sure than that I shall crack my skull against these walls." He implored his wife to fling herself at the Minister's feet and, if necessary, at the feet of the King, to win her husband back. "Tormenting me as they are doing they are simply pandering to the cruel outlook of your mother." His wife should not be deceived by Lady Montreuil's vain pretext that this imprisonment was calculated to make it easier to have the *1772* sentence quashed. Further, the prisoner expressed his fears that Lady Montreuil had got hold of the portfolio he left at the Danemark Hôtel and found in it "things which will have seemed unseemly to her", especially the talk written down in his hand to the dictation of a Mr Saint Pol whom he met in Italy. But Sade said he was ready to give explanations of all the papers in question and in the meantime Lady Montreuil should draw no vexatious conclusions.

March 4th 1777. "Everything is going extremely well and very smoothly—and high time too!" Such were Lady Montreuil's sentiments about her son-in-law's imprisonment. She imparted them to Gaufridy without any beating about the bush. Gaufridy was to write and tell her everything that Lady Sade wrote to her husband and anything he could find out at La Coste. He was to have no fears; Lady de Sade would never let on that he had told her; as additional safeguard his letters would be burned as soon as read. Gaufridy could have an easy mind—did he not address them to "a physician who works to cure"? She deplored the fact that all the moderation and tact she had showed her daughter had failed to inspire more willingness to co-operate and more confidence in her. However, for some days now Lady de Sade had seemed less "crushed", despite the scant results of her applications to ministers, for these not merely refused her permission to see her husband, but persisted in keeping from her where he was imprisoned—"which is all as it should be" was Lady Montreuil's opinion.

March 6th 1777. The Marquis to his wife: "Oh, my dear love, when will this horrible situation of mine end? Oh God! When will they let me out of this grave in which they have buried me alive? Nothing can equal the horror of my fate, nothing can tell all I am undergoing or convey the anxiety which torments me or the griefs which devour me. To console myself all I have are my tears and my protests. But nobody hears them.... Where are those days when my dear love shared them? Today I have nobody, it is as if the whole of Nature were dead to me."

March 13th 1777. In a letter to Lady Montreuil, Sade reproached her with having in one fell moment "betrayed every feeling that is sacred, every sentiment of humanity, having a son arrested on the request of his mother". He implored her to have him freed, lest he be reduced to utter despair. She should give him time to make up for his errors.

April 18th 1777. The Marquis to his wife: "I am in a tower, closed in by nineteen iron doors, with light reaching me only through two little windows, each with a score of iron bars." In sixty-five days he had had only five walks of one hour each, "in a sort of tomb about forty foot square, surrounded by walls more than fifty feet high". "How expect a man not to prize virtue when offered it in such divine hues?"

April 29th 1777. Sade wrote to his wife to tell her that the appeal to the Crown for annulment of the Aix sentence had reached him and he had signed it. But reading it had only made him "more furious still". What was the point in showing him that he was believed "as innocent as all that" unless they set him free at the same time? He was amazed that a Government could consent "in such a puerile way to serve the vengeance of a shrew".

The same day Lady Montreuil wrote to tell Gaufridy that Justine had recently left for Montpellier where she would arrive on May 1st or 2nd. She had had a private talk with the girl and had received her confidences and among other things the kitchen-maid had spoken of a fellow countrywoman of hers who had been at La Coste manor in secret. In case that business of the girls of Lyon and Vienne were brought up again some day, it would be a good thing if Gaufridy took care to see that certain "supporting evidence which it was dangerous to leave about" was removed.

May 9th 1777. In a letter to Gaufridy Lady de Sade complained of her mother's indifference about the miserable lot of her husband. Her mother's slowness in the matter made her frantic, but so long as she was able to feast her eyes on "her Dulcinea" (no doubt this referred to Lady Anne) "she was content".

May 10th 1777. The Marquis informed his wife and mother-in-law that he absolutely refused to sign the power of attorney proposed to him. However could anybody imagine that he would be so silly as to furnish Lady Montreuil with an instrument enabling her to manage his affairs while he lay suffering in the horrible prison into which she had cast him? The very suggestion was absolutely infuriating. All it had done was to make him desperate, because it showed clearly that his captivity was not near its end.

June 2nd 1777. Lady de Sade wrote to Gaufridy about her children. The young knight was going to be like his great-uncle. "He will be a very wise commander who will never act without due consideration." The eldest was "fly" and "of a quick temper and touchiness which are unparalleled". As for the girl, now in a convent, she made out she loved seeing her mother but she loved her nuns infinitely more: "that will have to be changed".

June 3rd 1777. Lady Montreuil informed Gaufridy that she had arranged to delay the release of Nanon "for various reasons which do not reveal the real one". This step seems to have related to the compromising discoveries made in that secret room at La Coste. Lady Montreuil seems to have been anxious to have every trace destroyed before the liberation of that girl now at Arles, because "she might talk". The uncertainty as to what "those traces" actually were had set Lady

Montreuil in a state of agonising perplexity. Gaufridy definitely must find out about it all. Were "those traces" writings? Or were they "mechanical devices which they were in the habit of using?" she asked. (No doubt here Lady Montreuil had in mind the chairs which many libertines of the period used: when a girl sat in one the seat tipped back and at the same time iron grips seized her legs and spread them wide).

June 4th 1777. Now at last Lady de Sade knew that her husband was in Vincennes Fortress. But she was still not allowed to see him and the only news she could have from him was in the form of unsealed notes, which had to pass through censorship. Whenever she wrote anything that "might mean anything" her own note was returned to her undelivered. She wrote to Gaufridy that if the Marquis was taken down to Aix to appear before the court, "his escape must be contrived". "Better to be free than merely to ask to be."

July 5th 1777. Lady Montreuil had clearly not grasped the new information that Gaufridy gave her about the compromising objects at La Coste. She wanted more details. What for instance did he mean by "some old pieces of furniture with fancy sculpturing"? And what was that about paper that had blown out of the window? Did Nanon know anything about that loss? This point absolutely must be cleared up, so that they knew what attitude to take regarding that servant-girl.*

August 11th 1777. Lady de Sade informed Gaufridy that her husband was suffering frightfully from piles. Would he kindly inform the Abbé? "That too will help to buck him up." Her efforts to be allowed to see the prisoner are still vain. "It is not

---

*Indeed, how was the Nanon business going to end? The girl's father, Annet Sablionnière, had lodged a plaint. Nanon had managed to inform an uncle, who was the *curé* of a village in the Auvergne, of her situation. She had got a message to him through an anniversary preacher to whom she had made confession, and the *curé* had found protectors for her. The matter was very prickly, and what Lady Montreuil pretended she was offering she could not withhold any longer.

Nanon was set free early in February 1778, by order of M. Lavilel, but she was not to be allowed to come within three leagues of Lyons or Vienne. In lieu of wages she was paid three hundred and fifty *livres* and in consideration of this she undertook not to say any more about what had happened.

His Majesty's desire," the Minister replied every time. As for Lady Montreuil, she insisted that she was just not interested. "I need the patience of an angel to deal with all these creatures." If her husband's fate were not dependent on them, Lady de Sade would long since have taken her revenge.

September 1st 1777. Sade expressed the horror of his situation in a letter to his wife. Before experiencing it he would never have believed it. Such cages should be reserved for savage animals, not human beings.

September 23rd and 24th 1777. Lady Montreuil and Lady de Sade both wrote to the Minister of the Royal Household (now de Vergennes) supporting the quashing of the 1772 sentence, and requesting this to be formally submitted to the King in his Council of Despatches on the 26th inst.

October 16th 1777. Police Deputy Le Noir visited the prisoner at Vincennes. Four days later Sade poured forth to his wife the story of the foul trick played on him. For six months now he had been told to look forward to this visit as to an event which would bring him all manner of consolations, but it merely increased his anxiety. Far from soothing him by the faintest hope of liberation, at any date whatsoever, Le Noir left him the most crushing uncertainty. True, he tried to convince Sade that his mother-in-law was making every effort to bring his case to an end, but Sade was going to believe that when he was liberated.

December 31st 1777. Jacques François Paul Aldonse de Sade, titulary Abbé of Ébreuil in the diocese of Limoges, author of the learned and elegantly written *Notes for a Life of François Petrarch* in three volumes, died at la Vignerme, his home in Saumane, aged 72 years 2 months, 10 days.

"The inheritance is most entangled," wrote P. Bourdin, from whom we have the substance of the evidence of Gaufridy's papers (now dispersed). "The Marquis' uncle left numerous debts and had a Spanish lady with her daughter staying with him which complicates it, since he had sold them the Vignerme land for ten thousand *livres,* no doubt with the legal subterfuge of a dummy husband. . . ."

Lady Montreuil was exerting all her powers of diplomacy

to have the inheritance recognised by the Commander, provided no liability in excess of the assets was involved and the Marquis' land and furniture, especially the library, the cabinet of medals and the natural history cabinet did not go with the property, since these were greatly prized by the Marquis.

Despite that business of the Spanish woman, the Abbess of Saint Benoît produced a fine eulogy of her brother and found pious solace in the manner of the Abbé's death, which was most relieving. Lady de Villeneuve, another sister of the late Abbé, found a still better way of preserving his memory. "She collared all the china, so that that too was to be the subject of legal argument for more than twenty years."

January 5th 1778. The Marquis de Sade wrote to Lady Montreuil in characters of blood to implore her to put an end to the horror of his captivity.

January 10th 1778. Since July 1777 Lady Montreuil had been telling Lady de Sade that she planned to make use of a pretended state of lunacy in the Marquis to acquire the right to represent him at the Aix Court. But when he heard of this suggestion the Vincennes prisoner was indeed vociferous. At the beginning of 1778, however, Lady de Montreuil returned to the proposal, which, she said, offered important advantages. As she assured Gaufridy, the plea of insanity lent a special colour to acts of libertinage, which after all could only be thus explained, and this, together with the lack of cast-iron evidence against Sade, eliminated any question of a second-degree crime. What Lady Montreuil meant by a second-degree crime was homosexual sodomy, which valet La Tour had sworn to high Heaven was not true, giving a very credible explanation of all that had been said about that. But La Tour would not be able to give evidence, as he was "somewhere, I don't know where, in the West Indies". So when the time came Gaufridy would have to take the necessary steps with the girls in the case. Lady Montreuil reminded him that Marguerite Coste had withdrawn her statement and in her re-examination also denied the question of buggery, and "the other girl, the one who gave such outrageous evidence on the second instance, being herself an accomplice according to what she said", could be challenged because of the demand she made for indemnification when she withdrew her charge. As for Mariannette Laugier, she herself agreed that she could not have seen anything, since she had been leaning out of the window.

A little time after this Lady de Sade was to intimate to lawyer Siméon that the insanity procedure was "the minister's idea", and she asked him to sound the First President and the Attorney-General of Aix about it.

February 28th 1778. Lady Montreuil informed Gaufridy that she had made all her arrangements for the big case. All was agreed with the two "chiefs" of the Aix high court, La Tour and de Castillon.

March 1778. Lady Montreuil informed Dr Mesny, of Florence, literary correspondent of her son-in-law, that it would from now on be pointless to send the Marquis de Sade any document for his work on the cities of Italy, for he would not be able to make use of it.

April 14th 1778. Lady Montreuil sent Gaufridy instructions about the Marseilles prostitutes. They were to be cross-examined and well drilled what to say, as the big case was soon coming on. It would also be necessary to make sure of the police, who might bring pressure to bear on the girls and try to secure evidence from them which suited their book when the time came.

May 2nd 1778. Jean Baptiste Joseph David, Count de Sade d'Eyguières, obtained from the King the post of Lieutenant-General of the provinces of Bresse, Bugey, Valromey and Gex, formerly held by the Marquis de Sade, but in suspense since 1773. Thus the name of Sade would still appear in the *Royal Almanach*.

May 23rd 1778. Faced with the necessity of choosing whether to be represented as insane or to appear himself before the High Court of Provence, the prisoner, who had consistently rejected any suggestion of a plea of insanity, chose the latter course.

May 27th 1778. His Majesty at Marly granted the Marquis de Sade papers of *ester à droit* [leave] to appeal against the sentence of the high court of Provence, notwithstanding the expiry of the legal period of five years. The papers were based on there being "no evidence of the alleged crimes of poisoning and pederasty" and further that the proceedings had been "marred by a number of acts definitely, indeed radically *ultra vires*".

June 14th 1778. Escorted by Inspector Marais, the Marquis de Sade left Vincennes Fortress to go to Aix.

THE SENTENCE OF 1772 IS QUASHED

June 20th 1778. On this Saturday, in the evening, the Marquis reached Aix-en-Provence, and he and his escort (Inspector Marais) put up at the Saint Jacques Inn, as it was too late for the Royal prison to accommodate the prisoner.

June 21st 1778. In the afternoon, "to obey justice and purge his contumacy", the Marquis reported at the Royal prison of the city. If we are to believe Inspector Marais, throughout his detention the Marquis never once ceased pestering him with countless "demands of a personal nature, though he was being treated as well as a man of quality could be in prison" and also was for ever insisting on "making gifts to all the other prisoners, to show how great-hearted he is". Here we may add that Sade spent as much as seventy-two *livres* in the prison canteen and did not omit to press his attentions on a young woman detained there. He called her his "Dulcinea at the mirror".

June 22nd 1778. On this Monday Milords of the High Court of Provence accepted the letters of *ester à droit* granted to the Marquis de Sade, "to be implemented in form and content". From now on, as may be seen, the new trial—completely a matter of form, all having been settled in advance by the court and the defence—proceeded at unusual speed. In three weeks the heads of the charge were reduced to nothing and on July 14th the sentence of death of 1772 was reduced to—a mere reprimand.

A most favourable transformation in the judiciary had in the meantime taken place. On November 12th 1774 the *parlements* or high courts which Maupeou had abolished were restored, but now with professional judges sitting in them in place of the men who in the Chancellor Maupeou's heyday had so hastily and so unfairly condemned the Marquis de Sade.

This malevolent persecution of Sade had been observable from the outset. It began with the Arcueil case, which was throughout based on Maupeou's hatred of Sade's father-in-law.

Throughout these momentous weeks Lady de Montreuil had actually contrived to keep her daughter in total ignorance of what was happening! This was to make sure that Lady de Sade did not appear in Aix. So on June 22nd we find the *Marquise* writing to Vincennes to tell her husband how worried she was to have no news from him. She was afraid he must be ill, which might explain his silence, for she could not imagine him to be indifferent to her. Did he not know that she would "give her blood at that very moment" if thereby she could set at liberty the man she adored?

June 27th 1778. Gothon, Sade's chambermaid,* who had stayed behind at La Coste and was "very sad and very often in tears" when she heard that her master was in the neighbourhood "felt inexpressible delight" and sent him flowers, fruit and sweets and a most touching letter.

June 30th 1778. Some time before eight in the morning the Marquis de Sade was removed from the Conciergerie Prison of Aix and taken in a sedan chair with drawn curtains to the Jacobin Monastery, where the High Court held its sittings. Entering, the prisoner knelt before his judges, but the president of the bench signed to him to rise. *Maître* Joseph-Jérôme Siméon, for the plaintiff, and General d'Eymar de Montmeyan as Royal Attorney, both spoke strongly in the plaintiff's favour. After deliberating, the court then quashed the Marseilles trial altogether as null and void by absolute lack of evidence of any poisoning, and for pure form they ordered a new investigation of the allegations of debauch and pederasty alone and the hearing of witnesses.

The session had lasted two hours. A crowd of two hundred

---

*A callipygous country wench, Gothon Duffé was a Protestant and a Swiss citizen who had been in Sade's employ at least six years. In a letter of April 17th 1782 to Mlle de Rousset we find Sade remarking genially that when his father-in-law stayed at La Coste in 1772 he was nothing loth "to spend a moment of leisure sweetly contemplating those lovely orbs," that is to say, "the loveliest backside that emerged from the Swiss mountains these past hundred years."

persons crowded round the door to see the Marquis both when he arrived and left, but the drawn curtains cheated them. At the close of the proceedings Gaufridy was received by the First President and the Attorney-General, who officially suggested he should leave for Marseilles that very day to make sure that the girls who were to be summoned as witnesses would deny everything relating to pederasty.

July 2nd 1778. Mariette Borelly made a statement to *Maître* du Bourguet, Councillor, as principal witness of the allegation of pederasty according to her statements made on July 1st 1772.

July 7th 1778. Cross-examination of the Marquis by *Maître* du Bourguet.

July 8th 1778. The court decision ordering a special trial was issued. The same day, for all that she was unworried about the final issue of the proceedings, Lady Montreuil nevertheless approached the principal magistrates of Aix to demand most energetically that the terms of the final sentence should not leave any stain on the accused and thus not damage the honour of any to whom he belonged.

July 10th 1778. Re-examination of the witnesses and confrontation with the accused.

July 14th 1778. Saint Bonaventure's Day. In the morning the Marquis was cross-examined publicly in the High Court chamber, returning shortly after to hear the judgment. The Court found no more than facts of debauch and extreme libertinage and ordered that "Louis Aldonse Donatien de Sade be admonished behind the bench in the presence of the Attorney-General in future to be of more seemly conduct" and to be prohibited "to live in or frequent the city of Marseilles for three years" and further condemned him to be mulcted of fifty *livres* in favour of the prison fund and the costs of justice, which fine when paid "the prison shall be open and his confinement barred". The admonishment followed at once.

July 15th 1778. Legally a free man, but still a prisoner of the King's in virtue of the *lettre de cachet* of February 13th 1777, which was still valid, to his stupefaction and anguish the Mar-

quis was taken from prison at three in the morning and heard
Inspector Marais require him to make the journey back to
Vincennes. The Berlin coach which was to convey him, together with Marais, Marais's brother Antoine Thomas and two
junior warders, set off briskly on the road to Avignon. It bowled
through Saint Canat, Lambesc and Pont Royal. When, after
a dozen leagues, they had climbed to Plan d'Orgon, it turned
off the main road towards the Rhône, thus avoiding Avignon,
where everybody knew Sade. At Tarascon the coach turned
north again through Comps, Remoulins, Rochefort forest and
Valliguières clearing, where they spent the night. The lay-out
of the inn or some other unforeseen obstacle prevented the
escape which on the way Sade had thought he would be able
to achieve here.

ESCAPE AT VALENCE

July 16th and 17th 1778. Leaving Valliguières at dawn on July
16th, the prisoner and his four guards travelled north. They
crossed the Rhône at Pont Saint Esprit and made for La Palud.
Throughout the day they took fresh relays of horses—at Pier-
relate, Donzère, Montélimar and Livron. Towards nine-thirty
that evening, on the outskirts of Valence, their carriage turned
aside into the yard of the posting inn which went by the name
of *The Louvre.* Sade was at once taken to the room destined for
him. With his elbows on the window-sill, he gazed out at the
main road and remained in that position till Inspector Marais
proposed he should dine. He declined. He had neither the
appetite nor the desire. So the Marais brothers set to work in
the Marquis' presence—the table had been laid for them too
—while he paced up and down.

It was about ten p.m. when the Marquis told Antoine
Thomas he had "an urgent need", and the inspector's brother
took him to a small privy opening off the corridor. Candlestick
in hand, the Marquis entered, while Antoine Thomas took up
a position at the head of the stairs, the only way down from the
upper floor. After five or six minutes the prisoner "crept
stealthily" up to his guard, who was sitting staring downstairs,
and at first did not notice him. The moment that Thomas did
see him, the Marquis contrived to trip on something and
apparently fell. Antoine Thomas ran to help him up, then he

too was tripped up by something. Instantly "heaving himself up with the greatest promptitude", the Marquis forthwith "slipped under the arm" held out to hold him back and was off, bounding four at a time down the stone stairs, which led straight out into the yard at a point only three paces from the street door. Thomas now recovered his wits and chased after him, followed by the inspector and the two other guards, who had heard the sound of running.

It was concluded that their fugitive had not managed to get out into the street, so they searched the stables and outbuildings, the cellars, the hayloft, "every corner of the place", even the roof and the gardens and houses all round, but not a sign of Sade. Inspector Marais requested the landlord to go and en-quire at the constabulary headquarters, but he said he could not, all the city gates were closed at so late an hour. After that two cabs set out in search, Antoine Thomas and one of the junior guards in one, took the Montélimar road, Marais and the other junior guard drove out in the other, down the Tain road.

The following morning, July 17th, as soon as the town gates were opened, the inspector called on Thyais, the constabulary quartermaster, told him what had happened, gave him a des-cription of Sade and with twelve men at his disposal Thyais did his best both in Valence and the country round. Indeed, he also sent a posse of mounted men to scour all the roads lead-ing to crossings of the Rhône. But all this searching brought them not even a hint of the road that Sade had taken.

By now the inspector had summoned the assessor in charge of the constabulary throughout the Dauphiné. This dignitary took his registrar, the rector of Valence University and Thyais, and went to the room which the Marquis had occupied for one hour. Marais' detailed statement was now taken down. An in-ventory was also made of the effects which Sade had left be-hind, Sade's trunk was wrapped in canvas and sealed with four seals, and the assessor imprinted the seal of his office in the hot wax.

In his *Story of my Imprisonment* Sade himself has related what happened after his escape. "I had taken refuge about half a mile outside the town in a shanty near a farmer's threshing-floor. Then two countrymen guided me. First we went towards

Montélimar, but after a league we changed our minds and made our way back to the Rhône, intending to cross it, but could not find a boat. At last, just as day was breaking, one of us crossed the river into Vivarais, where he found a suitable boat, and for a *louis* this took me down to Avignon."

Coming ashore a little before six p.m. outside the Papal city, Sade went to the house of a couple named Quinaut. He took supper with them and ordered a carriage to take him the same evening to his *château* at La Coste.

THIRTY-NINE DAYS OF LIBERTY AND REARREST

July 18th 1778. Sade reached La Coste at about 9 a.m. and stayed there "in peace till Wednesday August 19th", Mlle Marie Dorothée de Rousset acting as housekeeper. His first act before lunching and resting, of which he had great need, was to send Gaufridy news of his return.

> "I have got here, worn out, dying of exhaustion and hunger; I terrified poor Gothon. I will tell you all about it; quite a romance. Do please come and see me as soon as you can. And please send some lemons and all the keys by return."

There is another long letter which he wrote to Gaufridy one month after arriving, though he ante-dated it at least two days. This is an epistle which was well pondered beforehand, indeed, it was "specially put together", its author said, and in this "pre-arranged optimism" we find all the signs, as Paul Bourdin very aptly pointed out, "of a case stated, a narration specially concocted and angled", calculated to draw his enemies on to ground they had not counted on. Thanks to this diplomatic document, copies of which he sent to his family and his friends (including of course Lady Montreuil), and also thanks to other letters which are equally expressive of his confidence and gratitude, the Marquis thought by imputing feelings to them which were not theirs to disarm Lady Montreuil and the Minister and force them to be generous.

From July 18th to August 19th 1778. Intoxicated with liberty, Sade flung himself with exultant fervour into everything about him. "I have seen everybody. The parson and I are all attention to each other, I think he is in love with me." "Just look at what's being said," he wrote to his lawyer, the notary of Apt, "I don't think my arrival ever caused so much chatter before." Then again : "I am not going to tell you anything because there is too much to tell you. We shall need a few days for it all." If he thinks of one thing, he says, fifty more come into his head, and he does not know where to begin. He is all eagerness to go to Saumane to handle his rights as the Abbé's heir. He will put them all straight, he is all impatience to be on the road. Will Gaufridy be able to go there with him in the near future ?

The love affairs of the village interest him intensely. He finds the goings-on of his farmer Chauvin "very dirty indeed", seducing the daughter of Sambas his gamekeeper. He has not said the last word about that. There had also been a "rare business" between him and Reinaud, all about that pretty girl who was a prisoner at Aix. "He had sent one of my letters to my 'Dulcinea in the mirror' to her; the letter was intercepted in the prison and now Reinaud was known everywhere as the *Divine Messenger*. Killing !" A little later we find the lord and master of La Coste engaging the same Reinaud to pass a gift of seven *livres* 10 *sols* to "that poor lass".

A long unpublished letter of Sade's to his wife contains references to indefatigable kindness of Mlle de Rousset during this period. She does not quit the *château* and she renders the Marquis "all the services that friendship could suggest, even helping to wait on him, just as Gothon would have done, because there is no maid". "She is absolutely devoted to me," he added.

Meanwhile Lady de Sade, in Paris, had learned from Lady Montreuil's own lips of the event that this person had hidden from her for five weeks. This was a few days before July 25th. Her husband had been before the High Court at Aix. And when Lady Montreuil went on to tell her daughter the finding of the court, but that Sade was still under detention, a terrible scene between mother and daughter ensued. The older woman now revealed her intentions to her daughter "with such outrageous superciliousness and tyranny that Lady de Sade completely lost control of herself". Her mother did however hint that Sade would be liberated some day—but not at once.

For a moment, still ignorant of Sade's escape (after all, even Lady Montreuil had not yet had time to hear of it) the wretched wife toyed with the idea of rushing off south herself, to meet Sade on the road back. But when at last she got news of the return to La Coste of "her adored little love whom she loved endlessly", and spoke of going to join him without delay, it was Lady Montreuil's turn to boil over. She threatened very seriously to have her daughter too locked up. "She was like a wild tiger." She said she would not allow a daughter of hers to expose herself to fresh dangers and "to be still more debased and compromised than she has already been". "She wanted to help her husband? Very well. But let her stay in Paris to do so." And what "outraged" Lady Montreuil most in these violent altercations was to find that all these ideas and proposals arose spontaneously in Lady de Sade's own heart and were not the Marquis' suggestion at all "who, she had thought, prompted it all in her, just like a parrot".

Lady de Sade knew very well that her mother would certainly not hesitate to appeal to the authorities if, disobeying her, she did dare to go down to La Coste, so she resigned herself to patience, and while awaiting a better mood in her mother made it her business to haunt the magistrates of Paris and Ministers of the Crown, trying through them to secure an annulment of the *lettre de cachet* by which her husband was held in prison.

At La Coste the Marquis seems to have been the victim of his own game. As Bourdin put it, just like a child he got the stubborn notion into his head that all that had taken place was engineered by Lady Montreuil, and there was no general intention of hindering his enjoyment of his liberty so he refused to pay serious attention to an anonymous letter from Paris advising him to be seriously on his guard; he wrote to Gaufridy that this was all "a jape" on somebody's part and they now had no more intention of locking him up than he had of drowning himself.

On August 13th Lady Montreuil returned her daughter a letter without breaking the seal and indignantly rejected the suggestion that it was she who had had the Marquis arrested eighteen months previously. Further, she added, if there was any hint of her daughter's going down to join her husband she would have her locked up at once. From now on she refused to open any letter that Sade wrote her. It was out of the question for there to be any hint of correspondence with him, now he was flagrantly disregarding the Royal order. Why, she might even be suspected of having aided and abetted the escape!

August 19th 1778 (Wednesday). While Sade was strolling peaceably in his park with *Curé* Testanière and Mlle Rousset, the elder Sambuc suddenly came charging out of the little wood. He was a trifle in his cups, and spoke with great alarm and concern, but he implored Sade to make a get-away at once, the inn was beginning to fill up with suspicious characters. Mlle de Rousset went down to the village at once, to find out about it, and returned greatly relieved. There was nothing to fear. They were merely some silk merchants. However, the Marquis was not entirely reassured by this and decided to take refuge at Canon Vidal's house in Oppède, sleeping there that night. He begged Mlle de Rousset to write to him twice a day to tell him what went on.

August 21st (Friday)—August 22nd (Saturday). As the news reaching him began to be disquieting, Sade no longer felt secure at Oppède, so during the night of the 21st he took shelter in a disused granary, beside the road about a couple of miles outside the village.

August 23rd (Sunday). Sade now became extremely uneasy. He said that it was like "burying my wretched liberty in a cruel grave". Canon Vidal had sent a man to look after him and this person now fetched the good canon, who came at once. The following conversation took place, as reported by Sade himself : "Whatever is the matter?" "I want to get out of this place." "Are you very uncomfortable here?" "No, but I want to get away from it." "And where do you mean to go?" "Home." "You are mad, I am definitely not going with you." "You need not, I can go there quite well by myself." "Think twice before you do, please." "I have thought quite enough, I want to go home." "But that is to blind yourself to the danger, you know what news you have had." "All cock-and-bull stories. There is no danger. Let's be going." "But let us wait at least four days more." (At least the poor devil was right in the number of days he would have to wait !) "I do not intend to wait, I mean to go now !" At last the canon consented. When they reached La Coste they avoided more talk about the folly of his returning, so that he might get some rest.

August 24th 1778 (Monday). The canon spent the day at La Coste, vainly trying to persuade Sade to go back to his hide-out.

August 25th 1778 (Tuesday). Gaufridy received a message from Lady Montreuil and at her request communicated it to Sade. He now learned that the previous May 2nd he had been deprived of his title of Lieutenant-General of Bresse in favour of the Count de Sade d'Eyguières. This revelation absolutely dumbfounded him. But at the same time it served to convince him that he was now safe. He found it impossible to conceive that anybody would want to acquaint him with such "frightful news" on the eve of robbing him of his freedom. Further, there was a sentence in a letter of his wife's to Gaufridy, which came with that of Lady Montreuil, which helped to put his mind at rest. "The outburst of persecution is over, nobody talks about it any more, on the contrary, everybody finds it most natural that after such a long absence the Marquis should be busy with his estates." So after supper, having that day received two other letters from his wife which were not less reassuring, Sade went to bed both "very upset on the one hand" because of the loss of his appointment but "most reassured on the other", because his freedom no longer seemed to be endangered. (Later he was to reproach his wife with having "plunged him" into a dangerous sense of security. But was it not easy in all this to recognise the craftiness of Lady Montreuil? Anxious to allay his fears, so that he would not take flight, she had deceived her daughter as to her real intentions and made her believe in an imaginary forgiveness.)

August 26th 1778 (Wednesday). At four in the morning, "in her *déshabillé* and very agitated", Gothon burst into her master's room and shouted to him to run! In his nightshirt Sade locked himself in a lumber room. A great din was to be heard on the stairs. Was it an attack by bandits, who would cut his throat?

Very soon, the door was forced and Sade was seized by ten men, some pointing their swords at him, others their pistols.

They were four Parisian police officers and a brigade of six men of the constabulary of Salon. The leader of this grim little mob heaped insults and frightful lies on Sade, daring to address him in the singular of the verb and shake his fist under his nose. "Now talk, my little man! Now you're going to be shut up for the rest of your life, for having done so and so in a black room upstairs with dead bodies in it!"

The canon, the priest and Mlle de Rousset all three witnessed the outrageous conduct of this police officer. They found the proceedings so outrageous that they insisted on making a legal deposition about it all as soon as they could. Brigadier Simiot himself agreed that it was all wrong and threatened to withdraw his men.

Meanwhile Sade was bound and dragged outside. "From that moment all the way to Valence there was no cessation of insults and ill-treatment." As they passed through Cavaillon the whole town saw the prisoner. In the Papal city, where he had numerous relations, to Sade's great disgrace three hundred persons witnessed his sad humiliation.

"What a shock! Good God! What a shock it was!" Sade was to cry fifteen years later. "After having received the congratulations of all my relations and been urged to go to see them so that they might embrace me and compliment me in person, after the delight of spreading the news that it was all over, after that, I say, to see myself arrested in my own house, and with a fury, a savagery, a brutality and an insolence which would not be meted out to the worst dregs of the lower orders! To see myself dragged, bound and gagged through the heart of the province and the very places where my innocence and the judgement which established it had only just been published!"

September 1st 1778. From Lyons, on the way to Vincennes Sade sent detailed instructions to Gaufridy. (He also wrote a long letter to Gothon about how to look after La Coste.) He hoped that Gaufridy would spend a few days up at the house to put things in order a bit and reach an understanding with Mlle de Rousset on all the matters he has only been able to give her hasty indications about before he left. "She is a very dear and worthy friend," he wrote, "a man could not be more obliged than I am to her. Her decent, sensitive heart is certainly cast to render a man aware of all the delights of purest friendship. I am very attached to her and shall be all my life." Sade then asked Gaufridy to write at once to Lady Montreuil to say that his presence at La Coste was essential, to complete various matters of business, and so she should do all she could to speed up his release. Further, the quashing of the sentence of 1772 had terminated the powers of attorney given the *Marquise* and Sade meant to administer the estates himself through the intermediary of Gaufridy.

September 5th 1778. Still suffering from the shock of the dramatic arrest of the Marquis—she was "definitely ill through it"—Mlle de Rousset begged Gaufridy to support Sade's case in his dealings with Lady Montreuil. "Never forget the unfortunate man who now groans," she wrote to him, "and forgive his errors. He is your friend, he loves you sincerely, you are in a position to do him great service by shortening his penitence. Do so, I implore you!"

CHAPTER ELEVEN

Five Years and a Half in Vincennes Prison

1778 - 1784

September 7th 1778. After thirteen days' travel by post chaise to Lyons, a halt there of two days, then farther travel by stage coach, the Marquis was escorted by Inspector Marais to Vincennes Fortress, arriving there at 8.30 p.m. on September 7th. His luggage consisted of : a green surcoat, a white waistcoat, serge breeches, black stockings, two nightcaps, a pair of slippers, two shirts, two handkerchiefs, two towels. He was without gold, silver or jewellery. He was locked into Cell No. 6.

Here is how Mirabeau describes Vincennes Fortress or Keep. The physiognomy of Vincennes fort are familiar to everybody. It was begun by Philippe de Valois, finished by Charles V and so solidly built that there is still not the slightest hint of decay. There are two moats about forty feet deep and twenty wide. These are lined with masonry. Next come the outer walls, with a single entrance, guarded by two sentries and three large doors. The inner door cannot be opened independently of the outer one or *vice versa*. The sergeant of the watch and the turnkey have to operate in concert. Inside are the towers. Three more doors bar the sole entry to these. Only cannon could force these. Every hall connecting the towers, which contain the prisoners' cells, is also furnished with doors of the same thickness. Three other doors give final entry to each cell.

The door which any prisoner could touch is lined with iron. Each is armed with two iron locks, each with triple bolt, and each opening opposite to the next, so that each door serves as bar to this. Such is the security in this prison, with its sixteen-foot walls and arched ceilings more than thirty feet high. These gloomy abodes are wrapped in eternal night except for a ray of light let in by opaque windows. From the inside, iron bars prevent the prisoners getting at those narrow peepholes, while interlaced iron bars which are quite out of reach further reduce the passage of light and air, and in many cases there is another row of bars between these two sets. At nightfall the watch withdrew inside, the drawbridges were raised, the doors of the towers closed and locked. Two sentries were then stationed so that they had sight of all four faces of the quadrangle enclosed by the towers and a posse went round every half hour under the windows outside and also night and morning before the doors were closed or opened, and inspected the moats, where even the turnkey is not allowed to go without express orders.

The same day Lady de Sade, who, with breaking heart, had just learned of her husband's arrest, wrote to Mlle de Rousset, whose arrival in Paris she expected.

"Dear God, what a blow for me! In what abyss of grief am I thrust back again! How can I ever escape it? Whom can I trust? What am I to believe? With all I have been told and all that has been done I find it quite impossible to know where we stand or what the solution is. The contradictions, the deceptions, the air of good faith on some faces which look as though they could never deceive you —all this engulfs me without my being able to see any way out. If you have written to my mother to tell her the news, you have done very well, but if you are on your way here, still better. Since this event I have not been near her and in writing have sworn everlasting hatred and vengeance if within three days she does not enable me to see my husband wherever she has had him taken. She swears to high Heaven, by a third party who comes to see me, that she does not know what I mean . . . I am sick of being

tricked by everybody as I have been for the past eighteen
months. The ministers are nothing but stone walls. . . . I
have great need of your good counsel and light to get clear
of the frightful confusion I am in. If I am allowed to write
to him, I shall let him know when you arrive; that will
ease his mind. Adieu, *Mademoiselle*. My gratitude equals
all you are doing for us; this will tell you how grateful I
am."

September 15th 1778. In a letter to Gaufridy, Lady Montreuil
maintained that though she was falsely charged by her
daughter with having secured the arrest of the Marquis in concert with the Commander, she nevertheless approved of the
measure, for, while remarking that she was sorry he had destroyed "the rubbish, all those scraps of paper" which the Marquis left at La Coste and "those two volumes", she added that
these documents might have convinced her daughter of the
dangers from which the incarceration of her husband would
be a permanent protection. She also said that when she learned
from Mlle de Rousset how Inspector Marais behaved when he
arrested the Marquis, she at once lodged a complaint.

October 4th 1778. Desperate at finding himself back in his
dungeon after the intoxication of a month of freedom, Sade
now multiplied endless erroneous interpretations of everything
that his wife wrote to him. He declared her behaviour to have
been "execrable" and said he would curse her "as the last of
women" if she insisted on remaining silent as to how long he
was to be imprisoned. (This radical unfairness, understandable
enough but none the less cruel, had already begun to show
during the first six months of his imprisonment.) It was the
fruit of the tormented imagination of a prisoner and was not to
cease to appear with varying intensity both at Vincennes and
in the Bastille, till 1789 !*

*Later Lady de Sade was to utter the following moving reproach:
"You confuse me, I fear, with those who have done you many wrongs.
I cherish your letters so that I may show them to you when you come
out and prove how false your interpretations of what we are trying to
do have been and how fantastic you are. I can almost see you swing
round on your heels, but, no nonsense, I shall hold you back, I shall
shut you in my room and you shan't go out till you have read them all
and compared the facts and said to me: 'My darling, I admit you were
right.' Then you will no longer be able to say I was wrong."

In other letters Sade told his wife his many complaints. He was not allowed to take exercise. He was not allowed writing paper. His new cell was much worse than No. 11 had been. "Not only shall I not be able to have a fire all the winter, but to make it worse I am devoured by rats and mice, which never give me a moment's rest all night. . . . When I ask for the favour of a cat . . . to keep them down, the answer is that "animals are not allowed". To that I reply : 'You brutes, if animals are forbidden, so should rats and mice'."

October 1778, date uncertain. Accompanied by Mme Langevin, their governess, the Marquis' two sons left Paris for Vallery, near Sens, where the Montreuils had a country house. The boys now began school under the rule of the village *curé* and the supervision of their grandmother. Sade was very pleased to learn that Mme Langevin had gone with them and was looking after "the little one"—Madeleine Laure, born in Paris, April 17th 1771. This child had been put out to a wet-nurse and Sade had never seen her.*

November 3rd 1778. Lady de Montreuil expressed fear lest the presence of Mlle de Rousset might add to the *Marquise*'s worries. She definitely complained to Gaufridy : "This wench, with her superabundance of good will, and all that the Marquis as he parted from her, may have told her to tell my daughter, may well send her out of her mind rather than calm her."

November 6th 1778. Mlle de Rousset reached Paris and stayed with Lady de Sade, at the Carmelites' in the *rue d'Enfer.*

November 27th 1778. Mlle de Rousset wrote to Gaufridy to describe her first meeting with Lady Montreuil :

"I am very happy indeed because I have been to call on Lady Montreuil and she received me with all the courtesy, decency and frankness one could imagine. . . . She

*"I do not know whether I shall love her, but she certainly won't move me like the others," he wrote at the time. On January 15th 1779 he wrote to Mlle de Rousset: "In a word, my daughter is ugly; you have told me so in the kindest way, but she is ugly, that I can see. Well, so much the worse for her. But let her have intelligence and character; that'll be worth more than a pretty face."

began by saying that Marais has been punished, he has lost the costs of that journey.... Now imagine two cats matching up, the aggressor stroking the ground with his paws and stretching out his claws every now and then, just to stir up his opponent. Once we got to grips, without either of us showing the least sign that this was it, we thrashed about till the moment I thought fit to launch the attack. At this point, through all the confusion of ideas and the heat of the duel, I saw most clearly that the Marquis is the object of her affection and that her heart aches to see him where he is.... After the recital of all that the Marquis owes to her—and there she is right because he owes her a lot—came his ill-deeds. 'He agrees,' I told her, 'but he will never make recompense where he is.' 'Ah, *Mademoiselle,* if only you knew all he used to promise me. Why, in this very room we are in now, what oaths has he not sworn!' I said I believed her, and he had really intended to fulfil his promises, but, I said, 'Madame, man is a feeble creature, as you know, but the years and his misfortunes have brought about great changes.' 'I hope so too,' she said. 'But, tell me straight, *Mademoiselle,* would you be responsible for him?' Fortunately I had foreseen that very question. Without too great eagerness or hesitation I replied modestly : 'Yes, Madame, I would. But the fact remains, his family are against him, *not one of them has taken the tiniest step to ask for his release.*' Can you not hear me saying it, *Monsieur* ? ... I told her I had seen Lady de Villeneuve and Lady de Saint Laurent, that they all desired it and I imagined that the Commander felt the same and also the Cavaillon aunts. ...

Lady Montreuil is a delightful person, so elegant in conversation, still very fresh, rather daintily built, with a charming face and a most taking laugh and way of looking at you, and a sprightly mind too, with the wisdom and frankness of an angel, yet as wily as any vixen, though charming with all and quite taking in her way. She has won my heart, just as her son did. You must be won too. Lady de Sade called to see her mother a few days after me. They chatted lightly of this and that and she remarked 'I have seen that Mlle de Rousset, she is quite bright'."

November 30th 1778. Mlle de Rousset wrote to the Marquis to tell him the result of her first steps and expressed an optimism with which he was later to reproach her, calling it deceitfulness when the hope of liberation which this charming girl had raised when put to the test, proved vain. "I have seen the grand priestess," she wrote, "and shall see her again. I am not dissatisfied, but it would ruin everything hopelessly if I tried to rush things; people's minds are still too prejudiced. If we go gently and make a good case we shall win and at the worst our detention *will not last beyond the spring.*"

December 7th 1778. After three months' solitary confinement the prisoner was allowed to have paper and pens to write as he chose and to take exercise twice a week.*

January 1st 1779. Mlle de Rousset sent Gaufridy a compliment in verse which she received from the Marquis on December 13th. She limited herself to this for, she said, "it would take too long to copy all the Marquis' letters and you would find too much wildness mixed up in with the black and the sombre in them. We wrangle, we grumble at each other, I moralise," she adds, "and now he always calls me 'St Rousset'."

January 26th 1779. Mlle de Rousset to Gaufridy : "The Marquis' position is frightful, as you may imagine, knowing his nature and vivacity. The few brief moments of cheerfulness which he shows us from time to time are made up for by storms of hail which rake our hearts through and through."

She now suspected that it was Lady Montreuil's intention to leave the Marquis "inside" for a long time, and added :

"The whole of her family are really astounding. One of Lady de Sade's maternal uncles wrote to her on New Year's day : 'You are wrong to be against your family;

*Of taking the air at Vincennes Mirabeau wrote: "The most favoured (a very small number) walked for an hour in a garden thirty paces long, with only the turnkey to talk to. . . . The prisoner and his guard walked side by side, and the turnkey was not obliged to answer if the prisoner spoke. The moment the hour struck, in they went again. You may imagine how sick the turnkey got of those walks, and that because of this rule the number of walks or their length could not be extended for the Marquis. . . . To add to the sense of restraints one needs to remember the fifty-foot high walls all round, with the moats beyond them, so that only an angel with wings could ever have hoped to get out."

it is you who are to blame for being so mad about your husband. You ought to have remembered that you have brothers and sisters to set up and so forth. If all that crowd have had to get married off before he could be free it would be too cruel. . . . We should like to see the bird outside the cage. . . ."

Some date in January 1779. The Governor of the Prison, de Rougement, visited the Marquis in his cell for the first time.

Charles de Rougement was the issue of a liaison between the Marquis d'Oise and an Englishwoman, a certain Mrs Hatt. After litigation he was declared a bastard. Sade used to refer to him either as "that quarter Englishman" or "that mongrel" and spoke of making him "dance an English saraband" some day. Mirabeau asserted that he had paid a pretty penny for his post to Vrillière's mistress, Mme Sabbathin. But as in addition to the various forms of emolument his post brought him, amounting to eighteen thousand *livres* per annum, his illicit gains from his prisoners (so Mirabeau estimated) amounted to 15,400 *livres,* he ought to have been able to pay off that capital outlay fairly quickly.

In his correspondence Sade always spoke of Rougement with loathing. He called him "that toad in breeches and doublet who starves his prisoners to pocket a few more crowns". Rougement was, he said, one of "those automata, so idiotic, so slow-witted, that he could never think of any way to refuse a request, but by saying 'It has never been done, I've never known it to be done before'." Sade penned the following Martial-like reply :

"But, stupid brute that you are, if strange things so strike you, don't for Heaven's sake do strange things yourself, for if you do not wish to be astonished, you should not astonish others.

A thing that's never done and that I have never known to be done before is for example to wear an apple green coat at age sixty-five and have your hair done in six tiers of curls.

A thing that's never done and that I have never known to be done before is for example to prostitute your own wife to get prisoners and to bring up as if they were your own children you never had the power to beget.

*A thing that's never done and that I have never known
to be done before* is for example to make a disgusting
gaoler one's pet and to show that gaoler such confidence
that he becomes your mistress and your reader and your
scribe and your intimate friend.

My old friend Rougement, when singularity is pushed
as far as that one really ought not to be astonished at other
people's petty foibles, or else be resigned to being
accounted a f—— brute. But that's not what scares you,
is it? Your mind's been made up on that a long time, and
that plucky decision of yours is the only good point I know
about you."

Mirabeau did not spare Rougement any more than did Sade.
In the second part of his *On Lettres de cachet and State Prisons*
we find the Governor of Vincennes stigmatised on every page.

February 8th 1779. The Marquis to his wife :

"So now you're going through a delightful attack of 'deaf
ear' or when you're asked to do something. Very nice, I
am sure, very smart, very fashionable! There's only one
thing wrong with it; it gets monotonous. The delightful
gesture comes too often. This means that it ceases to be
your *nature,* as you would like it to be . . . being animals
with only a sign language, you all try to run after the
appearance of being natural. . . . But wait a moment, my
good sign-folk. Do you really not know that lies and nature
have never married up and that the more people try to
give the first the appearance of the latter the more clumsy
and ridiculous they become? But I am sure you do not
know this and no doubt there are many other things too
of which you are ignorant.

For a sign-person by very nature must be extremely ill-
read, very ignorant, very crochety, blockheaded and ponderous, very pedantic, idiotic and dull."

These words call for commentary. In a great many of the
Marquis' letters written from Vincennes or the Bastille we find
statements in figures which are more or less incomprehensible
and which he calls *signs*. What was the meaning of his strange
arithmetic? Imprisoned as he was by *lettre de cachet*, which

meant being in the absolute power of his persecutors, Sade was tragically unable to gather the slightest notion of how long they would keep him there. Because of this uncertainty he invented a system of deduction based on calculations which may be ludicrous to us, but which to him seemed to give indications of that date of release which he so frantically craved.

The author has discussed elsewhere* the phenomenon of a "psychosis of figures". In reality the Marquis' bizarre arithmetical exercises were a sort of mental defence reaction, a subconscious struggle against the despair which would have taken possession of him without recourse to such a defence mechanism. (Do not some psychoanalysts think that the persecution mania which follows the obsession of guilt is a lesser evil simply because the human mind is better organised to combat the hostility of the exterior world than the aggressions of the ego?) "The impossibility of expressing sexual pleasure in figures led Sade to base his calculations on the most unexpected bases," Maurice Heine observes. "Everything seemed to him to be an indication of the fate awaiting him or possibly a secret hint which had slipped through the censorship. His mind fastened wildly on the number of lines in a letter or the number of times that this or that word appeared, even on some word which by its mere sound suggesting a figure." But the calculations he made were not solely aimed at discovering the date when he would be set free. He also tried to obtain guidance regarding his daily life as prisoner. When would the prohibition of exercise be removed? When would his wife be allowed to see him? And so on.

It was usually his wife's letters that provided the basic data for his reckonings, and often when the deductions to be drawn from them seemed grim, or were self-contradictory, he charged Lady Montreuil** or her "lackeys" (especially Albaret) of having put into his wife's mind *signs* calculated to demoralise him or leave him utterly puzzled. In the same way some ges-

---

* *Aide-Mémoire de la Vie de Sade.*
** "'Your mother must be either tipsy or *stark raving mad* to risk her daughter's life to form a 19 *and* 4 or 16 *and* 9 and not to tire of it these past twelve years. Oh what a dyspepsia of figures that foul Termagant has! I am convinced that were she to die before the entry [sic] and were opened up, millions of figures would gush out of her bowels. Unbelievable what a loathing it has given me for figures and subterfuges!'"

ture, either of a warder or of a member of the Fortress military staff, was held to be a *sign,* which had really been concocted at the Montreuil mansion.*

The Night of February 1779. Towards midnight, just when the Marquis had fallen asleep, with his uncle's *Life of Petrarch* beside him, his ancestress Laura appeared to him in a dream and spoke to him in terms both mysterious and noble. The very next day, most upset by it all, the prisoner wrote to tell his wife. He prefaced the story with an expression of the great admiration which he felt for the poet of the sonnets and also for all that Provençal love-making that the Abbé de Sade described.

> My sole consolation here is Petrarch. I read him with delight, with a passion like none other. But I read him just as Madame de Sévigné read her daughter's letters: *I read him gingerly, for fear of having read him.* How well written the book is! ... Laura turns my head; I am like a child, I read about her all day and dream about her all night. Listen to what I dreamt of her last night, while the whole universe was taking its pleasure.
>
> It was about midnight. I had just fallen asleep with those biographical jottings at my side. Suddenly she appeared to me ... I could see her! The horror of the grave had not changed the brilliance of her charms, and her eyes still had the same fire as when Petrarch sang of them. She was completely draped in black muslin, her lovely fair hair flowing over it. As if to make her still beautiful, love tried to soften the essentially gruesome form in which she appeared to me. 'Why do you groan on earth?' she asked me. 'Come and join me. No more ills, no more worries, no more trouble in the vast expanse in which I live. Have courage and follow me there.' When she said this I flung myself at her feet and addressed her, calling her "my mother", and sobs shook me. She held out her hand to me and I covered it with my tears. Then she too

*"On March 28th he [de Rougement] sent a man to borrow 6 nightlights from me, and on April 6th 6 more—I lent him only 4 . . . On Thursday January 6th, 9 months after borrowing those nightlights, on precisely the same day I was returned 25 in place of the 10 I had lent, which seemed to indicate without any doubt 9 more months of prison, making 25 in all."

wept. "When I dwelt in that world which you loathe I used to like to look into the future, multiplying my descendants till I reached you, *but I did not see you so unhappy."* Then I was completely engulfed in my despair and affection, and flung my arms round her neck, to keep her with me, or to follow her and to water her with my tears. But the phantom vanished. All that remained was my grief.

> *O voi che travagliate, ecco il cammino*
> *Venite a me se'l passo altri no serra.*
> *Petrarch, Sonnet LIX.*

March 14th 1779. The Marquis wrote a statement, which in the absence of a notary public he had the Governor of the prison witness, signifying that he refused to discuss or conclude any business while held in prison, and by this ban on any management of his property "he tied them all, hand and foot", as Mlle de Rousset put it.

March 22nd 1779. The Marquis had seen the portrait made of him by Mlle de Rousset (whom he now regularly called "the saint"), using a canvas by Van Loo as the basis.

"This portrait which the saint has made is indeed unique. I never before heard of anybody doing such a thing without a sketch. . . . She does whatever she wants with those five fingers of hers. There is only one thing I wanted to get her to do with those same fingers at La Coste, but she never would. . . . Ah, Dear Ladies, now we've said it, haven't we? Now you're about to hear something really shocking, yet it's the simplest thing in the world. I would say it to the Virgin herself, were she to ask me, it is so simple and decent. Were you to ask me to enlighten you, I would. . . . Meanwhile, tell her I was even more gratified than she was by her efforts, and will keep this portrait to the end of my days. Also tell her that it is wrong to go away when one likes people to the point of drawing their portrait. . . ."

March 29th 1779. The prisoner was visited by de Rougement for the second time, and his exercise periods were increased to three times a week instead of twice.

April 22nd 1779. Canon Vidal wrote from his home at Oppède to give the Marquis news of La Coste. The manor orchard was in full bloom. The apple and pear trees were coming on magnificently. The cherries, in bloom, called for their master. Finally, the author of this Georgic assured the Marquis of his unbreakable attachment and said he never ceased to sigh for the friend who was so dear to him.

May 19th 1779. The Marquis was granted four walks weekly.

A date in May 1779. Sade told his wife that the story of Lady de la Vallière had made him "weep like a child". He would like to be at the nunnery to see the fine portrait of that heroine. But for all that he loved Louis XIV's mistress, he loved his own wife no less. She must come and see him. They would *measure each other up.* And let the Governor of the prison hold the candle for them. Oh indeed she must come. But the Marquis is doing some "measuring" in advance; she is forewarned. . . .

A date in May 1779. The Marquis to Mlle de Rousset, reproachfully.

"This Sunday evening, having received your letter. . . ." What? She was after all going to leave him? She had promised to wait. He would not delude himself by thinking he could hold her back; he would only tell her that if she did leave Paris before he was set free, he would never see her again, no, never again. Then, after two pages of reproaches touching on two other points, suddenly there came an emotional volte-face. In lines of exquisite sensitivity he recalled the gentle conversation they had held in August 1778 on a bench in La Coste park ("our bench . . .") He reminded her of the frankness and directness which persuaded him to open his heart, as to a woman friend who was all solicitude for him. "Go to La Coste in August, I sentence you to do so . . . go into the little green sitting-room and say : 'That is where my table was, that is where I wrote all the letters . . . and he sat in that armchair . . . and from there dictated. . . .' You will think you see me and it will merely be your own shadow, think you hear me and it will be merely the voice of your heart."

A date in May 1779. The Marquis wrote to Mlle de Rousset to inform her of several grudges he nursed against her. One was

to have deliberately deceived him when she led him to hope
that he would be released in the spring. As if he had not told her
so plainly at La Coste that the greatest torture that existed was
for a man who was wretched to be given hope and then see it
snatched away, and that if one were to "examine the root cause
of all the suicides twenty-nine out of thirty had no other origin
but this". Happily however she had not waited till the last
moment to destroy that "chimera about the Spring". And the
Marquis was grateful to her for that. But what he "did not
like" was the "idiotic way" in which she had done it. "*Had
you but been wiser . . . had you not written*" and so on—why,
that was the way people "punished a small boy, giving him
strokes with the ruler when he does not know his lesson. That
was a very stupid way to set about it".

May 29th 1779. Mlle de Rousset was touched to the quick by
the Marquis' complaining that this strange friend of hers had
denounced her to the Ministers for having given secret advice.*
She was indeed tempted to break with him at once. But people
were so prejudiced against the Marquis that "it is impossible to
mention his name without the very flags of the floor threatening
to rise up and smother you". "The events of twelve years, in
essence almost nothing, but swollen by men's malice, were as
fresh as if they had happened but yesterday."

A date in May 1779. After passing through all the degrees of
ill humour the correspondence between Sade and Mlle de
Rousset reached a peak of exasperation and further letters became impossible. The two friends decided to stop writing. "Let's
face it, we had better stop writing to each other. It is not worth
while saying harsh things one to another. It is too embittering.
I do not want to hate anyone." Sade too asks her not to write
to him. "After a request so courteous . . . she will surely not
have the heart" but to fall in readily with his wishes.

July 15th 1779. The Marquis' weekly days of exercise were
now raised to five—Monday, Wednesday, Thursday, Saturday and Sunday.

---

*This would seem to refer merely to an imprudence of Sade's. That
he had deliberately told on Mlle de Rousset would seem so outrageous
a step on his part that it is impossible to credit that he did so.

August 22nd 1779. The prisoner asks to be allowed to spend the daytime "in a room with a view", that is to say, in one above the outer wall, so that he might "have a little distraction from the festive Vincennes round" which he had now "had quite a sufficiency of" in the course of two years at the window of No. 11.

September 23rd and 29th 1779. Carteron *alias* La Jeunesse, *alias* Quiros, *knight,* addressed two fine epistles to the Marquis, missives which witnessed both to the sweetness of his character and the simplicity of his mind. Since February 1777 this Harlequin had lived at the Carmelites', where he waited on Lady de Sade. Gothon's ex-lover had frequent bouts of debauchery. He would even spend three or four days out in the town, and then the cook had to do the rooms. But his disorderly manner of living did not prevent his furnishing Mlle de Rousset with medicaments (she was spitting blood) maintaining an emotional and agreeable correspondence with his master enclosed "in a bitch of a cage" and copying out in an elegant hand those comedies which Sade was now writing in his cell to while away the grim hours.

There are two of La Jeunesse's letters which are interesting because in them he writes about an eruption of Mt Vesuvius (much in the news). These letters go to confirm the masochistic pleasure which the volcano's activity suggested to Sade. In *La Nouvelle Justine* the monk Jérôme, when he sees flames belching forth from Etna, cries : "Mouth of all hells, if only like you I could engulf all the villages that surrounded me, what tears I could cause to flow !" We may also recall that after Juliette and Lady Clairwil have thrown la Borghèse into the crater of Vesuvius, they resort to Lesbian love made all the more pleasurable by the nature of the murder they have just committed.

October 4th 1779. Sade gives a burlesque reply to points in the two letters his valet had written him. The text of this would immortalise him as a forerunner of a supreme manner of symbolism in writing, genuine or pastiche, in which he was fully a century ahead of his time, both in the workings of his mind and in the unique quality of his language.

December 11th 1779. Mlle de Rousset had spat blood and been

bled in the arm. She was on herbals and "frightful potions"
that La Jeunesse pressed upon her.

January 1st 1780. The courteous valet sent his imprisoned
master New Year's greetings.

Early January 1780. Sade's remarkable reply to the good wishes
of "*Don Quiros, knight-at-arms*".

"*Señor* Quiros, I make all haste to make use of this New
Year's occasion to wish you and all who interest you the
peak of happiness in it. At last, *Señor* Quiros, my tribu-
lations and misfortunes are coming to an end and thanks
to the kindnesses and protection of Milady *La Présidente*
de Montreuil, I hope, *Señor* Quiros, I may be able
to offer you the same in the flesh the day-after-tomorrow
five years hence. Three cheers for influence, *Señor* Quiros! Had my accursed star allied my fortunes to any
other family, I had enough for life, for as you know, *Señor*
Quiros, in France there is no lack of 'respectable' respect
for whores. A man may slang the administration, the
King, religion, all that is of no consequence. But a whore,
Señor Quiros, hell's buttons! a whore? one must take fine
care not to offend a whore, or in an instant your Sartines,
Maupeous, Montreuils and other brothel lackeys come
with brutal soldiery to support the whore and unflinch-
ingly lock up a noble for twelve or fifteen years for one
whore. Hence nothing so glorious as the *French police*. If
you have a sister, niece or daughter, *Señor* Quiros, counsel
her to be a whore, for I defy her to find a finer occupation.
For indeed where can one find the girl able to call upon as
much support, as much credulity, as much protection as
the most respectable lady of substance, not to speak of
already enjoying luxury and soft living and a constant
intoxication of debauch? That's what you really can call
encouragement of decent living, my dear friend, that is
indeed the way to make a decent girl loathe filth. Heavens
alive, how well thought out! *Señor* Quiros, what intelligence our age does possess! For, speaking for myself,
Señor Quiros, I give you my word of honour that had
Heaven not set me in a station which will enable me to

support my daughter, I swear by all I have that is most sacred in the world that I would at once make a whore of her.

I hope, *Señor* Quiros, you will allow me as New Year's gift to offer you a new little work selected by your dear mistress's imps and well worthy of their taste. Indeed, I have come to the conclusion that this little work might interest you, and I deprive myself in your favour. It is anonymous, great authors, as you know, being anxious to be veiled. But as we book-lovers enjoy guessing who it is, I think I have assessed this one well, and if it's not the work of the ruffian at the corner of your street, it is certainly that of Albaret. That worthy child's father certainly must have been one or the other of those two great men of the market or the law court, there's no other source. It is the extreme likeness of these two that confuses me. It is so easy to attribute to one what comes from the other that it is also easy to get it wrong. It is like the pictures of Caraccio and Guido; these two illustrious masters rise into sublimity so equally that it is sometimes possible to mix up their brushes. Hell's flies! *Señor* Quiros, it's a real pleasure to discuss the fine arts with you! Your Palmieris, Albanos, Solimenos, Dominicanos, Bramantes, Veroneses, Lanfrancs, Espagnolets, Luc Giardinos, Calabreses and so on, all these personalities you know as well as Sartine knows the whores and Albaret the pimps. But here when I try to talk of all this they do not grasp it at all. Only *Monsieur le lieutenant Charles,* a most learned person, who whenever you like will tell you that *in the twelfth century* the Keep of his Fortress was besieged *by cannon fire.* Only one lacks the fortune of sufficient conversation with him. . . . He is like Molé, he only acts on great days.*

I have enriched the enclosed book with some notes to elucidate the text which I hope, *Señor* Quiros, will not displease you, and I like to imagine that you will preserve this little present of mine all your life. I have attached a little song which is a little old and a little bawdy, but which

---

*Francois René Molé (1734-1802) of the *Théâtre Français*, was much admired in lovers' parts. Sade may have known him personally (and was perhaps even his pupil).

will be no less good to enliven you and your friends, *Señor* Quiros, when you are dining off veal in white sauce or rabbit and bacon at Vincennes, La Rapée or La Redoute.

By the way, *Señor* Quiros, do kindly tell me if you are in the fashion, if you have racing pumps, frogged trimmings and a windmill on your head. I have a particular longing to see you garbed in that style, and you must be very entertaining so. The other day it was my whim to adorn my head with one of those windmills. It was that of milord the Lieutenant Charles, who was *gambling*, on this occasion (it was a lovely day); well, *Señor* Quiros, you just would not believe what a cuckold I looked as soon as my forehead had that bit of felt drawn over it. Oh yes, and where was the look, *Señor* Quiros (for it existed)? Was it in the hat? Was it on my forehead? Or was it in my lieutenant? That is a question I leave it to you to decide.

Señor Quiros, I would be most sincerely obliged to you if in recognition of the attention I am showing you you would kindly send me a little paper model of the *rogue-cap* of your friend M. Albaret. I have all the eccentric whim of a woman in the family way to see a specimen of that sort of diadem. Do get the address of his hat, I pray you, for the first thing I shall do when I get out is go to him to head-dress me.

And your little pleasures, *Señor* Quiros, what of them?

> *Bacchus or Cupid, which the name*
> *Now your victorious concern?*
> *Or do you hope to earn the fame*
> *Of fêting both of them in turn?*

I certainly think you quite capable of it, and the wines of Meursault, Chablis, l'Hermitage, Côte-roti, Lanerte, Romagna, Tokáy, Paphos, Sherry, Montepulciano, Falerno and Brie tickle your parts lubriciously on the chaste thighs of Pamphale, Aurora, Adelaide, Rosette, Zalmira, Flora, Fatimah, Pouponne, Hyacinth, Angelica, Augustine and Fathmé. Wonderful, *Señor* Quiros! Believe me, that's how a man should live, and when the creator of Nature produced vines on the one hand and c——s on the other, you may be quite sure that he intended us to enjoy them all. As for myself, *Señor* Quiros, I too have my little pleasures, and though they may not be quite so lively as yours, they are no less sensitive. I wear my shoeleather out both ways and to entertain me at table I have a man (this by great favour) who regularly, without any exaggeration, takes ten pinches of snuff, belches six times, clears his nose ten times and hawks *good thick throat phlegm* at least fourteen times, and all this in half an hour. Don't you find that most suitable and stimulating, especially when I am on the lee side of it all? ... True, every fortnight a big disabled soldier comes to bring me a new form to fill in and once a year Lieutenant Charles comes to be rude and in most occult signs too. Away with you, *Señor* Quiros, be assured that these pleasures are worth all yours, yours befoul you with all the vices, mine lead to all the virtues. Ask Lady Montreuil, just ask her, if there is a better way of producing virtues than locks. I am well aware that there are animals—like yourself, *Señor* Quiros, you'll pardon me—who say and argue that a man may try prison once and when it doesn't succeed it is very dangerous to try again. But that's a stupid blunder, *Señor* Quiros. This is the proper argument : prison is the only remedy that we know in France, hence prison must be good, and since prison is good, it ought to be applied in every case. But it didn't work, neither the first nor the second nor the third time. ... Well, they reply, then all the more reason to try a fourth time ! It wasn't the prison that was wrong, because we have just, well, not exactly proved, but *established* that prison is good, hence it is the subject of the cure that's wrong and he should be put back into prison. Bleeding is good for fever, we know nothing better in France; hence bleeding is a sovereign remedy. But a *Señor* Quiros may have sensitive nerves or lack blood, so that bleeding does not do him any good and some other treatment should be found. Not at all, your doctor will say, bleeding is excellent for fever, we have established it to be so. *Señor* Quiros has fever, therefore he should be bled. And that is what is called *powerful argument*. ... To which people much more sensible than

yourself, *Señor* Quiros (who are an ox, if you'll pardon
me) say: *Pagan, atheistic, impious creatures! How can
you confuse physical ailments with those of the soul?
Can't you see there is no connection whatsoever between
soul and body?* The proof of that is there in your case,
you being a *whorer and a drunkard,* your soul in the
devil's hands while your body is in St Eustace's cavity.
Hence there is a great difference between soul and body,
so that no conformity can be established between the treatment of one and that of the other. Besides, being a doctor
myself, I earn money by bleeding you, I get so much
every time my lancet goes in, so you must be bled. And I,
Sartine, earn by having you put in prison, I get so much
per prisoner, so you must be shut up. What have you to
say now to this argument, *Señor* Quiros? Come on, take
it from me and hold your tongue and don't meddle in
producing your rejected objections here; prison is the
finest establishment of the monarchy.... Had I not kept
my son-in-law in prison, Lady Montreuil will say, could
I have matched 5's, 3's and 8's together, could I have
fitted together 23's and 9's? And so arranged things that
when my daughter first visits her husband, when she visits
him for the last time and when she goes to fetch him,
more than forty-eight numbers are the same? Oh you
blockhead! Lady Montreuil will go on to say to you,
would I have been able to do that if I had cared about my
son-in-law's happiness, the treatment of his head or his
return to virtue? And are not matchings of figures well
worth all the stupid steps you now suggest? *Happiness,
virtue and head cures* are to be seen any day. But matchings of figures, relationships, resemblances only my pet
Albaret and I can achieve. At this profound piece of argument, *Señor* Quiros, you drop your hands, your big mouth
grins till it tickles your ears, your right eyebrow creeps
across to the left, your nose swells, your forehead sweats,
your knees begin to knock and in your enthusiasm you'll
suddenly cry: *Oh, I always maintained that that female
b—— had more sense than I or my cousin Albaret have!*
Right then, *Señor* Quiros, cough away, blow your nose,
spit, fart and strike up that little ditty: *Margot's done time.*"

February 1st 1780. Anne Marguerite Maillefer, *alias* Gothon Duffé, daughter of Pierre Isaac Maillefer (of Ballaiagne, Berne canton) made preparations to receive absolution of the sin of heresy from the hands of the Grand Vicar of Apt, as preparation for her abjuration of Protestantism. This act of apostasy was essential for her to be able to marry young Grégoire, of La Coste, born at Nîmes.

April 21st 1780. M. Le Noir* called on the prisoner, and the Marquis said he was very satisfied by what this police chief told him. The official had in fact told Sade that very soon his wife would be allowed to visit him.

A date in May 1780. Sade expressed misgivings lest, thanks to Gaufridy's good offices, Lady Montreuil had got hold of certain manuscripts of his, licentious in nature, which he had left locked up in his study at La Coste. In grand defiance he declared that he would reconstitute them all from memory.

June 26th 1780. "To vent his spite," a gaoler was extremely insolent to the Marquis. A violent scene was the result. Sade was so upset that he fainted and was unconscious for some time, then spat blood till the following morning. After this quarrel (the gaoler told the Commandant that Sade had struck him, whereas Sade had merely menaced him) Sade's right to exercise was taken away from him and he was to be shown "no services whatsoever". On the 28th, a few hours before a new incident, Sade informed his wife what had happened and asked her to go all the way up to the Minister to complain about the shocking treatment to which he was being subjected.

June 28th 1780. The Captain of the Guard, M. de Valage, "Chevalier of St Louis", came to Sade's cell to tell him that by order of the Minister his daily walks had been curtailed. Immediately, every foul word that came to Sade's tongue was showered on this elderly soldier and on the Commandant of the Fortress. Sade threatened to make luncheon-meat of the

*Charles Le Noir, (1732-1807) *Lieutenant Criminel* and *Lieutenant de Police* of Paris (June 1774-May 1775 and 14 June 1776-August 11 1785), that is, Police Chief and Chief of the Criminal Investigation Department—created the municipal pawnshop, improved the hospitals and abolished torture. He lived outside France from 1790 to 1802. He was known as a very fair-minded, kindly personality.

Captain the moment he came out of prison and yelled at the top of his voice to tell the other prisoners about the horrible treatment meted out to him by depriving him of air and light, calling on them to stand by him in their common interest. Then, repeating several times that it was the Marquis de Sade, Colonel of Cavalry, who was being treated in this wise, he launched into a most insulting tirade against his mother-in-law and all the Ministers of the Crown. While this was going on, he suddenly heard somebody out in the garden, rushed to the window and saw M. de Mirabeau, who was knocking at a door to ask for fresh water. He yelled down that it was Mirabeau's fault that he, Sade, was being deprived of his walks and called Mirabeau the "commandant's toady" and said he might go and kiss his protector's backside. Then he called on the b—— b—— to reply and say who he was if he dared, because he was going to lop his ears off as soon as he came out of prison. This prompted Mirabeau to say: "My name is that of a man of honour who never dissected or poisoned women and who will be only too pleased to write his name on your shoulders if you're not broken on the wheel before I am able to do so," and Sade inspired only one misgiving in him, that Sade might put him in mourning on the place of execution."*

Reporting on this on July 30th to the Chief of Police, Mirabeau being indeed toady enough to add his own complaint, de Rougement wrote to the Minister, asking for instructions, and reminding him that this was not the first time that Sade had tried to stir up the other prisoners. On one occasion he had shouted to de Whitte as he passed his door : "Comrade, take care what you eat, they mean to poison you!" Further, de Rougement informed his superior that he did not intend to reply to any attack the prisoner might make on his person, "any such response being beneath the dignity of an officer whom His Majesty has deigned to honour with his confidence."

*July 7th 1780.*** Mlle de Rousset had requested either the prisoner's release or some weighty reasons for his detention. Almost all the ministers had received copies and supporting

---

*Sade and Mirabeau were distant cousins.
**At about this time the *Marquise* was getting ready to leave the Carmelite Convent to take up an apartment in the *rue de la Marche*, in the Marais quarter.

letters and some princesses had supported Sade's case with de Maurepas. But should the Ministers make too close an enquiry, Mlle de Rousset wrote to Gaufridy, they were "done", for the prisoner was behaving very badly and attacking all the ladies in a frightful way, in letters which they might read or which might be brought to their notice, "for letters of the sort are not made to be sent". For instance, the "saint" herself was now regularly called "a whore". She needed great steadfastness of purpose to dare persist in her application.

July 24th 1780. The motives for holding Sade prisoner were examined and debated at Versailles. "The first Minister ordered another, his junior, to present him with all the evidence. He would not give his reply till he had read it all, but in words he had been most obliging." His reply was going to throw light on many points of which Lady de Sade and Mlle de Rousset were ignorant.

July 27th 1780. Sade sent some books back to his wife, after having read them. Among them was the *Abbé Prévost,* also *d'Alembert* : "What a man ! What a pen ! There you have men I would like to be my arbiters and judges, not the imbecile gang who propose to command me. I would not have any misgivings about being whitewashed by such tribunals as they would make. . . ."

The prisoner was most insistent that his wife should get his walks restored. He was suffering frightfully from lack of air. "It is infamous to deprive a man of what any animal has." And his hair was falling out now it was not being tended. Not that he was all complaint about that; he had had "these forty delightful years", in which he had always been promising "to renounce Old Nick and his worldly delights" and the time had now come for him to begin to assume "a bit of coffin hue".

September 17th 1780. The prisoner was told in the morning that his walks would be restored, but "it didn't happen so". He at once took his pen and reported the event to Lady de Sade.

"This morning the so-called major came and told me that *the King* has granted me my walks. 'Very much obliged, *Monsieur,* I thank you and the King too.' 'But, *Monsieur,* that is not all, you see, you have no right. . . .'

'What's this, *Monsieur*?' I interrupted. 'A little sermonising? Please spare me; about morals I know all there is to know.' 'But, *Monsieur*, you see. . . .' '*Monsieur*,' I went on, 'in so far as the man you speak of (the gaoler) is decent, he will find me gentle. When he ceases to be, he will find a man most disposed to put him right, not being made to put up with the insolence of any man and least of all a rascally gaoler. . . .' Then he raised the siege and since, he made out, I refused to listen to the moral homily of *Monsieur* the Disabled One . . . no more walks. Thus, my dear one, I thank you for nothing and reserve all my gratitude for when the favour comes to me without conditions, that is, without the homily."

October 21st 1780. No doubt thanks to a clerk with enough courage to have given her or copied the whole or part of the file relating to the Marquis, Mlle de Rousset had now learned the real reasons, or what she thought were the real reasons, for the Marquis' detention. She wrote to Gaufridy about this.

"The matter stands where it did before and *I believe it will for a long time to come*. After many delays and vague promises, I tried to see and inform Lady de Sade of the reasons for the Marquis' detention. It was not easy. The person who was bold enough to do it took a chance and now runs the risk of the galleys or life imprisonment. . . . This daring step has anyway informed us that the dear Lady Montreuil is not as much to blame as we used to think. He has much more powerful enemies, whom he has merited. We must hope that some will die and the others be forgotten before we can count on anything."

October 23rd 1780. In another letter to Gaufridy Mlle de Rousset came back to the reasons for the Marquis' imprisonment:

"There are serious reasons, very serious reasons, which make me fear a long captivity. Whether they are true or false, they are none the less the main forces the Minister wields to seal the lips of all decent folk. Lord and Lady de Maurepas, two princesses and some others, after seeing and reading these motives, said : 'He is in the proper place;

his wife is either mad or as guilty as he is to dare to request his liberty. We have no desire to see her. . . .' The various police officers who visited La Coste house have made shocking statements. Very coarse persons they are. The Marquis' whole life is written in a folio volume (let us omit the title); the man is for hanging! Certain details which I thought very few people knew are now in broad daylight and, dear God, many other things which call for the most profound silence make me think his captivity will be long."

November 15th 1780. Mlle de Rousset told Gaufridy what a sad life Lady de Sade was now leading. Exhausting though the journey might be she herself would be very glad when in the spring she returned to Provence. Then she would no longer have "this hell upon earth" before her eyes; she would be ten years younger.

December 13th 1780. On leaving Vincennes prison, Mirabeau made out his official discharge on the reverse of the record of the Marquis de Sade's arrival at the prison.

December 14th 1780. "Today Friday December 14th 1780 is the 1,400th day, the 200th week and the end of the 46th month of our separation, during which I have received from you sixty-eight fortnightly payments and one hundred letters, this being the 114th I have written." This was Sade to his wife in a long letter in which married love found the most moving expression.

December 24th 1780. Sade sketched out his comedy *The Inconstant One.*

December 30th 1780. Less than a week after the words of fond gratitude and the relatively philosophical reflections expressed in the letter of December 14th, the captive in this the last day but one of the year felt rage and desperation welling up within him. He reproached Lady de Sade for her "loathsome lies", by which he meant the vain hopes of liberty with which she had not ceased to feed him. "It will be vain for you to fall back on the explanation that you yourself were deceived," he wrote. "Either you should have said nothing or spoken when quite sure of your facts. In a couple of words, you are an idiot and

let yourself be led by the nose, and any who so led you are monsters fit for the gallows and what is more to be hanged there
till the crows gnaw their flesh from their bones." He ended
this letter with the ugliest of behests; "May you and your execre-
able family and their scum of valets all be bundled into a sack
and pitched into the water. Then give me the news without
delay and I swear to Heaven that that will be the happiest day
I have ever known. There, Madam, you have my behests and
my wishes to you—which includes your whore de Rousset, from
head to foot."

February 20th 1781. In his "grand epistle" to his wife Sade
listed all the lying charges made against him which made him
seem a criminal, refutes these in detail, and concludes with an
apologia from which let us quote the following : "Yes, I am a
libertine. I admit it frankly. My mind has encompassed everything possibly conceivable in that sphere, though I have certainly not done all I have conceived and certainly never shall.
I am a libertine, but I am neither *a criminal* nor *a murderer.*"

March 9th 1781. After thirty-six weeks of curtailment, the
prisoner's hours of exercise were restored him.

March 10th 1781. Lady Montreuil to Gaufridy : Lady de Sade
had told her that Gaufridy had written to say the Marquis
was needed on his estates, but Lady Montreuil had told her
daughter that she washed her hands of that request and all she
could do was to let Lady de Sade do what she chose without
opposing her. But how could Lady de Sade hope to obtain her
husband's release? Above all, however could she want it? Lady
Montreuil reproved Gaufridy for having "brazenly" gone
so far as to suggest liberation, when he more than anybody
else *knew* so positively what the Marquis had done and what
he would still be capable of doing.

March 31st 1781. Thanks to the support of the *Marquise* de
Sorans, Lady-in-Waiting to Elizabeth of France, sister of the
King, Lady de Sade now obtained the Royal consent for her
husband to be transferred to Montélimar Fortress, to be closer
at hand to his affairs. Lady Montreuil was very annoyed to
learn of the success of an application made apart from her.

April 1st 1781. A letter from Lady de Sade brought the prisoner the news of his forthcoming transfer to Montélimar. Not merely did the Marquis not express any pleasure, he even saw in the news a First of April trick played by Lady Montreuil, and pretended to deny that any such fortress existed.

No doubt Lady de Sade misunderstood. It could only have been Crest Tower, near Montélimar. But this keep was a gaol "quite definitely more frightful than Vincennes, more extremely unhealthy" where only prisoners they wanted to get rid of quickly were sent. "It is an abominable sewer in which a man can scarcely see daylight at all, in the heart of a fever-infected marshland." If this really was the dwelling place intended for him, for the favour of which he was now supposed to offer the *Marquise* de Sorans his "humble" gratitude, might he be permitted to do nothing of the kind, the more so since the style of the letter suggested to him was that which the lady in question's footman would use if she had dismissed him and he was trying to get back into her good graces. "Take it from me," the prisoner wrote to Lady de Sade, "we have been exhibited enough in the Dauphiné and in Provence. Valence has recorded me in its archives in letters of gold, as well as Mandrin and Vienne, Grenoble and other places. Let us leave it there."

In short, in no uncertain terms Sade told his wife that he refused any sort of transfer and would only express his gratitude to the *Marquise* de Sorans when that lady had obtained him unadulterated liberty, not an exchange of fortress, for as between the two he preferred Vincennes to anything but a return to his property.

April 12th 1781. The Marquis informed the police chief that if they did not wish to give up the idea of Montélimar, he was ready to leave, but would escape, whatever precautions they took, and go out of the country. "I have a ruler prepared to adopt me, you may count on that, Sir, and that a monarch who does not have his subjects locked up to suit whores and does not hand them over to pimps." Once thus safe, he would bring public shame down on Lady Montreuil by what he published and would reveal that the only reason that he was a prisoner so long was "for not having a hundred thousand francs to spend per annum to purchase the toadies of Themis" as did those to whom the State had sacrificed him. Further, he would still have "a reliable means of stripping his children of any moral existence" and not leaving them "more than the breath their mother gave them". Let M. Le Noir kindly ponder all this and be kind enough to work for his liberation. He, the Marquis de Sade, would give him his word all his life "to behave most discreetly, in the most orderly, in the most model way that even an angel could live, thinking solely of the happiness of his wife and children, of repairing the breach in his fortunes that his misfortunes had made, in a word, of blotting out the past so that never a memory of it should emerge".

May 10th 1781. Lady Anne, sister-in-law of the Marquis, fell ill of smallpox, the eruption appearing on Friday evening.

May 13th 1781. Lady Anne died of her illness, or possibly of peritonitis, at one p.m.

Some days before May 19th. In receipt of Sade's letter, Mlle de Rousset thanked him sarcastically for having at last, after two years, remembered to write to her. She was on the point of leaving for Provence. Had he any instructions regarding La Coste house?

June 13th 1781. Lady de Sade wrote to Mlle de Rousset, who had returned to La Coste, to keep an eye on Gaufridy.

July 13th 1781. On this day occurred the first visit that Sade's wife was able to pay him. Even so she could only see him in the presence of a witness, despite his express wish they might be alone. Thus after a separation of exactly four years and five months they were allowed to meet in the presence of police officer Boucher, in the Council room.

FROM JULY 13TH 1781 TO FEBRUARY 29TH 1784

From July 13th to the Beginning of October 1781. The period from July 13th 1781, when Lady de Sade first visited her husband in Vincennes prison, and the beginning of October, when for a time M. le Noir objected to the couple's seeing each other, is almost entirely preoccupied by the attack of husbandly jealousy which took possession of the prisoner.

On July 27th, a fortnight after visiting Sade, the *Marquise* wrote about it to Mlle de Rousset :

"Since I saw him he has made me miserable with count-less silly fancies he has taken into his head; for want of something better to do he is jealous. I can see you laughing at this distance. 'And of what?' you ask. Of Lefèvre (he honours me greatly, don't you think?) because I men-tioned that Lefèvre had bought me some books for him. He is also jealous of Lady de Villette, just because I wrote to tell him that she asked me to stay with her. . . . Do tell me, I pray, where he gets it all from."

What do we know of this person Lefèvre and of Lady de Villette who thus distinguished themselves by making the Mar-quis jealous?

First, the lady. The name may not have surprised the con-noisseur of eighteenth century letters. Reine Philiberte Rouph de Varicourt was born at Pougny on June 3rd 1757, daughter of a cavalry officer of the Gex country to whom Voltaire, her neighbour, on occasion offered hospitality. A lovely woman of pleasant character, she was taken up by Mme Denis, who welcomed her at Ferney. Then Voltaire himself took her up and began to call her the *"belle et bonne"*—as beautiful as kind. It was under his wing that on November 12th 1777 in Ferney chapel she married the rich Marquis de Villette, twenty years her senior and notorious for his not being above intimate rela-tions with small boys. At first he manifested great love for the young wife he had taken, but this domestic bliss of theirs did not last long, because the Marquis was not slow to resume his old ways.

In due course the couple followed Voltaire to Paris and provided him with a home in Villette Mansion, a luxurious town house on the Seine embankment which bears that name to this day. A few months later he was to die there. So much for the lady's rôle in literary history, though it is said of her that throughout her life she showed many examples of benev-olence. And that "the fair Lady Villette", as Sade called her, at the same time showed herself to be "a great f——r" and per-haps also "a bit of a Sappho" is not in the least incompatible with the gentleness and goodness for which she was famed.

However, it would seem that the prisoner was less jealous of Mme Villette herself than of the considerable company which frequented her mansion. Here was the principal reason for Sade's forbidding his wife to accept the hospitality of her delightful friend.

Now for the principal object of the Marquis' jealousy. M. Lefèvre, who had been his secretary in 1771 and 1772, was a young Provençal of rather low social class, a "small farmer" of Mazan come to town to make a career. His first job was valet to the Abbé de Sade, who taught him to read and write. Later, probably after Sade's flight in 1772, he worked in the offices of M. d'Albertas of Aix. Lefèvre's "ignoble" origin is confirmed by the stories with which Sade tricked out his imaginary rival's portrait and by such language as the following in a letter from Sade to his wife : "And it's a rapscallion of that sort, a paltry clodhopper on my estates, a little squirt who pickled himself in filth at Aix, to whom you have recourse to be false to me, is it ?"

During the Revolution Lefèvre was turn and turn about Jacobin and Moderate, as circumstances demanded. He attained some political notoriety and after Vendémaire 13th, Year IV was appointed assistant to Frérom when that person visited Provence as Representative the second time. By the Year XII Sade's former little secretary had become Assistant Prefect of Verdun, and was the author of a recently published *Essay on Eloquence*.

A private collector (who wishes to remain anonymous) possesses an unpublished letter of the *Marquise* to her husband in Vincennes which is blotted all over with blood and annotated by Sade in furious and obscene terms. Lady de Sade is called a wh ... and procuress, la Montigni's establishment is recommended her as her "nunnery". Further, the dimensions of Lefèvre's penis are calculated from the date in August which the letter bears—the 5th. "And there's the figure that fine fellow is classed with a 5, with a 7 ! which one supposes are his measurements."* (What this sort of preoccupation indicates will be discussed below.) Finally, to his wife's signature: *Montreuil de Sade*, the jealous man added his rival's name, producing the startling result of *Montreuil Le Févre de Sade*.

*Inches : circumference and length.

However, despite such insulting language to her, Sade does not forget to thank her for her last letter and even to thank her for the copied-out oath which he had indicated to her and which he himself insisted "soothed him". But then with haughty severity and in terms of a remarkable dignity that his ancestor Richard de Sade, Chamberlain to Urbain VIII and subsequently Bishop of Cavaillon would not have disdained, the Marquis goes on to say that he reproves his spouse for the frivolity of her appearance and her hair style, which he says were not at all those that became the wife of a man who had been held for five years in the most horrible of prisons.

"What sense is there in the excuse 'If only you saw the others?' The others have not got husbands in prison, or, if they have and do behave like that, they are hussies that do not merit anything else but insults and scorn. Tell me, would you go to Easter Sunday service in that get-up, like a common actress or a woman selling quack cures at the fair? Now, tell me, would you? Well, reflection ought to act in the same way; grief and sorrow ought to produce in this case what piety and respect for the Deity would produce in the other. However extravagant the fashion, you are not going to tell me there is no style that suits a woman of sixty? Imitate that, however far off that age you may be. Bear in mind that my misfortune makes us all but that age, if not entirely so, and in conduct and dress leaves us no other fashion to follow. If you are a decent woman, I am the only person you ought to be pleasing to, and you certainly are not going to please me except by a manner and by acting with the greatest possible circumspection and the most perfect modesty. . . . I insist on your coming in what you women call a *house gown,* in a large, in fact very large bonnet, without any fancy hair-do under it, your hair merely combed. Not a hint of false curls, no bun, no false tresses, no exaggerated curves, with your bosom in particular covered and not shockingly flourished as it was the other day; and let the colour of your gown be as dark as possible. I swear by all I hold most sacred in the world that you will make my head boil to such a point that there will be a frightful scene if you depart in any detail from all I have just prescribed."

However, the most really sensational manifestation of Sade's jealousy, exceeding even the cynical comments he made on that letter of Lady de Sade's of August 5th, is offered by the assassination of an effigy of his supposed rival. The effigy was a pencil drawing of Lefèvre that Mlle de Rousset had made. It has been described elsewhere by the author.* Sade had torn it thirteen times. It was bloodstained. And all round it the Marquis had written titles expressive of his scorn and hatred and of an unsurpassable virulence. Let us glance at a fragment of one only of the descriptions :

> "The woman who solely for either vile vengeance or, which is perhaps worse still, for the turgid, coarse craving of satisfying her bodily lust, shamelessly gives herself to a valet, to a peasant of the vilest breed to whom her husband's father gave *largesse,* that woman, I say, has no longer even the right to be called wife. She is but a shameless she-wolf made for universal derision, a woman a thousand times more to be scorned than those in whom the right to live justifies such loathsome things—than a wretch, in short, who no longer has any rights, save to ignominy and filth and what is base—than a monster who dishonours simultaneously her children, her husband and herself, and who should no longer think she can do other than just exist in the filth and mire in which she has found the vile instrument of her crime."

Yet all this time Lady de Sade never ceased countering her husband's savage charges with the noblest and most touching patience, reminding him again and again in the most convincing language of her love and her constancy :

> "It is not enough for me that my conscience can reproach me with nothing—I need your happiness and contentment. I would rather you told me your suspicions, your

*It was placed at his disposal by M. Xavier de Sade in 1948, at his *château* of Condé-en-Brie.

uneasinesses than have you harbour them, for it is very easy for me to clear myself. . . .

. . . The way you now think of me crushes me, annihilates me, humiliates me, when I live and think only of seeing you. To see myself thus suspected and abused! I say nothing but you lacerate my heart. It will never heal. I have nothing to answer. My conduct is hidden from nobody. No, it is not possible that, knowing me as you must, you really mean what you write. . . .

. . . My heart has not changed: it worships you and will ever worship you. The only revenge I reserve is, when you come out, to make you admit, when you have been able to verify everything and find out the truth, that all that has passed through your head while you are in prison is the most fantastic extravagance. . . ."

Some time after this, finding that all her assurances merely increased the prisoner's fury, not only did the *Marquise* decline the hospitality that Lady de Villette offered her, but in order to remove the last possible reason for jealousy decided to leave the apartment she occupied in the *rue de la Marche* and withdraw into a nunnery.

"I give you my word of honour," she wrote, "that I will not go to live with Lady de Villette. I am going to find a nunnery, so I may at last remove any reason for your tormenting yourself as you do. The friendship and interest that she takes in my situation had made me fond of Lady de Villette, but the friendship is over; the fact that she displeases you is enough for me to break with her."

Writing on August 18th to Mlle de Rousset that her husband's letters have not reached her, Lady de Sade told her too that she had decided to take a room in the Nunnery of St Aure in the *rue Neuve Ste Geneviève*. In this nunnery she had found a girl named Martin who knew the Marquis when he was small and even boxed his ears, because he teased her.

At the beginning of October we find M. Le Noir—despite Lady de Sade's pleas,—refusing to allow her to visit her husband because of his mad jealousy, and just when there was some sign of this obsession leaving the Marquis, one day towards the end of October innocent words of his wife's suddenly made him suspect she was pregnant because of having "seen too much of her dyer".

*   *   *

Knowledge of Lady de Sade's character inclines one to think that her husband's jealousy rested on very slight foundations. Yet on the other hand it must be pointed out that seeing the orgies at La Coste between 1774 and 1777, particularly those with the young girls of Lyons and Vienne and the young secretary—and there seems no doubt that, however little he might expect his modestly brought up wife to approve, he compelled her to take part—were all calculated to result in a dangerous stimulation of her imagination. (It is worth noting that the extreme freedom of language in Sade's letters to his wife does suggest a sort of understanding on the matter between the pair.)

Two-dimensional psychology, *plane* psychology, to use Marcel Proust's happy expression, can only provide a very incomplete answer to the problem of these unjustified suspicions of Sade's. Sade had been locked up in Vincennes for nearly five years. In such long-drawn-out and frightful isolation, what man but would not have tended to be jealous? This is what *plane* psychology would say. Added to this over-simplified view of the matter we may suggest the following : in order, by conjuring up pictures of Lady de Sade's imaginary adultery, to lend some body to the only pleasures of the flesh available to him, the Marquis quite unconsciously built up a foundation for his jealousy.

It has often seemed to us that in the heart of this jealous man his rage more often than not merely served to cloak an unconscious craving to be deceived. This paradoxical position would appear implicit in a dream which Sade had one night (in which in addition orthodox psychoanalysis would certainly detect traces of the Oedipus complex).

"I dreamt of you much older than when I left you," he wrote to his wife, "before that visit of last July, when you had a secret you had to tell me but about which you would never say any more; and you were constantly being unfaithful to me, in the full meaning of the term." He added : "I think I have dreamt that particular dream five hundred times."

Now what is the pathogenic principle of the sort of jealousy here in question? It would seem quite justifiable to say it was homosexuality, whether completely unconscious, (as in some men), or overt and free from misgivings (as in Sade's case),— homosexuality, whether completely unconscious (as in some men), or overt and free from misgivings (as in Sade's case),— and his bizarre insistence on cylindrical objects,** to leave any doubt as to the manner in which he "obliged" his valet Latour during the Marseilles debauch.)

To resume our story: We can only be jealous about pleasures which we know, or of which at least we have some deductive sense. The more violent our jealousy becomes, the more we know or sense that pleasure of which we are frustrated, which is not always solely—in the case under discussion—that pleasure which we most resent being deprived of. Husbands or lovers who are bi-sexual, or are mental hermaphrodites, are, by reason of the nature or the degree of their homosexuality, not only envious of the pleasure which their rival obtains, but also, whether consciously or unconsciously, they are also envious of the pleasure which their wife obtains, a pleasure which they either know directly, through having experienced it themselves, or through sensing it in some obscure way, constitutionally, so to speak. Put otherwise, they have a terrible knowledge, which is more or less conscious, of what the other man's penis, which they abominate and admire at the same time, means to their wife, so that in the same way they both abominate and admire the free enjoyment of her sex by the woman whose betrayal of them tortures them.

The rival's penis then becomes almost the only object of the fantasies of this sort of jealous man. We have seen how the Marquis with a sort of bedazed hatred conjectured the "measurements" of young Lefèvre who had "rotted in the filth

---

*For instance, in a letter of November 23rd 1783 he thanked his wife for sending him the portrait of a "handsome boy" which he had asked for, in the following term: "My *darling turtle-dove*, so you have sent me the lovely boy. *The lovely boy*—how sweet those words are to my slightly Italian ear. *Un' bel' giovanetto, signor*, they would say to me, were I in Naples: *Si, si, signor, mandotelo lo voglio bene.* You have treated me as if I were a cardinal, *my little mother* . . . But unfortunately, it is only a painting . . . The case, then, at least, the casket, since you reduce me to illusion!"

**Caskets and flasks.

of Aix", as he said in another place, no doubt to add the fascination of the dregs of society (very frequent, as we know, in homosexuals) to the image of the *Marquise* unfaithful "in the full meaning of the term", which already raised him to such frightful heights of emotion.*

And now, lest it should seem that the author is here indulging in the abuse with which he has reproached more than one biographer of Sade's, namely, that of identifying Sade with the characters created by his imagination, it is not without interest to throw a little more light on the above line of thought by recalling an episode in both *Justines* in which the sensuous enjoyment of dishonour is enjoyed to the full by a husband who is both masochist and homosexual.

In the version of 1791 Sade offers a first sketch of the way of life of Count de Gernande, whose regular form of sexual indulgence (apart from bleeding his lovely wife every day) consisted in compelling her to submit to the barbarous assaults of young men of his choice, with himself looking on and then bringing them to final orgasm orally. And in *la Nouvelle Justine,* in which the episodes of the first book are taken up again and developed deliriously till they reach a paroxysm of action and language, de Gernande's passionate revelling in his own marital dishonour is enriched by a further proliferation of imagination which is both demoniacal and magnificent. However, this version of *The Life of Sade* cannot accept this orgy at its most extravagant. One cannot help but abhor the Count de Gernande's summary of the matter in the frenzied slogan on his scarlet banner of *Nothing gives me such pleasure as working for my own dishonour.* Yet is this not a most succinct profession of faith, which should serve after all as summary to the story of Sade's jealousy?

Nevertheless, yet to prove once more that it is completely

---

*With his usual eloquence Sade praised adultery in *Juliette.* "Adulterous wives, that's the position: in your husbands' arms you yield only your bodies to them, while the sensations of physical enjoyment which they give rise to never belong to any other but your lovers. Your husbands deceive themselves, thinking the intoxication which their movements cause in you belongs to them, whereas the fools really haven't a spark of the fire which burns. Enchanting sex, go on with your trickery, it is in nature itself; the flexibility of your fancies proves it, so in this wise, since you have no other, recompense yourselves for the ridiculous chains of modesty and the marriage bond."

wrong to judge of the Marquis' own personality by the acts or the words he attributes to his heroes, let us add this bestial picture of a husband what is at once the purest possible praise— and the most chastely erotic praise—that the institution of marriage ever inspired. There is something fine in the fact that this passage, redolent of the breath of the Heavenly Twins, was penned by the same hand that depicted—for our horror but also for our lyrical delight—the lacerated anguish of the Countess de Gernande.

"Ah, do not imagine that sexual enjoyment can quench the flame when this is the work of love, for then the more a wife yields her charms to us the more does she excite our fire and the bond which one mocks when one does not love one's wife becomes so sweet when one adores her, for it is such bliss to match the movements of one's heart to the desires of Heaven, of the Law and of Nature. . . . No, no, there is not the woman in the world that can equal her who belongs to us. In free abandonment to the fiery promptings of her soul, on her one showers with such delight all the epithets which promise to confirm those with which she is already endowed. She is at once our wife and our mistress, our sister, our Goddess; she is all that could add to the most exciting bliss of our life; every passion is enflamed, coming together in her and for her alone; one exists only by reason of her and one desires none other than her. Indeed, my friend, there is no bond so pleasing, there is no pleasure of such value as those of the marriage bond and not one on earth the details of which reach such a point of bodily pleasure; misfortunate he who has not known them, misfortunate he who would choose some other kind, for such a man tastes everything in life but never finds happiness."

Towards October 20th 1781. Gothon gave birth to a boy, baptised at the cost of her masters. Soon illness ensued, no doubt puerperal fever, taken at first to be "phthisis".

October 26th 1781. On this Thursday Gothon's end was felt to be near and the sacraments were administered her. There was fear lest she infected the whole house. There was a sharp interchange between her husband, Grégoire, and Mlle de Rousset, when the latter requested him to remove her elsewhere.

The same day the Marquis (who had recently written to his wife to defend himself against the charge of having threatened her, as Le Noir had been told by the Fortress personnel), protested his innocence a second time.

October 27th 1781. The Marquis either threatened his gaoler or actually struck him. As reprisal his room was not to be swept and he was deprived of the services of a barber.

October 27th or 28th 1781. Gothon passed away, outside her masters' walls, in the arms of Mlle de Rousset herself, who did not shrink from nursing her, despite the danger of infection.

Learning of this death Sade despite his atheism at once ordered a religious service for Gothon, though he asked that Gaufridy should not be told about the *louis d'or* which the ceremony would cost. It had however been thought better to conceal from the "*Chevalier* Don Quiros", who had been much aggrieved by his mistress's marriage, that she was no more but he had "a peculiar dream" and was worried about her.

Towards the end of October 1781. From a harmless phrase in one of his wife's letters, Sade suddenly got the idea into his head that she was pregnant, therefore adulterous. "I am delighted to inform you," she had written, "that I am putting on so much weight that I am mortally afeared of becoming a fat old sow; when you see me you will be surprised." Immediately jealousy seized Sade's mind again and in a rage he noted in the margin : "Through too much tumbling with your cleaner man ! Putting on weight ! With what, eh?"

No doubt he could not refrain from shouting out loud, and he was heard by the turnkey. Very soon the chief of the police was informed and hastened to tell Lady de Sade to what an insulting suspicion her husband was subjecting her.

"Madame," he said, "if in spite of this you persist in wishing to see him, I shall in future refer matters to the Minister and put all the circumstances before him, for I have no desire to be responsible for concealing such matters."

"What would you have replied to that ?" Lady de Sade asked

Mlle de Rousset on November 1st; "I dared not insist lest unguardedly I harmed my husband."

Even this new trial did not prevent her writing to tell the "saint" that she was distressed that Mlle de Rousset should have such thoughts about the Marquis, for whatever he did, her own attachment to him could never diminish.

October 31st 1781. From modesty and to ease any sense of remorse which the Marquis was sure to feel, Lady de Sade wrote to tell him that she did not believe a word of what Le Noir had told her. She also intimated to the prisoner that in two days' time she was going to apply to the chief of police for permission for the Abbé Amblet to pay his old pupil a visit.

November 10th 1781. Lady de Sade told her husband that it had not been possible for her to obtain permission for the Abbé Amblet to go to Vincennes. No outside person was allowed there. She begged him to keep in good heart and be patient and said that La Jeunesse was still busy copying out his plays. As for the books they sent him, would he very kindly not tear them up when he did not like them, because he had to pay for them, and it all came out of his money.

December 15th 1781. Lady de Sade requested the police chief to withdraw the ban he had placed on her visiting Vincennes. Le Noir should not judge the prisoner by what he wrote. He had behaved in a most seemly manner the last time she had had the satisfaction of seeing him. "His desperation may make him wild, but a little kindness and patience would restore calm and would make him a different man."

April 17th 1782. During the night of March 28th unidentified persons at La Coste had had the "rascality" to split in two twenty-eight fruit trees in the manor park. The Marquis, when he received this news from Gaufridy, replied by a letter of exquisite tomfoolery. (One looks, alas, in vain for anything so amusing in his comedies.)

End of April 1782. The Marquis suggested to Lady de Sade that she should use all possible means of persuasion to get Mlle de Rousset to agree to take up quarters in the *château* and look after it.

May 14th 1782. Mlle de Rousset says she moved in to the manor house a few days since and is sleeping in that "far from chaste" bedroom in which the keeper used to have his fun.

June 23rd 1782. Letter from Sade to his wife—the letter heading marked the occasion as the "two hundred and tenth week" of his captivity. He affected the most philosophical detachment regarding his worldly goods and declared himself satisfied too that his wife's conduct had been perfect, she was incapable of deceiving him. "Six visits sufficed to rescue me from my wild imaginings. They were insulting to you and that is enough for me never to get such ideas again. Now I am better able to prize what I love."

June 30th 1782. Mlle de Rousset complained to Gaufridy about Sambuc's insolence. She had spoken to the gamekeeper's mistress about not feeding the rabbits properly, when the yokel had shouted that she was "worse than Gothon" and he was surprised people who were not the masters there, but "b—— f—— of people" should dare say things like that to her.

In the same letter Lady de Sade's friend communicated an odd item of interest, that Canon Vidal of Oppède had "so well confessed his housekeeper that she is smitten with the nine months hydropsy". Malicious wags were constantly plying her with poems and ditties on the subject.

July 12th 1782. The Marquis de Sade completed the exercise book containing his *Dialogue between a Priest and a Dying Man*.

July 31st 1782. A violent altercation between the Marquis and his gaoler. The gaoler was either threatened or had his ears boxed. As a consequence, not only were walks forbidden the Marquis, but he was not even allowed out into the corridor which had provided him with some relaxation.

August 6th 1782. All books were taken away from the prisoner, because they "overheated his head" and made him write "unseemly things". His wife pleaded with him to restrain himself in his writings, which did him "infinite harm". He should "adjust the wild things that come into his mind" by a "decent fashion of thinking which should match his inner heart".

Some days after August 19th 1782. Extract from a letter from Sade to his wife:

... "As for me, *personally,* I promise you nothing. The animal is too old. Take my advice and stop trying to improve him. Julie made no headway with de Wolmar, and yet he loved her dearly. There are systems too intimately tied up with being, especially when one has imbibed them at the breast, for it to be possible ever to give them up. It is the same with habits—when they are so tremendously bound up with the very constitution of a person all that ten thousand years of prison and five hundred pounds of chains would do is give them greater strength. I expect I shall surprise you when I say that *all these things* and their remembrance are always what I call to my aid when I want to dull myself to my situation. Our behaviour does not depend on ourselves, but on our make-up, our organisation. What does depend on us is not to spread our poison abroad and not only that what surrounds us should not suffer, but that it should not even notice it. A conduct so flawless with one's children and with one's wife that she is unable, even when she compares her lot with that of other wives, to even be able to suspect her husband's evil ways, that is what depends on us, and that is what a decent man should contrive, because one is not called a rascal merely for having some peculiarity in one's pleasures. Hide it in public, above all from your children, and let your wife never even faintly suspect it, letting your duties to her be fulfilled too *in every way.* That is the essential and that is what I promise. One cannot give oneself virtues nor is one any longer able to adopt this or that taste, any more than a hunchback can make himself straight, or a man can make this or that opinion his general system or make himself auburn-haired when he is born ginger. That is my permanent view of life and I shall never give it up.— Nevertheless, in 1777 I was still fairly young; the height of misfortune I found myself in should have been a preparation. My heart was still not hardened and inaccessible to kindly feelings in the way you have since taken care to make it. A totally different plan on your part could have done great things, but you did not wish this. I thank you for it. I much prefer only having to clear my head of your figures than to have to banish an infinity of things and details from it which I find very delightful and which are so capable of easing my misfortunes when I let my imagination play on them. I might say that you have been very badly advised, but I must truthfully say I would much rather it had not been so."

There is indeed very little likelihood that by normal logic one would deduce from this admirable profession of faith that since 1782 Sade had been working deliriously on his *120 Days of Sodom,* but this fragment nevertheless is ardent and compelling evidence that by now the prisoner of Vincennes had found salvation and a lightness of heart outside of time in his cruel erotic meditations, packed as they were with those details "which I find very delightful", a lightness of heart which heralded his masterpieces to come.

September 25th 1782. Resumed after January, Lady de Sade's rare visits had once again been curtailed because of the prisoner's bad behaviour. Learning this from the lips of M. Le Noir, the *Marquise* was "crushed"; she had asked to see Le Noir to complain that she had not seen her husband for a long time and to ask that officer to secure her permission to visit.

End of September 1782. Mlle de Rousset was beginning to be chary of sleeping at La Coste house every evening, as the high winds were threatening to reduce the place to ruins. There were cracks in every corner, something new collapsed every quarter of an hour and the tiles and lumps of plaster coming down like peals of bells all added to her terror. Further, the chimney of her room had collapsed and the terrible wind which shook the windows and tore the frames from their sockets "turned and tossed" poor Mlle Rousset in her bed "as if she were a feather".

October 8th 1782. Lady de Sade instructed Gaufridy to have the repairs which Mlle de Rousset had indicated at La Coste house proceeded with at once.

Towards December 15th 1782. Four months and a half after his altercation with the gaoler the Marquis was again allowed

to walk up and down the corridor which had been closed to
him.

Towards the end of January 1783. Lady de Sade's younger
sister, Françoise Pélagie, born October 12th 1760, married
the Marquis de Wavrin. Lady de Sade could not but make her
a present and this had left her "without a *sou*".

February 4th 1783. Recently the Marquis had been suffering
from trouble in one eye, and begged his wife to send him in an
oculist, the best to be found in Paris.*

End of March 1783. The Marquis sent his wife the final manuscript of his tragedy *Jeanne Lainé,* followed by a short blank
verse curtain-raiser entitled *A Foolish Test, or the Credulous
Husband.* He beseeched her not to deprive him any longer of
visits and to obtain restoration of exercise in the garden "for this
is the time of the year when that becomes more necessary than
life itself".

End of March 1783. The prisoner asked his wife to tell the
oculist he wished to be examined because the state of his eye
was beginning to worry him very much. "The inflammation
was extreme and was working inside; half my head on that
side is on fire, you could not imagine it; I suffered terribly last
night from the discomfort and pain of it." There was no satisfaction to be had from the prison surgeon, M. Fonteillot. Not
that Sade blamed him; it was not his fault; it all came from the
orders given by de Rougement, which amounted to a prohibition of any treatment which gave the domestic staff any trouble
"because they will grumble if you prescribe any such". How
did they expect any surgeon, whatever his powers—and Fonteillot was far from being without—to perform his task with
such restrictions? He was afraid of becoming very ill indeed.
And looking ahead, he begged his wife to secure a woman nurse,
not a male. "I would die of sheer lack of patience were I to be
ill and looked after by a man. And besides, what a man it would
be! Do you realize? I have been told. Some ex-guardsman who
happens to have helped male nurses in army hospitals! Those
are the hands I would be left in the care of! Oh, but not for

*Apparently Sade was suffering from that most common complica-
tion, a corneal opacity.

long! A filthy, stinking veteran! With my sensitivities, my vapours and my anxieties when I am ill! It would be enough to kill me in three days."

June 18th 1783. Lady Sade told the prisoner that the letters which he wrote were not being delivered to her because of the improprieties which they contained and until he wrote decent letters she would not be able to see him or get anything done in his favour.

Towards June 25th 1783. Extract from a letter from the Marquis to his wife:

"... Refusing to let me have Jean Jacques' *Confessions* is fine, especially after sending me Lucrece and Voltaire's dialogues; it is proof of great discrimination, a profound sense of judgment in your authorities. Alas, they do honour me, thinking a deistic author could be bad reading for me; I wish I had reached that point. You are not exactly sublime in your methods of cure, my dear authorities! You must learn that it is the stage one has reached that makes a thing good or bad, not the thing in itself. Russian peasants are cured of the fever with arsenic, but the stomach of a pretty woman would not be cured by such a remedy. There you have the proof that everything is relative. From that point, Gentlemen, you should have the wit to understand, while sending me the book I ask for, that Rousseau can be a dangerous author for dull-headed bigots like yourselves, yet become an excellent book for me. For me Jean Jacques is what an *Imitation of Jesus Christ* is for you. Rousseau's ethics and religion are severe matters for me, and I read them when I need edifying. If you do not wish me to become better than I am, very well then! Good is a painful, troublesome condition for me, and I ask nothing better than to remain in my cesspit, it suits me. You, Gentlemen, think your particular *pons asinorum* should serve and work with everybody, and you are wrong, I will prove it to you. There are countless occasions when an evil has to be suffered to destroy a vice. For instance, you have got it into your head that you have done wonders, I'll bet, reducing me to frightful abstinence in *the sin of the flesh*. Well, you have made a mistake, you have heated my head, you have made me conjure up phantoms which I shall now have to realise. This was beginning to pass off and now it will have a fine revival indeed. If you overboil the stew, you know, it may well boil over.

Had I had *Monsieur No. 6* to cure, I would have set about it in a very different way, for instead of shutting him up with cannibals, I would have incarcerated him with some whores, I would have provided him with such a great number that the devil take me if in the seven years he had been inside he would not have used up all the oil in his lamp. When a man has a horse that's too restive, he gallops it over ploughed land, he doesn't shut it up in a stable. That method would have put him on the *right path,* the one they call the *path of honour.* Enough of those *philosophical trickeries,* those enquiries disowned by nature (as if nature cared at all about that), those dangerous flights of too fiery an imagination which, for ever chasing after happiness without ever finding it in anything, ends by putting fantasies in place of reality and *indecent détours* in place of decent sexual indulgence ! ... No. 6 in the heart of a *seraglio* would have become *the friend of women*; he would have recognised and *felt* that nothing is more lovely or *greater* than sex and that outside sex there is no salvation. Exclusively busy with serving the ladies and satisfying their delicate desires, No. 6 would have sacrificed all his. The habit of only experiencing what is seemly would have trained his mind to overcome those leanings which would have prevented his having pleasure. All that in the end would have left him a tamed man, and there you have the way in which in the bosom of vice I would have brought him back to virtue. For, once again, to a very vicious soul virtue is merely a lesser vice."

July 2nd 1783. A lightning conductor was placed on one of the towers of Vincennes Fortress. That very day (or the following day) this was struck by lightning. Paris spoke of this as a catastrophe.

With July thus beginning, it was nearly a year since Sade was last deprived of the right to take exercise out of doors. This caused him terrible suffering, because of the excessive heat of the past few weeks.

During the first days of July 1783. Mlle de Rousset was very ill. But though she was wearied of pain, she still thought life very precious.

September 2nd 1783. The victim of a terrible depression which now frequently took possession of his spirit, despite the disturbing but delightful fantasies he now constantly bred, though now, it would seem, precisely because of those fancies, the prisoner approached Lady Montreuil in the most supplicating terms. He believed, or pretended to believe, with extreme sorrow, that his wife, whom he now saw dagger in hand, out to cut him up, would never come to see him till after he was free. And, whether consciously or unconsciously, affected by the pressure of normal marital love, and apparently solely in the hope of reunion with a woman who had become so desirable in his sight through having been the cause of his sufferings, Sade did not shrink, in terms of utter contrition, from imploring his pitiless mother-in-law to get Lady de Sade to come to see him, without any witness and as soon as possible, in the room in which every day the delirious images of his erotic imagination were consumed and reborn.

September 19th 1783. The Marquis suggested to his wife four points "of extreme beauty" invented by himself, Christophe de Sade.* The first was "cutting off the b—— of Cadet de la Basoch (Albaret)" and sending them to the prisoner in a box. The second was to serve to indicate "2, double, duplicata"** "a lovely woman in the posture of the Kallipygous Farnesian"*** should be placed in his room. The third would be to set fire to the powder-store, to imitate the thunder which was frequent that summer. The fourth was "the finest of all"—Lady de Sade was to get two skulls—he "might have said *six*, but though he

---

*By this assumption of the name *Christophe*, Sade may have intended an ironic comparison of his trials with those of Christ.

**Probably "doubling" the act, an image of heterosexual sodomy.

***The Venus Kallipygous in the Farnese collection, which Sade was able to admire during his stay in Naples in 1776.

served in the dragoons, he is modest". She would tell her husband it was a parcel from Provence, he would hasten to open
it and "*that*" would be it, he would be "scared to death".

Early November 1783. Extract from a letter from the Marquis
to his wife :

> "You say my train of thought cannot meet with approval.
> And what does that matter to me? The man who adopts
> any train of thought to suit other people is certainly a
> madman. My train of thought is the fruit of my reflections,
> it is connected with my existence, my make-up. I am not
> able to change it, and I wouldn't if I could. This train of
> thought which you blame is the sole consolation my life
> contains, it alleviates all my tribulations in prison, it com-
> prises all my pleasures in the world and I cling to it more
> than to life. It is not my manner of thinking that has
> caused my misfortune, but that of other people."

November 23rd and 24th 1783. Of all the years of Sade's letter-
writing it is 1783 that offers the finest fruit. An outstanding
example is that written on these two dates. To describe its
wealth one could find no better phrase than one which Sade's
valet Carteron wrote him on one occasion, though intending it
in another sense altogether—and quite unaware how well he
had put it : "Anyone might think a swarm of bees had come
down on your paper." The erotic daring with which he begins
the epistle and the note of delicate raillery in this, the exquisi-
tely lean vigour of his language, and the enchanting grace
which he maintains throughout suggest comparison with the
music of Mozart, who knew so well how to express the dignity
of being a man. At the same time here once again Sade appears
as a forerunner of the studies of sexology of our day and
would seem to be pleading the very justifiability of his future
enterprise.

"I have respect for tastes, for fancies, however baroque they
be, I find them all worthy of respect, both because we are not
their masters and because the most extraordinary and bizarre
of them all can, if well analysed, be seen to have its origin in a
principle of sensitivity." Now this is precisely the thesis which
a century later Havelock Ellis was to put forward when he

said that the phenomena of erotic symbolism, which strip the individual human being naked, "presuppose a highly developed plastic power of the imagination and are the supreme triumph of human idealism".

It is remarkable indeed that in 1783 Sade should so explicitly have formulated the very spearhead of the philosophy which Havelock Ellis advanced. "You know that nobody analyses as well as I do," is how the Marquis thought fit to begin his letter and we are bound to admit that not only his major works but also his marvellous letters brilliantly justify this frank declaration at which only foolish men would laugh.

End of November 1783. In a letter to his wife Sade indulged in a pen-portrait of himself, and difficult it indeed is to conceive a better one in five lines :

"Imperious, choleric, impetuous, extreme in everything, of a disorderly wealth of imagination on human conduct such as life never saw the equal of, there you have me in a couple of words; one thing more, you must either kill me or take me as I am, for I shall not change."

December 29th 1783. Sade's elder son, Louis Marie, on the eve of joining up in Rohan-Soubise's recently formed infantry regiment, wrote to give his father New Year's wishes and also tell him how impatient he was to begin his career as officer.

Beginning of January 1784. Furious when he learned that his son was preparing to don a different uniform from that he himself had worn in 1757, Sade twice wrote to his wife to tell her that he categorically objected to this proposal. He intimated as much to de Rougement and would "tell all Europe, if necessary". Louis Marie was to serve nowhere else but in the carabiniers; Sade had sworn this when his son was born, and if twenty or forty thousand francs were required, he was ready to give them and would sign any authorisation whatsoever to sell, mortgage or borrow for the purpose. He also enjoined his wife to indicate to Lady Montreuil that she might in future refrain from interfering in a matter regarding which solely the father of the young man had the right to decide. He had no need for these "little services" of Lady Montreuil's or for the "great support of her younger one"—his brother-in-law

Marie Joseph—to get Louis Marie into the service. Further, he had many times declared that none of his children was to leave school or home without having spent a year under his personal control. As it was quite possible that this lady's "head", which always went "a long way", had "planned some fine marriage", the prisoner most solemnly swore that he would agree to no such marriage till Louis Marie was twenty-five, and it was his intention that he must marry somebody either from Lyons or Avignon.

"Long since, I told you, Madam, that after all this I propose to live in my own country. Without question my children will join me there, and most certainly they will have no other marriage or settlement but those." To his letter he added the following postscript:

"Madam, now that your elder son has become a sort of personage in society, I must warn you that it is my intention to follow the custom established in all families, for the head to take the title of Count, leaving that of Marquis to his eldest son."

This postscript requires some explanation. As we have seen, it was Donatien Alphonse François' grand-father, Gaspard François de Sade, who died in 1739, who was the first of the family to bear the title *Marquis*. But ever since Sade himself came of age there was utter confusion about his style. In the army and in the letters of Ministers of the Crown about the Arceuil affair, his imprisonment in Savoy and so forth he appears as *Count,* but in his marriage contract, the arrest warrant of October 29th 1763 and the proceedings at both Arceuil and Marseilles and elsewhere he is described as *Marquis*. However, notwithstanding his own desire, thus expressed in 1784, we shall continue to call him *Marquis,* because it would be odd to call him anything else. As far as that goes, all but one of the elder sons of the family since the demise of the author of *Justine* have with horror refused the title of *marquis*. It was too reminiscent of that shocking ancestor, only to be mentioned in whispers. The present Marquis Xavier de Sade, the first after five generations to allow access to the unpublished manuscripts, was the first not to shrink from making use of the glorious name which had so shocked his immediate ancestors.

To come back to Louis Marie, we may note that it was quite

beyond his power to obey his father and become a carabinier, and we find him listed as a sub-lieutenant in the regiment his father so loathed, garrisoned at Port Louis.

January 13th 1784. No doubt thanks to a new minister, de Breteuil, a more humane man than his predecessor, Lady de Sade at last obtained permission to make frequent visits to Vincennes.

January 25th 1784. Mlle de Rousset, who had for a long time been suffering from pulmonary tuberculosis, died at La Coste at the age of forty years, nineteen days.

In the last days of February 1784. The prisoner became convinced that representations had been made to the King to obtain an appointment as ambassador abroad for him, so as to get him out of France. But Lady Montreuil had given him such a horror of her cypher signs (which he called "conjuring tricks") that he thought it wise at once to swear on oath, "on all that was most sacred in the world", that even if His Majesty were to offer him the top embassy of the realm he would without hesitation refuse it. What he wished for was to live where he himself chose and to give himself up exclusively to the arts and sciences, in the bosom of his family. But what he required at the moment, however, was Lady de Sade's opinion on his dramatic poem *Tancredi* and he hoped she would give him it when she next came to see him. But in this dangerous cold snap that "ugly little white bosom" of hers must be wrapped up, or he would be very angry.

He ended by a punning reference to the *embassy* question— would she very kindly not forget to bring him the cotton stockings he had asked for several times—the *"bas de coton"*—because he was badly off in stockings, "bien mal EN BAS" to which words he added his signature "SADE", so that the letter could also be read that he was *"bien mal en bas, Sade"*, i.e., *"bien mal ambasade"*—a very poor ambassador !

*   *   *

However, far indeed from offering the Marquis an ambassador's post, His Majesty had in mind another fortress, one which was still grimmer than Vincennes. The proposal to close down Vincennes as a state prison had been kept a close secret, and when Sade went to bed on February 28th he had not a notion that this was to be the very last night that he would spend in that bed.

CHAPTER TWELVE

Five and a Half Years
in the Bastille
(1784-1789)

IN THE SECOND LIBERTY

February 29th 1784. "Mr Surbois, inspector of police, removed the Marquis de Sade from Vincennes prison at nine o'clock of the evening. Countersigned by Breteuil, the Royal Order was dated January 31st. He was lodged in the second Liberty."

*   *   *

In the second Liberty? This meant on the second floor of Liberty tower, no doubt thus called by way of contrast. With Bertaudière Tower, Liberty tower formed the St Antoine Blockhouse, the first stone of which was laid April 22nd 1370 by Hugues Aubriot, Provost of Paris. At the time of Sade's imprisonment there, Liberty Tower comprised two dungeon cells, half underground, six rooms, one above the other and a "ring" of narrow cells. Over these came a platform furnished with thirteen cannon, which were fired on public holidays, the birthdays of members of the Royal family, victory days and so forth.

There was only one single room on each floor. These rooms were octagonal, fifteen or sixteen feet in diameter and fifteen to twenty feet high. The walls and ceiling were lime-washed, the floor of bricks. Three steps led up to a window with triple bars. The furniture consisted of a bed with green serge curtains, one or two tables, a number of chairs, andirons, a shovel and tongs. Prisoners were however allowed to bring in furniture. "The result was that some of the rooms in the Bastille were furnished very elegantly. . . . The Marquis de Sade draped his bare walls with long brightly coloured hangings."

One of the best descriptions of the Bastille is that given by H. Monin, in his preface to the Memoirs of Linguet and de Dussaulx.

"In the free outer precincts, adjoining the *rue Saint Antoine* and the Arsenal gardens, the eighteenth century packed shops and dwellings, from all of which the Governor drew rents. In the second precinct, which was not open to the public, was the Governor's residence. . . . The most important change had taken place in 1761, when in the interior of the eight towers, between that of the Chapel and the Liberty Tower, a three-storeyed building was erected to house the staff and the records and contain a council chamber.

The Bastille and ancillary buildings thus comprised four towers, two outside the fortress proper and two inner ones.

A plaque on No. 232 in the *rue Saint Antoine* now shows where the main entrance was situated, leading to the first outer yard, to which there was also access by a small door opening on the other side on to the Arsenal gardens. Anybody had access to this first yard. A drawbridge led to the second outer court, in which the Governor's residence was situated. Here on the left, at right-angles, two further drawbridges, a larger and a smaller, side by side, led into the fortress proper. Going straight on, one crossed the court lengthwise. On the right, on the Saint Antoine side, were the Comté tower, the Trésor tower and the Chapelle tower, on the left the Bazinière, Bertaudière and Liberté towers. The two others, on the right the Corner tower, on the left the Wells tower, were hidden by the staff building. The first inner court was 102 feet by 72, the second, the Wells Court, 72 by 42. To get to one from the other one had to pass through the staff building, from one side to the other.

In the final years of the Bastille the main courtyard was the only one that the prisoners used, the Wells Court and the Wells and Corner towers were principally used by turnkeys, warders and the garrison. . . .

The towers, of various heights, were all round. . . . There were eight underground dungeons, two in the Bertandiére tower, two in the Liberté tower, and one each in the other four towers. The turnkeys stated in 1789 that for the past fifteen years nobody had been confined in those damp, unhealthy underground cells. The top storey of each tower was a domed gallery open to all the heat of summer. Reaching from dungeons to the gallery were stairs, with doors at intervals opening on to the single rooms on the various floors. These rooms were almost all octagonal. Some were good, others bad, but not one of them had more than one outer window, with triple bars. The chimney of each room was carefully barred throughout its length, and the doors were solid, with triple locks. There was no direct contact between one room and another, but an empty space, or drum. The towers contained altogether 37 usable rooms, not counting closets and cupboards. In the staff building there were five 'privilege' cells.

The thickness of the walls varied greatly. The lower parts were fifteen or more feet thick, the walls of the structure connecting the towers nine feet thick, and the towers themselves between five and seven feet thick. The highest tower was 73 feet high, usually shown in exaggerated perspective in old drawings of the Bastille. . . .

There is no doubt about it, this was an imposing building, but its chief features were its clumsiness and ugliness,* and the whiteness of the recent buildings in the outer yard and the teeming life round the shops there merely accentuated the grimness of the building."

Memoirists as a whole agree that the food in the Bastille was as a rule very good. "Three meals a day were served** in the

---

*The decision had in fact been taken to pull the Bastille down, and this would have followed in due course, had the Revolution not broken out. The Carnavalet Museum possesses a plan drawn in 1784 by the architect Corbet, Architect-Inspector of Paris City, giving his work an official character. He had designed a "Louis XVI Square" to take the place of the old fortress.

**At 7 a.m., at 11 a.m. and at 6 p.m.

rooms, and if the regularity with which the changes were rung had a distressing effect on some minds, the dishes were plentiful in number and quantity and the wine was drinkable. It might even be said that "the Bastille diet was too rich for the sedentary, confined life to which one was restricted". It ought however to be pointed out that though the diet was acceptable even at its worst, what was actually served depended on the prisoners' social rank, all laid down in a tariff of charges. Funck-Brentano informs us that the Governor received three *livres* a day for lower-class prisoners, five *livres* for members of the bourgeoisie, ten *livres* for a financier, a judge, or a man of letters; fifteen *livres* for a Councillor of the High Court and thirty-six *livres* for a Marshal of France. This allowance for keep, in exceptional cases (such as that of the Cardinal de Rohan), reached the enormous sum of one hundred and twenty *livres*. But the Marquis de Sade fell in another category of prisoners altogether—those imprisoned by *lettre de cachet* on the request of their families! There was no allowance for him. He was boarded by his family, and they paid 800 *livres* quarterly.

What were the arrangements for exercise? It could be taken either on the top of the towers, or in the first inner quadrangle. Thus on November 24th 1785 in addition to his evening hour in the quadrangle Sade was allowed to take the air for one hour on one of the towers. This however seems to have been a rare occurrence, and in the main his exercise was restricted to that evening hour in the courtyard. When, in his letter of March 8th 1784, he said that exercise meant more to him than food, he definitely complained about that restricted quadrangle in which all a man could breathe was the breath of the guardroom and the kitchen. "It is a quadrangle 106 feet in length," wrote Linguet in *Mémoires sur la Bastille*; "the walls enclosing it are over one hundred feet high, without any opening in them, so that to face it is no more than a deep well in which the cold in winter is unbearable, because it catches the cold north-east wind, while in summer the heat is just as unbearable, because as there is no draught through it, the sun makes a regular oven of it." As all walks were solo walks, with the escort of a warder, their frequency and duration depended on the number of prisoners and the availability of warders.

We own a list of the prisoners held in the Bastille between 1782 and 1789 to Alfred Bégis. There were on the average sixteen in any one year. In May 1788 the number rose to twenty-seven. This was the peak reached in those eight years. In December 1788 there were nine, and on July 14 only seven. On March 1st 1784—that is, the day after Sade's entry—there were no more than thirteen, which was two less than the number of warders in charge of them.

March 3rd 1784. Le Noir wrote to the Governor of the Bastille as follows : "Milord the Marquis de Beauvau, as well as Milords de Sade and de Solages, recently transferred from Vincennes Fortress to the Bastille, used there from time to time to be allowed to take exercise. I see nothing against this privilege still being accorded them, provided the customary precautions are taken."

March 8th 1784. The first letter from the prisoner of the Second Liberty : Sade informed his wife of the cruel conditions at the Bastille. It was much more severe than Vincennes. What was more, he had been allowed to bring nothing from Vincennes. He was "naked" and asked his wife to let him have clothing and prime necessities.

March 16th 1784. "Milady the *Marquise* de Sade came at four o'clock and stayed with Milord the Marquis, her husband, till seven, on a permit dated this day allowing her to see her husband twice monthly. She is to come again on the 27th. She brought him six pounds of candles."

April 29th 1784. Sade was allowed to have his books and other effects, sent from Vincennes on April 22th by de Rougement.

May 4th 1784. Lady de Sade told Gaufridy that she would not allow anybody to handle the Marquis' papers which had been left in a sealed chest at La Coste and asked the lawyer as a precaution against any infringement of this to place seals on the door of her husband's study. "The Marquis and his children are in reasonably good health. However, he constantly complains about his eye."

May 24th and June 7th 1784. Lady de Sade visited her husband.

July 16th 1784. Le Noir allowed Granjean the oculist to attend the Marquis.

September 12th 1784. Lady de Sade told Gaufridy that she was very put out, because the nuns at Sainte Aure had just taken her rooms, to turn them into more cells, and were giving her other accommodation "in the barn", which was "a wretched hole". How ironic it was, when she possessed three *châteaux* which were going to rack and ruin through being unoccupied! Yet she would put up with ten thousand such trials, if only her husband could obtain justice.

February 1785. Sade told his wife that he wanted neither letters nor outside visitors. True, he would very much like to see Reinaud, the Aix lawyer, who was passing through the capital. Yet on the other hand was it a good thing to let him see the wretched lot of his compatriot, with the possibility of his spreading the news in Provence of the "outrageous treatment" to which the Marquis de Sade was being submitted in the Bastille? So he would ask her not to send Reinaud to him. Yet there was one visit which it greatly incensed him not to have had—that of Le Noir. "Is it not a first duty of his to respond to the desires of a prisoner who has for days on end been demanding an interview with him? But Madame Jeanne's backside has quite turned the man's head, has it not? And far rather make much of the flabby c—— of a whore than give a suffering wretch any attention."*

March 17th 1785. Lady Montreuil wrote to tell Gaufridy that she was still of the same views regarding the detention of her son-in-law. He was of just as ebullient a temperament as ever and the only thing to do was to leave him where he was, because new scandals would certainly arise if he were set free. "This is a matter in which I do not think I need dabble any more, after having intervened so many times, and obtained it too, I mean freedom for him, out of kindness of heart for his wife who has had such good reason to regret it; you know what you know, *Monsieur,* and after that there is nothing to be said, only to make the best of it."

---

*Pamphlets published against police chief Le Noir do indeed charge him with buying the "unclean remnants of their charms rotted by debauch" by giving them his protection.

May 2nd 1785. Lady de Sade to Gaufridy : "My elder son has had measles. He has made a good recovery. His palate had to be slit, and he has been ill more than a month, but at last he has come through it and now it is only a question of patience, as he will be a long time convalescing."

May 24th 1785. Lady de Sade informed Gaufridy that "poor La Jeunesse" had died, after an illness of six weeks; "he was quite conscious to the end and passed away in great piety." The *Marquise* needed money. This illness had cost her a great deal and she owed still more. "Notwithstanding his short-comings," she wrote, "I was very sorry to lose him, for he was very loyal. I have not been able to bring myself to find somebody else and it will not be easy to do so."

June 16th 1785. Lady de Sade to Gaufridy : "I am ill; I no longer have poor La Jeunesse to write for me; my daughter is a real lazybones and cannot. Since I have had her with me I am more pleased with her, but it will need a lot of time to shape her, she has no natural gifts."

July 22nd 1785. Lady de Sade informed Gaufridy that the Marquis was still the same. "He cannot restrain his pen and that does him unbelievable harm; in addition it makes it impossible for me to see him and hear his news."

Towards August 1st 1785. Le Noir was replaced by de Crosne, as "lieutenant-general of police".

August 15th 1785. Cardinal de Rohan was imprisoned in the Bastille. The presence of this ecclesiastical dignitary stopped all private visits to prisoners.

October 22nd 1785. The Marquis began the final revision of his draft of his great work *120 Days of Sodom* or *The School for Libertines.**

November 12th 1785. In twenty evenings of work, from seven to ten, he completed one side of a twelve-metre (39 feet 4 inches long) roll of paper which he had had made for this purpose.

*In this diary only the few works of which Sade himself gave dates are mentioned. For a review of his literary activity in Vincennes prison and the Bastille see Chapter Thirteen.

November 28th 1785. Sade completed the famous manuscript of the *120 Days* in the form in which it has come down to us.

July 7th 1786. De Launay wrote to de Crosne :

"I have received the letter which you honoured me with regarding the request submitted by Lady de Sade.

It is true that when her husband first came here from Vincennes she had *Monsieur* Le Noir's permission to see him once weekly. But the prisoner, who is difficult and violent in the extreme, constantly made scenes, particularly one day when he refused to conform to the rule here which is to speak out loud.* And he attacked M. de Losne with the greatest violence. The police offices are full of letters packed with the most outrageous things about his wife, his family and ourselves. It was because of his bad conduct, which seemed to get worse after his wife's visits, that M. Le Noir considered it proper to deprive him of those visits, at least for some time. In my opinion, *Monsieur,* it would be a service to his wife and his family not to allow such permission more frequently than once a month. If he does not abuse the privilege, visits might possibly be made more frequent later. Since he has seen nobody his conduct has improved. Lady de Sade's kind heart and decency persuade her to ask to see him, but almost invariably all she gets is a torrent of insults and idiocies. The truth is that she fears for her life, were he one day to be set at liberty. This is my observation on the matter, with which the views of my staff coincide."

October 5th 1786. M. Gibert senior and M. Girard, notaries, called on the Marquis to get him to sign a power-of-attorney which his family wished to give, but he refused.

November 25th 1786. The Marquis was getting impatient. He had asked his wife for the answers to a series of questions about Spain and Portugal. He must now have been writing the novel

---

*Visits to prisoners at the Bastille as a rule took place in the Council Chamber with a prison officer present, but if the chief of police gave permission, could take place in the prisoner's cell "privately and without the presence of a prison officer," and this privilege was apparently allowed the Marquis after this.

Aline and Valcour, several episodes of which take place in those countries, and he had received no reply.

February 17th 1787. The *Marquise* visited her husband from 4 to 6 p.m.

February 26th, March 11th and 27th, April 10th and 23rd 1787. Lady de Sade visited her husband.

End of April 1787. The Commander de Sade, "Bailiff" of the Order of Malta, was appointed Grand Prior of Toulouse.

At about this time the Commander spent some time in the *Comtat,* getting to know his aunts and female cousins, then at La Coste, where his vassals gave him a joyous welcome with firing of mortars and cannon, after which the young knight set sail for Malta.

May 7th 1787. Lady de Sade visited her husband.

May 11th 1787. The Commander de Sade reached Malta on May 9th, to begin his formal receptions.

May 21st 1787. Lady de Sade visited her husband.

May 23rd 1787. The Marquis, who hitherto had been allowed only one hour's walk every other day, was allowed one hour daily on probation and seemed to be pleased by the concession.

May 25th 1787. Lady de Sade told Gaufridy that the Marquis was in fair health, but getting very fat.

June 4th 1787. Lady de Sade visited her husband.

June 18th 1787. Lady de Sade visited her husband.

June 21st 1787. Simple decree of the Châtelet court providing for administration of the property of the Marquis de Sade "absent for the past ten years".

July 8th 1787. Sade on this day completed the 138 pages of his philosophical story entitled *The Disabilities of Virtue,* begun a fortnight before this, and made the following marginal note on the last page : "My eyes troubled me much all the time I wrote this."

July 23rd and August 6th 1787. Lady de Sade visited her husband.

August 20th 1787. Lady de Sade spent two and a half hours with her husband. The same day, the Marquis received his wife's portrait, a miniature framed in tortoise-shell. He wrote at once to tell her what great delight "this precious, divine present" gave him, "the ever newly engendered sensations of which, in spite of malicious folk to the very last moment of my life will crown its thorns with ever fresh blossoms".... "I embrace you and will thank you still more warmly when I am able to take you into my arms : portrait and tortoise-shell together, the whole thing is exquisite, the whole thing delights me and affords me incredible pleasure."

October 1st 1787. Lady de Sade visited her husband.

October 10th 1787. Major de Losme-Salbray, who had on February 20th 1787 replaced Major Chevalier as Reversioner, reported to the chief of police :

"Sir,

I had the honour to inform you on the 7th inst. of the violent outburst of the Marquis de Sade when he insisted on being allowed his hour of exercise although he had been informed that certain business of the Bastille made this impossible. It was the moment when a prisoner was to arrive, and the Royal Lieutenant and I were present. I had to inform you yesterday of the unseemly and threatening tone which this prisoner assumed towards the Governor when he came with his Adjutant to inform him that, because of the representation he made that nothing should interfere with the hour of his exercise, Milord the Baron de Breteuil had withdrawn in his favour. I have nothing to add to my two letters on this subject except that he is afraid he will not be able to be visited by his spouse on Monday, though Milord the Governor seems to be inclined because of the persons concerned not to make any change without orders of the Minister or whatever you decide."

October 15th 1787. Lady de Sade and M. Demour, oculist, visited the Marquis.

October 23rd 1787. Right to exercise reaccorded the Marquis.

March 1st 1788. Sade began his story *Eugénie and Franval,* finishing this in six days.

June 5th 1788. Major de Losme-Salbray reported to the chief of police :

> "Sir,
>
> I have the honour to inform you that the Governor having given orders to suspend exercise of the Marquis de Sade I intimated this in writing and as precaution stationed a junior officer at his door, counting on his not regarding the order, which was what happened, for he tried to come down. It was only when the officer pointed his gun at him that he kept back, swearing volubly. . . .
>
> I beg, Sir, to remain
>
> Your very humble and obedient servant, De Losme."

June 15th 1788. Lady de Sade informed Gaufridy that she had just lost her maternal grandmother, Pélagie Partyet, widow of Lord Jean Masson de Plissay, at the age of ninety-two years, three months.

IN THE SIXTH LIBERTY

September 22nd 1788. "The Count de Sade having requested transfer to another room and to be in No. 6 in the same tower, the Governor granted the application."

October 1st 1788. Sade drew up an *explanatory catalogue*— the *Catalogue raisonné*—of his writings, which at this date amounted in volume to sufficient to fill fifteen octavo books, not including the clandestine manuscripts.

Early October 1788. The Marquis was granted a disabled man to do for him and run errands and tend him when ill. The prisoner asked his wife first for eight *louis,* then twenty more, to furnish his new cell. In particular he required coloured wall hangings and a "reliable" bed, "like my old camp bed".

October 20th 1788. Lady de Sade visited her husband.

October 22nd 1788. The *Marquise* wrote to Gaufridy. She had just learned that the Dauphin was ill, "so ill he cannot last long".

This was going to mean six months' mourning for the nobility. Lady de Sade would require a black outfit, all her black clothes being worn out, and her daughter too being without. For this reason the lawyer was requested to pack in a chest all the black gowns he could find at La Coste and send her, that would be cheaper than buying new clothes. She was in fairly good health, but found difficulty in walking and travel by carriage fatigued her.

October 28th, November 10th, December 19th and 22nd 1788. Lady de Sade visited her husband.

November 24th 1788. Report by Major de Losme to the chief of police :

> "Milord the Marquis de Sade was today visited by his wife. Since your letter arrived this prisoner has been enjoying one hour's exercise on the towers apart from his walk in the quadrangle. As for the permission which your letter granted to see his wife every week, he does not seem disposed to take advantage of it since I remarked to him that as he was now having more frequent visits they would be of the usual length of one hour though as far as that went he would be allowed to choose whether one hour every week or two hours every fortnight and he chose the latter, till his wife obtains more from you."

January 5th, 12th, 19th, February 3rd, 9th, 16th and 23rd, March 2nd, 9th, 16th, 22nd, 23rd and 30th, April 6th, 13th, 20th and 27th, May 4th, 11th and 18th, June 1st, 8th and 15th 1789, Lady de Sade visited her husband.

June 22nd 1789. Lady de Sade, bedridden, wrote to tell Gaufridy of the news that had reached her of the *Jeu de Paume* meeting and that the infuriated populace were crying that "those damn priests want stringing up" and even some bishops had been insulted.

July 2nd 1789. "A number of times the Count de Sade shouted from the window that the Bastille prisoners were being slaughtered and would people come and rescue him." Thus the brief note in the Bastille logbook under July 2nd 1789. We find a more detailed account of this event in a letter which de Launay wrote to Lord de Villedeuil, Minister of State, the following day:

> "I have the honour to inform you that being obliged by momentary circumstances to suspend taking exercise on the towers, which privilege you were kind enough to grant the Marquis de Sade, yesterday at midday he went to his window and at the top of his voice, so that he could be heard in the whole neighbourhood and by passers-by, yelled that he was being slaughtered, that the Bastille prisoners were being murdered, and would people come to their aid. He repeated his cries and vociferous complaints several times. This is a moment when it seems very dangerous to have this man here and where he will tend to be detrimental to good service. I feel it my duty, Sir, to suggest that it would be most advisable to transfer this prisoner to Charenton, or to some such establishment, where he could not disturb order, as he constantly does here. This would be a propitious moment for relieving ourselves of this person whom nothing can subdue and over whom no superior officer has any influence. It is out of the question to allow him exercise on the towers, the cannon are loaded and it would be most dangerous. The whole staff would be most obliged if you would accede to their wish to have the Marquis de Sade transferred elsewhere without delay.

> (signed) De Launay

> P.S. He had been told that he would not be able to walk on the towers, that he would have morning and evening exercise in the quadrangle, which he indeed was granted, but which did not satisfy him, and he threatens to shout again."

Here we may observe that on *Frimaire 6th, Year II,* on the eve of being imprisoned in the prisons of the Revolutionary régime for "moderatism", Sade asked the Minister of the Interior, Paré, to get him a copy of this letter, and presented it to the *Committee of General Safety and the Rule of the People* as "one of the finest testimonials of civic spirit that any Republican could offer".

A second account, which Manuel had from the lips of a

warder named Lossinote, gives us further details, particularly the bizarre episode of the stove-pipe used by the prisoner as a megaphone.

> "At a fixed hour the Marquis was allowed to walk on the towers. The disorders in Paris, which were increasing daily, compelled the Governor to take precautions, having the cannon loaded, and consequently putting the top of the towers out of bounds to all the prisoners. The Marquis was not satisfied with these reasons and lost his temper and threatened to make a terrible row if Lossinote did not bring back a favourable reply to a request which he asked him to take in that sense to the Governor. M. de Launay stuck to his refusal. Then the Marquis took a long tin-plate pipe at one end of which was a funnel, the whole having been fitted up to make it easier to drain water from the moat. With this as a sort of megaphone which he stuck up at his window which overlooked the *rue Saint Antoine* (he being in the so-called Liberty Tower) he yelled till he gathered quite a crowd then poured out vituperation of the Governor and called on the citizens to come to his aid as we meant to cut his throat. Furious, the Governor sent a runner to Versailles, obtained an order, and that very night the Marquis was transferred to Charenton."

On *6 Messidor, Year II*, in the statement on his own political conduct since 1789 made to the Committee of the People, Citizen Sade, detained at the time at Picpus, rather garnished his act of rebellion. He made out that he was outraged by the reinforcement of the garrison of the Bastille and said that during his walks he had not been afraid to talk to the soldiery. "I asked them if they would ever be infamous enough to fire on the people and being dissatisfied with their reply I resolved to prevent that act of treason to the people and through my window, using a tin-plate pipe, I warned the *rue Saint Antoine....*"

July 4th 1789. At 1 a.m., following the report on the Marquis' conduct sent to de Villedeuil on July 2nd, Sade was taken to Charenton by Police Inspector Quidor and Commissary Chénon sealed his cell at the Bastille.

How the Marquis was transferred we know from his own account, and with that let us conclude his five years in the Bastille : pistol in hand, six men tore him from his bed, scarcely allowed him time to dress, bundled him into a cab and took him off. He was allowed to take nothing with him. "Furniture, suits of clothes* and outfits of linen worth one hundred *louis,* six hundred books, some of them very expensive, and, irreparable loss, *Fifteen volumes of my own manuscript works,* all ready for the press, all these effects ... were sealed by the Bastille Commissioner and Lady de Sade dined, went to the closet, said her prayers and went to bed."

*"A number of suits all embroidered and adorned with gold and silver facings, and even with characters, which were found in the Bastille, belonged to the Marquis, but we do not know what use he made of them." (Manuel).

CHAPTER THIRTEEN

Posthumous and Unpublished Works Written in Vincennes Fortress and in the Bastille

IN THE ten months which preceded the storming of the Bastille a number of de Sade's major works began to stand out from the imposing mass of his manuscripts. These were the *Dialogue between a Priest and a Dying Man*, the *120 Days of Sodom*, *Aline and Valcour* and the first *Justine*, to which ought to be added the best of his stories, long and short.

It was towards 1780, when he was forty years old, that the prisoner of His Majesty's personal prisons began his enormous work as author. In this work Sade definitely found "salvation" and in course of time began to see that this was the purpose of his life. As Heine says, "Thus though well able to protect a family from the prodigality and wild living of its head, by results which could not have been foreseen, the King himself forged the instrument of a great philosophical work which was directed against himself and the whole of society, the most formidable weapon of war that materialism ever created to achieve the absolute liberation of man."

On October 1st 1788, in his Bastille cell, at the beginning of his one hundred and fortieth month of captivity in the fortresses of the French monarchy, the Marquis de Sade with justifiable pride drew up the annotated catalogue of what was already a considerable work, one which, taking account of the frightful conditions in which he built it up, was evidence in the author of a steadfastness of spirit which was quite extraordinary.

It is impossible to find a devotion to literary creation to match it in all the history of fine writing. In his catalogue, which was limited to works which he wished to sign publicly, thus excluding the clandestine texts of the *Dialogue* and the *120 Days,* Sade assembled the matter of fifteen octavo volumes, comprising two volumes of plays, five novels, four volumes of stories and four of sundry items (*Portfolio of a Man of Letters*).

With four of the five works listed in the Catalogue we shall have to deal separately. Because of the biographical circumstances of their publication consideration of *Justine* and *Aline and Valcour* must be left to the proper chronological place in our story (Chapter Sixteen), and the stories collected as *Crimes of Love* also come in there, while the plays will come under a separate heading of the present chapter. For the moment they will only be listed. It is the miscellaneous works of the *Portfolio* that we must now look at. But first, here is what Sade listed in his *Catalogue.*

A. Two volumes of plays.
B. *Aline and Valcour,* or *The Philosophical Novel.*
     (Four volumes).
C. *Justine,* or *The Misfortunes of Virtue.* (One volume).
D. *Stories Long and Short* (Four volumes).
E. *The Portfolio of a Man of Letters.* (Four volumes).

Here is the framework of the *Portfolio* : "Two sisters, one a cheerful flirt, the other a grave intellectual, leave Paris for the country, charging a friend who stays in Paris—a man—to provide them with entertainment in the country. The flirt promises her favours to the man of letters who can entertain her."

Only the first two volumes of this were ready, the others still being merely roughed out. Sade was not going to make the final draft till he had "tested the public taste" with the first two volumes.

Synopsis of Volume One. The "lighthearted letters" which provide the background include a love tangle, a dissertation on the death penalty, followed by a plan regarding the use to be made of criminals to keep them useful to the state, a letter on the dangers of lavish living, one on education, sixty-two reflections on morals and philosophy, an analysis and discussion of

Molière's comedies, a letter on novels, and a philosophical essay on the New World.

Synopsis of Volume Two. Likewise against a background of "lighthearted letters", one on the art of comedy writing, the plot of a verse comedy, fifty play-writing precepts, ninety features of the history of all countries interspersed with reflections and terminating in the massacres of Mérindol and Cabrières, one hundred and twelve examples of delightful repartee and sententious remarks, sixteen anecdotes and one dozen poems.

Synopsis of Volumes Three and Four. "Similar background letters between the same three characters," stories of French life from the establishment of the monarchy to the reign of Charles IX, inclusive, critical descriptions of Florence, Rome, Naples and their environment, a journey to Holland, twelve tales in verse, and some philosophical reflections.

Of this peculiar compound, in which that framework of the two sisters and the man of letters did little to conceal its hybrid nature, what fragments have reached us?

1. *A Reflection on God* (published by Maurice Heine), intended as part of the philosophical reflections.

2. Some philosophical reflections and unpublished literary jottings, together with the *Reflection on God* appear in the manuscript of the *Dialogue between a Priest and a Dying Man*.

3. The *Subject of Zélonide* (published by Maurice Heine), which is the plot of a comedy mentioned in the second volume.

4. Unpublished historical fragments, one of these being the rough draft of *The Mérindol Massacre,* which is in ms. 12456 of the Bastille Archives, now in the *Arsenal* library.

5. Eleven *Anecdotes (Historiettes)* Published in 1926 by Maurice Heine out of the sixteen listed as in the second volume (five of them have never been found).

6. Some unpublished poems from the manuscript entitled *Miscellaneous Works** which Sade no doubt included in the *Portfolio.*

*It was in 1949 that the author had the good luck to find this precious manuscript, fair-copied between 1764 and 1769. Sade went to the trouble of having it bound in calf, like a book. The marking of this Vol. I in gilt on the spine makes it clear that there was to have been at least one other volume.

7. Unpublished matter of the *Critical and Philosophical Descriptions of Florence, Rome etc.*, in some forty notebooks of varying size. These notebooks, some in Sade's hand, others in another, contain little more than brief descriptions of notable public buildings, statuary and pictures, mostly copied out of Italian works and supplied to the author by Dr Mesny, of Florence, and Dr Giuseppe Oberti, of Rome.

8. The unpublished *Journey to Holland*, written variously in Brussels, Antwerp, Rotterdam and The Hague, in the form of letters addressed to a lady between September 25th and October 23rd 1769. It appears in the manuscript entitled *Miscellaneous*.

9. Finally, of the *Portfolio* we have the draft *Foreword*, published for the first time in the French original of this work, a piece which shows a certain philosophical boldness, for all that there is a list of titles which at first sight would suggest only the most ordinary contents.*

* * *

In Sade's literary production during these years in Vincennes and the Bastille which has either been lost or destroyed should be included the *Diary* mentioned by Michaud in his *Universal Biography* as one of the author's manuscripts which remained in the possession of his descendants. According to Michaud, out of thirteen volumes of this diary running between February 1777 and April 1790, the first (1777-1781) and the twelfth (1789) were missing. Part of the work was in cypher. It was no doubt on the basis of this diary that Sade later wrote the *Confessions* which have also been lost and allegedly referred to his periods of captivity in the phrase : "The intervals between the acts of my life have been too long."

DRAMA

While the letters which Sade wrote during his long captivity abound in requests for plays and allusions to his own comedies,

---

*Since we are here concerned with Sade's literary activity in Vincennes and the Bastille, mention should also be made of the *Philosophical New Year's Gift* addressed to Mlle de Rousset, published for the first time by P. Bourdin. This charming, lively little work dates from January 26th 1782. It really merits separate publication. It is of considerable interest, since it shows that Sade's philosophical outlook was already clearly formed in his mind by that date.

the catalogue of 1788 still more clearly reveals his special attachment to dramatic literature, for the thirty-five acts of which at this point he was the author take the place of honour, at the head of his works, and in the analysis of the *Portfolio of a Man of Letters* we read of three didactic works on the theatre. As we have seen, the Marquis had his own private theatre at La Coste, where in January 1772 he put on a play of his own, while eight years previously he organised a society theatre at Évry *Château,* the residence of one of his wife's uncles. In 1791 he spoke of himself as being "buried in his study, surrounded by Molière, Destouches, Marivaux, Boissy and Regnard, whom he was examining, contemplating, marvelling at, but never completely grasping."

As we shall see below, Sade made tremendous effort to get his plays put on during the Revolution, and the melancholy of his declining years was somewhat lessened by performance of some of them in the Charenton Asylum of which he was made an inmate. Here at last his plays had their audience....

In his heyday and his old age alike he looked, with great naïvety, upon play-writing as his *forte.* Look at what he wrote to his old master, the Abbé Amblet, in 1784: "I simply cannot resist my inspiration; it leads me up that line of life despite my will, and whatever anybody does I cannot be turned aside from it. In my portfolio I have more plays than many of the boasted authors of our time and more than twice as many on the stocks. Had I been given the peace, I would have had fifteen comedies ready when I came out of prison. They thought it the more handsome way to mock me, but it is the future which will show my executioners whether they were right or wrong."

By the evidence we now possess, the Marquis de Sade was the author of seventeen plays.* It seems unlikely that he wrote more, for the truth is that all that he wrote in this form was so humdrum that neither his family nor the authorities thought it worth consigning to judicial flames.

Of these seventeen plays, only one has ever been published —*Oxtiern* or *The Misfortunes of a Rake's Way of Life,* which appeared in the Year VIII. Here is a list of the others:

*In this account *La Ruse d'Amour,* a crude compound of five one-act plays, has been treated as one play.

A. A one-act prose comedy, *le Philosophe soi-disant*, which is included in the manuscript *Miscellaneous Works* (1763-1769), but which the author did not include among his plays in 1788;

B. Eight plays written in Vincennes and the Bastille between 1780 and 1788, part of the Marquis Xavier de Sade's collection;

C. Two plays written in the same period, but since lost, one entitled *l'Égarement de l'Infortune* (in prose, three acts, written in Vincennes some time before 1781) and *Tancrède*, a "lyric piece", of which a few lines of verse remain;

D. Four plays written during the Revolution, or in Charenton Asylum, now part of the collection of the Marquis Xavier : *les Antiquaires,* a prose comedy in three acts; *Franchise et Trahison* and *Fanny ou les Effets du Désespoir,* prose plays in three acts; *Les Fêtes de l'amitié,* which "included a prologue and a vaudeville play entitled *Hommage de la reconnaissance,* the whole comprising two acts, with a mingling of prose, verse and Vaudeville";

E. A three-act prose play, *Cléontine ou la Fille malheureuse,* written either during the Revolution or in Charenton Asylum, but lost, as well as an earlier one-act version of the same.

Thus we have eight dramatic works dating from Vincennes and Bastille days, still unpublished. It must however be bluntly stated that here we are in a realm in which one never ceases marvelling—how could the author of *Aline et Valcour* and *Justine,* the least preparatory fragment of which is eloquent of the brilliance of the hand that traced it, how could he have contrived to remain so invariably mediocre in this other form? For reading Sade's plays serves marvellously to reveal the merits of such minor dramatists as Boissy, Barthe or Saurin. Such plays as *Les Dehors trompeurs* and *Les Fausses Infidelités* become masterpieces in comparison with Sade's. Nevertheless, let us give a brief glance at each in turn :

1. Henriette et Saint Clair

The title in the 1788 catalogue is longer : *Henriette et Saint Clair ou la Voix de la Nature*—"Henriette and St Clair or the Voice of Nature", though finally the "Voice of Nature" turned into the "Voice of the Blood". Written in Vincennes before 1781, this play is about incestuous love, which however remains chaste, between a brother and sister ignorant of their parentage. Written in the cloying sentimental vein of the worst of Diderot, it is far removed indeed from the powerful boldness of Sade's novels.

2. *Les Deux Jumelles (The Twin Girls).*

This title was ultimately expanded by the addition of "Or a Difficult Choice". A one-act piece in verse, composed in Vincennes before 1781. This is one of Sade's most insignificant works and needs only be mentioned. Even he himself realised how poor it was, despite his blindness regarding his own dramatic sense, for on April 26th 1781 he wrote to his wife to ask her not to judge *l'Inconstant* (become *Le Capricieux*) by *Les Deux Jumelles.*

3. *Le Capricieux*

In letters from Vincennes this play is called *l'Inconstant.* It is a five-act comedy in alexandrines, headed by a four-line epigraph :

> *He will, he won't, he grants, rejects,*
> *Guided by hate and prompted by love,*
> *Promises, withdraws, condemns, excuses*
> *What pleases now, displeases next.*

On the final page, copied by La Jeunesse, but with important corrections in Sade's hand, the author painstakingly noted the various stages of composition: "This play was begun on December 24th 1780, the draft was completed January 8th 1781 and the work completed in the evening of January 24th. It had taken exactly one month to work out and was then corrected between January 24th and April 5th of the same year and between April 5th and 14th clear copied. Which makes six weeks of work in all. It then contained eighteen hundred and eighty lines of verse." Further, on the stuck-in reverse of page one of the cover there are two further notes which show the interest which Sade still took in the comedy : "Good, revised and corrected in August 1803" and "Read and corrected for the last time June 6th and 7th, 1811."

In the 1788 Catalogue this play appears with a new title : change into *l'Homme inégal* and finally become *le Capricieux.*

The second manuscript of this play is the work of an unknown copyist. It includes a long preface written at Charenton in which Sade outlines his ideas on comedy as a form and tries to bring out the difference between the character of his hero, who, he thinks, is "absolutely new" and that of Destouches' *l'Irrésolu* (performed in 1713). "The undecided character is one who can make up his mind on nothing, the capricious, one who cannot stick to his decision; one both desires and does not desire, the other desires, then ceases to do so. Destouches' Le Dorante is only incidentally capricious, because indecision is the daughter of caprice, whereas the Marquis de Fonrose is capricious by taste, habitually so . . . It was not at all easy to make such a person interesting, for he tends more to irritate than entertain us, so all the interest had to be transferred to those whom he lets down and those who show him to be what he is."

In 1795 Citizen D. A. F. Sade drew up a leaflet intended to whet the appetite of the theatre managers of Bordeaux, Toulouse, Lyons, Besançon, Rouen, Caen and Rennes and outlined the fine qualities of the thirty-five acts of which he was the author, and here *le Capricieux,* at the time known as *l'Homme inégal,* was brought to the benevolent notice of the theatre managers in the following terms : "A comedy of character, this play offers three fine characters; the changeable man himself is very vigorously depicted, the character contrasts are excellent and the versification of a fine finish. It was accepted at the *Théâtre Français* subject to correction, and the corrections have been introduced into it."

Alas, we are obliged to point out that despite the praise which the Marquis lavished on his play, the characters are dismal automata and in spite of the patient toil given it the versification is muddled and unmelodious.

Writing to the Abbé Amblet towards the end of April 1784, the Marquis remarked what great delight he would experience, were his plays to be performed in Paris. "The reputation for it which I would acquire would perhaps cast to oblivion the setbacks of youth and would in a sense rehabilitate me, occupying my mind and making me lose sight of all else."

4. Le Prévaricateur

Writing to his wife on March 18th 1783, Sade begged her not to delay in acknowledging receipt of a manuscript which he had sent her. The letter incidentally shows that by this time he already had this play and also *l'Inconstant, l'Égarement de l'Infortune, Henriette et Saint Clair* and *Les Deux Jumelles* in his portfolio. This new play, *la Double Épreuve ou le Prévaricateur,* was after 1789 to be known as *Le Prévaricateur ou le Magistrat du temps passé.* Sade's leaflet sent to the theatre managers gave the following indications : "A four-act comedy in hexameters, this play depicts the foibles and evils of the old magistrature, and is to the gentry of the long robe of the old régime what *Tartuffe* was to pious hypocrites. It is entertaining, the leading part stands out, and there are pleasing details. The *Théâtre Louvois* accepted it while this was performing serious plays, but I withdrew it when I learned that the manager did not pay anyone."

The author took care not to mention that the Reading Committee of the *Théâtre Français* had rejected it on February 28th 1791.

On November 7th 1791 the *Marais Theatre* also rejected the play.

It is hard indeed to believe that this is the work of the man who wrote letters to Carteron which so magnificently combined boisterous humour and lucid moralising. However, there is a passage which is perhaps worth quoting. At first glance it would seem to be ascribing to Shakespeare Sade's ideas on the novel. It is however not praise but satire in question, and once again we realise how absolutely infantile Sade's mind was as soon as it turned to the theatre :

"In the wise man's eyes rule is the death of pleasure.
Imitate Shakespeare and you will be sublime.
Show us the victim sobbing on the scaffold;
Before our English gaze rip his side open,
Let us hear his cries, make his blood gush out,
In frightful dungeons, in utter darkness
Hang daggers and funeral lanterns
By strips of flesh or on piles of corpses . . .
There you have the swift springs of great talent.
I shall soon be like that wonderful model
And my workshop at this moment contains
A character who raises me to the level of my model. . . ."

5. Jeanne Laisné

This is Sade's only tragedy. He did indeed "sketch out" a *François I* and in a letter in February 1784 declared flatly that this was going to be a "sublime piece". But it was never written.

Completed in 1783, *Jeanne Laisné* is taken from history. "The Women defending Beauvais under Louis XI who made Charles the Bold raise the Siege." There is the known letter of Sade's written to the *Journal de Paris* on July 21st 1798 in which he claimed the honour of having been the first to discover in the Beauvais archives that the heroine was not Jeanne Hachette. The claim is supported by letters patent of Louis XI and historical notes. An epigraph evinced the author's patriotic intention : "Let us carefully note these various cases and may they one day prove to the world that loyalty, the sense of glory and valour were always the virtues of France."

After such an effusion it is not surprising to learn that, while in the Bastille, the Marquis obtained permission to recite his tragedy to the Fortress staff assembled in his cell. This we learn from a note of 1813, which further informs us that there was a first reading at the Governor's mistress's apartment, in the presence of the actors Saint Prix and Saint Phal. However, it was a better qualified audience which the author managed to assemble some years later. It was November 24th 1791 when thanks to the support of Mlle Raucourt, Sade gave a reading of *Jeanne Laisné* before the Committee of the *Théâtre Français*. But they turned it down by eight against five, and even three of those five wanted "corrections" made. It was in vain that nine years after this Sade tried to get Goupillard de Montaigu, a member of the Convention, to support his tragedy. "I am offering you a tragedy . . . a work which will stir patriotic emotions in the heart of every man," he wrote.

Sade never tired of hoping that his play would have the same success as De Belloy's *Siège de Calais,* for which the King gave the author a gold medal and a nice little sum, and only a year before his death Sade once again put the tragedy before the men of the *Théâtre Français*. Alas, once again they rejected it, and the report, dated February 28th 1814, was cruelly frank. They pulled the play to pieces. This is hardly surprising. One really must admit that in all the dramatic literature of the eighteenth century, so rich in mediocrity, it would be difficult to find a play as clumsily put together, as dull, or as platitudinously written as this.

6. *Le Boudoir ou Le Mari Crédule*

This was a one-act comedy which Sade—so his Catalogue tells us—intended to be given after the tragedy. A copy of the play was seized by Le Noir, the police chief. It was originally called *Le Mari crédule ou la Folle Épreuve*. Sade first turned it into *l'Ecole des Jaloux ou la Folle Épreuve,* then in the *Year III,* into the definitive title. In blank verse, it was rejected by the *Théâtre Français* on August 25th 1790 and the *Feydeau Theatre* on 22 *Prairial, Year III.* Is the manuscript of which we now possess a fair copy in La Jeunesse's calligraphy, with the author's corrections, the one which the Marquis submitted to that delightful actress Julie Candeille, famous for her beauty and also for her histrionic gifts—who inspired Sade with passionate desire?

Julie wrote the Marquis this little note :

"The little play entitled *le Boudoir* is pleasantly written, but I doubt whether the subject, in itself rather free, is capable of being dealt with on the stage without some risk. We all know that a crowd is far more severe about the morals shown them than they would be as individuals. I doubt whether they would stand for Mme d'Olcour's *course of morals,* and I urge the author to exercise his gifts on some other subject.

J-ie Candeille."

This note is most astonishing. One seeks in vain for any reason for such alarm in the comedy concerned. The ten scenes of the *Boudoir* are far removed indeed from the "philosophy" which at this stage Sade had just published under the same title and signed as "the author of *Justine*".

In the play, d'Olcour, "a personality in the realm of high finance", has chosen to frown on the frequent meetings taking place between his young wife and her cousin, "sprightly" Sérigny. Lucile, Madame's maid, tries to reassure him. The couple, she says, only meet in the *boudoir* to indulge in a mutual "course of morals". But however much one studies the play, it is impossible to establish whether Mme d'Olcour is or is not

Sérigny's mistress. All that takes place between them is the most trifling flirtation. D'Olcour decides to hide behind a big armchair, to hear what their morals are about. But the flirtatious wife is tipped off by Lucile and loses no time telling Sérigny. After the discussion on morals, d'Olcour emerges from his hiding-place, flings himself down on his knees, and implores his wife's forgiveness for his unjustified jealousy. This feeble stuff is what the author of *Justine* chose to claim as the most solid monument to his fame in the years to come!

As it is most unlikely that Sade's dramatic works will ever appear in book form (and we must confess that we certainly should not recommend such a publication, which could add nothing to his reputation) at one time the author did toy with the idea of publishing just one of Sade's plays, for the edification of enthusiasts, and choice had fallen on the *Boudoir*—because it was so short. But now that one Sade play has appeared, the author lacks the temerity to add another, let alone one so ridiculous, as far removed from a Marivaux as a cheap chocolate-box picture from a Watteau.

7. Sophie et Desfrancs

So it stands in the 1788 Catalogue. In the final version it became *le Misanthrope par amour ou Sophie et Desfrancs*. It was a blank-verse comedy in five acts. "With extracts showing the action it was accepted by the *Comédie Française* unanimously on September 16th 1790, after five years repeated offering." But it was never performed. Whether it was written at Vincennes or the Bastille we do not know. There is however a detailed outline of a first version entitled *Sujet de Zélonide* with Sade's note: "Completed July 12th 1782." This mere outline, published by Heine, contains all Sade's free fantasy and is of incomparably greater value than the finished comedy, cramped as this is in the cast-iron stays of the classical conception of a play, so far removed from Sade's own wild, vigorous fantasy.

8. La Ruse d'Amour ou les Six Spectacles.

This was an "episodic comedy in six thousand lines of verse of various measures and of prose, lasting five hours in performance". Originally it contained five one-act plays—*Euphémie de Melun ou le Siège d'Alger*, tragedy, *le Suborneur*, comedy, *la Fille malheureuse,* drama, *Azélis ou la Coquette punie,* comedy-pantomime, *la Tour enchantée,* comic opera, and as final entertainment piece a *pantomime ballet.* The manuscript which has come down to us, entitled *l'Union des Arts ou les Fuses de l'amour,* contains neither *la Fille malheureuse** or *la Tour mysteriéuse,* of which there is a separate manuscript, and is in any case the subject matter of a new addition to *les Crimes de l'amour.*

Accepted in 1791 by the *Théâtre de la rue de Bondy, Azélis* seems never to have been performed.

Le Suborneur, the manuscript of which bears another title, *l'Homme dangereux,* was accepted by the Italian theatre on August 3rd 1790. There were rehearsals on January 24th, February 3rd and March 3rd 1792. It was performed on March 5th and killed after the first few exchanges of dialogue by the hissing of the Jacobine faction, solely because it was the work of a *ci-devant,* an ex-noble. But the truth is that it merited no better fate. We shall however return—for other reasons—to that stormy performance, in Chapter Sixteen.

9. *Appendix: Tancrède (a lost work)*

Tancrède must have been completed some time in January 1784, for at this time Sade told Lady de Sade that he was awaiting her opinion on the play. It was a lyric scene in one act of hexameters combined with music, the subject drawn from Tasso. But all that has remained is a dozen lines which the author quoted in an unpublished letter to the Abbé Amblet. Sade was replying to his former tutor's criticism.

At the close of the same letter there is a most interesting reference. " ... she [i.e., Lady Montreuil] lives in constant fear of my putting her into a play. Let her mind be at rest. Calibans are Shakespeare's job. They don't come off on the French stage." When we recall the passage we have quoted above from the *Prévaricateur* and the reminiscence of the *Merchant of Venice* which *le Carillon de Vincennes* contains, we can have little doubt but that Sade was familiar with Shakespeare's works, no doubt in La Place's translation, published in 1746.

It was pointed out at the beginning of this chapter that

*The manuscript of this is lost, just as is that of the three-act version entitled *Cléontine ou la Fille malheureuse.*

examination of Sade's dramatic works is not calculated to add to his literary glory. The fact is, Sade's dramas were never on the stage, but merely in his self-created conception of his brilliance as dramatic author. We feel the greater regrets at this failure since it is Sade's dialogue that is one of the strongest points in his novels. One needs take only his story *Augustine de Villeblanche,* for example. Without any major alteration or suppression, the parts which are not dialogue being given to a new character—a sort of narrator—this story could be cut down into a most disturbing little one-act piece of real character.

CORRESPONDENCE :

THE EAGLE, MADEMOISELLE . . . LE CARILLON DE VINCENNES, MONSIEUR NO. 6

A voice supreme in sense and delirium : that lashing, comminatory voice of the Marquis de Sade.

The invaluable bundle of letters which the author had the supreme good fortune to discover in January 1948, in the *château* of Condé-en-Brie, residence of the direct descendant of the Marquis de Sade, revealed a completely new aspect, or at least one hitherto difficult to glimpse, of the literary gifts of the author of *Justine*. It consists of one hundred and seventy-nine letters, to which may be added lists of things ordered, notes and receipts, bringing the total number of pieces up to about two hundred and fifty. They classify as follows :

(a) Forty-two letters written from Vincennes prison between February 1777 and June 1778;

(b) One hundred and twenty letters written from Vincennes between September 1778 and February 1784, after a period of liberty lasting some weeks;

(c) Seventeen letters written from the Bastille between February 1784 and September 1785.

Three-quarters of these letters are to his wife, the others in order of frequency being to Lady Montreuil, Mlle de Rousset, police chief Le Noir, Sade's valet Carteron *alias* La Jeunesse *alias* Martin Quiros, notary Gaufridy, the Abbé Amblet, police commissary Martin, Commandant de Rougement, Grandjean the oculist, and his eldest son, young Donatien Claude Armand de Sade.

Of these one hundred and seventy nine letters, at the moment of writing ninety-one have been published by the author, in three collections, bearing the following titles: *The Eagle, Mademoiselle; The Vincennes Carillon;* and (edited with the help of M. Georges Daumas), *Monsieur No. 6.*

Most of these letters of Sade's are not dated, or merely bear the day, but not the name, of the month. Careful cross-checking in most cases nevertheless enables us to assign fairly precise dates to them all. Most of them consist of one double sheet covered with close-packed lines of writing on both sides. The calligraphy is invariably of extreme elegance. The longest letter, however, is of sixteen pages, while some have only two.

Sade clearly wrote letters without a preliminary draft, just as his despair, his indignation or his tragic humour dictated. There are very rare erasions and often none at all. Four or five letters stand out from all the others in the moving roughness and clumsiness of the writing—for instance, Nos. 36, 37 and 38 of *Monsieur No. 6.* They belong to one of those periods of acute eye trouble, of which Sade experienced the first attacks in February 1783.

To these letters should be joined an unpublished bundle of some thirty letters which Lady de Sade wrote the prisoner at Vincennes. (A number of these have been quoted or sum-marised in chapters ten, eleven and twelve of this work.)

The absence of any least common measure between Sade's letters, which are real Shakespearean monologues, and the great epistolary classics, even at their most brilliant, is such as to strike any reader so vividly that we thought it proper to head each of our published volumes of them with a title suggestive of the exceptional nature of Sade's correspondence. *The Eagle, Mademoiselle* are the three first words of a letter to Mlle de Rous-set. The choice seemed inevitable to the author, so beautiful and so unusual did the words sound, making a title of quite heraldic significance. The title of the second collection finds justification in the following: "Since a prisoner always takes everything to himself and invariably imagines that everything that is done concerns him, that everything said has a meaning, I did not need to ferret deep in my mind to discover that those accursed chimes were talking to me and saying—and very clearly, too: *'Sorry for you, sorry for you/now there's no more ending for you/but dust to dust/but dust to dust'."* And *Monsieur No. 6* is of course Sade himself, suggested by that passage in a letter which has already been quoted, in which Sade said that he would have cured No. 6 in a different way, with so many wenches that they would have used up all his energies!

Most of Sade's letters published prior to these three collections—principally those which Paul Bourdin published—belong to the period between Sade's leaving Charenton, April 2nd 1790, as a result of the Decree of the Constituent Assembly regarding persons imprisoned by *lettre de cachet,* and his imprisonment in *Sainte Pélagie* prison on April 5th 1801 by the police of the First Consul. His twelve years in Vincennes and the Bastille (1777-1789) were represented solely by four letters in Bourdin's collection and the letter of October 4th 1779 to Martin Quiros published by Maurice Heine (one need only make cursory mention of the confused fragments quoted by Jean Desbordes "which even their progenitor would not recognise"). But it is precisely the first nine of those twelve years to which the letters discovered at Condé-en-Brie *château* belong —twelve years of tribulation when his enemies had "swallowed him up alive"—at the height of his powers, in the prime of life, with an erotic imagination which had been fed on intoxicating experience—buried first in one then in the other of the two most sinister of the living tombs of the French monarchy.

The letters which Paul Bourdin has published are of vital interest both regarding the attitudes assumed by Sade during the Revolution and what he did, and for the high literary quality of some of them. But they are almost all letters to his lawyer, Gaufridy, which means that requests for money and discussion of property worries take first place. And for all Sade's weakness for this man with whom he had played as a boy, Sade rarely enough felt he could confide any really intimate thought to him. It had not been long before he discovered to what extent Gaufridy had been Lady de Montreuil's secret agent— since 1775, indeed—and uninterruptedly from then up to the Revolution.

Those letters which the author has now been able to publish breathe a different atmosphere altogether. They were almost all of them letters to the only person whose profound devotion, a devotion which showed great courage, Sade had experienced through thick and thin—his wife. The bitter irony and the attacks of real fury to which Sade was provoked by the slightest frustration of his wishes should never be allowed to deceive us either as to Lady de Sade's part in it all or what his feelings for her really were. Despite all his reproaches and that never-dormant suspicion of his—though perhaps some of the manifestations of this were a deliberate attempt to spur her to greater efforts towards securing his release—he could never lose sight of the fact that his wife's whole existence was now based on securing his release from prison and that to achieve this she would shrink from nothing. She never once ceased to bombard the Royal ministries with the most moving pleas. The result was that, as far as he could hope his letters might escape police censorship or his mother-in-law's unjustified interference, he never hesitated to open his heart to Lady de Sade, even to the point of confiding his most inmost desires to her, ever confident that this woman from whom he had had such clear proof of devotion could never stir a finger against him.

* * *

Vincennes Fortress is a monstrous tomb, flanked by four towers. A spiral staircase leads to a tortured life. The cells are heartbreakingly grim. They are small in area, disproportionately high, and set in eternal twilight, since their narrow windows can only let in light past a double set of iron bars. It was in the heart of that awful tomb, in one of these icy cylinders, that the Marquis de Sade wrote these letters, which reach such heights of eloquence and of imagination. The only works that will bear comparison with them, in these respects, are the works of Shakespeare himself.

What fills one with admiration at the very first reading is that after the first rage and despair of their author in the first months of detention had died down he could offer such a magnificent lesson of steadfastness. On the one hand we have an unbroken adherence to the ideas which had earned him this solitary confinement. On the other we have the development of a superb sense of humour which was at once the most courageous and no doubt the most efficacious defence a human being could find against the aggression of the world without.

Never for a moment did Sade consent to deny any trait of his mentality, of his conception of morals, his philosophy of life, despite the obvious risk that such stubbornness would imperil his hopes of liberation. "Impérieux, colère, emporté, extrême en tout, d'un dérèglement d'imagination sur les moeurs qui de la vie n'a eu son pareil, athée jusqu'au fanatisme, en deux mots me voilà, et, encore un coup, tuez-moi ou prenez-moi comme cela, car je ne changerai pas." That is how he put it himself.* And one can find a score of other declarations of the same sort in the letters of this indomitable captive. For instance : "My way of thought is the fruit of my own thinking; it is dependent on my being, on the way I am built. I have not the power to change it, but even if I had, I would not. This way of thought which you criticise is the only solace of my life; it alleviates all my trials in prison, it constitutes my every pleasure in this world and I cling to it more than to life itself. It is not my way of thinking that has brought about my misfortune, but that of others." If in his *Prière du soir*—"evening prayer" —Sade pretends to turn to that creator of the world of whom he had always "denied the usefulness and hence the existence", it was in an attempt for once to reduce his persecutors by turning their own weapons against them. At the same time in this "prayer", so grandly expressive of his awareness of his lofty role and unprecedented isolation, Donatien Alphonse François's appeal to a superior instance which he called "god" should not be ignored. In this place that instance may well be poetry itself. Or rather, in a period in which the very notion was unfamiliar, it was a cry torn from him telling of an avenging truth before which those unreal prisons of man would be shattered and his own primordial sword restored to him, endowing him with the most transcendental powers.

We have referred above to the essential part which humour plays in the unpublished correspondence of this man. To resume the thread of our thought, it has always been our view that in the hierarchy of our feelings tears are more beautiful than laughter. The Count de Lautréamont supported that preference when in the fourth canto of his *Maldoror* he cried: "Oh, what awful abasement it is ! When we laugh we look just like goats." Yet laughter can on occasion attain the beauty of

*For translation, see p. 256.

tears, and that is when it is in the form of a humour that transcends all else as it becomes an expression of human courage. "Humour," Freud has put it, "has in it not only a liberating quality ... but also a quality of sublimity.... The invulnerability of the ego ... finds triumphant expression in it. The ego refuses to let itself be impaired, to be made to suffer by exterior realities, it refuses to admit that the traumata of the outer world can affect it and, what is more, it makes it manifest that those traumata can even provide it with pleasure."*

The genius of Sade's response exactly fits this definition of Freud's and his letters offer us the most modern aspects of that *humeur noir*—that "black humour"—of which André Breton's anthology under that title included many instances.

Lautréamont, Jarry, Nietzsche—those are the names which come to our lips when we glance through Sade's letters for the first time. What an unparalleled delight it is to picture the stupefaction of those to whom Sade addressed these letters when they saw the contents, which so boldly flouted all their concepts of life. We have already noticed how on January 1st 1779 Mlle de Rousset apologised to Gaufridy for not telling him all she had received from Vincennes ... " ... it would be too long to copy out for you all the Marquis' letters and in them side by side with the profoundest gloom you would find too much that was frivolous...." On every page Sade proves himself a century before his time, both in the way he dresses outer reality and in his manner of turning things upside-down, utterly strange to the eighteenth century. "Your mother must be either *tipsy* or *stark raving mad* to risk her daughter's life to form a *19* and *6* or *16* and *9* and not to tire of it these past twelve years. Oh what a dyspepsia of figures that foul termagant has! I am convinced that were she to have died before this eruption and been opened up, millions of figures would have gushed out of her entrails."

One of the major "discoveries" of the Count de Lautréamont was the introduction into an ordinary piece of literary prose of disjointed fragments of phrases drawn from works of medicine or the natural sciences. Now, in Sade's letters we find precisely the same surprise device, which was in due course to be

---

*Need one point out that the pleasure of which Freud spoke here should in no way be taken to refer to any sort of masochistic pleasure.

one of the principal tricks of the surrealist manner. "The restricted capacity of my little brain," Sade wrote to his wife "somehow refuses to accommodate the notion that the mere act of asking for a case should excite those nerves which in you carry the sensation of pain to the mind. You say you are considered crazy. But that is just what I do not grasp, for I cannot admit that a *little* woman asking for a *big* case should provoke any disorder in the pineal gland where we atheistic philosophers find the seat of ratiocination."

All the disturbing gravity of Mervyn's father, the Commodore, seems already to have been contained in that passage in the tenth letter of *The Eagle, Mademoiselle* concerning Lady de Sade's manner of dressing, but the Marquis' comminatory cursing is none the less most moving, for the source of it was his tragic acquaintanceship with jealousy.

What comment should one make concerning that puzzling appearance in 1784 of a female Ubu in the form of "Lady President Cordier" with her "sublime reasoning"? The dialogue form of the beginning of this letter and the presence in it of a dummy in the form of the Major of the Bastille add up to a resemblance which does equal honour to the Marquis de Sade and Alfred Jarry.

Again, in the seventeenth letter of *The Eagle, Mademoiselle,* which might well be entitled the "Poem of the Signs" Sade seems to have adumbrated—and certainly in sheer rhetoric surpassed—that letter of Frederic Nietzsche's of January 4th 1889, which André Breton characterised as the "supreme lyrical explosion" of the philosopher. Is it going too far under the thundery skies of Sade's letter, to see all that Nietzsche tried to do, even with "that semblance of euphória", that enterprise which Breton defined in the following terms : "Pessimism presented as a form of goodwill, death as a form of freedom, sexual love as the ideal realisation of the unity of opposites?"

In numerous other places in Sade's letters we find passages, or even whole letters which, if not exactly meriting the modern definition of "black humour" (at least, not in themselves, though the fact that Sade could write so at all during his terrible imprisonment might well be considered to earn them that definition), nevertheless belong to a superior order of wit, with an element of the lyric in it, at times certainly suggestive of certain pages of Aristophanes and Shakespeare. To our definition of this kind of humour, which might be called *sunshine humour,* to make it quite clear that it has nothing in common with the lower forms of laughter, that is, laughter considered as an end in itself, we can add a general observation which would seem to throw a new light on Sade's major erotic novels : those of Sade's letters whch derive from this unexpected form of his genius suggest an element of transcendental trickery which *La Nouvelle Justine* and *Juliette* both contain, though—need it be said—not at all to the detriment of the marvellous compound of lyricism and descriptive psycho-pathology which those two works offer us.

The discovery of Sade's letters, unique of their kind in any language, constituted no less remarkable a revelation than the discovery at the beginning of this century of the roll containing the *120 Days of Sodom.* It is without question that in our day Sade's great novels have earned him a fame for their very language which very few French writers have merited. But despite the erotic daring of their vocabulary and despite the unequalled subversiveness of their substance, *La Nouvelle Justine* and *Juliette* do still adhere to a number of conventions of manner which all eighteenth century novelists obeyed and even so bold a spirit as Sade's could not conceive completely giving up. But no preoccupation of *taste* or composition, no lurking concern for their *literary* quality ever appears in his letters, which he was very far from thinking would ever be published. Nobody ever wrote with such freedom before the romantic period, unless it was the Duke de Saint-Simon. How chill and timid, too, Rousseau's *Confessions* seem, however sincere they may be, however perfect their style, after Sade's letters ! In *The Eagle, Mademoiselle,* in *The Chimes of Vincennes* and in *Monsieur No. 6,* a century in advance of them, we behold that triumph of personal writing which was to reach its highest point in the Count de Lautréamont, Arthur Rimbaud and Alfred Jarry.

Every day new minds feel drawn to Sade, but not without a certain uneasiness which diminishes their ability to understand work which knows so few limits. Thus hesitant, they never manage to achieve that fusion of extremes which makes it possible to read the *120 Days, Justine* or *Juliette* without blanching.

However, the publication of these letters may now at last help to free from misgivings in their subconscious that admiration which they otherwise feel for Sade's literary work. With these twenty-four letters, such very human documents, before them, they will find liberation in the moving diversity and the very intonation of these lines penned under such tragic circumstances. They will be able at last to "admit" the genius of Sade and rank him with Shakespeare, Pascal or Nietzsche. Without looking back they will be able to feel affection for his black erotic paradise, whether they see his books in the light of descriptive psychopathology or purified by that double use of language and the dialectics of contraries with which long since they credited that other great pessimist aristocrat, Count de Lautréamont.

Despite all the hue and cry which every age starts up against him, the three little volumes of the Vincennes letters will, to the rare delight of those who already know him, once again mark Sade as one of the stars of the first magnitude of poetic realism. In them we have a symphony wrested from Hell itself. With the hot and savage breath of a great protagonist of love are mingled the accents now of Ariel, now of Falstaff, as from the eternal dusk of those cruel walls a new language emerged and the cells became full of eternal visions.

DIALOGUE BETWEEN A PRIEST AND A DYING MAN

Drawn from a notebook of rough drafts which contained a number of other small works, this *Dialogue,* written in Vincennes during the summer of 1782, was first published in 1926 by Maurice Heine.* One wonders whether Sade ever made a final version of this dialogue, the melodious eloquence and sarcasm of which are often reminiscent of the divine Plato.

In an exhaustive introduction Heine draws a contrast between the inexorable atheism of the Marquis and the antireligious sentiments of which his contemporaries produced such timid expression, with their free deisms and their belief in a benevolent Nature. On this fundamental question, which con-

---

Dialogue entre un prêtre et un moribond, par Donatien-Alphonse-Francois, marquis de Sade, publié pour la premiere fois sur le manuscrit autographe inédit, avec un avant-propos et des notes, par Maurice Heine; Paris; Stendhal and Company, 1926. It is a small quarto volume.

cerns not only the *Dialogue,* but also almost all that Sade wrote, the author feels it hardly possible to add to his predecessor's analysis. First, however, let us quote some essential passages from Heine :

" ... *What is an Atheist? It is a man who destroys chimaeras which are detrimental to the human species and brings men back to Nature, experience, and reason. It is a thinker who, having considered matter, its energy, its properties and its reactions, does not need to imagine ideal powers, fictitious intelligences, reasoning beings to explain the phenomena of the universe and the workings of nature, for far from making nature more comprehensible, they merely make it capricious, inexplicable, unknowable, of no service to the happiness of men.*"

This definition by the Baron d'Holbach (*Système de la Nature,* 1770) may be taken as one of the clearest and most explicit that his age produced. But do his apparent words of rejection do any more than conceal the sentimental conception of a Nature which is at the service of human beings and is concerned with their happiness? And do we not find, a few pages farther on, monotonous as any church litany, invocations of those *ideal powers* and *imaginary intelligences* on which Holbach frowned so sternly under other names? *O Nature! Lord of all beings! and you her divine daughters, Virtue, Reason, Truth! Ever be our only Divinities, it is to you that the incense and worship of this earth are due.*

This atheistic mythology was well suited to be somehow tacked on to the *natural philosophy* set out in the opening essay of the *Encyclopaedia,* but only to the greater confusion of the philosophers of the Academy. In works published over their names Diderot and d'Alembert showed no indulgence for that atheism of which their dangerous opponents suspected them, or for atheists, whose ruthless frankness threatened to compromise everything. ... This philosophy deserted them—worse, it condemned them, called for their execution. ... *The most tolerant of men would not deny that a judge has the right to repress those who dare profess themselves atheists, and even con-*

demn them to death, if there is no other way of freeing
society of them . . . if he can punish those who wrong a
single person, he doubtless has as much right to punish
those who wrong the whole of a society with their denials
that there is a God. . . . Such a man may be looked upon
as the enemy of all men.

If the *Encyclopaedia* of 1751 did not hesitate to utter a
verdict like that, can one complain of the cautious reserve
expressed by a La Mettreie, or such a man as Helvetius,
uttering a humble apology after the condemnation of his
work *De l'Esprit*? Both the one and the other had
as much reason to fear the condemnation of *natural right*
uttered by their friends as the thundering of the high courts
uttered by their enemies. Sylvain Maréchal was right
indeed when in the *Dictionnaire des athées*, published in
the Year VIII of the Revolution, he pointed out to the
nascent nineteenth century *to what extent, with all its*
enlightenment and its claims, its liberal notions and its
boldnesses, the eighteenth century was still servile and hide-
bound in its outlook.

It would be out of the question to complain of this
judgement had the Marquis de Sade not existed—or
rather, had his work, which was persecuted as rigorously
as he himself was, not partly escaped the fury of those who
would have destroyed it. . . . For though Sade may
still refer to Nature as to a personality, it is in him no
longer the benevolent man-loving goddess of the *Système*
de la Nature, which was still too much for Voltaire, but
that divinity of the catastrophic which haunted the crater
of Etna. Here is how Almani the chemist put it in *La*
Nouvelle Justine : *"The more I seek to find out its secrets,*
the more I find it bent on man's destruction. Just follow
all its workings and you will see that it is invariably vora-
cious, destructive, malevolent, invariably inconsequent,
hostile, destructive. . . . Does it not indeed seem that the
only purpose of its murderous devices is to have victims,
that evil is its only element and that it is endowed with
the power of creation solely to drown the world with
blood, tears and mourning? One of your modern philos-
ophers declared himself the lover of nature, but I, my

dear friend, will say I am its executioner. Mark its ways, see what it does, nature is frightful; you will never see it create but to destroy, never attain its ends but by murdering, and like the Minotaur it ever battens on nothing but man's unhappiness and annihilation."

One must never lose sight of the fact that Sade is *absolute* and follows a straight line to the very end of his thought, to the extreme limit of its logical results. . . . He does not merely write, whenever he can, that there is no God, he thinks and he acts without cease, and leaves us his word, whatever the cost, and that inexorable certainty of his pride is without doubt what men have least been able to forgive in him. But this is precisely how he reaches up into the heights and his curses become prayers. O Thou, they say, who hast created all that exists in this world, thou of whom I have not the faintest idea, thou whom I know only by hearsay and by what men who are deceived daily may have told me, strange, fantastic creature that they call God, I declare formally, authentically, publicly, that I have not the faintest belief that you exist, and this for the excellent reason that I find nothing to convince me of such a ludicrous being, the reality of which nothing in the world supports. (*Histoire de Juliette*).

One could adduce ten, twenty, thirty pages of quotations from Sade in this spirit. His work as a whole overflows with them. But let us confine ourselves to noting that the last statement of Sade's vigorous atheism that we have in writing—at least, among the material which has come down to us—is in *Personal Notebook* (1803-4) of which the author has recently published a summary. There is a fragment entitled *Phantoms (Fantômes)* in all probability intended as the introduction to his *Refutation of Fénelon* which puts it very clearly —we shall return to it in Chapter Eighteen.

In that fine work by Pierre Klossowski, entitled *My Neighbour Sade (Sade, mon prochain)* we have a first attempt at research into the latent contents of Sade's work. In Klossowski's book we find the Christian mentality, paradoxically enough, engendering the most profound psychoanalytical enquiry. Two years previously, *The Eagle, Mademoiselle* collection of letters had brought to Klossowski's notice a strange *Prière du soir* (Evening Prayer), addressed to the Almighty and written at Vincennes in 1782 ! This at first sight seemed to support Klossowski's theory about the ambivalence of Sade's anti-religious sentiments. At the end of it Sade wrote *Fructus belli*—the fruits of war. What did he mean by that, if not : "To what means of defence am I now reduced? To show the injustice of my enemies and slash their cruelty I am forced to make use of a notion which I loathe, to explode their hypocrisy I have to tackle them with their own loathsome weapons, invoking that absurd deity in the name of which they make bold to persecute me. . . ."

Let us here note that in a letter to his wife on one occasion he used the notion of God in just the same way to match up to the trickery of Lady Montreuil and scare her. Further, to understand the meaning of the prayer we should note that it was written only three months before the *Dialogue,* which was completed on July 13th 1782.

But since the reality of Sade's atheism has been questioned, may we now glance at the matter from a different angle. First, with all due recognition of the homage paid to the author of the *120 Days of Sodom* by Klossowski's book of 1947, Klossowski's assertion is open to grave doubt. God? No, the presence of that metaphysical excipient in *My Neighbour, Sade* is no more disturbing than it is in Simone Weil's *La Pesanteur de la Grâce,* nor does it prevent both books from being greathearted or affect the rigorous intellectual standards under which they were conceived. But there was a most unfair suggestion which does deserve refutation. When Sade made one of his characters say : "If atheism wants martyrs, let it say so, and I am absolutely prepared to shed my blood," Klossowski protests and says : "This is pure rhetoric. Atheism does not want martyrs. Still less Sade's blood." With this we simply cannot agree. We do not know if atheism wants martyrs, but we certainly know very well that during the sixteenth century, torture and the stake produced a steady flow of them. One needs cite only one example—Lucilio Vanini of Taurisano had his noble tongue torn out with episcopal tongs. And in Sade's protest there is surely no hint of rhetoric. If in Klossowski's eyes thirty years' imprisonment was not sufficient to warrant the title *martyr* for this man who scorned the deity, perhaps Paul Claudel may be quoted—here being childish, uncharitable and above all most unworthy of the author of the *Soulier de Satin* : "At least it was a good piece of work putting Sade away for half his life !" When all is said and done, it was clearly for his insistence on disregarding all the moral precepts of a society still ruled by the Church that the Marquis spent the greater part of his adult life, including his last fourteen years, in prison. If Klossowski should still question this relationship of cause and effect, the eloquent protest which will follow must have been made to convince him.

But first we must make it clear that Sade's atheism, which is our subject at the moment, did not consist merely in a metaphysical rejection of religious dogmata. He was equally opposed to the *secular* power of the Church, that is, equally against those prohibitions of society which under the monarchy resulted from the omnipotence of the Church. "Oh no !" he cried, "by all that I hold most sacred I shall never accept the tutelage of the disciples of a deity which thinks it has a right to insult the products of creation merely to honour the alleged creator of them. Build your impious chapels, then, and worship your idols, you miserable heathen ! But so long as to achieve that end you put a brake on the most holy laws of Nature, do not forget that you will merely succeed in forcing me to hate you and scorn you."

Were the Marquis de Sade to be resurrected today, in his eyes the anti-religious struggle would not seem more than a philosophical jousting, and there is reason to believe that it would even fail to interest him at all. In the man who qualified Robespierre as "infamous" the complete theistic plurality of the past twenty years would indubitably fan his fury in a different way. If Sade's atheism invariably appears so violently expressed that M. Klossowski feels himself justified in drawing the conclusion that it was ambivalent in nature, this was not purely and simply, as M. Maurice Blanchot maintains, because "dizzy with his power and his lust" he would not submit to the shame of "self-annulment before God"; it was also—and in our opinion before all else—because to the author of *Juliette* the word *atheism* meant equally a savage condemnation of anything which in his eyes seemed to entrammel man's inborn freedom, whether it was a religious, a political or an intellectual tyranny. Such a many-sided atheism, concerned with the essential spirit of man, seems rich enough in cogent reasons for us to feel no astonishment at his lack of "sangfroid" and to make it unnecessary to have recourse to any ambivalence or even "the heat of pride" to explain the passionate hatred which inspired Sade's language every time that his pen traced those four letters of the word *dieu* (God). The conclusion to be drawn is that Sade against God means Sade against the absolute monarchy, Sade against Robespierre, Sade against Napoleon, Sade against anything which immediately or even remotely seemed in any way to lay a restricting hand on the golden fleece of human personality.

THE 120 DAYS OF SODOM OR THE RAKE'S SCHOOL

It was on October 22nd 1785 that the Marquis de Sade began making a fair copy from the first sketches of the *120 Days of Sodom*. Fully aware of the powerful originality of his work, no less than of the dangers of seizure to which such a manuscript was daily subject, he decided, without waiting to complete it, to make a careful copy in a form which would be most easily concealable. For twenty evenings, from seven to ten p.m., the prisoner of the Bastille covered one side of a roll of thin paper with microscopic writing. The roll was thirty-nine feet, four and a third inches long, and was made up of little sheets four and three-quarters inches wide stuck end to end. Completing one side, without a break he started on the other, till on November 28th he had completed the provisional manuscript, exactly as it has come down to us one hundred and twenty-five years later. To him it was to seem "a precaution useless for myself, if not for posterity", for after the pillaging of the Bastille neither the rough draft nor the roll ever came into his hands again. We may add that the loss of such a work may well have been not the least cause of the "tears of blood" which he spoke of shedding in May 1790.

However, the lost roll was one day discovered by Arnoux de Saint Maximin, and in the very cell in which Sade was a prisoner! It came into the possession of the Villeneuve-Trans family, which looked after it for three generations. It was then, at the beginning of the present century, sold to a collector beyond the Rhine, and in 1904 the unpublished manuscript was published by the Berlin psychiatrist Iwan Bloch under the pseudonym of Eugène Dühren.* But although the great scientific importance of the *120 Days* "to doctors, jurists and anthropologists" did not escape its publisher, who in his notes many times pointed out the "astonishing analogies" between instances cited by Sade and those by Krafft-Ebing, the version which he published remains to all intents useless because of the thousands of errors which distort the text.

After Bloch's death the manuscript remained in Germany, till January 1929, when Maurice Heine went to Berlin to obtain it for the Viscount Charles de ————. In 1931-5 Maurice Heine's excellent three-volume edition at last appeared. Because of its complete accuracy it should be looked upon as the real original.** Unfortunately, the critical notes which are promised in the introduction are missing from Vol 3, which was to have contained them. A work of this quality, the fruit of Maurice Heine's scrupulous learning, whose notes on the "little sheets" give us a notion what it would have been like, would have greatly enriched our knowledge of Sade.

Let us recapitulate the setting and the actors in this terrific work of imagination. Towards the end of the reign of Louis le Grand four psychopaths, whose ages ranged from forty-five to sixty, and whose great wealth was the fruit of murder and thuggery—they were the Duke de Blagis, his brother, a bishop, the president of the high court of Curval and a financier named Durcet—locked themselves up for a nameless orgy in a *château* buried somewhere in the Black Forest. With them they took forty-two objects of their lust, who were in their complete power, first, their very young and wonderfully beautiful "spouses", Constance, daughter of Durcet and wife of Blangis (in fourth marriage, he having killed all his previous wives), Adélaïde, Curval's daughter and Durcet's wife, Julie, Blangis's daughter by her first husband, now Curval's wife, and Aline, il-

---

*Paris; Club des Bibliophiles (real publisher: Berlin; Max Harrwitz). This was a limited 8-vol. edition.

***Les 120 Journées de Sodome, ou l'Ecole du Libertinage, par le marquis de Sade. Edition critique établie sur le manuscrit original par Maurice Heine. A Paris, par S. et C., au dépens des bibliophiles souscripteurs, 3 vol., in-4°.* (396 copies were printed).

legitimate daughter of the bishop and Blangis's second wife, with a "seraglio" of eight young lads and eight young girls ravished from their parents, "their attractiveness beyond expression", and eight sodomistic "f——s", selected by reason of their monstrous dimensions, four sexagenarian duennas, eaten and ravaged by chancres, cess-pits of every crime, six kitchen-maids and servants and finally four narrator-procuresses, grown grey in the service, La Duclos, la Champville, la Martaine and the frightful Desgranges. Between a certain November 1st and the following February 28th these four, taking turns by months, each told one hundred and fifty tales of perversions, which the lord of the *château* and his guests in many cases put into immediate practice, reaching the heights of excitation. In the course of countless orgies, a *crescendo* of horrors which lasted in fact twenty days beyond February 28th, thirty victims, drawn from all the categories mentioned with the exception of the story-tellers, died in frightful torment. Only twelve returned to Paris with the Duke and his three accomplices.

The form of the *120 Days* is clearly modelled on Boccaccio's *Decameron* and Marguerite of Navarre's *Heptameron*. A lengthy introduction is followed by four parts, in diary form, corresponding to November, December, January and February and divided into passions described as "simple", "double", "criminal" and "murderous", the story of which is interlocked with the actual "shocking events in the *château*". Only the introduction and the first part were worked out in detail, the three other parts remaining in the form of a detailed plot and notes. But let us note that it is this plot with its cursory listing of psychopathological facts, all painstakingly numbered, and in an order the sense of which is at once clear, that does so much to give the *120 Days* that medical treatise quality which indeed perfectly corresponds to the author's own preliminary remarks.

If, as we shall see below, Sade's work deserves consideration from both the scientific and the literary standpoint, we have to observe that in a third sphere the rare philosophical passages in the *120 Days* are a succinct outline of those theories on morals and of obsessional views of the world that throughout his career as writer Donatien Alphonse François never tired of adding to and refining.

His *Misfortunes of Virtue,* written in 1788, was a first step.

We find a sketch of these views mainly in an outburst of the Duke de Blangis: he loathes virtue; since youth he has been clear how "empty and void" it is; only vice, in his view, can provide man with "that mental and physical thrill whence arises the most subtle sensual enjoyment". "I have abandoned myself to it," he cries, "at an early age I rose above the fanciful notions of religion, being completely convinced that the existence of a creator is a revolting absurdity. . . . I have no need whatsoever to curb my leanings with the aim of pleasing him; Nature granted these urges to me, and to resist them would be to outrage it. If Nature provided me with urges that are bad, that means they must have become bad to suit nature's ends; in nature's hands I am only a piece of mechanism that nature moves as it will, and there is not one of my crimes but serves it. The more nature suggests them, the more it needs them. . . ." As for the very machinery of Sadian sensual enjoyment, as far as can be deduced—less from the partial and curiously physiological explanation in a passage of the *120 Days* than from the arguments of Sade himself in the course of his later works—it seems to boil down to the following question: if we above all draw our sex satisfaction from the emotions by which the person we possess is moved, what engine could be more powerful than pain as a means for causing those emotions, and consequently our sexual satisfaction at its most intense?

It was no doubt of his *120 Days* that Sade was thinking when in *Aline et Valcour* he wrote: "I wish instead of those fancy pieces of furniture which suggest nothing at all people in their homes had a sort of tree in relief with the name of a vice on every branch, starting with the slightest overstepping of the bounds and working up to that crime which springs from scorning the most fundamental obligations. Would not such an ethical table have value? And would it not be equal to a Teniers or a Rubens?"

However, the opening passage of the *120 Days* had already revealed the author's didactic intent, at the same time as it expressed the disturbing novelty of his proposals: "Now at once, dear reader, you should dispose your heart and soul to the most impure story told ever since the world began, there being no such book either among the ancients or the moderns. Realise that all decent bodily indulgence is prescribed by that beast of which you are always talking without knowing it and which you call *nature,* that such indulgence in any of its forms is, I say, to be expressly excluded from this collection and that whenever you happen to come upon any such this will only be in so far as they are accompanied by some crime or coloured by something outrageous. . . . As for the diversity of it all, rest assured that it is exact; make a careful study of the diversity of passions which may seem to you to be closely alike one to the other and you will see that there are always differences and that however slight they may be, they are endowed with just that subtlety, that sensitivity, which marks the kind of lasciviousness which is here in question."

"Losing his *120 Days,*" wrote Maurice Heine in his introduction, "Sade lost his main thread, and knew it. The remainder of his literary life was dominated by concern to remedy the consequences of that accident. So with painful perserverance and insistence he went on striving to attain the mastery which was his when at the height of his solitude and misanthropy." And the same author, whom one cannot help quoting because it would be vain to try to compete with him in succinctness, elsewhere wrote: "It is a document of singular value at the same time as the first definite attempt (apart from the work of priests in the confessional) to classify sexual anomalies. The man responsible for this initiative in methodical observation of such phenomena and in their systematic description, a century before Krafft-Ebing and Freud, certainly deserves the honour which the learned accord his name by calling the most serious of these psychopathic conditions *sadism.*"

Yet even though in that natural history of paraesthesia,* the *120 Days,* Sade gives proof of his pioneering genius, and even though some of his psycho-sexual descriptions must, quite apart from their eminent literary value, be recognised as masterpieces of their kind, one should point out that there is one persistent error which in many places reduced the didactic value of his work—namely, the monstrously exaggerated place which he gave to the coprolagneic aberration carried to the extreme of excess. For out of the six hundred cases of abnormality re-

---

*Paraesthesia is the excitement of the sexual urge by inadequate things.

lated by the female story-tellers—leaving out the pure fiction in which that disgusting practice is common—more than half involve the eating of excrement, either as act pure and simple, or coupled with some other form of lust. Now, whereas visual coprolagneia, olfactive coprolagneia* and tactile coprolagneia (which seems to have origins in both fetishism and sado-masochism) are fairly common anomalies, their paroxystic sister coprophagy must be classed as one of the less wide-spread sexual aberrations. With one single mention in the nine hundred pages of Krafft-Ebing's collection of cases, it belongs rather to the sphere of real lunacy, quite a different field of investigation from that which Sade set himself. Thus in the *120 Days* verisimilitude is very often diminished by the quite unnecessary superimposition of the ugliest of depar-tures from normality, in place of which many other essen-tially erotic variations might equally well have stood. Apart from the monotony which results from such an abuse, some of the most striking cases, such as that of the necrophilous judge who only liked dealings "with women who are going to be executed", are somehow deprived of their universal application by the coprophagous element which Sade thought necessary to graft on to the main perversion.

Nevertheless, despite these reserves which one has to make, the *120 Days* contains the finest pages that Sade ever wrote. The texture, the breadth, the sweep of the sentences, all seem more comparable with the style of his letters, that true tape-recording on which the very sound of his voice is imprinted, than that of his other works, the style of which has been much more worked by the author. The introduction, in which we see all the re-sources of his art, in its newest and most spontaneous form, is unquestionably his masterpiece : Take only the portrait of Blangis, in sparkling black amid the magnificent nudity of the wives and the demoniacal loveliness of his sermon to "feeble, entrammelled creatures", or that gallery-full of procuresses and duennas, drabs and nymphettes, equal in every sense to Goya's album of *Whims of Fancy* (the *Capricios*). And to take a great name for comparison with the perfection of the pageant of morals which we have in *Part One,* one only needs to mention the subtlety of the clever, natural colouring of Petronius's

*This was one of the aspects of the great Marseilles case.

Satyricon. And how skilled Sade is in making his characters speak in character and according to their status. Take that episode in which Duclos tells of the first steps of his own rake's progress—the disquisition which his sister delivers him on what is to be gained by submitting to the manifestations of a man's depravity is masterly in its realism, and defeats Restif de la Bretonne on his own ground.

M. André Rousseaux maintains that in Sade he does not find "that Satanic grandeur which has found lofty expression in literature". He thinks Sade lacking in the poetic gift. On the contrary it is precisely their Satanic grandeur that lends Sade's works an exceptional fascination. Indeed, practically every one of them has yielded some passage for a striking collection of prose poems, selections which, torn from the argument of their context, have all the wonderful tragic quality which glows in such a work as *Maldoror.* Very many passages have come from the *120 Days,* among them that tortured avatar of human idealism, the sadistic indulgence in necrophily arranged by the Duke de Florville. Such diamonds of Sade's delirium, however fortuitous, in isolation cannot fail to strike the sensitive modern mind as outstanding poetry. For that matter, without realising it, did not this lifelong prisoner depict himself in the very pose of poetic meditation, however unsuitable the subject of those meditations might seem? "All *those things* and remembrance of them are always what I call to my aid when I want to drown my miseries . . . it so soothes my unhappiness when I let my imagination play with them again."

"All *those things*" indeed make him quite rapturous : "Two delightful young girls were violated and murdered in their mother's arms, to which countless other horrors were added. . . ." "With a mail-coach whip he chased her about the garden till she fell from exhaustion, and that was the moment when he flung himself upon her. . . ." Larger than life as Constance and Adélaïde were, what barbaric fury their big-bottomed, queenly bodies had to suffer before death came !

If prisoner Sade did not give satisfaction to his gaolers, the fact is—he did not want to. The only sword he possessed in his gloomy habitation to avenge himself on the world which kept him a prisoner was that of being subversive to moral judgments and sensitive standards. What reason was there then for him to refrain from thrusting it up to the hilt into the heart of man? However, the aesthetic preaching of evil excluded the accomplishment of his intention. It was the virtuous Robespierre who killed, he who indirectly slaughtered a thousand young women, not Sade of the lovely voice. "Behind that curtain of blood," wrote René Char, "was the scorching cry of a force which was to destroy itself, because it had a horror of force, its own sterile inner sister".

But for those exquisite victims, brought back to life at dawn on the hundred and twentieth day, the French language will utter thanks.

LES INFORTUNES DE LA VERTU
ANECDOTES, STORIES AND LEGENDS

Despite their date of composition, here these two posthumous works which Maurice Heine has published will only be placed on record. For it seems to be a sounder approach (a) to treat the story entitled *Les Infortunes de la Vertu* (The disadvantages of Virtue), which is really the first sketch of that work, together with the first section of Chapter XVI of the 1791 *Justine,* (b) to examine the *Anecdotes, Stories and Legends* and the collection of *Crimes of Love* together with section 6 of the first chapter of the 1791 *Justine* and in the light of MS 4010 of the *Bibliothèque Nationale* and Sade's 1804 notes on the recasting of his work as story-teller.

CHAPTER FOURTEEN

Under the Revolutionary Régime

(part one)

(1789-1792)

NINE MONTHS IN CHARENTON SAINT MAURICE

July 4th 1789. Charenton Asylum, where the untamable prisoner of the Bastille was transferred during the dark hours "naked as a maggot", a pistol held to his throat, was an establishment run by the Charity order of Friars known as the Petits Pères, or "minor fathers". Here is the report they made on the new inmate of their institution :

> "CHARITY ORDER CHARENTON ASYLUM : *His Lordship the Count de Sade (Louis Aldonce Donatien).* Order of July 3rd 1789. Period—without limit. Signed : de Villedeuil. Deprived of his liberty since 1777, on request of his family, following a criminal trial on a charge of poisoning and sodomy, of which crimes he proved himself innocent, and further because of his extreme immorality, indulging in much debauch and with periods of loss of sanity to which he is subject and which give his family cause to fear that in one of his attacks he may in the end disgrace them."

July 9th 1789. The Marquis de Sade signed an authorisation to break the seals on the cell he had occupied in the Bastille, as required of him by Commissary Chenon, the operation to be performed in the presence of the *Marquise,* whom the prisoner had appointed his representative. At the same time he wrote to the Commissary to make it clear that it was not a question of making an inventory, but of handing Lady de Sade his papers, furniture and personal effects. He also gave notice to the Commissary that "one of the soldiery sent to do this violence", namely, the treatment to which he had been submitted in the Bastille that night of July 3rd, had stolen two *louis* from his pocket. Would the Commissary have this sum handed to Lady de Sade?

July 14th 1789. The Bastille was stormed. Governor de Launay, Major de Losme-Salbray and Adjutant Miray were hauled off to the *Place de Grève* and put to death. With a clasp-knife a scullery boy named Desnot cut off the Governor's head and carried it about on a pike.

This same day Lady de Sade, who had still not carried out her errand at the Bastille, wakened from her "lethargy". Overtaken by events, she sent an authorisation to Commissary Chenon, empowering him to do the best he could and requested the delivery of her husband's effects, so they should not be sacked and seen by all and sundry. Having done this, she removed herself to the country, determined not to return "till there be a decision which may ease my mind".

And Sade's former cell was sacked. His library of six hundred volumes, "some of great value", his suits and his linen, his furniture and his portraits, totalling two thousand *livres* in value, and also his manuscript works, amounting to fifteen volumes "ready for press" were all "torn up, burned, carried away, pillaged". Worst of all, that irreplaceable roll containing the *120 Days of Sodom* was lost, never again to be seen by Sade himself.

July 19th 1789. Back at Sainte Aure, Lady de Sade informed Commissary Chenon that for personal reasons she did not consider she could be held responsible for the papers and effects of the Marquis de Sade.

End of July 1789. The Grand Prior, Sade's uncle, had a stroke, at his town house, in Toulouse.

August 2nd 1789. Receiving news of her brother's illness a little before 8 p.m., at Avignon, and suspecting that death would shortly ensue, the Countess de Villeneuse decided to protect her own interests before everything was signed and sealed. That same night, before the representative of the Order of Malta (Sade's son) who was her brother's heir, could arrive, she drove to Saint Cloud *Château,* near Varpentras, with two waggons and removed the more valuable pieces of furniture, taking them straight to Mazan *Château.*

September 20th 1789. Death of the Grand Prior at Toulouse. Some days before this he handed his almoner, the Abbé Audin, his diamond crucifix, to give to the young Marquis de Sade.

October 8th 1789. Lady de Sade to Gaufridy, recounting her escape from Paris on October 5th:

" ... I escaped from Paris with my daughter and a chamber-maid, but without a valet, following the general flood in a hired carriage. I preferred not to be dragged out by the women of the people, who were seizing all the womenfolk in town houses to make them march through the rain and mud to Versailles to seize the King. I arrived here safe and sound, travelling by little side roads. The King is in Paris. He has been taken into the town, the heads of his two bodyguards on pikes in front of him, and thence to the Louvre. Paris is in a state of intoxication of delight because people think that the presence of the King will assure them bread."

November 26th 1789. Lady de Sade to Gaufridy:

" ... : We are daily menaced with bloodshed. The clergy and the nobility—very few of them—in vain agree to everything, but are still detested. So far, since the event at Versailles, nothing has happened, but one cannot go to bed with any certainty of the morrow. Two days ago at the *Palais Royal* and *la Halle* they were taking people's shoe buckles and earrings and making them empty their pockets on the pretext of taking it all to the treasury. . . . History will never believe all that is happening. . . ."

January 12th 1790. Eusèbe Boyer, Prior of the Charity Friars, implored the President of the National Assembly to relieve him of a certain inmate of Charenton who, unless they were allowed to lock him up, might well bring misfortune on the Asylum.

March 11th 1790. Lady de Sade to Gaufridy:

> "The shops refuse to sell, because people are buying things just to get rid of the paper money.... There has been frightful bloodshed at Meaux; the Mayor was hanged, I hear, and the Bishop has fled. The misery is extreme, it could not be otherwise. The password for crime is: 'He's an aristocrat, he means to steal the King away.' The victim is strung up at once without any trial."

March 13th 1790. On a proposal submitted by de Castellane, regarding *lettres de cachet*, the Constituent Assembly decided within six weeks to release all persons detained by such secret Royal orders, except those condemned to death, found guilty on a charge or insane.

March 18th 1790. Louis Marie and Donatien Claude Armand de Sade, whom their father had not seen for nearly fifteen years, visited him at Charenton. They informed him of the Decree passed by the Assembly. ("I hope it makes him happy, but I very much doubt if he is capable of so being," was what Lady de Montreuil said to her grandsons, when they told her their intention of informing the prisoner). The friars allowed the Marquis to stroll about with his children and entertain them to dinner.

March 23rd 1790. Lady Montreuil warned Gaufridy that the Marquis, her son-in-law, might soon be set at liberty. Nevertheless, the wording of the Decree of the Assembly did "envisage the possibility of there being exceptions". The sole question was whether in certain circumstances a family "could create such an exception". It was however her opinion that in some cases it was better to remain neutral. "That is the only way to be sure of being beyond reproach". The thing to do was to remain neutral and let the authorities decide. Then one "would have nothing to explain, whatever happened".

April 2nd 1790. On this Good Friday ("the better the day, the better the deed!") by the Decree of the Assembly concerning prisoners detained by *lettre de cachet,* the Marquis de Sade recovered his liberty and left Charenton—without a penny, "dressed in a black rateen waistcoat and *no breeches*"—

breeches being the mark of the nobility. He went straight to
see the man who was handling his affairs in Paris, namely,
M. de Milly, Attorney of the Châtelet Court. De Milly provided him with bed and board and six *louis*.

THE FIRST YEAR OF LIBERTY

April 3rd 1790. Lady de Sade, resident in the Nunnery of
Sainte Aure, refused to see her husband. She was definitely resolved to seek a separation order.

For a long time Sade had observed "a certain attitude in
Lady de Sade's behaviour" when she came to see him at the
Bastille which had "caused him alarm and sorrow". The need
he had then had of her had compelled him to conceal his awareness of this. But he had quite positively detected things "to
which her Father Confessor" had prompted her and been clear
in his mind that liberty was going to "become a period of conjugal separation".

April 6th 1790. Sade had found a new lodging—in the same
street—a room in the *du Bouloir Hôtel*. On the same day, furnished with an authorisation given by his father, Louis Marie,
Count de Sade, he withdrew the furniture and other effects
left in the care of the Charenton friars.

April 12th 1790. Lady Montreuil had lent her son-in-law
a few *louis*, on condition that he wrote to Gaufridy at once to
send him some money, both to repay the loan and to have the
funds on which to live in future. Sade however had not waited
to be thus provided with advice by Lady Montreuil on this
subject. On April 6th he had written to his lawyer to send him
"at least one thousand crowns" *instanter*. Now he wrote again
for the money, "my need for which is as extreme as promptitude of despatch is essential".

April 17th 1790. The Marquis applied to the Provost's Office
in Paris for the *Châtelet* court order disposing of management
of his property to be revoked, and this was done at once.

April 28th 1790. Lady de Sade applied to the *Châtelet* Court
for a separation order.

May 1st 1790. *Maitre* Tay, Court Registrar, delivered Lady de Sade's application to the Marquis at his domicile.

May 2nd 1790. The Marquis, whose principal thought, despite his marital troubles, was to get his plays put on, called on Molé the actor, who had given him an appointment.

Early in May 1790. Sade informed Gaufridy of his wife's treachery. Before doing so he took pains to clear the ground between himself and his lawyer and convince the latter of his unflagging friendship. If he had not written to him while a prisoner, it was because he had been "deprived of the means". How could Gaufridy ever have thought that his childhood's friend had forgotten him? This was something that the Marquis could not forgive. It was solely because of their old friendship that he had asked Gaufridy to go on handling his affairs. What reason had he to withdraw his confidence?

> "It was not your fault that I was taken at La Coste [September 1778] but mine; I believed myself too safe and did not know how abominable a family I had to do with. I like to think that it is quite clear to you that I am only speaking of the Montreuils; you just could not conceive what Satanic and anthropophagic tricks that crowd have been at concerning myself. Even had I been the worst creature on this earth I would not have deserved the barbaric treatment I was the victim of through them; in a word, sight and lungs ruined, and through lack of exercise I have become so corpulent that I can scarcely move, my senses are all deadened, I have lost all sense of taste, I care for naught, the world I was so mad about seems an utter bore to me ... a wretched bore! ... There are moments when I have the mind to become a Trappist, and I will not promise not to vanish one of these days without anybody's knowing where I have disappeared to. I was never such a misanthrope as I am since I have returned to human society and if I seem strange when I present myself to people they can be sure they produce the same impression on me. I was very busy while imprisoned. Do you realise, my dear lawyer, that I had fifteen volumes ready for the press? But I have come out of prison without even one quarter of those manuscripts. By unforgivable

carelessness Lady de Sade allowed some to be lost and have the others seized, and that's thirteen lost years! Three-quarters of my works remained behind in my Bastille cell; I was transferred to Charenton on July 4th; on the fourteenth the Bastille was taken and ransacked, and my manuscripts, six hundred books, two thousand *livres* worth of furniture, and precious portraits—all torn up, burned, carried away, pillaged, and no possibility of my finding a straw, and all that by reason of Lady de Sade's unadulterated negligence. She had ten full days to get my effects away. She can have had no doubt but that the Bastille, which during those ten days was being packed with weapons, gunpowder, soldiers, was preparing either for *attack* or *defence*. So why ever did she not make haste to get my things away? ... My manuscripts? ... My manuscripts, over the loss of which I shed tears of blood! ... You can replace beds, tables, commodes, but you cannot get ideas again. ... No, my friend, no, I can never tell you how desperate that loss has made me; for me it is irreparable. Since then sensitive, fine-sentimented Lady de Sade refuses even to see me. Another woman would have said: 'He is unhappy, I must wipe away his tears,' but that is a logic of the emotions she knows not. I have not lost enough; she wants to ruin me utterly, and now she is applying for a separation! By that incredible step she is going to set the seal of truth on all the slanders conspued out against me, she is going to cover her children and me with unhappiness and opprobrium, or rather, go into a nunnery, so as to be able *sweetly to vegetate*, as she would put it, and where no doubt some *father confessor* will provide her with consolation, smoothing for her the path of crime, the path of horror and infamy in which her behaviour is going to engulf us all. Were the woman to accept the counsel of my worst enemy, it could not possibly be viler or more dangerous.

My dear lawyer, you will easily understand that with the sums already spent on my wife's allowance (one hundred and sixty thousand *livres*) all of which my property will have to meet, this separation is going to ruin me altogether, and that is just what these monsters are after."

May 19th 1790. Writing to Rinaud the lawyer, of Aix, Sade gave his views on the French Revolution and the character of the French nation.

... "Essential business to be completed here and the fear of being strung up on *a democratic gallows* in Provence will keep me here till next spring. Then, that is to say, early in March, I count on coming to Provence with my children. There you have my plans, my dear sir, which I shall carry out, if God and the enemies of the nobility let me live. But in this connection, please do not take me for an embittered man. I protest, I am nothing if not impartial, sore at having lost much, more sore still to see my sovereign in irons, aghast to see what, my dear sirs, you just do not feel in the provinces, that it is impossible for good to be done and to continue so long as the sanctions of the monarch are constrained by thirty thousand armed scoundrels and twenty pieces of cannon—though for that matter I have few regrets for the old order; it certainly made me too unhappy for me to weep over it. There you have my confession of faith, and I make it without fear.

You ask news of me. The most important thing today is the Assembly's having refused to allow the King to have anything to do with peace or war.* As far as that goes, it is the provinces which provide us with what engages us most: Valence, Montauban and Marseilles are scenes of horror, where cannibals daily enact plays in the English manner such as make a man's hair stand on end. ... Ah! Long since it is indeed that I for my part declared that this lovely, gentle *nation* was only biding its time for the chance to be galvanised into action and show that, balanced eternally betwixt savagery and fanaticism, it would revert to its natural mode as soon as circumstances allowed!

But that is enough of this, we must be prudent in our letters. The régime of the despot was never such a ruthless prober into private secrets as liberty is."

*This letter, though dated May 19th, must have been broken off and continued three days later, after the Decree concerning the Royal prerogative of making peace or declaring war—a decree which, for that matter, still left the King the right to take up arms and declare sanctions. (Note by P. Bourdin).

End of May 1790. Once again reminding Gaufridy of his
reasons for complaining of his wife, responsible as she was for
the loss of his writings, the Marquis outlined to the lawyer the
new grievances that this lady had provided him with. She was
refusing to let her husband have those manuscripts which he
had secretly passed to her when she used to visit him in Vincennes and the Bastille, and had even passed them to persons
who had burned part. What was more, she had just presented
him with a separation order based on all the lies to which the
Arceuil and Marseilles affairs had given rise. He had resolved
to make no reply to that "monumental shamelessness" and let
it be condemned by default. But after this tragic picture, in
order to deck his letter out with "some roses", he told Gaufridy
that for some time now he had been living with a delightful
lady (the wife of Court President Fleurieu) a person full of wit
and genius, who was "smothering him with kindnesses". But
that delightful company was not his only solace. He could not
but congratulate himself on the attitude of relations and
friends: the Countess de Saumane, First Lady-in-waiting of
Queen Elizabeth, and the Clermont-Tonnerres* were showing
him every possible kindness. Finally he came across a number
of old friends, including some women friends, who were very
kind to him. But all this took place in the greatest "tranquillity".
His philosophy was now "that of the Stoics"; there were "no
more unclean pleasures". Having once upon a time been all
hot on them, today he was merely disgusted by them, for now
"his physical strength was scarcely enough to cope with all the
ills which had overcome him".

---

*Count Stanislas de Clermont-Tonnerre (1747-1792) and his wife.
He was Colonel of the Royal-Navarre Regiment when the Revolution
broke out. One of the principal architects of the union of the three
orders, he voted for the abolition of privileges, then for civic rights for
Protestants and Jews. A moderate reformer and a disciple of the English
school, like T.G. de Lally-Tolendal et Malouet; together with this
person he founded an anti-Jacobin society supported by the *Journal des
Impartiaux*, which for a time Sade frequented. Wounded by a scythe
cut on August 10th 1792, the Count de Clermont-Tonnerre took refuge
in the town house of a woman friend in the *rue du Vaugirard*. Worked up
by a valet pursued for theft, the crowd found the wretched man there
and threw him out of the window.
  Born at Sorans, the Countess was a cousin of the Marquis' on his
mother's side. She eventually married the Marquis de Talaru.

June 9th 1790. On Lady de Sade's application, the Châtelet Court issued a separation order *in contumaciam* and ordered the Marquis to pay her back 160,842 *livres* received as marriage settlement.

June 13th 1790. Lady de Sade informed Gaufridy that it was only "after mature and well weighed reflection" over some considerable time that she had decided to seek a separation from her husband. As for her reasons, if the Marquis would only "probe to the bottom of his heart", he could not but agree that she was justified. If he wished to make it a public scandal, that was up to him. "To justify myself I shall only say what I am forced to say, *but if forced to, I shall say it.*"

July 1st 1790. The Marquis obtained an identity card as an "active citizen" of the *Place Vendôme* section (later to become the *Section des Piques*).

August 3rd 1790. The Italian Theatre accepted *le Suborneur* (The Briber), a one act play in octosyllabic verse.

August 17th 1790. Sade gave at the *Comédie Française* a reading of his little *vers libre* one-act play *le Boudoir ou le Mari crédule* (The Boudoir or the Gullible Husband). (On August 25th he received their rejection, only one member of the committee being in favour! However, they agreed to a second reading, subject to certain changes to be made by the author.)

August 18th 1790. Writing to his Apt lawyer, Sade discussed his daughter, Madeleine Laure, with utter frankness : "I assure you, my daughter really is as ugly as I once told you. I have seen her three or four times since and paid close attention to her and do assure you that both mentally and bodily she is, to put it plainly, just a good plump country wench. She spends all her time with Milady her mother who, no doubt about it, imparts neither manners nor wit. As far as that goes, she is very well off as she is, seeing what she will have to be, and there's nothing else to be done about her for the present."

August 25th 1790. Sade formed an alliance with a young actress of under thirty, *née* Marie Constance Renelle. Her husband, Balthazar Quesnet, had abandoned her, leaving her with one child. From now on our story is that of their faithful love and mutual attachment to each other.

September 3rd 1790. The Marquis was now on rather cool terms with Milady de Fleurieu, whom the attentions which a new liaison involved had compelled him rather to neglect. He required her to sign a receipt for two hundred and twenty-five *livres,* being the rent he had paid her for nine months lodging (from Easter to January 15th of the following year).

September 16th 1790. Le Misanthrope par amour ou Sophie et Desfrancs, a five-act *vers libre* comedy, was accepted "unanimously" by the *Comédie Française.* But it was never produced.

September 23rd 1790. The separation order of the Sades was followed by tiresome bickering on the business side. An intermediary was found in lawyer Reinaud, on his way through Paris, and before two notaries of the Châtelet Court the couple agreed on the following terms: 1. The Marquis accepted the separation order made *in contumaciam*; 2. he recognised his debt to Lady de Sade of 160,842 *livres,* which he had received on account of the marriage settlement; 3. Lady de Sade undertook not to demand repayment of that sum during her husband's lifetime, on condition that she received the interest on the sum, agreed upon as a flat 4,000 *livres* per annum, "consideration taken of the limited revenue from the estate"; 4. as guarantee of payment in six-monthly instalments of 2,000 *livres* Sade agreed within eight days to give Lady de Sade an order to his bailiffs to pay; 5. any litigation on the matter between the two was "quashed and settled completely".

November 1st 1790. The Marquis, who had completely broken off with Lady de Fleurieu "to the point of deciding never to see each other again", set up house in a maisonette at 20, *rue Neuve des Mathurins,* off the *Chaussée d'Antin,* where he proposed to live jointly with Marie Constance Quesnet.* A few days later, to give Gaufridy some idea of the new situation, Sade asked him to imagine "a good stout country parson in his parsonage". He had engaged a housekeeper, a woman cook and a valet. "Is that excessive?"

---

*The property consisted of two houses. One gave on to the *rue Neuve des Mathurins*, the other on to the *rue de la Ferme des Mathurins*, with a garden between them. Sade himself took up quarters in this latter house

November 26th 1790. The new "fiancé" who had written to Gaufridy for furniture to equip his "little shanty" was getting impatient, because there was still no signs of its arriving.

December 18th 1790. The Marquis had definitely come to the conclusion that the Montreuils had given him a false picture of the revenue from his estates and that his wife had not taken into account what she had received from his mother's estate while he was in prison. He therefore addressed her a letter. Gaufridy was to endorse it and ensure delivery. His demands were clearly set out: as he needed at least ten thousand *livres per annum,* Lady de Sade would receive as her dowry interest, only whatever revenue he obtained in excess of that sum, while she would also have to make up to him what had been received on his mother's legacy.

Second half of January 1791. It was apparently now that Marie Constance, for whom Sade's pet name was "Sensitivity" moved in at the little house in the *rue Neuve des Mathurins.*

We have to leap five months to hear Sade himself speaking about his "little set-up". He had told Reinaud about a little theatrical affair, very brief, but wonderful, and the lawyer ventured to tease him about it, said he would do well not to get too mixed up in the wings, and then, no doubt apropos of Marie Constance, herself an actress, whose sway over the Marquis was known to him, either referred directly to la Beauvoisin or in some other way provoked memories.

"Me beware of actresses?" cried Sade in reply. "Oh yes, sir, I can assure you that I will do. Once a man has experienced that breed he despises it for what it is worth. Far from it! We are anything but stage folk and nothing was ever more virtuous than my little set-up. To begin with, there's no hint of love-making. She is just a decent, kindly, matronly person, sweet and good, and with an excellent mind, who, being separated from her husband, who is in business in America, has undertaken to look after my little home for me. Here she lives on the scanty allowance her husband makes her, but I supply board and lodging and that is at present all she gets out of it."

Marie Quesnet was no calligraphist and her handwriting was clumsy. But so was Lady de Sade's. If however she lacked education, she made up for it in her exquisite sensitivity. This is how it was that the dedicatory introduction to *Justine* was addressed to her. What was more, Sade got into the habit of regularly reading her every chapter "hot from the oven", and the observations his "dear friend" made struck him as so apt that he would put them straight down in his *Notes littéraires*. In the novel *Delphine* he prefaced some of his reflections by a thumbnail sketch of his companion. For instance, writing of Mme de Staël, he said : "In a woman domestic cares have a special charm. The loveliest of women, the most outstanding in wit and beauty, was not above those simple, kind little attentions which it is so sweet to find in one's home."

Despite difficult periods, despite anxious, critical moments, Marie Quesnet's plucky devotion never once failed in nearly twenty-five years. "I do declare, this woman is an angel sent me by Heaven", Sade declared in February 1799. But it was never one-sided care, for throughout their life together these two adoring companions vied with each other in kindness one to the other. From now on Sade thought of no other woman, heaping kindnesses on her, while she remained ever faithful to the strange person whose true heart only Lady de Sade and she ever understood. Perhaps hers was still the lesser merit, since she never had to undergo the wildnesses of his youth. But these two were only parted at last by death.

February 28th 1791. Le Prévaricateur ou le Magistrat du temps passé—The Prevaricator or the oldtime Judge—a five-act comedy in alexandrines, was rejected by the reading committee of the *Théâtre Français*.

March 6th 1791. The Marquis wrote to tell Reinaud that he was sending the four volumes of his novel *Aline et Valcour,* for him to have printed at Easter. What worried him a great deal was that he could not trace his Bastille manuscripts anywhere. Finally, in his present ignorance of the fickleness of theatre managers, he remarked that he now had five plays accepted by various theatres, *Sophie et Desfrancs* at the *Théâtre de la Nation, l'Homme Immoral* at the *Italian Theatre, le Jaloux corrigé ou l'Ecole des Coquettes* also at this theatre (this being the same play as the *Boudoir*), *le Criminel par vertu,** at the *Palais Royal* Theatre and *Azélis* at the *Theatre of the rue de Bondy*.

March 15th 1791. Lady de Sade informed Gaufridy that she intended to make the Marquis honour his undertakings. He could not possibly back out of his undertaking of September 23rd. Far from having cause to complain, he should think himself lucky, paying only 4,000 *livres* annual interest on the 160,000 *francs* that he owed. It was not her fault if his estates did not produce enough to leave him 10,000 *francs* income, especially seeing that her funds had been used to pay his debts. She had her children to maintain and she could not possibly abate any part of the agreement.

May 12th 1791. Sade had received some of his furniture, rather damaged, during March. He had then asked Gaufridy to send him three chests, which should contain his papers, also his library and some local delicacies. Now this second consignment arrived, in still worse a state than the first. "A jar of preserve had been upset all over the blue tapestries, the Chinese jars leaked and it all gummed up the books, the Marquis is heartbroken." With "theatrical costumes" there would be a third despatch, and a fourth consignment was in question, but Gaufridy was going to be so careless over it all that the *château* would be completely ransacked before he completed the work.

May 22nd 1791. The Marquis received "terrible news"—his Villeneuve aunt had been dragged off to prison by the revolutionary "brigands" of the *Comtat*. He was profoundly upset, outraged by such a "frightful abomination", just the sort of thing those villains would do. He at once offered the old lady any service he could render her, as, for instance, to take refuge in his *château*, where she would be more safe, for he himself was not in Provence, he was in France.

Some date in June 1791. People were beginning to refuse to accept paper money in Paris. It was worth only twenty-one per cent of its face value. As nobody would supply anything without cash, the Marquis this day went to bed without having either dined or supped. At the same time *Justine or the Mis-*

---

*Indicated by Sade as "three prose acts," and probably the play also called *Franchise et Trahison*.

fortunes of Virtue was being published. For the first time Sade was to see himself bound in leather.

June 12th 1791. Sade to Reinaud:

"If [Mme Quesnet] joins me, to interest her in prolonging my life, I shall make her a little annuity *every five years,* a neat way of securing her interest in my living, so that by sheer self-interest she will look after me, but of *love-making* not a thought. Could I live alone, with two or three valets who would have robbed, perhaps killed me? Was it not essential to put some *reliable* person between those rascals and myself? Can I skim the saucepan or add up the butcher's book when buried in my study with Molière, Destouches, Marivaux, Boissy, and Regnard, whom I look up to and study but never reach? Besides, do I not need some person to whom I can read things *piping hot*? Well, my companion does all this. May God preserve her for me, and spite the amazing cabal which never ceases working to take her away from me. The only fear I have is lest, losing all patience with so many shady montreuilian manoeuvres, the poor woman gets sick of it and takes the huff and leaves me. . . .

At the moment a novel of mine is being printed, but it is too immoral a work to be sent to so circumspect, religious and modest a man as yourself. I needed money, my printer said he wanted it *well peppered* so I gave it him fit to plague old Nick himself. It is being called *Justine or the Misfortunes of Virtue.* Burn it unread if by chance it comes your way. I am renouncing it, but you shall soon have the philosophical novel which I certainly shall send you."

June 21st 1791. When Lemoine, the King's personal valet, entered his room at the Tuileries at seven a.m., it was to find the bed empty. The news of the flight of the King and his family swept through the capital at once. The Municipality had three volleys of cannon fired, to sound the alarm. The National Assembly issued an order for Louis XVI's arrest after reading the *Declaration to all Frenchmen* which he had left behind him.

FROM VARENNES TO THE SACKING OF LA COSTE

June 24th 1791. Is Citizen Sade to be believed? Detained at
Picous, he made a statement and asserted to the Commission
of the People on the 6th Messidor, Year II, that "When that
scoundrel the Capet [i.e., Louis XVI] came back from
Varennes, I penned a fulminatory letter to him ... it was all
over Paris, people read it on the streets, in the Tuileries, *and
I saw to it that it was* tossed into his carriage as it was crossing
the *Place de la Révolution."*

There is no doubt about it, the letter exists, and Sade was
certainly the author of it. He had it printed by Girouard, who
was publishing *Justine* for him. But did Sade really throw it
himself into the wretched Louis's carriage?* Not that this was
an act completely beyond our hero. Was it perhaps a sort of
communal exhibitionism, or did it result from the contagion
of mass madness? Perhaps both together. There seems nothing
incompatible between this "patriotic" gesture which Citizen
Sade claims to have made and that profession of faith of May
19th in which he made himself out to be so indignant against
the brigands who had "put irons on" the King, or those references to "brigands" and the term "frightful abomination"
which he used to describe the Jacobins of Vence and their
crime of taking the aged Countess de Villeneuve to prison. We
should merely raise one eyebrow at something so little in keeping with Sade's character, suggesting a sort of cowardice of
which we know no other instance in his life. We have already
observed—and it was to show out still more clearly in the years
to come—that when faced with the misfortune of others Sade's
immediate reaction was usually one of generosity. This reaction
never failed him, even regarding the Montreuils, even when for
fifteen years he had sworn that he would take dire vengeance
on them.

Neither a biographer's intuition nor his personal preference
should ever be allowed to play any part in his assessment of the

---

*The original statement runs "par mes soins". The author interprets
this to mean that Sade claimed that he threw a copy of the letter into
the carriage himself. But all that Sade wrote was that he made sure it
would be thrown in—i.e., either he paid somebody to do so or else
otherwise made sure that it would be thrown by a partisan of the
Revolution. (Translator).

facts, but here perhaps two arguments (each of them after all based on concrete observations) may be allowed.

The first reason for questioning the veracity of this statement touches on the moving aspect of that June 24th recorded by memoirists. This was the attitude of dignity—unique in the course of the Revolution—shown by the three hundred thousand Parisians who stood still and watched the Royal coach pass in utter silence. On the walls had been chalked up the warning : ANY PERSON CHEERING THE KING WILL BE FLOGGED, ANYBODY INSULTING HIM WILL BE HANGED. In the circumstances of stolid decorum which resulted it is difficult to place this wild, highly-strung act with which three years later the Marquis chose to embellish his political record.

But, quite apart from whether the incident really took place or was a subsequent fiction of the imagination, why did Sade boast of it? This is our second *caveat.* We must observe the circumstances in which the prisoner at Picpus made his statement. He had been under detention for seven months in the gaols of the Terror. The Decree of the *22 Prairial,* passed a fortnight before this, had laid down one penalty only for those who came before the Tribunal—death. Robespierre's slaughterhouse was becoming greedier with every day that passed. The Committee of Public Safety was actually negotiating the purchase of fresh land for disposal of the bodies! Had not the ex-Marquis, charged with having formerly tried to serve in the Royal *garde constitutionelle,* in itself a crime that had brought a number of men to the scaffold (to which were added the venomous accusations of several witnesses of his district), the most urgent interest in cashing in on any title whatsoever to be at one with the Revolution, and even to deck out that claim in the most vivid colours, to impress a committee of the people and obtain a ticket of patriotism which would save him from the grasp of Fouqier-Tinville? (That order to the people of Paris three years since to remain calm was no doubt long since forgotten by the members of the committee. The spirit of that stage in the Revolution was already very remote.)

Thus, to the honour of the Marquis, the author does not hesitate to claim that on June 24th 1791 he did *not* add insult to injury by throwing any pamphlet at all into Louis XVI's carriage. Outspoken in its language the supposed pamphlet may well have been, but Sade could never be reproached with having written or published it. However contradictory it may have been to what he had said previously, quite possibly this letter did express his mood of the moment, and, as we shall see, his "way of seeing things" on the following December 5th.

But what about the letter, what was really contained in that thin ephemeral little booklet which has never been reprinted? The vigour of Sade's style and the excellent flow of his rhetoric certainly show through in several places. But otherwise this *Address of a French citizen to the King of the French** is about on a level with most of the pamphleteering of the French Revolution. Even the idea is not at all original, and it is far below the quite powerful *Idée sur le mode de la sanction des Lois* (Thoughts on the manner of approving the Laws) which Sade published in October, and also poorer than his petition of June 1793 against the formation of a revolutionary army in the capital. One part is apparently a reply to Louis XVI's complaints about personal insults set forth in his *Déclaration à tous les Français* issued immediately after his flight (which Beauharnais had read to the National Assembly):

> " . . . You complain of your situation, you are cruelly constrained in irons. . . . Ah, but what Sovereign, whose soul was pure and decent, what Sovereign enlightened enough to prefer the well-being of his peoples to the vain pomps of despotism, would not consent to sacrifice a few months of physical comfort to the spiritual comforts such as those which the work of the Nation's Representatives is preparing you. Besides is one so badly off in the loveliest palace of the loveliest city in the world, when the situation above all is but temporary and when it is the certain means of attaining the perfection of the happiness of twenty-five million men? Thus placed as you are in a position which to many another would be happiness, do deign to give a moment's thought to the well-being of the former victims of your despotism, those wretched individuals whom, as a result of somebody's tricking you or of your own lack of thought, your mere signature tore weeping from the bosom of their families to cast them for ever into the dun-

---

*Girouard, printer, *rue du Bout du monde*, 8 pp. 8°, no date.

geon cells of those grim Bastilles which reared all over
your Kingdom. . . ."

How much sincerity was there in this Address? Let the
Marquis himself answer, the Marquis who was also a citizen
of the *Place Vendôme* section, later to be known as the *Section
des Piques,* and also intimate friend of Stanislas de Clermont-
Tonnerre, one of the leaders of the "monarchist" party. On
December 28th 1791—six months later, that is—he wrote to
Gaufridy, who had asked what his attitude really was, so that
he, Gaufridy, might follow suit. Sade assured the lawyer that
there was no subject so "touchy" (*si délicat*) and that as a man
of letters "*the daily necessity of working first for one party,
then another, results in a mobility of opinions which affects
my inmost mode of thought.* And if I really do probe into it,
it proves to be for no party at all, but a compound of them all.
I am an anti-Jacobin and hate them to the death; I worship the
King, but I loathe the old abuses; I love very many articles of
the constitution, but others revolt me; I want the nobility to be
restored in its brilliance, for taking that away does no good; I
want the King to be head of the nation; I do not want a national
assembly, but two houses, as in England, which gives the King
a modified authority balanced by the support of a nation neces-
sarily divided into two orders—the third order* is useless, I
want none of it. There you have my profession of faith. Now
what am I? Aristocrat or democrat? Tell me, please, my dear
lawyer, for I myself have no idea at all."

To have a fair notion of Citizen Sade's behaviour and of his
writings during the Revolutionary régime, though one should
not exclude (for it is a matter of journalism) basic acceptance
of the notion of servitude as inherent in the trade of a man of
letters (though Sade himself gave the lie to that suggestion
countless times in his own works by the undying fire of revolt
that suffuses them) the profession of faith of December 5th,
a veritable retraction of the *Address,* should be kept constantly
in mind.

July 9th 1791. The Marquis wrote to tell Gaufridy that he
refused to re-build the walls at Mazan to satisfy the whims of a

*Obviously, the clergy!

population of "brigands" and "imbeciles" from whom he in any case did not take orders.

July 13th 1791. Sub-lieutenant Louis Marie de Sade, commanding a detachment of the 84th Infantry Regiment at Pornic, resigned his commission.

July 21st 1791. The Commissaries of the *Garde Nationale* of Paris gave the Marquis a receipt for 18 *livres,* sum paid *in lieu* of "personal service" up to July 1st.

Towards September 11th 1791. Louis Marie de Sade left France.

October 14th 1791. The Marquis got news that his cousin, Lady de Raousset, proposed to go to La Coste in March "to enjoy the good season". He implored Gaufridy to do all possible to persuade her not to do so. He spoke from experience. If that woman entered his house, the *château* would be in ruins, from cellar to granary.

Next, having learned that no mail was interfered with between Aix and Paris, the Marquis begged the lawyer to send him "a certain little case" which he greatly counted on obtaining. It contained "certain manuscripts" which he "absolutely must" get back.

He wound up with a passage about his children. His younger son was now nearer to Provence, being in garrison in Lyons. The elder, having resigned his commission, had left the Kingdom and since his departure three weeks since had sent no news of himself. "That young man seems to be harbouring a secret grouse. He is uneasy, restless, he wants to go to the ends of the world, he loathes his fatherland, nobody knows quite what the reason is, but he is unsettled. The other is calmer and better behaved. . . ."

October . . . 1791. Only a few days after putting his lawyer on guard against Lady de Raousset, the Marquis learned of her sudden demise! "I have mourned my dear cousin," he wrote to Gaufridy, "and for many reasons would like to bring her back to life; my dear lawyer, she was my playmate in childhood. She was known as *Pauline* then, and came with you to play in my grandmother's downstairs drawing-room." This expression of the grief that was due was however at once followed by "the business side". After a little flash of fire about her estate, Sade bluntly observed that she left a husband and a mother. It would therefore be necessary to see that the Countess de Villeneuve drew up a good will in his favour, augmented by a third part of what Lady de Raousset left. To this end Gaufridy was to "work body and soul to see that the cash does not evaporate" just when the Marquis went "to tickle my said aunt's right shoulder. They will get round her, all round her. . ." Cannot the lawyer contrive to "detach her from them, talk to her, get others to talk and talk about her nephew" and his "most sincere" devotion? Meanwhile he should as soon as ever possible send the young knight [i.e., Sade's younger son] that six thousand *livres* cross that Lady de Raousset promised him. "I have told him about it. The poor boy won it by the sweat of his loins. That is a love story of dear Lady de Raousset's of which you perhaps never heard, but now we can laugh over it; *it was she had his virginity*. So, that cross, I beg you! . . ."

October 22nd 1791. First performance of the three-act prose play *Le Comte Oxtiern ou les Effets du libertinage* (*Count Oxtiern or the Effects of a Rake's Life*) on the stage of the Molière Theatre in the *rue Saint Martin,* (formerly the *Passage des Nourrices*).

Some days later, the Marquis wrote to Gaufridy:

" . . . At last I have been performed, my dear lawyer. Last Saturday the 22nd one of my plays was put on, the success, thanks to cliques and hirelings and certain women I had insulted, was very modest. It is being repeated on Saturday the 29th with modifications: pray for me; we shall see. Adieu."

The second performance was however postponed till November 4th. When the curtain went down, there was a call for the author, and Sade appeared. On November 6th *Le Moniteur* wrote:

"*Count Oxtiern or the Effects of a Rake's Life,* a three-act prose play, was successfully shown in this theatre.

Oxtiern, a great Swedish noble, is a determined rake. He has seduced and abducted Ernestine, daughter of Count de Falkenheim, securing the imprisonment of her sweetheart on a false charge. He brings the wretched girl to a place one league from Stockholm, but the proprietor of the inn is an honest man. Ernestine's father finds her. Then to have her revenge of the monster who has dishonoured her, Ernestine challenges him to a sword duel in the garden at eleven o'clock at night. The letter is written as if from Ernestine's brother. But her father also challenges Oxtiern, and the latter, aware of Ernestine's plan, conceives the frightful device of getting father and daughter to fight each other. The two arrive on the scene and fight fiercely, but Fabrice the innkeeper has got Ernestine's sweetheart out of prison and the young man separates father and daughter. He then fights Oxtiern and kills him and thus, avenging his mistress, marries her.

This play is interesting for its vigour, but the character of Oxtiern is a revolting atrocity. He is a worse, viler rascal than Lovelace, with none of his more likeable qualities.

A small incident threatened to disturb the second performance of the play. A dissatisfied or malicious member of the audience cried: "Lower the curtain" ... The stage hand made the mistake of doing so more than half way, when many other members of the audience had it raised again and cried "Turn him out!" ... This resulted in some measures of dissension in the audience. A very weak minority hissed while the author was well recompensed by the considerable applause of the majority. He was called for after the show; it was the Marquis de Sade."

The following extract from an undated letter to Gaufridy completes the picture:

"The frightful disturbance that *Oxtiern* caused resulted in its not being repeated with the same title and I delayed further shows. People were at each other's throats. The ushers had to be in constant readiness whenever it was played. I preferred to suspend it. We shall put it on again in the winter."

The story of *Oxtiern* was taken from *Ernestine, a Novel of Sweden,* written in the Bastille by the Marquis and part of the *Crimes of Love* collection published in the *Year VIII*.

The climax of the novel, writes Maurice Heine, was "both more sombre and richer in content" than that of the drama.

"Not only is Ernestine's sweetheart imprisoned. He is also condemned to death, though innocent, and executed on a scaffold erected in front of Oxtiern's windows at the very moment when that person is violating Ernestine! The duel between father and daughter follows, each thinking to be fighting Oxtiern, and Ernestine is mortally wounded. At last her father obtains justice and Oxtiern is reprieved, only to go to forced labour in the mines."

Let us add that *Ernestine* is qualitatively better than *Oxtiern,* which rarely rises above the mediocrity of Sade's unpublished plays. Not, as has been observed before, that Sade could not write dialogue. *La Philosophie dans le Boudoir* and the novels and stories contain excellent dialogue. But the moment he cut his quill to write drama he became flat and clumsy. One needs only to compare the dialogues in *Ernestine* with the corresponding scenes of *Oxtiern!*

November 7th 1791. The *Théâtre du Marais* rejected *Le Prévaricateur.*

November 24th 1791. Sade gave a reading of his tragedy *Jeanne Laisné ou le Siège de Beauvais* to the *Comédie Française* theatre. It was rejected by eight votes to five.

Early January 1792. Sade wrote to Gaufridy. It had been impossible for him, leaving Charenton naked, to be the possessor twenty-one months later of "eight complete outfits of clothing ... fairly good linen, a house which though small is delightful, pleasing enough to be admired in Paris, where people's eyes are sick of luxury ... and with three or four decent houses where I am welcome to dinner or supper whenever I wish, free entry to all the shows, and a measure of literary esteem, a circle of friends who are decent and most attentive to me and some pretty good wine in my cellar" in fact it was impossible for him to have risen from liberated prisoner to his present level, without "much expense, care, work, effort and pluck", all of which had "inevitably" involved incurring debts. He had thought he would be able to settle them with the 10,000 *francs* which Lady de Sade owed him of his mother's legacy, but in vain had he "pleaded, shouted, got angry", she had got away with 4,800 *francs* and because of his "dear spouse" he still had more than 4,000 *livres* of debts. So Gaufridy was requested pressingly *to sell anything* to help the poor marquis. He might frown and cry two or three times [in Provençal] "*Ah! ché peste l'homme ès isso*—do I get my dialect right? I don't know, but pay up quickly and all will be for the best."

January 24th 1792. First rehearsal of the *Suborneur* at the Italian Theatre.

End of January 1792. All business matters between the Marquis and his wife were now completed by court judgements and a "well stuck together" deed.

February . . . 1792. The Marquis honoured a bill of exchange which his son Louis Marie de Sade, *émigré,* had drawn on him.

Early March 1792. As his younger son, garrisoned at Lyons, had paid a few days' visit to Lady de Villeneuve, before going on to Strasbourg, Sade got it into his head and sounded the alarm to Gaufridy, that Donatien Claude Armaud had been prompted by the Montreuils and had gone down to Provence merely to trick his father out of whatever the old Countess had, and collar all the ready cash. However, early in March Sade received reassuring news from Gaufridy about his son's conduct. He made his apologies and even went so far as to say he was annoyed to hear that "the poor little devil" had only got three hundred *francs*. "The visit was worth more than that, why, it won't cover his expenses down there."

However, though wrong about his younger son, Sade need have had no doubts about Lady de Villeneuve's intentions and he expressed the wish that his aunt should outlive him, he would not have two griefs at once, "that of *losing her* and that *of being disinherited by her*". But in order somehow or other to get out of the Countess the money he absolutely needed to buy his house, he began to fix his mind on going down to Provence in the early spring. But where was he going to establish his head-quarters? "Mazan? Uninhabitable. Saumane?

"I am afraid of it." La Coste? He felt a sense of disgust—for the *château,* that is. "My choice would lean towards some house in the village. On the other hand, would that not look like fear and pusillanimity? Although favoured for reasons of equality, goodwill, democracy, would it not be both condemned by my equals and maliciously exposed in its principle by my inferiors?" He would take with him his friend who was "most positively" no more than that to him. "Not the slightest hint of anything wrong" either in the lady's conduct or in his attitude towards her. Since she had decided she would come to Provence, she had read all Gaufridy's letters, so the Marquis advised his lawyer not to make any mention of her which might upset her or be a snub to her, for "this is an extremely decent and very sensitive woman".

March 5th 1792. At the *Italian Theatre* a Jacobin cabal— on this occasion all donning red wool bonnets with the point forward, brought the performance of *Le Suborneur* to a noisy end—because it was by an ex-noble.

On March 10th 1792 the *Journal des Théâtres* wrote: "On Monday March 5th this theatre put on a one-act verse comedy entitled *le Suborneur*. There was a hubbub during the first scene. We could not tell why, for nobody had listened, with talking going on in the stalls as if the curtain had never gone up. With the second scene the din grew greater; at the third, it reached its height, and with the fourth the actors gave up. What was the purpose of this? We had no idea and could not even hear the explanation. But during the interlude we saw patriots donning the red bonnet with the tip turned forward, like the Phrygian *corno*. One of those thus bedecked said in a loud voice that from now on this red bonnet in public places was going to be the signal for rallying all patriots, especially in theatres. . . ."

End of March 1792. An unexpected visit of Sade's younger son, whom he had not seen for two years. "He had just sent a letter from one hundred and sixty leagues' distance and all at once here he was entering the room and throwing his arms round my neck. He had been sent by the Marquis de Toulongeon, to whom he is *aide-de-camp*. He had brought an important letter, as courier, and left at once with the answer. We had scarce four or five hours together."

April 18th 1792. The ex-Marquis, requested to do so by the municipal officers of La Coste, wrote a long letter giving expression to the many reasons for which he felt loyalty to the French Revolution and the Constitution.

April 19th 1792. The following day Sade had firm news that the Constitutional Club of the same commune had passed a resolution that the pinnacles of the old house were to be taken down. At once he addressed an eloquent protest to the President of the society, signing it *Louis Sade*—we shall see later what difficulties Sade had caused himself, for later, in the Year VI, by thus bedecking himself with that little name which did not figure in his christening certificate! In his protest he called on the local patriot not "to give the whole province an example of inconsistency which it would find much too difficult to understand".

" . . . for, *Monsieur le Président,* I am sure you will concede the point that it would certainly be most peculiar in the brief space of three *lustra* to see my unfortunate house La Coste simultaneously sullied by the unworthy myrmidons of ministerial despotism and degraded by the enemies of those myrmidons, whence it would result that the man who has the most of all men reason to loathe and detest the former régime would not know what attitude to adopt, being nevertheless forced to regret the old régime, if among those who ought to share these same sentiments he were to find it impossible to discover friends or defenders. . . . Do you not think those who would thus have mistreated me would not be charged with injustice? . . .

If one single stone of the house which I own in your area is removed, I shall take the matter to our law-givers, I shall take it to your brethren the Jacobins in Paris and request to have it inscribed with these words: 'A stone of the house of the man who made those of the Bastille fall and which the friends of the constitution tore from the dwelling of the most ill-fated of the victims of the tyranny of the kings. Passers-by, include this outrage in the history of human inconsistency!'

Leave my old walls alone, *Monsieur le Président*! Examine my heart, open my writings, read the letters I had printed and distributed throughout Paris when the great ladies of France departed and the King took flight; you will see there if it is right to cause the author of such writings vexation regarding his possessions.... Have I become an émigré, sir? Have I not throughout regarded such a step with contumely? Am I not an active citizen of my section? ... Have I ever been known to claim any other title than *man of letters*? Write to my district and you will see what they think of me there! But you say you don't like my pinnacles? Very well, gentlemen, please be calm. Here I address the community as a whole. All I ask is the honour of having sacrificed them myself, the first time I come to your *département*. The constitution in one hand, a hammer in the other, I would have us make the demolition *a civic occassion*. Let us hold our hand till then, gentlemen, and *respect private property*. These words I take from the very Constitution. I am sure you will have the same respect for them that I have. As I wrote to your honoured councillors yesterday, Brutus and his friends had neither stonemasons nor house-firers in their train when they gave Rome the precious freedom that tyrants had robbed it of."

April 20th 1792. The Marquis urged Gaufridy to send that fourth consignment which he had asked for as far back as December 5th. He begged the lawyer not to forget to include "countless little things" from his natural history cabinet, such as "gold and copper coins and medals of the Roman emperors", "that superb Priapus on a ring", his father's letters, and above all that little box of manuscripts. "Do not fail to send all this, I ask that kindness of you, since I tremble to think of it all in a house threatened by Jacobin masons and incendiaries...."

May 3rd 1792. The municipal officers of La Coste replied to that letter so full "of the fire of patriotism" which they had received from "M. Louis Sade" on April 18th. Read out at the last meeting of the Constitutional Club, it had been received with "the greatest applause" and had been recorded in the minutes. Let their childhood friend have no fears; his properties would be placed under communal protection and that sacred right would never be violated at La Coste.

May 11th 1792. The twenty members of the society of Friends of the Constitution "deeply stirred by the sentiments and constitutional principles" which with the Marquis' letter of April 19th was imbued, and convinced of its sincerity, confirmed that his properties would always be respected. They therefore wished to inform him, over all their signatures, that he enjoyed the "affection and fraternal and inviolable friendship of all the citizens of La Coste".

A date in May 1792. The Marquis de Toulongeon's *aide-de-camp,* Sub-lieutenant Donatien Claude Armand de Sade, deserted. . . .

A date in June 1792. Informed that the Célestins Priory of Avignon was in all probability going to be demolished, the Marquis de Sade wished to provide his ancestress Laura, there interred, with a resting-place which would never be disturbed, in one of the parishes of his estates, for example. But yet would this proposal, "exclusively philosophical" though he conceived it to be, not be interpreted by the "patriots" as an aristocratic gesture? What was Gaufridy's opinion? The Marquis also thought that the friars had "some papers or records" relative to Petrarch's great love, such as the original manuscript of the epitaph verse which François I had written. These should all be secured.

July 10th 1792. A young woman of La Coste (one of Soton's daughters), reached Paris on horseback, to submit to the National Assembly a memorandum against Gaufridy, the former curé and two or three others. The Marquis hastened to tell the lawyer about that strange and not a little disturbing expedition and also about all that Mme Quesnet and he had set moving to get the wretched Soton girl to hold her peace.

A few days later Sade wrote to Gaufridy to tell him that the Soton girl was still causing a lot of trouble all round and had come to see him, with much weeping. He thought "the hussy" was very dangerous. She insisted on going ahead with her memorandum and now said *she could not stop herself* from implicating him as well. This rustic amazon had had a memorandum drawn up by a lawyer, who had forbidden her to let the Marquis see it. Clearly they wanted to involve him "in their thieves' den".

Even as Sade was writing, the Soton girl was at the door again, accompanied by a soldier, whose presence she refused to give any reason for. He had them sent away and gave instructions that the woman was not to be admitted to his house again. "She can think only of attacking us both, but she will see what I shall reply.... Adieu, send money, money, for Heaven's sake."

August 10th 1792. Sade to Gaufridy: "The 10th has been my unlucky date—robbed me of everything, relatives, friends, family, protection, assistance; three hours stripped me of it all, I am alone. . . ."

August 18th 1792. The day after that menacing tenth of August, in order to be prepared for anything, Sade had Citizens Macarel (employed in the state bank-note press) and Girouard (printer and publisher) attest as faithful copies the transcript of three letters which he had just written, one to Lord Montreuil, one to Lady de Sade and one to his two sons, all concerning their having gone abroad as *émigrés*.

He reminded Montreuil of the decree which menaced the relations of *émigrés* with the sword of the law. Thus the Marquis, who had throughout been most outspokenly opposed to his children's desertion, once again found himself victim of the "imbecile acts" of the Montreuil family. "Was it as proof of your own *high nobility* that you insisted on your children and your nephews ranging themselves among the *nobles*? For my part, sir, never having suffered from that ridiculous form of insanity, all I have wished my family to have has been patriotism and honesty.

"That your ambitious half, lady Montreuil, should sacrifice everything, betray everything, in an attempt to put life back into the diseased skeleton of that revolting lawyerocracy and into the poisonous clutches of ministers armed with secret prison orders (*lettres de cachet*) is not at all hard to understand; but in my own indignation, Sir, at the line you have compelled my sons to take, I do assure you that if in a fortnight you do not make them come back to their duties (I cannot do so, because their address is hidden from me)—if in a fortnight they are not in Paris and, like their father, armed for the defence of their fatherland, no consideration will halt me and I shall at once denounce you to the National Assembly and all France as the instigator of their criminal emigration."

Need one point out that this threat is pure form and was written exclusively as a safeguard? Not only was Sade never going to carry it out (and would in fact have been incapable of such meanness?) but the following August he even inscribed his family on a list to be cleared of guilt, whereas a single word from him could have been their ruin.

Finally, to his sons he wrote that the cause they had embraced was a dishonour and an infamy. The King was "a rascal and traitor" and "only lunatics" could still rally to the banner of "such a rogue". But to make things worse, the National Assembly made parents responsible for their children's conduct, and dealt severely with them if those children did not return promptly. "I ask you if it is right for you to stay any longer in a situation which holds a sword dangling over the heads of those who gave you life." He ended his letter: "In a word, my boys, I order you at once to return and you risk my hatred and my curse if you hesitate even a day to obey me."

Let us recall that in February the Marquis had honoured a bill which son Louis had drawn on him abroad. But all was well. Covered now by *sans-culotte* verbiage which was all fake, our trickster of the *Place Vendôme* section thought he could safely await the further developments of France's magnificent "national" events.

August 30th 1792. "M. de Sade" of the 4th battalion, the 5th Legion of the National Guard, was called upon to report to HQ at 11 a.m. on Saturday September 1st, to do twenty-four hours guard duty at the Tuileries.

September 1st 1792. Sade conjured Gaufridy to send him his fourth quarter's revenues. He was sick, he had guard duty in his section to cope with, and that Soton girl was threatening to blazon abroad all his rake's doings between 1773 and 1777!

September 3rd 1792. During the massacres, Sade was for the first time Secretary of his section.

September 6th 1792. Sade to Gaufridy:

" ... Ten thousand prisoners were slaughtered on September 3rd. Nothing can equal the horror of the massacre committed [Sade interpolated 'but justly', in case his letter were opened]. The former Princess de Lamballe was one of the victims. Her head, stuck on a pike, was shown to the king and queen and her poor body was dragged through the streets for eight hours after being subjected to the most savage debauchery,* the refractory priests had their throats cut in the churches where they were kept locked up, among them the Archbishop of Arles, most virtuous and respectable of men. . . ."

It was at about this time that the house which Sade rented, and which he wanted to buy, was bought by a courtesan named Palza for 77,000 *livres*.

September 13th 1792. Informed that Gaufridy and his son Elzéar had been obliged to take refuge in Lyons,** Sade at once offered them the warmest hospitality. He would provide his lawyer with board without asking a *sou,* the son could obtain board elsewhere at 60 *francs* per month, and he would bed them both and provide lighting and heating.

September 17th-21st 1792. On two occasions, Monday 17th and Wednesday 19th, some dozens of people of La Coste village men, women and children, forced their way into the former manor-house, and this was ransacked and pillaged without the national guard being able to do anything to stop it.*** On the Monday they had begun at ten in the morning. To speed up the pillage of the furniture, they had thrown the heavier pieces out of the windows. Whatever could not be taken away had been

*We know, for instance, that one of the princess's executioners cut off her *mons Veneris* and stuck it on his upper lip as a moustache, much to the hilarity of the "patriots."
**Gaufridy and his son had fled together with ten other plotters of Apt (including his colleague Fage) when troops sent to crush the South-Eastern plot arrived, following the arrest of Monier de la Quarrée at Grenoble.
***Writing to the Marquis on October 21st, Paulet, prominent citizen, informed Sade that almost all the big houses of those parts had suffered the same fate. He did not mean to excuse his fellow citizens, he merely remarked that these excesses had been instigated by a handful of ne'er-do-wells of Lauris and that after committing the same outrages in their own locality they had passed on to La Coste.

smashed to splinters. The glass was all broken, partitions were broken down, doors and shutters were taken off their hinges and smashed on the rocks all round. The horde, which that day consisted of eighty-four persons, frightened the national guard the more because they drank the stocks of wine in the Marquis' cellar. On the Wednesday it was about fifty who came back to complete the ruin. Fortunately, Citizen Ange Raspail of Apt, authorised by the communal authorities to intervene, succeeded in preventing the demolition of the floor-boards and the roof. By a mixture of speeches, proclamations, and threats and a judicious use of what forces it did dispose of, the municipality thus succeeded in reducing the destruction of Sade's property as much as they could. They now had all the doors of the *château* walled up, and thanks to their efforts the furniture and other effects which the mob had taken away were reassembled and housed in the vicarage. Not, as we shall see, that this ensured very prolonged security.

September 21st 1792. The legislative Assembly handed over authority to the National Convention, which it had established by decree on August 10th. The new body immediately voted for the abolition of the monarchy in France.

September 23rd 1792. Jean Gardiol, a member of the La Coste council, convicted of having played a part in "the horrors latterly committed at the former manor-house" was reported by his colleagues to the *département's* administrative officers for dismissal.

September 28th 1792. Bearing a requisition order signed by Jacques Montbrion et Bergier, Commissaries of the Administration of the Département of the *Bouches-du-Rhone,* Louis Honoré Raspaud and Laurent Raspaud his son, bailiffs of Apt, called on the municipal offices of La Coste, in order to take from the vicarage and load on to four waggons the furniture and effects belonging to the ex-Marquis. When the Council protested its "sorrow" at the "shocking treatment" inflicted on a citizen whose model patriotism was beyond doubt, the two bailiffs assumed a dictatorial tone and threatened the Council. Notwithstanding this, they were unable to prevent three national guards and the municipality's attorney, with a list of the property, going with the waggons to the outskirts of Apt.

September 30th 1792. At a little before 3 p.m. at La Coste, Citizens Daniel Bas, municipal employee, and Jean Etienne Béridon, a prominent citizen, were informed of a new outbreak of destructiveness at the former manor house. They immediately went there, to see what was happening, and found that Charles Béridon of Goult had torn off the main door and was smashing it up, to get all the iron work. When the two citizens proposed to arrest him, the culprit took to his heels. The same evening the authorities again proclaimed in the village that nobody was to enter the manor precincts, under pain of immediate arrest.

October 10th 1792. Sade implored Gaufridy to give him as much information as he could on the sacking of La Coste. There were incredible details that the younger Gaufridy had given him, such as the removal of certain pieces of furniture which could not be moved without a crane, so the story seemed very queer and incredible. But "the dagger is in my heart" if the news were true, for the loss would be immense.

A few days later, Sade received the resignation of Lions Senior, in insolent terms, and from Mazan the news that everything there was in disorder and that Ripert could no longer be responsible for managing the farm. Sade was obliged to hand it over to a man named Quinquin, a fanatical Jacobin of the town, who however "accepted the task with a mixture of assiduity and impudence, made a muddle of it all, did shady deals with the administrative offices and did not pay a *sou.* ..." These losses, added to the situation at Saumane, were enough to make Sade commit suicide. Indeed, he told Gaufridy that two or three times he had been on the point of blowing out his brains. The lawyer by his flight had prompted a "real conflagration". Once again, "with tears in my eyes", Sade implored Gaufridy to go back, if not to Apt, at least to somewhere in the district, and not to leave his "wretched friend" in such a cruel situation. Did this mean that he, the Marquis, had regained his freedom only to die of starvation? Was he going to live to regret the cells of the Bastille?

Then a frightful letter came in from Reinaud. Sade "shook

all over" as he opened it. It contained the "ghastly details" of what had happened at La Coste.

"That's the end of La Coste for me! ... What a loss! I cannot express it! There was enough furniture in that house to furnish six! ... I am in despair! If you had not been so tardy with your infernal despatching, I might have saved the whole inventory. ..." In addition, Sade now learned of the requisition of the furniture which the municipality had saved.

"If they go on like that, those rogues will soon make their rule a hated one." He was told that the municipality's behaviour had been excellent. He would write to thank them. ... "Adieu, adieu! I have death in my heart."

October 17th 1792. Louis Sade, soldier of the 8th Company of the *Section des Piques (formerly Place Vendôme)*, and commissary for organisation of the cavalry of the same section, lodged a complaint with Rolland, Minister of the Interior, against those who caused and carried out the sacking of his house and against the commissaries of the *département* who had taken away the furniture and other effects temporarily housed at La Coste vicarage.

CHAPTER FIFTEEN

Under the Revolutionary Régime

(part two)

(1792-1801)

CITIZEN SADE OF THE PIQUES WARD

October 25th 1792. The General Assembly of the *Piques Ward* (former *Place Vendôme Ward*) appointed Citizens Sanet *senior* and Sade Commissioners, to discuss with the Commissioners of other wards the necessary steps to make the various managements of the hospitals more appropriate to the public cause.

October 28th 1792. Citizen Sade presented the assembly of management of the hospitals of Paris the five *recommendations* drawn up by himself, and the Piques Ward decided that these recommendations be printed and circulated to the forty-seven other wards of Paris.

October 30th 1792. Sade to Gaufridy: in the last consignment sent by Gaufridy before the sack of La Coste, Sade had found the little case he had been so impatiently awaiting. Alas, it was *empty*! Yet there was no sign of its having been interfered with. What had happened? There was the Montreuil hand in this. They had been after Lady Laure de Launay's letters! However, here was the position as far as his in-laws went. There had been a general comb-out of Paris, and as the Montreuils were absent, their mansion had been sealed. They now wanted the seals removed. Think! They were domiciled in the same ward as Sade himself, and he was on the point of being made Commissioner, to carry out the removal of seals!!!

Was Gaufridy aware, indeed, that now his client was very popular in the Piques Ward? Never a day but what he was entrusted with something! Enclosed, his lawyer friend would find a little screed of his which his colleagues had thought quite a lot of. It still passed Sade's comprehension that Gaufridy could have been harassed so, when he was the legal representative of a man whose patriotism, "built as it is on ten years in the Bastille", was beyond question. Could there any longer be doubts? The one-time marquis had "abandoned all pretensions to aristocracy". Instead, he was "body and soul up to the neck in the Revolution". Yes, indeed, up to the neck. But not with any certainty above it. The guillotine—which on *9 Thermidor* he escaped by a sheer miracle, would have shown him that! But let us not be too sarcastic about a declaration clearly made to placate the *sans-culottes* of Apt.

November 2nd 1792. Having heard two readings by Citizen Sade of his paper entitled: *Consideration of how to support legislation by sanctions, by a Citizen of this Ward,* published by the *Piques Ward* and printed at the press of the *rue de Saint Fiacre,* the general assembly of the ward unanimously agreed to print the same and send to the other forty-seven wards, inviting them to "express their opinion at their earliest convenience on so important a subject". The work was then printed (an 8vo pamphlet of 16 pp.).

This essay was by far the most serious and original of the various little political works of the author of *Aline et Valcour* as citizen of his ward. Every paragraph glows with a powerful sense of liberty and the concluding sentences are most moving in their evident sincerity and sense of fraternity. "Here is what I propose, to reach the indispensable approval of the people by the most prompt and majestic of means. . . ." is how Sade introduces his proposal—an elaborate system of reference of proposed legislation to popular approval throughout the country.

November 4th 1792. Citizen Sade was called upon by the Armed Ward des Piques to report the day after tomorrow at nine a.m. at the National Convention post to do twenty-four hours guard duty and warned that by law this service must be performed in person under pain of twenty-four hours' imprisonment.

December 10th 1792. Two important matters called for Sade's presence in Provence—the disorder of his affairs at La Coste and Mazan, Saumane and Arles, and the state of health of Lady Villeneuve, a legacy from whom might still not come to him. Lady Villeneuve had expressed a desire to see her nephew. But was such a journey quite safe for an ex-marquis, a *"ci-devant"*? Ripert and Reinaud assured him it was not. But Provençal folk, coming in to Paris, expressed the contrary opinion. Who was to be believed? Gaufridy had been back home for some days now, and Sade asked him his opinion, "hand on heart". For there was something alarming about the sacking of La Coste. It showed clearly that there were enemies, "definite enemies, old enemies, clear enemies". He had lodged complaint against them and would prosecute them when he got there. But if they proved the stronger, what insults would he not have to suffer? If they were found guilty, they would kill him. If the lawyer was loth to decide on his own what was to be done, let him take two colleagues as counsel, one of them to be Reinaud, and discuss it with them "coolly".

At the same time, to ease his mind on money matters, Sade would like Gaufridy to send him a note of hand that he had drafted, which would "set his mind at rest, or at least, enable him to wait with less uneasiness". The lawyer was to swear on oath first, that he would achieve the impossible and send the marquis the two thousand *francs* which he needed to take his silver out of pawn, secondly, that he would not give up the management of the estates before the spring of 1794 (Gaufridy before going to Lyons had written that he had secretly been warned to give up Sade's affairs!) and thirdly, that between May 1793 and May 1794 would find eleven thousand and ten *livres* in three equal instalments.

December 13th 1792. Either by error, or in malicious intent, Sade was entered on the *Bouches-du-Rhône département* list of émigrés under the name of *Louis Alphonse Donatien Sade.*

December 26th 1792. Sade complained to Gaufridy about the impudence of young Lions. Lions had sent him only eight hundred and forty *francs* out of the sixteen hundred which he had received from the man who farmed Cabanes. The King had been made to appear before the bar of the Assembly for the second time.

A few days later, reduced to borrowing money at seven per cent weekly interest, Sade enjoined Gaufridy to send a draft. He also remarked that he had been aghast to hear that his name had been stuck up on the boards at Marseilles as an *émigré*. While awaiting certificates for which he had asked, as to whether anybody doubted that he was in fact permanently residented in Paris, he sent his lawyer a printed document issued by the *Piques Ward* which showed that he was a ward secretary. Gaufridy might do worse than show this to people. It was clear that he was a servant of the cause of the people, not the *émigrés*.

January 21st 1793. "Louis Capet, aged thirty-nine, profession: last King of the French", was guillotined in the *Place de la Révolution*, at 10.22 a.m.

February 26th 1793. Together with colleagues Carré and Désormeaux, Sade signed the report he had drawn up about their inspection of five hospitals which the Hospitals Commission had entrusted to them on January 17th.

Though sold at an auction on April 25th 1858, this document has never since come to light. All we know is that it consisted of eighty-eight foolscap sheets with five little lines in Sade's handwriting asserting that he "had never worked but on his own observation and the notes he had made himself or received from his colleagues". If we are to believe Dr Ramon, it was as a result of this report that in future every wretched patient of the hospitals was given a separate bed and people were no longer made to sleep two or three in a bed.

March 1st 1793. Citizen Sade informed the actors of the Théâtre de la Nation (sometime *Théâtre Français*) that if they would agree to perform his one-act comedy in *vers libre* known as *Le Boudoir ou le Mari Crédule* at once—the play which he said they had rejected eighteen months previously, though in fact it was two and a half years—and the manuscript of which, corrected as they had suggested, he now sent them, he would renounce all rights or royalties.

March 15th 1793. Having had no reply to his offer of March

1st, Sade sent the secretary of the *Comédie Française* the following missive:

"If the *Comédie Française* does not accept the offer I made it ... kindly return the play, I never once thought one would have to wait for an acknowledgement of what one *gave* for as long as for what one *sold*. ..."

April 6th 1793. In the late afternoon the former President of the Montreuil court came to the Ward Assembly of which his son-in-law was secretary. The two had not seen each other for nearly fifteen years. They had an hour's talk. "It all passed off as pleasantly as you could wish; I saw that at any moment he was going to invite me to visit him. ..." Imparting this news, Sade pressed Gaufridy urgently for funds.

April 8th 1793. The name of Sade appeared on a list, drawn up and signed by him, of twenty citizens of the ward who were to serve as special jury in the forged banknote case.

April 12th 1793. Informed that the *Théâtre de la Nation* was irritated by his note of March 15th and preparing to return his play, with intimation that they never accepted plays without paying for them and their work excluded such rapid reading as he was demanding, the Marquis got in touch with the Secretary and told him what a pity it was to quarrel; he had held them in high opinion for twenty-five years, which M. Molé could confirm. He asked the Secretary to put the matter straight and ended by pleading in a manner which ill suited his dignity as author. Meanwhile, however, there was a comforting message from the Secretary. His play was going to be read at once. So now the Marquis added a P.S.—was he, the Secretary, going to read the play, or would it be M. Saint Fall; if the latter, would he kindly send him the play back, to run through it once again.

April 13th 1793. Sade informed Gaufridy he was appointed a court assessor.

"I have two items of news which will surprise you. Lord Montreuil has been to see me! And guess the other! I'd give you a hundred tries! I am appointed magistrate, yes, magistrate! By the prosecution! Who, my dear lawyer, would have told you *that* fifteen years back? You see how wise in its old age my head is becoming. . . . But do at least congratulate me, and above all do not fail to send *Monsieur le Juge* some money, or, confound it, he'll be *condemning you to death*! Spread that news about a bit, will you, so they realise that I really am a good patriot, for I assure you, I really am that, body and soul."

May 5th 1793. Gaufridy had still not sent Sade either his quarter of the 3,670 *francs* or the 2,000 which he wanted to get his silver out of pawn. Penniless and unable to find anybody to lend to him, he was "frankly dying of hunger". The "detestable tardiness" of his lawyer was indeed "a stab in the back".

May 7th 1793. The Minister of the Interior addressed a letter to "Citizen Sade, at *871, rue de la Ferme des Mathurins*". He would have the honour of receiving him and his colleague the following day.

May 13th 1793. A certificate of residence was delivered by the *Piques Ward* to "François Aldonze Sade, man of letters and sometime Cavalry Colonel, aged fifty-one years, five foot two inches high, grey haired, with rounded, full face, open forehead, blue eyes, short nose, medium mouth, round chin".

May 26th 1793. On a petition presented by *Louis* Sade, supported by the opinion of the Apt *département* (both dated April 23rd) the central administration of the *Bouches-du-Rhône département* decided that Sade had satisfactorily established his continual residence in France and ruled that his name should be forthwith erased from the list of *émigrés,* and his full right to his estates and other possessions recognised.

A month later, Vaucluse *département* was established as an administrative unit separately from the *Bouches-du-Rhône département*, but by accident or mischief the new *district* was supplied with a list of absentee *émigrés* on which Louis Sade's name still stood.

This was to have grave consequences in 1798, made all the worse by the whimsical way in which Sade's Christian names had always been treated, so that now he appeared as Louis, now as Aldonze Donatien Louis, now as merely Aldonze François. . . .

June 15th 1793. Citizen Sade, secretary of the assembly of the wards of Paris meeting at the Bishopric, was appointed one of the four delegates who the next day were to present an address to the Convention, calling for annulment of the decree which established a Parisian army of six thousand men at forty *sous* a day.

June 16th 1793. On this Sunday Citizen Sade read the address of which he was the author. It was signed by Pyron, Chairman of the Committee, and Sade himself as secretary, and published by the *Piques Ward* printing-press, a four page octavo document. There is also another edition entitled Draft Petition, which contains fragments of sentences and even whole sentences which are not in the final version.

June 17th 1793. The general assembly of the Piques Ward came back to the question of this Parisian army. It was astonished that Adjutant-General Muller, adjutant of the Minister of War, should have issued orders that six thousand muskets and six thousand pikes should be set aside for this force, though the wards had almost no weapons at all. The assembly called for a share-out among the wards of Paris, which were all invited to join in, and appointed Citizens Sade and Vincent to submit an extract from the day's minutes to the Minister of War. We can imagine who wrote the extract! This too was printed, as a four-page pamphlet in 16°.

July 11th 1793. At the conclusion of the deliberations of the General Assembly of Hospitals, Citizen Sade (who took the chair on this occasion) decided that each ward should provide the Committee charged to reform abuses with the names of all its sick in hospital, so that a thorough check could be made of how they were being treated.

July 19th 1793. Another document was printed: *The Piques Ward to its Brothers and Friends of the Society of Liberty and Equality of Saintes, Département of the Lower Charente* (four pages, 8°). It was signed by Pyron, (chairman), Girard, (vice-chairman), and Artaud, Sade and Clavier (secretaries). It was a reply to an address delivered to the Ward on July 3rd. It ended:

"In advance, Brothers and Friends, accept the fraternal

greetings that we are preparing for you for August 10th, which the *Parisians,* your loyal friends, your faithful comrades, will repeat amid the most affectionate embracings."

Oh, those "delights of the new régime" which the printed message assured the men of the Lower Charenton *département* they were all going to enjoy! Sade was soon to know them quite well—in Robespierre's prisons. As for those "affectionate embracings" of those "faithful comrades and loyal friends", such as those of the *Piques Ward,* as we shall see, less than six months later they were prepared to snuff him out for ever, merely to appease the Committee of General Security with another victim.

July 23rd 1793. Sade wrote to Gaufridy. He had been made *chairman*! ("See yet another step up!") And yesterday "papa Montreuil was in the hall".

August 2nd 1793. Meetings of the Piques Assembly had become so stormy that Chairman Sade was "a wreck, worn out". He had been spitting blood. Today, after having twice been obliged to put on his cap, he had handed over the Vice-chairmanship. They wanted him to put "a horrible proposal, utterly inhuman", to the vote. "Not on your life! Ye Gods, I am through with it all!"

Telling Gaufridy this news the next day, he also remarked that he had had the Montreuils put on the list of those who were cleared of plotting against the Revolution. "It only needed a word from me, and they were finished. I held my tongue. That is the sort of vengeance I take!"

There is no question about it, Sade did use his position as vice-chairman to intervene wherever he could in favour of those under his jurisdiction who had been denounced, and it is equally beyond doubt that this attitude of his, which the above instance illustrates, was the cause of that hostility of his fellow members who were without doubt responsible for his arrest the following December. One only needs glance at what they had to say of Citizen Sade when they were cross-examined in the Committee of Public Safety.

September ... 1793. Sade was busy writing to Gaufridy, with characteristic sarcasm reproaching him about owing some hundred and twenty *francs,* when a letter from Quinquin was brought him which left him aghast: worried by the Jacobins, and about "the Marseilles business", Gaufridy was in flight!

However ridiculous Citizen Sade might find it this "Marseilles affair" was quite real. The lawyer had been put in a difficult position by his own son, Elzéar, who was a supporter of the federal idea, and in June joined the separatist army of the *département.* Paul Bourdin furnishes us with some information on Gaufridy's stay in Toulon, a city which had been won over to the idea and served as asylum to its victims. He tells us of the timorous lawyer's subsequent misfortunes as despite himself he became involved in events quite alien to his nature:

> "There were a few men of Apt, Gaufridy and Fage among them, who took refuge at Toulon after the back of federal movement was broken and Carteaux entered Marseilles, but while they were busy acclaiming Louis XVII there and sporting white cockades, they were recognised by two soldiers who were from Apt, but were prisoners at the time, and these men denounced them some months later. They were imprisoned and only escaped the death penalty by the production of certificates of residence supplied by obliging municipal officers. Fage indeed was re-arrested a second time, together with his family, while for some time Gaufridy and his son moved 'from pillar to post' on Mt Luberon. This was probably where they still were when at the beginning of *Year III* Goupilleau and the Marquis obtained a pardon for them."

Let it be added that all the time Gaufridy took advantage of favourable moments to go back home for a few days. Letters exchanged with Sade in November 1793 and January 1794 certainly show that at those dates he was back at Apt.

August 28th 1793. Promised the purchase for forty thousand *francs* of a house in the *rue de Miromesnil* in the Roule quarter, Sade empowered Citizen Quinquin Le Veuf to dispose of his Mazan *château,* to obtain the necessary sum. He enjoined Le Veuf to press the matter forward. He was also to remind Gaufridy to send his September draft, because he had no news of the lawyer.

August 29th 1793. The Health Committee appointed Sade to

ensure the good working of the hospital services, both on the clinical and the management sides.

September 20th 1793. Down at Apt on official business, as Commissioner of the Vaucluse *département* Sade signed a summons served on the Chairman of the Society of Friends of Liberty and Equality, with headquarters at Sault. Were it not for revolutionary slapdash ways, it might have struck somebody that the signature was that of a man on the *département*'s list of *emigres*!

September 29th 1793. "Approving the principles and the vigour" of a *Speech to the Shades of Marat and Le Pelletier*, written by Citizen Sade, the General Assembly of the Piques Ward decided to print this and to send it to the National Convention, to all *départements*, to the armies, to the central public authorities of Paris, to all the forty-seven other wards and to all societies of the people. The *Speech* had been delivered by the ex-Marquis standing on the plinth of the monument in the *Place des Piques* on the occasion of the public commemoration of those "great men" who fell at the hand of "slaves".

This is the most disappointing of Sade's little political works. Not that it lacks his native eloquence, not that the familiar grandeur of his prose is missing (as sheer music, apart from its meaning, it would delight the ear) but in the gush of revolutionary commonplaces such words as *virtue, happiness, patriotism* and *liberty* are frivolously used, to express *falsehood* and *ignorance*. One might even imagine that Sade had intended the thing as a parody, some twisted sort of satire on that ghoul of the Revolution, Marat.

But though while imprisoned under the Terror Sade many a time wrote such exorbitant rubbish that the men who held his life in their hands were really deceived, we are obliged to admit here that this paean of praise of Marat and Le Pelletier was genuinely meant and sincerely delivered.

At the same time, as we have seen, in his work as Ward Chairman, he showed all the features of a moderate. We have to agree with Dr Marciat. The speech in question "was no doubt an expression rather of the collective will than any individual emotions". To this may be added that in it we have the unconscious blindness to reality of the dramatic author whose work so many a theatre had rejected, who had been hissed off the stage by redcaps at the Italian Theatre, but was now able to revel in the applause of the masses assembled on a stage of such scale as the *Place Vendôme*. Sade himself had once written of the "fanaticism" which was so to be regretted as perhaps the natural emotion of what he ironically called his "lovely, gentle nation". Soon enough this was to show him how clear-sighted that earlier judgment had been. Meanwhile, here is an extract from his set piece on Marat:

> "Oh, timid, gentle fair sex, how could it be that your delicate hands could take up that dagger? Ah, but the eagerness you all show, coming to cast your flowers on the tomb of that true friend of the people, has made us oblivious of the fact that the hand that struck sprang from among you. Like those mixed creatures which belong to neither sex, vomit of hell of universal ill omen, the barbaric murder of Marat belongs to nobody. Let a funeral veil hide her memory for ever, let nobody ever more depict her, as has been done hitherto, under the seductive sign of loveliness. Too credulous by far, you artists, destroy, deface, smash the features of that monster, or show it to us solely amid the demons of Tartary. . . ."*

Thus as "Citizen Sade" the man who had sung the praises of the amazon of Beauvais and who later was in *Isabelle de Bavière* to pay a tribute to Joan of Arc, outraged the recent memory of that other heroine, Charlotte Corday, whose retort to her judge (Montané) was in no wise feebler than that of the girl of Domrémy—"With him [i.e. Marat] dead, the others may feel fear." How different from André Chénier's undaunted lines to Charlotte Corday which are to be compared with what in his *Feuillets d'Hypnos* René Char wrote about the Nazi monsters. "This is the time when a poet feels the meridional vigour of ascension rise within him!"

> *The sword shall arm you, oh maiden great and sublime,*
> *To shame the Gods and make amends for their crime*
> *When they gave that monster human shape. . . ."*

*The speech was printed by the Ward printing-press: *Discours prononcé á la Fête décernée par la Section des Piques, aux mânes de Marat et de Le Pelletier, par Sade, citoyen de cette Section, et membre de la Société populaire—29 September 1793, l'an II de la République française, une et indivisible.*

In due course we shall have to relate what sheer luck it was that ensured that the man who thus sullied Charlotte Corday's name did not mount the scaffold himself exactly three days after the Chénier who thus praised her. Chénier was executed on the 7th Thermidor and Sade was on the list for the 9th Thermidor! Another astonishing coincidence was that had not Marat been thus knifed by lovely Charlotte, Sade would soon have known at his own cost how efficiently that man worked whose "sublime deeds" (Sade's own words) were devoted to "human happiness" and the Marquis' headless trunk would by several months have preceded the earthly remains of Chénier into one of the common graves of the Revolution. For there could be no man that the "green enemy of the people" loathed so much as Sade, whom he would know from Delaure's list of former aristocrats. It was about a month before his death —on June 2nd 1793, to be exact—that, misled by the similarity of the names, Marat denounced the Marquis de la Salle in his paper. In due course he discovered his mistake, and had it not been for the devil's attention, would soon enough have repaired the error by handing over the hero of Arceuil and Marseilles to the virtuous blade of the guillotine.

Of all this Sade was no doubt in ignorance, or he would indeed have been made to thrust laurels on the man who would have liked to have him cough his last gasp into the bag.

October 16th 1793. Marie Antoinette was executed.

Sade's sentiments regarding the Queen would seem to be contained in a jotting among his *Literary Notes.*

"*Spoken by Antoinette at the Conciergerie Prison:* 'The savage brutes who surround me, daily invent some new humiliation to add to the horror of my fate; drop by drop in my heart they distil the poison of adversity, counting my every sigh with delight and quenching their thirst with my tears before they come to feast on my blood'."

Obviously enough, these words were copied out as apposite to Sade's own fate. But was the quotation not intended also as genuine respect for a woman greatly to be pitied? There would be nothing astonishing in this from the man who, when a little later he came out of the gaols of the Revolution, was to cry: "My detention by *the nation,* with the guillotine before my eyes, hurt me a hundred times more than all the Bastilles in the world could have done." The profound humanity shown in those words—among a dozen other such pronouncements—is in striking contrast to the smug words of that jackal, Citizen Restif de la Bretonne, who quoted a shocking remark about the Queen's martyrdom, and apropos of the frightful end of the Countess du Barry could say: "She went to execution like La Fontaine's sow, squealing."

November 14th 1793 (24th Brumaire, Year II). Citizen Sade, man of letters, sent Gaufridy a new statement of his income. That which he had sent recently was worthless. Would the lawyer have the figures certified by the authorities of La Coste, Mazan, Saumane and Arles? From his fine figuring it appeared that when all deductions were made he had 100 *francs per annum.* Among the deductions were the 4,000 *francs* which he had never paid Lady de Sade and an annuity of 1,000 *francs* to Citizeness Quesnet, described as his "natural and adopted daughter".

November 15th 1793 (25th Brumaire, Year II). Sade was the leader of seven other delegates (Vincent, Artaud, Becq, Sanet, Bsoir, Gérard and Guillemard) at the bar of the National Convention, to read the *Petition* of the Piques Ward which he himself had written (it was published by the Ward press) proposing the idolatrous worship of the Virtues, complete with hymns and incense, at the deserted altars of the Catholic faith. The Convention received the paper favourably, passed a resolution to include it in the minutes and decided to pass it on to the Committee on Public Education.

End of November 1793 (Frimaire, Year II). Nine cases of belongings of the former Marquis, which good Paulet of La Coste had sent to Gaufridy some months previously, were seized by the authorities.

December 4th 1793 (14th Frimaire, Year II). Minister of the Interior Paré to Citizen Sade, Military Welfare Commissioner of Hospitals:

"Citizen, you asked me on the 6th inst. to obtain for you a copy of a letter written by Launay, Commandant of the

Bastille concerning yourself to Villedeuil, then Minister of State; I have had search made for this letter in the archives of the Home administration, and one has been found dated July 3rd 1789, which may be the one you request and I am having a copy sent you."

PRISONS OF THE RÉGIME OF LIBERTY
(MADELONNETTES, CARMES, SAINT LAZARE AND PICPUS)

December 8th 1793 (18th Frimaire, Year II). In re a "note in the form of a list" in the hand of Citizen Pache, former Mayor of Paris, under the heading *Extract from the Brissac Letters** in which Citizen Sade figured as having applied for service in 1791 for himself and his sons in the Royal Constitutional Guards, a warrant of arrest was issued against the same as suspect by the Department of Police of the Commune of Paris. Bearing this warrant, Citizen Juspel applied to the Revolutionary Committee of the Piques Ward at 10 a.m., to obtain one of its members to go with him and effect the arrest. Michel Laurent was appointed for the purpose, and together the two went to the *rue Neuve des Mathurins.* Citizen Sade was found in the company of Citizeness Quesnet. The house was searched, seals were placed and left in charge of *sans-culotte* François Tijot as bailiff. The suspect was arrested and taken to the Madelonnettes Prison.

As soon as he reached the prison, Sade sent an agonised appeal to his colleagues of the Piques Ward. But they were far from leaping to his assistance. Rather were they concerned to please the masters of the day. The Watch Committee hastened not to deny, but *to add to the charges—though later on, after Thermidor,* the same citizens were with equal eye to the better chance just as eager to certify to Sade's good qualities and civic spirit!

But first, a few words on the prison in which during the six weeks that he spent there the Robespierrian "rascals" made the former marquis sleep in the privies! The *Madelonnettes* was

---

*"Brissac" was Louis Hercules Timoléon, Duke de Brissac, General Commander of Louis XVI's Constitutional Guard. The accusation was serious indeed. Any convicted of being in this force were at that time being guillotined. We give Sade's own explanation of the letter to Brissac below.

originally a convent hostel founded in 1720 by the Order of the Daughters of St Michel. Under the monarchy it was intended as a sort of Reformatory for four classes of inmates: girls sent there to do penance, called the daughters of St Martha (grey robe), prostitutes who, having shown evidence of mending their ways, were admitted, to take their vows, prostitutes sent there by authority (lay gown and violet veil), and loose-living girls of good family whom it was hoped to reform. Thus there was a great assortment of delightful ghosts of nearly a century of sexual indulgence who may well have proved enchanting to the author of *Justine* while he was held there. Nor on rather a different level can he have been quite unresponsive to the French actors who as Talma's political opponents were incarcerated in this place when at the beginning of 1793 the convent was first made a prison.

After the Revolutionary period the Madelonnettes building was still used as prison. Between 1848 and 1866 it was reserved for political prisoners. In 1866 it was demolished. The buildings which line the *rue Ste Elizabeth* and the *rue Turbigo* now stand on the site.

January 12th 1794 (23rd Nivôse, Year II). In the evening Sade was taken from the Madelonnettes prison to his home, to be present at the opening of the seals and examination of his papers. This operation took place shortly before midnight. Fourteen country letters were seized, to be passed to the department of police. The Commissioner decided not to re-seal the house, as Citizen Sade declared himself unable to go on paying *sans-culotte* Thiot to mount guard over the seals.

January 13th 1794 (24th Nivôse, Year II). The municipal police department ordered the transfer of prisoner Sade to the Carmelite Convent in the *rue du Vaugirard*. He spent only one week there, but it was a week shut up with six persons suffering from malignant fever, two of these dying in his presence.*

---

*This convent, founded in 1611 to carry out the new ideas of St Theresa, was made a prison during the Revolution. The building still stands, No 70 in the *rue du Vaugirard*, but the garden has been built on. On September 2nd 1792 one hundred and fifty priests who would not take the oath were imprisoned there and Danton's murderers slaughtered them with pikes, axes and clubs. Among them were the Archbishop of Arles and the Bishops of Saintes and Beauvais. Later Josephine de Beauharnais was imprisoned there.

January 22nd 1794 (3rd Pluviôse, Year II). By an order of the 1st Pluviôse, Sade was transferred to the Saint Lazare Hostel.*

March 8th 1794 (18th Ventôse, Year II). A "Report on the political bearing of Citizen Sade" made to "the representatives of the people of the Committee of Public Safety" in the form of a questionnaire filled in by the Watch Committee of the Piques Ward : *(to be filled in within eight days of receipt)*.

"1. Name of prisoner, residence before arrest, age, number of children, their ages, where they are, and if he is a widower, bachelor or married man: Sade, 36 *rue Neuve des Mathurins*, married, about 60.

2. Where held, since when, for how long, on whose order, why. Madelonnettes, last *Frimaire*, by order of police administration, as suspect.

3. Profession before and after the Revolution. Former Count.

4. Income before and after the Revolution. Own income, stated by same to be 8,000 *livres*.

5. Relations, connections. With Brissac, Captain of Capet's Guard, trying to obtain service in it for himself and family; letters at the Mayoralty under seal say this man was in correspondence with enemies of the Republic.

To give his patriotism an air of validity, makes much of having been imprisoned in the Bastille, under the old régime, whereas he would have suffered another condign punishment, had he not been of noble caste. In short, by all showings, a very immoral man, most suspect and unworthy of society, if one is to believe the remarks against him in volume three of *L'Espion anglais* or Volume 1 of the list of former nobles, p. 89, No. 28.**

6. What character and political opinions did he reveal in

---

*Built in 1632 as a Lepers' Hostel, under Saint Vincent de Paul, then a hospital and place of retirement, this eventually became a place of punishment. Sacked in July 1789, it went out of use in 1792, but was used to house suspects from January 18th 1794. Among the unfortunates who spent some time there were the Duke de Beauvilliers and his wife, the Princess of Monaco, André Chénier, Roucher, the Trudaine brothers, Suvée and Hubert Robert the painters, the Baron de Trenck, the Marquis de Montalambert, the Count de Bourgeilles and Marie Louise Laval, Abess of Montmartre. From 1818 to 1935 it was a hospital and women's prison—the notorious Mata Hari was imprisoned there. It was demolished in 1940. No. 107 *rue du Faubourg Saint Denis* stands on the site.

**Dulaure's libel, Year II.

May, June, July and October 1789, on August 10th, when the
tyrant fled and when the tyrant was executed, on May 31st
and when war threatened, and did he sign petitions or decisions
destructive of liberty?

Since he first approached this Ward, subsequent to August
10th he has throughout pretended to be a patriot, but the
members of the ward were not deceived by this. *Primo*, he revealed his true colours in a petition which was counter to the
principles of the Revolution and opposed to the formation of
the army of the Revolution decreed by the Convention.

In October 1792, when he came to the Ward, he first was
against the decision taken by the Assembly to the effect that
Roland had lost the confidence of the Ward and was unworthy
of that of the French nation, his specious pretext for this being
that he had not sufficient material proof and one would have
to wait before condemning a man of such virtue. Enemy of the
Republican clubs by principle, and making frequent comparisons in his conversation with the history of Greece and Rome
to prove the impossibility of establishing a democratic and republican Régime in France.

The Committee in session having re-read the present ques-
tionnaires and the facts set forth in it has after due consideration
decided that the same should be signed by all members and
forwarded to the Committee *instanter*.

[signed]Laurent, Vaillant, Montonnet. Crespon.
Garnier. Belloiel. Lhullier. Philippon. Moulin.
Chatard. Georges. Langlois."

Either on the same day (*18th Ventôse*) or the 8th of the
following *decade* (*28th Ventôse*)—it is not quite clear which
—Sade submitted his own statement. This is certainly dated
the 28th, but the folder in which we find it contains the covering note of the Piques Ward, which is dated *18th Ventôse*.
Either Sade's date is an error, or perhaps the date of a copy.
The former seems the more likely.

Here are the main points of Sade's statement, which is in
the main written sarcastically. If in 1791 he wrote to Brissac
to ask for a post in the guard, that was because at that date
he had no notion of how scandalously that guard had been
formed. Since 1789 his conduct had been inspired by his loyalty
to the Revolution. Even before the capture of the Bastille, he

had harangued the people from his cell window. On August 10th he had fought. He was delighted when the King was executed and the country delivered from "the most immoral, most rascally and most shocking tyrant". His ward had recognised his patriotism, appointing him to the most important posts and engaging him to draft almost all the *memoranda* it submitted to the Commune, finally selecting him to speak when the busts of Marat and Le Pelletier were unveiled. Where his children were he had no idea. If they had emigrated, let them be publicly cursed. He was concerning himself with the up-bringing of the son of the mistress of his household, Citizeness Quesnet, in the spirit of patriotism. The "purest civic sense" would always inspire their household. "When it is for the good of the country, the true patriot can suffer without complaint." He had "never been noble". His ancestors had been either in business or had cultivated the land. As soon as he was set at liberty he was proceeding to a divorce, and then he was going to marry "a tailor's daughter, one of the finest women patriots of Paris".

Who would dare to reproach Sade for this ingratiating ser-vility, this deliberate deception, rather, by which he hoped to maintain head and body in direct contact, now that he was face to face with the voracious jowl of the *Committee of Public Safety*? After all, with all its imitation of the *sans-culotte* manner, the only sentence really worthy of the former marquis in this statement seems almost deliberately ambiguous. "Sade, do bear in mind the irons which the despots made you wear and rather die a thousand times than drag out an existence under any régime which consented to revive them." But there was little risk that an Amar, a Vouland, or a Moïse Bayle, brutalised as they were by so much blood, would see any double meaning here.

March 27th 1794 (7th Germinal, Year II). The prisoner of Saint Lazare was transferred "for reasons of illness" to the Picpus hospital, known as Coignart House, near the *Barrière du Trône,* a prison quite recently opened.

G. Lenôtre's *Jardin de Picpus* contains valuable information on Coignart House, formerly the convent of the Canonesses of St Augustine, who had been obliged to move out in May 1792.

"In October of this year," he says, "Citizen Riedain became tenant of the vacated convent. After eighteen months in March 1794, he found a sub-tenant in Citizen Coignard, who had the notion of profiting by the reputation of the Picpus district, which was famous for its clean air. He proposed to establish a *prison hospice* there—a lucrative business during the Terror. It was the notorious Belhomme, who had an establishment of this sort in the *rue de Charonne,* who was the initiator of that lucrative business. By an agreement with the officials around him, more or less paid for, Belhomme acquired the right of housing rich prisoners who under excuse of illness were transferred to him—and forgotten. Board was excellent, but expensive; by going to Belhomme men purchased their lives. By sub-renting the former convent and its lovely garden, well enclosed in high walls, more than twelve hundred feet by two hundred, with straight avenues of trees enclosing plots with vegetable garden, fruit trees and bushes and vines, Coignard dreamt of rivalling Belhomme. As soon as the place was ready, that same spring, there was no lack of boarders, as may well be imagined. All were suspects who, still in possession of their revenues, preferred paying a high price in cash to being dealt with by the guillotine."

May 23rd 1794 (4th Prairial, Year II). In the general list of Vaucluse émigrés drawn up on this day, *Louis* Sade, who had been struck off the *Bouches-du-Rhône* list on May 26th 1793, was entered on page 29 with the Christian names of Louis Aldonze Donatien and the note: "Noble, last domicile La Coste, Apt district" and the additional note "declared émigré by the Bouches-du-Rhône *département*".

June 10th 1794 (22nd Prairial, Year II). In the National Convention Couthon made a statement on a decree which had just been incubated in the bosom of the Committee of Public Safety:

"The régime of despotism had created a judicial truth which was neither moral nor natural truth ... evidence alone had no right of conviction without witnesses or documents. ... Indulgent counter-revolutionaries would have liked to submit the people's justice and the course of the revolution to such rules of justice.... Everything conspired to soften or divert justice.... Without surprise wives would demand that Liberty should be sacrificed in favour of their relatives, their husbands, their friends.... The result of that was that popular justice never showed that awe-inspiring attitude or developed the energy which was its duty and it was considered a fine thing to be just towards individuals without caring much for being just towards the Republic.... The life of criminals was here set against that of the people; here any accommodation or unnecessary formalities are a public danger. The only delay in punishing the enemies of the fatherland should be to the time required to recognise them.... Indulgence to such is atrocious, clemency is parricide."

The same gentleman then read out the new decree, the principal sections of which were:

1, 2 and 3: the revolutionary tribunal was to be quadrupled.

6. The category of "suspects" included anybody who "tried to divert opinion astray... to ruin morals, corrupt the conscience of the public or adulterate the energy and purity of revolutionary or republican principles". (A free hand for the police!)

7. The penalty for any crime with which the revolutionary tribunal dealt was to be death.

9. Any citizen had the right to arrest and bring before the courts any conspirator or counter-revolutionary. He was required to denounce them as soon as he knew them.

16. The law gave calumniated patriots, patriot jurors for their defence, but did not grant such privileges to conspirators.

20. The Convention abrogated any disposition of any preceding law which did not conform to the present decree and it was understood that the laws concerning the set-up of ordinary courts did not apply to counter-revolutionary crimes or the working of the Revolutionary Tribunal.

Despite the requests for postponement which came from Ruamps and Lecontre (of Versailles), this "slaughter-house ruling" was passed when Robespierre made an angry speech supporting it.

June 24th 1794 (6th Messidor, Year II). Sade submitted to the Convention of the People a statement on his political conduct. In this he went into rather more explanation than he had in his replies of 18th Ventôse to the General Committee of Public Safety. To his statement he took care to attach some score of supporting documents, such as the copy of Villedeuil's letter to de Launay and of his own speech on the shade of Marat and Le Pelletier. He said he had all these papers, and was ready to submit them if required to. In a postscript he added that his arrest on 18th Frimaire had been made by order of a police officer of the old régime, which had now to a man been imprisoned and even guillotined.

July 24th (6th Thermidor, Year II). Sade's file as drawn up by the Piques Ward was forwarded by the Committee of Public Safety to the Revolutionary Tribunal in covers bearing the following inscription : ALDONZE *SADE* EX-NOBLE AND COUNT, MAN OF LETTERS AND CAVALRY OFFICER CHARGED WITH CONSPIRACY AGAINST THE REPUBLIC.

July 26th (8th Thermidor, Year II). Fouquier-Tinville, public prosecutor of the Extraordinary Revolutionary Criminal Tribunal, drew up the indictment against twenty-eight accused persons, among whom was Aldonze Sade, No. 11 on the list. Here is the paragraph concerning Sade:

"Sade, former Count, Captain of Capet's guard in 1792, corresponded and communicated with the enemies of the Republic. He has continuously fought against the republican régime, maintaining in his ward that such a régime will not work. He has shown himself to be a supporter of federalism and the protector of the traitor Roland. Finally, it would seem that the proofs of patriotism which he has given have on his part merely been the means of escaping enquiry into his complicity in the tyrant's plot, of which he was a vile adherent."

July 27th 1794 (9th Thermidor, Year II). Bearing a warrant with the names of the twenty-eight accused, the court bailiff went to the various prisons to summon the prisoners and take them for trial. But as despite all the bailiff's efforts Arpajon, Forceville, Montfort, Serre de Saint Romans and "Aldonze *Sade*" could not be found, only twenty-three persons were brought before the second section, presided over by Scellier. A cursory debate, which—in Couthon's words,—lasted just long enough *to identify the enemies of the fatherland,* and all the band of accused were condemned to death except two. Aviat-Turot, a farmer, was acquitted while Perrine Jeanne Leroux Maillé, (whose late husband was related to Sade through his mother, *née* Maillé de Carman), had a fit when she entered the court and was for this reason taken back to the Conciergerie prison.

The fact is, there were already so many prisons and the mounting disorder in the records was such that transfers could not be all entered up to date! No doubt the bailiff tried to find Sade in the Madelonnettes prison, the Carmelite House, or at St Lazare. There can hardly be any other explanation for his not getting his man. He certainly went to Picpus, (where Sade was), for he extracted Béchon d'Arquian, second on the list, from that prison.

Thus Sade escaped the guillotine by pure accident. It was also by sheer accident that he was spared the most frightful moral test of all during the reign of Terror. For here is what happened. Immediately after sentence the twenty-one victims of Sade's batch were bundled into waggons, which were to take them to the *Barrière du Trône* with other victims. Somebody had meanwhile called on Fouquier-Tinville, to point out that there were disorders in Paris. Did it not look like a complete change of policy? Would it not perhaps be wise to hold up the executions?

"Nothing shall halt the course of justice" was the public prosecutor's reply.

"And so the waggons left," the historian Campardon relates, "and passed through Paris, the people in the streets watching their passage in grim silence. In the *rue du Faubourg St Antoine,* where hitherto it had been usual for the victims to be insulted and jeered at by the Tribunal's paid men, people tried to stop them and unharness the horses, to set the poor creatures free. Everybody knew that Robespierre had just signed the arrest warrants. The armed escort hesitated. They would no doubt have given way. But at that point some uniformed men came galloping up. It was Hanriot with his staff. He was scouring the town, to rally Robespierre's supporters. He was completely drunk. With their sabres his men drove the crowd away from the waggons and the hesitant executioners. After that, the procession continued on its way and after those moments of hope the condemned were executed at the Vincennes bar."

The Vincennes bar was the Barrière du Trône, or the *Place du Trône-renversé*—the Square of the Overturned Throne—thus christened after the execution of Louis XVI. The site was only a few hundred yards from Picpus hospital. It may be recalled that the guillotine had been transferred here because people whose houses bordered on the *Place de la Concorde* could no longer bear the stench of the blood. When the guillotine was moved a modification in the apparatus was made, to enable the executioner's men to drain off the blood to the Picpus charnel-house. A lead-lined vat was placed under the knife to catch it!

Thus this party, which should have included Sade, was executed five hundred yards away from him. Sade was inwardly torn because he had the impression that some double of his had suffered in his place. On November 19th 1794, a month after he was finally set free, describing his experience of four revolutionary prisons, he wrote:

"An early paradise, a lovely building, a magnificent garden, choice company, charming women, then all at once the guillotine set up directly under our windows, and they began to dispose of the dead in the very middle of our garden. My dear friend, we buried one thousand eight hundred in thirty-five days, one third being taken from our own unfortunate home. At last my name came on the list, and I was to be eleventh, but the sword of justice became heavy the day before over the new Scylla of France. From that moment, things became much easier, and by the efforts, as vigorous as they were urgent, of the delightful partner who has shared my heart and life these

five years now, I was at last set free, on the twenty-fourth
Vendémiaire last."

"My imprisonment by the people, with the guillotine under
my eyes," he was to write to Gaufridy on January 21st 1795,
"hurt me a hundred times more than all the bastilles in the
world."

July 28th 1794 (10th Thermidor, Year II). To thunderous
cheering, thrice repeated, Maximilien Robespierre was
executed. With him also went to the scaffold Dumas, Couthon,
Hanriot, Saint-Just, Payan and sixteen other terrorists, commencing at seven thirty p.m.

August 22nd 1794 (5th Fructidor, Year II). Committee of
Public Safety members Dubarran and Vadier received a petition from Sade protesting his innocence and demanding his
liberation and forwarded the document to the Piques Ward,
for this to give its opinion on the prisoner of Picpus.

August 25th 1794 (8th Fructidor, Year II). The Piques Ward
returned Sade's papers to the Committee of Public Safety, with
the following certificate, written in the new Thermidorian spirit
—in strange contrast with the Piques Ward's effort of 18th
Ventôse:

"We, the Undersigned,
    Citizens of the Piques Ward, certify that Citizen Sade
is known to us, as we knew him to fulfil a number of functions in the said Ward and in the hospitals with fervour
and intelligence, and we attest that nothing came to our
knowledge of him which might be contrary to the principles of a good patriot and make us doubt his civic spirit.
    Paris, this 8th Fructidor, the second year of the one and
indivisible French Republic.

    [signed] Sverin, Touchard, Cabanès, Capt. Noel
        Thomas, Anterne, Secretary of the Military
        Office, Ladoucette, Surgeon, Chenevoz,
        Drapier, Bourgeois, Ract, Sané, Rogé,
        Simez, François, Stalport."

September 30th 1794 (9th Vendémiaire, Year III). Citizen
Sade, man of letters, referring to the decree providing for the

liberation of "patriotic artists devoted to the public cause" demanded his liberty of the representative citizens who were members of the Committee of Public Safety.

October 11th 1794 (20th Vendémiaire, Year III). Citizeness Quesnet requested Citizen Bourdon (of the Oise), representative of the people, to intervene in favour of Citizen Sade.

October 13th 1794 (22nd Vendémiaire, Year III). The Committee of Safety and Safeguarding of the National Convention decided that Citizen Sade should be set free at once.

October 15th 1794 (24th Vendémiaire, Year III). Liberated at last, after three hundred and twelve days detention, Sade returned to his house in the *rue Neuve des Mathurins* where, despite being a former nobleman, he was in view of his patriotic work given authority to reside on the 5th Brumaire, on the request of the Committee of Public Education.

FROM LEAVING PICPUS TO THE EVE OF ARREST ON THE 15TH VENTÔSE

Between October 15th and 21st 1794 (the last days of Vendémiaire, Year III). As soon as he emerged from prison the Marquis sent a legalised copy of the decision of the 22nd Vendémiaire—which also removed the sequester placed on his property—to the Apt district council and tried to re-establish contact with Gaufridy. But both Gaufridy and his son Elzéar were still in hiding, and Sade became most concerned lest his old friend was suffering, "which would grieve me greatly".

November 12th 1794 (22nd Brumaire, Year III). Writing to Citizen Esprit Audibert, farming La Coste, Sade with some indignation expressed surprise that despite the quashing of the sequester, Audibert had not sent the rent, especially since nothing had been paid for so long a time and Audibert must be aware how necessary funds were to him in Paris. He warned Audibert that if a draft was not forthcoming at once he would complain to the Committee of Public Safety. Working as he did "unceasingly" for the "cause of the people", he could count on the full support of the Committee. And moreover, let Citizen Payan of La Coste not imagine that as heretofore he could do just what he wanted; it was easy to prove to the authorities in Paris that "whoever bore that infamous name was working solely to betray the fatherland". Had not a Payan been one of Robespierre's creatures, guillotined on the 10th Thermidor, together with his master? Meanwhile Audibert was to find Gaufridy. Sade was in a position to help him—Gaufridy merely needed to say how.

November 19th 1794 (29th Brumaire, Year III). A letter had come in from Gaufridy, home at last! Sade was delighted and hastened to tell his friend so. Thus "the death of the rascals has scattered all the clouds, and the tranquillity we can now enjoy will heal all our wounds". After recounting his own sufferings in prison, he said he could now help Gaufridy: "My detention found me friends in the Convention and I shall be glad at any time to make use of them for you. My dear companion is moved of deputies, and is equally eager to be of service to you in something. You need only tell either of us."

November 30th 1794 (10th Frimaire, Year III). With 2,000 *crowns* of debts on emerging from prison and not a penny coming in, Sade rated Gaufridy for having slipped back into his old "lethargy". If Gaufridy did not help soon, he would blow his brains out. Let him hurry up with the sale of the Grand-Bastide of Saumane, but properly, as properties were fetching "crazy prices" in the south.

December 5th 1794 (15th Frimaire, Year III). Sade wrote to the *département*'s representatives, asking for the half-completed edition of his novel *Aline et Valcour*. The books were under seal, as Girouard the printer had died, but his widow was now having the seals removed.

December 12th 1794 (22th Frimaire, Year III). His energy curiously in contrast with his lawyer's lack of it, Sade obtained a pardon for Gaufridy. He assured his lawyer that Citizeness Quesnet was to be thanked, not he himself.

January 21st 1795 (2nd Pluviôse, Year III). Sade informed Gaufridy that Lord Montreuil had just died (about six months after being released from prison, where he and his wife

spent the days of the Terror). He had done his best for the two
"charming friends" from Provence who had come armed with
a letter from Gaufridy, but he did not know Rovère, so had
been able to do nothing for them. The younger was Mlle de
Rousset's nephew. How nice to see a relation of that "charming old friend of mine". "The winter is frightful, it seems colder
than 1709 or 1740, everything is short." A fortnight earlier he
had written to say that the ink in his inkpot froze and he had
to keep it in a bowl of hot water. "And no wood, only one load
every two months at forty *francs,* and everything else the same,
you spend 25 *francs* a day and die of hunger."

February 26th 1795 (8th Ventôse, Year III). On his beam
ends, the Marquis approached deputy Jacques Antoine Rabut
Pommier, to find him a job, either as diplomat or as keeper of
some library or museum.

End of March 1795 (Germinal, Year III). Sade had just
learned that M. de Murs, a relation, had died five months previously. He rated Gaufridy for his "accursed negligence". How
could he have been so dilatory? But meanwhile Grand Bastide
of Saumane had been sold—to Gaufridy's father-in-law,
Archiais, of Aix, who was to get it for 60,000 *francs.*

April 6th 1795 (17th Germinal, Year III). Sade had decided
to spend two months in the country, to complete an essential
work requested of him.

Sade's son Louis was back in Paris. As neither he nor his
brother had been listed as *émigrés,* he was held to have been
travelling in France, studying botany and engraving. The other
son was at Malta, on duty. But an order of *25th Brumaire, Year
III* was still most worrying. Even the relatives of *émigrés* might
be sentenced to death. And had not Sade honoured a draft for
Louis while abroad? So he wrote to Gaufridy to instruct him.
If anybody asked any questions, he was to say how glad he was
that Sade's sons had never become *émigrés,* one was at his post
on Malta, the other with his father, after travelling about
France, and so on and so forth.

June 10th 1795 (22nd Prairial, Year III). The Theatre of
the *rue Feydeau* rejected *Le Boudoir.*

August 26th 1795 (9th Fructidor, Year III). Sade requested

Gaufridy to send the various sums he owed him. He could invest the 60,000 *francs* from the Saumane property, and they would bring in 3,600 per annum. Gaufridy was ruining him. He also remarked that now *Aline et Valcour* was printed, and he was sending two copies, one for Gaufridy, the other for his best friend. "A work, of which people say much is expected, and which may well interest you."

March 14th 1796 (24th Ventôse, Year IV). Louis Sade, man of letters, and Constance Renelle, divorced wife of Balthasar Quesnet, rented a country house at Clichy la Garennee, in the *rue de la Réunion,* opposite the castle stables. The rental was for one year, at 300 paper *francs.*

April 19th 1796 (30th Germinal, Year IV). Sade on his son Louis: "A very nice boy who comes to see me often, I am very fond of him. . . . Very active, a passionate lover of the arts, does nothing but paint and make music, but he does not conceal that when peace is signed he will make the world his country. Did I not restrain him, indeed, he would be off to New England at once."

October 13th 1796 (22nd Vendémiaire, Year V). Sade sold La Coste, lock, stock and barrel, to the Rovères, for 58,400 *livres* plus a little *douceur* payable directly to himself. He was soon to buy Granvilliers, in Eure et Loire and Malmaison, Seine et Oise, total value 73,000 *livres,* rent from them 4,000.

January 2nd 1797 (13th Nivôse, Year V). Sade to Charles Gaufridy, who since Germinal had taken his father's place as manager of the estates:

> "All I think I owe you, Sir, for the blatant rudeness I have from you, is the most utter contempt. It is not seemly for me to speak to a mere boy like yourself of my misfortunes. Those misfortunes, which make me of interest and worthy of respect to decent folk, should remain unknown to you, for you were having your backside tanned when I was experiencing them, so kindly remain silent about them because it is most unseemly of you to mention them. . . .
>
> "All that, Sir, displeases me greatly. I request you to desist from handling my business and to request your

father to resume control over my affairs, quietly and
reasonably until the 1st May. Everything is about to change
and I hope he and I will always be friends, but as for you,
Sir, you are not to my taste, and I beg you not to write to
me further. Limit yourself to despatching the money; I
have not had a *sou* for a month."

March 5th 1797 (15th Ventôse, Year V). Lady de Sade was
not at all sure about the income which her ex-husband's new
properties would bring her, and took legal precautions, of
which she informed Gaufridy. "My mother," she wrote, "is
well. She and my poor father, whom we lost six months after
his liberation, were under arrest. . . ."

April 20th 1797 (1st Floréal, Year V). Sade moved into
Citizeness Quesnet's house, *3, Place de la Liberté,* at St Ouen.

Mid May 1797 (Floréal, Year V). Sade and Mme Quesnet
arrived in Provence.

*Between mid-May and mid-June 1797 (Floréal-Prairial, Year
V).* Sade visited Apt on business, seeing Gaufridy. He went to
La Coste, to Bonnieux, where Simon Stylite Rovère, brother of
Joseph Stanislav, at the ancient Recollect Priory, received him
courteously, and also to Mazan, where the municipality turned
out in full force to call on him, though they also did not omit
to establish a bailiff at his lodging to make sure he paid his
taxes.

*June 18th 1797 (30th Prairial, Year V)—13 July 1797 (25th
Messidor, Year V).* Sade was rash enough to accuse Perrin the
tax-collector, of Carpentras, of theft and malversation, and
was eventually obliged by court procedure to apologise publicly in writing and pay the costs.

End of July 1797 (18th Thermidor, Year V). Sade and Gaufridy's son Françoise went to Arles to try to sell the Cabanes farm.
He found separation from Mme Quesnet irksome, and hastened back to the "sincere friend whose existence was more
precious to him than his own". He thanked Gaufridy, with
whom she had stayed, for his kindness to her. But he was
anxious because he had had no letters, and was apprehensive
"lest new pleasures made her forget old ones".

September 4th 1797 (18th Fructidor, Year V). The *coup d'état* of Barras, Rewbell and La Revellière was followed by arrests and deportations, and on the list were Siméon, who had once defended the Marquis, and Rovère, who had bought La Coste. But what was more alarming still was that the laws about *émigrés* and priests were brought back!

October 22nd 1797 (1st Brumaire, Year VI). Sade and Mme Quesnet returned to Saint Ouen.

November 11th 1797 (21st Brumaire, Year VI). Sade had just learned that he was listed in the Vaucluse *département* as an *émigré*, despite clearing himself from the Bouches du Rhône *département* list. This made him liable to arrest under the laws passed immediately after the *coup d'état*. The situation was serious. On the one hand his property might be placed under sequester at any moment. On the other hand sections 15 and 16 said plainly that anybody on the list and not finally cleared was required to leave the territory of the Republic at once, or face a military tribunal! Sade had only one course— to get his name struck off the list again. To avoid arrest he obtained a medical certificate that he could not travel and also requested an enquiry. He now applied directly to the Minister of the Police, Citizen Doudreau.

November 13th 1797 (23rd Brumaire, Year VI). Sade lodged a file of five hundred items to prove his uninterrupted residence in Paris since July 4th 1789 with the police. The file included extracts from registers, extracts from the minutes of the Piques Ward, certificates of non-emigration issued in Paris and La Coste, certificates of residence, and so on and so forth.

December 7th 1797 (17th Frimaire, Year VI). Sade tried to move Gaufridy's heart. "Sensitivity"—Mme Quesnet—was starving and it was all Gaufridy's fault, for sending no money. She was sparing no effort to get Sade's name struck off the list of *émigrés*.

... *1797*. The year of the publication of *la Nouvelle Justine ou les Malheurs de la vertu, suivie de l'Histoire de Juliette, sa soeur January 2nd 1798 (13th Nivôse, Year VI)*. Raffelis, chairman of the Mazan authorities, wrote to tell Sade that notary Quinquin had been censured for not placing the ex-Marquis' property under sequester. Raffelis was not to blame, he would do anything for M. Sade. Otherwise, things were beginning to be quiet down in the south. . . .

January 10th 1798 (21 Nivôse, Year VI). Secretly won over to Lady de Sade's side—he and his son Charles had indeed been vexed that Sade should not pay the dowry interest punctually—Gaufridy had been doing all he could to prevent the sale of part of the Arles property, a transaction which Sade had begun to negotiate while down in Provence. Citizeness Cordier-Sade thanked him warmly. "You may be sure that I shall in no way involve you, and my gratitude for your loyalty to the interests of my children (the elder son was back in France, at Lyons, where he was to spend the winter) heads all my feelings of respect and consideration."

January 16th 1798 (27th Nivôse, Year VI). The ex-marquis wrote to Gaufridy about the many steps he had taken with the authorities. His fear was lest Barras (prompted by some friend) raked up old scandals. Further, since he still owed 10,000 *francs* on the Malmaison and Granvilliers properties and the seller's lawyers were threatening to seize, he had entered an earlier injunction in the name of a friend—would Gaufridy do the same down in Provence when the opportunity occurred? He also wrote to say that his daughter had been to Saint-Ouen to dinner with a cousin, and Mme Quesnet had been present. The other girl had been niceness itself, but Madeleine Laure was "stupid and touchy as a goose".

May 3rd 1798 (14th Floréal, Year VI). The lawyers had seized the Beauce revenues and also put a seizure on Sade's furniture, and the wretched Sade conjured Gaufridy not to deny his assistance.

June 16th 1798 (28th Prairial, Year VI). M. Darbaud, with authorisation, made a request of the Minister of Police: while awaiting justice to be done to Citizen Sade, the latter's personal safety demanded that he should be given protection by the *1st Arrondissement,* which had witnessed his great deed on July 2nd 1798.

July 5th 1798 (17th Messidor, Year VI). The appropriate

organs of the Ministry of Police informed Citizeness Quesnet, acting for Sade, why the Ministry was against striking Sade's name from the list of *émigrés*. The reason was the difference in Christian names! Without the proper proofs that it was indeed the Sade whom she represented who was struck out of that list on May 26th 1793, the Minister could not take any steps with the Directory concerning the request.

July 21st 1798 (3th Thermidor, Year VI). Writing to the *Journal de Paris,* Sade claimed the honour of being the first to establish that Jeanne, the heroine of Beaurais, had never been called Hachette, as historians said, but was Laisne, daughter of Mathieu Laisné. Before writing his tragedy he had taken the pains to check Louis XI's letters patent, preserved at Beauvais.

September 3rd 1798 (17th Fructidor, Year VI). Citizeness Quesnet requested of Barras an early decision regarding the protection which Sade had requested. He was in a wretched situation. On the one hand the slowness with which the sequester on his property was being removed compelled him to "die of hunger", on the other, almost infirm, and quite beyond travelling, he was the victim of a law which his condition made it impossible for him to obey.

September 10th 1798 (24th Fructidor, Year VI). Lack of funds compelled Sade and Mme Quesnet to leave Saint Ouen. She stayed with friends while he found shelter at Beauce, one of his farmers putting him up.

October 1798 (Vendémiaire-Brumaire, Year VIII). The sellers of Malmaison and Granvilliers had not been paid in full and they secured an injunction on the transfer of their properties. Sade's farmer refused to put Sade up much longer. He found himself obliged to move from pillar to post, wherever anybody would give him a meal or a bed. To crown it all, the eye infection which had attacked him in Vincennes prison and the Bastille had come back again and he suffered a great deal.

December 1st 1798 (11th Frimaire, Year VII). Mme Quesnet's application was at last granted. But as Sade now lacked funds to live at Saint Ouen, he was obliged to plead illness, as preventing his "enjoyment of the protection".

January 24th 1799 (5th Pluviôse, Year VII). Sade went to Versailles for the winter. This was one of the towns near Paris where life was less expensive. "Here," he wrote to Gaufridy, "at the back of a barn, my dear one's boy and I and a maid live on a few carrots and beans and warm ourselves (not every day, but when we can) with some faggots which we buy on tick most times. We are so wretched that when Mme Quesnet comes to see us, she brings us something to eat in her pocket."

Giving Gaufridy this frightful picture, which, he hoped, would frighten him, so that he might be prompted to do something and end it by sending some funds, he outlined to Gaufridy the rascally intrigues to which Louis Marie, "that rascal who calls himself my son," had resorted, "from now on I do not account him my son. Where decent relations no longer exist, blood means nothing, and were my own arm to be gangrenous, I would cut it off tomorrow."

March 28th 1799 (8th Germinal, Year VII). Sade mortgaged his estates to Marie Constance Renelle Quesnet for 28,200 *francs.*

August 5th 1799 (18th Termidor, Year VII). Clich Municipality issued Sade a certificate of residence and citizenship, countersigned by Commissioner Cazade, still in charge of his security.

August 29th 1799 (12th Fructidor, Year VII). In the *Ami des Lois* ("friend of the Laws") newspaper the author of the *Tribunal d'Apollon* column ("Apollo's Court") published the following note:

> "We are assured that de Sade is dead. The mere name of that shameless writer exhales a corpse-like odour which is murderous of virtue and inspires loathing, for the man is the author of *Justine or the Misfortunes of Virtue*. The most depraved of hearts, the most degraded of minds, the most fantastically obscene of imaginations could invent nothing which would so outrage reason, modesty and humanity. This work is as dangerous as the Royalist paper entitled *le Nécessaire,* because if it is bravery that founds republics, it is good morals that preserve them and their ruin always drags down empires."

After this charming little obituary notice, while waiting for his reply to the *Ami des Lois* to appear, Sade published a brief protest in other papers:

> "Why it pleased Paulthier to kill me and at the same time declare me the author of *Justine* I know not. He must have made murder and calumny a habit, to write such frightful lies. Kindly insert in your paper both this proof of my existence and my most formal denial of that infamous work *Justine*.
>
> (signed) Sade."

September 24th 1799 (2nd Vendémiaire, Year VIII). The *Ami des Lois* published Sade's rejoinder:

> "No, I am not dead, and I would like to imprint proof of my non-equivocal existence on your shoulders with a very vigorous stick. I would really do so, did I not fear the plague miasma of your mephitic corpse. But when all is said and done, scorn is the only weapon that a decent man need use to repel the banalities of a blockhead like yourself. It is not true that I am the author of *Justine*! To any other than a dolt such as you I might take the trouble to prove this, but what emerges from your stinking mouth is so stupid that refutation would dishonour more than accusation.
>
> A sensible man, when barked at by curs of your type, spits on them and continues on his way.
>
> So bark away, bray, howl, distil your poison; your inability, like that of the toad, to throw beyond your own nose, causing it to fall back on yourself will succeed in covering none but you with the poison you would like to sully others with."

October 1st 1799 (9th Vendémiaire, Year VIII). In a long letter to Goupilleau de Montaigu, Sade announced that he wished to offer the Republic the "vigour" of his "pen" and his "means" and asked if he might read him his tragedy *Jeanne Laisné*, a work most fitted to stir up "love of the fatherland in every heart". If the play pleased him "it would be essential to speed up its performance; this is the moment . . . absolutely the moment." And Sade begged Goupilleau to use his influence as deputy to "have the *Theatre Français* given categorical orders" to put the play on without delay.

October 27th 1799 (5th Brumaire, Year VIII). Sade to Gaufridy: Louis Marie is "a thoroughpaced rascal, well known to be such, whom the other day a deputy showed the door because of the shocking things he was saying about his father". So Sade felt no responsibility whatsoever towards the scoundrel and had no desire to take the food from his own mouth to improve his son's condition. Further, Gaufridy had sent a bill of exchange dated one month hence. How was he going to live, without losing one quarter in discounting?

December 10th 1799 (19th Frimaire, Year VIII). By a decision similar to that of the 4th February issued by the *Vaucluse* authorities, the *Bouches du Rhône* prefecture raised the sequester on Sade's property.

December 13th 1799 (22nd Frimaire, Year VIII). Revival of *Oxtiern* under the new title, *Oxtiern or the Misfortunes of a Rake's Life,* on the stage of the Dramatic Society of Versailles, the author playing the part of Fabrice.

January 3rd 1800 (13th Nivôse, Year VIII). Having kept Sade going for a time by selling her wardrobe, Mme Quesnet found herself obliged to work to keep herself. Frantic from the cold and hunger that were his lot as the nineteenth century broke, Sade was taken in at Versailles Infirmary. Otherwise he would have "died at a street corner". The wretched man had written to tell Gaufridy, whose son Charles had written to say he had money for him, but took it upon himself to hold it back! Reduced to accepting public assistance, Sade was infuriated. "What degree of ferocity is this to which you have sunk?"

January 17th 1800 (27th Nivôse, Year VIII). It was unbelievable that Charles Gaufridy could have gone to Arles after the annulment of the sequester and had not brought back any funds, "because it was cold". "Poor little Abbé Charles! Easy to see he's a soldier of the Pope. He doesn't go out when the weather's bad." But was not Sade himself more to be pitied, in a public infirmary, without any heating and only the food given to paupers to eat? Despite the cruel cold, Mme Quesnet was still trying to do what she could for Charles' brother. "But then, we in Paris are not so chickenhearted as you in Provence."

January 26th 1800 (6th Pluviôse, Year VIII). Sade to Gaufridy:

> "All who see my condition here are disgusted by your behaviour; there is nobody whom it does not make shudder and if I show anybody what Charles writes to me they condole with me for being in the grasp of such a maniac.
>
> In a word, I can wait no longer. Send me my money, or I will go to any steps to wrest it from your hands, as *crooked* as they are *savage.*
>
> 6th Pluviôse. Dying of cold and hunger in the public infirmary of Versailles for the past three months.
>
> It is Sunday today. When you went to mass I hope you at least asked God to forgive you for *lacerating* me, *slicing me up* and *torturing* me as you have been doing these three years now."

February 20th 1800 (1st Ventôse, Year VIII). Worthy Commissioner Cazade, under whose guard Sade had been placed, came to Versailles to inform Sade and Mme Quesnet, who was apparently living with him again, that two bailiff's men at twelve *francs* per diem were in their Saint Ouen house, as they had not paid instalments due. At the very same moment a bailiff appeared and wanted to take Sade to prison for non-payment of two court orders to pay a caterer who had supplied him for a year. Happily however, Cazade claimed that Sade was in his care and could not be taken to prison unless he took him himself.

April 5th 1800 (15th Germinal, Year VIII). Sade was back at St Ouen, whence Commissioner Cazade wrote to Sade's general manager Gaufridy whose inertia seemed most reprehensible. Gaufridy replied to the Commissioner's questions with "a monument of twisting, jesuitry, sophistry and bad faith which made the worthy fellow lose all faith in him."

April 15th 1800 (25th Germinal, Year VIII). "D. A. F. Sade, aged sixty, infirm and poor" requested the Minister of Justice to recommend his being struck off the list of *émigrés.*

May ... 1800 (Floréal-Prairial, Year VIII). Sade had twice accused Gaufridy of being bribed by Sade's tenants and had threatened legal action against him. Gaufridy now resigned his post as Sade's steward.

June 1800 (Prairial-Messidor, Year VIII). On February 20th Sade had warned Gaufridy that if he did not pay up he would send somebody down "with a dose of emetic sufficient to clear your gullet for you". Now he put the threat into execution. Mme Quesnet travelled to Provence with a legal representative armed with full powers to go through all the accounts and inspect the estates.

October 22nd 1800 (30th Vendémiaire, Year IX).   In the *Journal des Arts, des Sciences et de Littérature* an article by Villeterque appeared, very hostile to the *Crimes de l'amour*, which had just appeared, and to Sade, whom he treated as the author of *Justine*. Sade was shortly after to reply by a pamphlet in the form of a letter addressed to his character, Zoïle.

January 16th 1801 (26th Nivôse, Year IX). The Minister of Police issued a certificate of amnesty which made it possible to remove any sequester on Citizen Sade's property. But still not a hint of being struck off the list of *émigrés*! This was only to follow implicitly, when France became a monarchy again.

But, as we shall see, much later, even in June 1808, under the reign of the self-styled Emperor, Sade's family was to cite Sade's name as on the list of *émigrés* in order to establish that *he had lost all civic rights* and consequently could raise no legal opposition whatsoever to the marriage of his son Donatien Claude Armand !

CHAPTER SIXTEEN

Works Published During the Author's Lifetime

JUSTINE OR THE MISFORTUNES OF VIRTUE (1791)

THERE ARE three versions of the story of Justine. They differ so much that they should be treated as separate works. There are the 1791 novel, our present subject, the 1797 novel (*La Nouvelle Justine*), and a posthumous story entitled *The Misfortunes of Virtue*.

Between June 23rd and July 8th 1787, while in the "second Liberty", despite a painful eye trouble and writing without interruption, Sade completed the hundred and thirty-eight sheets of a philosophical story entitled *Les Infortunes de la Vertu* (The Adversities of Virtue). It was planned as one of a proposed collection of *Contes et Fabliaux du XVIIIth Siècle* (Tales and Legends of the 18th Century) but not a year had passed before Sade made important changes in it. The heroine continued her adventures, till Sade felt that the story was growing into a novel, and struck it off the list of tales. It became the draft of the *Malheurs de la Vertu* (Misfortunes of Virtue), though we lack the full text of that work, some episodes of which were roughed out in a volume of additions which has not been found.

By a process of painstaking analysis and comparison of emendations of the first draft and the later additions or corrections which turned the tale into a novel, most diligently deciphering passages which were heavily crossed out, Maurice Heine succeeded in deducing the text of the *Justine* of 1791. "The least," he wrote, "that we can say of it is that in place of the conventional lover it introduced the total human being into literature."

The Adversities of Virtue was first published in 1930 by Heine, with an excellent introduction, which should be consulted.

On June 12th 1791 Sade wrote to Reinaud that a novel of his was being printed "but it is too immoral a work to be sent to so circumspect, religious and modest a man as yourself. I needed money, my printer said he wanted it *well peppered,* so I gave it him fit to plague old Nick himself. It is being called *Justine or the Misfortunes of Virtue.* I renounce it. . . ."

But it is quite untrue that *Justine* was thus written to order. As we have just seen, the transformation of the *Adversities of Virtue* into this form had been completed three years before. We may add that the book appears in Sade's own *Catalogue raisonné,* which he drew up on October 1st 1788. No, those words of Sade's to Reinaud were merely intended to conceal from an old friend whatever disturbing mental compulsion had made him write it. As far as that goes, Sade's introduction to *Justine*—entitled *A ma bonne amie*—it was dedicated to Mme Quesnet—makes it perfectly plain that Sade was well aware of the exceptional value of the book he was about to publish. To Mme Quesnet he said : "Yes, Constance, it is to you that I address this book. You both exemplify and honour your sex, combining as you do the most sensitive heart and the most modest and most clear-seeing of minds, so yours alone is the honour to know what alleviating tears unfortunate Virtue produced."

Of the novel itself, in his introduction, he wrote:

> "The plan of this romance (not so romantic as one might expect) is undoubtedly new, the ascendance of Virtue over Vice, the reward of Good, the punishment of Evil, that is the usual course of all the works of this kind; surely it has been dinned into our ears enough!
>
> But to show Vice everywhere triumphant and Virtue the victim of its sacrifices, to show a wretched woman staggering from misfortune to misfortune, a toy of wickedness, the butt of every form of debauch, the plaything of the most barbaric and monstrous of tastes, dazed by the most outrageous sophistry and the most specious, the prey of the most cunning seduction, the most irresistible consent-

ment, and with nought but a sensitive heart, and unspoilt mind and a need of courage to set against so many setbacks, so many scourges and reject so much corruption— in a word, to venture the boldest of descriptions, the most extraordinary situations, the most terrifying maxims, the most vigorous brush strokes, with the sole purpose of drawing from it all one of the most sublime lessons of morals that man has ever had given him—this, it will be agreed, was to attain one's aim by a road little trodden hitherto."

The first work which Sade published was handled by Girouard, of the *rue du Bout du Monde* in Paris, in 1791, apparently in the autumn. The original edition of *Justine* (two octavo volumes) and an allegorical frontispiece representing Virtue between Self-indulgence and Irreligion. The title page does not bear the author's name and as in the case of many unlicensed books, in place of the publisher's name bears the words: *In Holland, at associated Booksellers.* Six prints in ten years are eloquent evidence of the contemporary success of the *Misfortunes of Virtue.*

In the supplement of "notices, announcements and miscellaneous information" of the *Journal Général de France* of September 27th 1792 the author has discovered an article which is an excellent expression of the alarm which the unusual appearance of the Marquis de Sade in the world of letters must have produced, though, notwithstanding the denigrations which such a work as *Justine* could not fail to produce, it is clear what respect the anonymous author felt for the "rich and dazzling" imagination of the author :

"All that the most disordered imagination could invent that was indecent, sophistical, even disgusting, has been dragged into this strange novel, the title of which might engage the interest of and deceive sensitive and decent folk.

Though most disordered, the imagination which produced so monstrous a work is, one must at the same time admit, *sui generis* both rich and brilliant. We have the most amazing happenings, the most extraordinary descriptions, all in profusion. If it was the author's intention to use his intelligence to develop the sole true principles of the social order and of nature, we have no doubt but that he would completely succeed. But his *Justine* is far from achieving that praiseworthy aim, which any writer should adopt. To read it is both wearisome and revolting. It is often difficult not to close the book from disgust and indignation. Young people, you whose sensitivity loose living has not yet calloused, avoid this work, a menace both to heart and senses. You, mature men, whom experience and the tranquillity of all the passions has placed above danger, read it to see to what point the delirium of man's imagination can go, but immediately you have done so, throw it in the fire; that is the advice you will give yourselves if you have the strength to read the whole of it."

The 1791 *Justine* is the only one of Sade's works of which Heine published his analysis. What he wrote is too well put for the present author merely to reshape it. Here is what he said:

"It is somewhere about 1775. Justine is fourteen years old. Her convent has discharged her because, suddenly orphaned, she is no longer able to pay. In Paris she lives a life of poverty and struggles to maintain her virtue. Falsely accused of theft by her employer, Du Harpin, a moneylender, she is imprisoned in the Conciergerie prison, but escapes, and avoids being raped only by taking flight in Bondy woods. Here she finds a good situation in a *château* and works there for four years, till one day young Count de Bressac sets his mastiffs on her because she refuses to poison his aunt for him. She is taken in by Rodin, as skilled in medicine as he is in debauch. He brands her and then turns her out when she tries to prevent him from dissecting alive a baby of which he is the father. At twenty-two we thus see her on the turnpike again. She reaches Sens, then Auxerre, which she leaves August 7th 1783. She goes on a pilgrimage to the miracle-working Virgin of Sainte Marie des Bois, where she is kept a prisoner six months by four lubricious and murderous monks. Escaping in the spring of 1784, in two days' time she falls

into the hands of a Count de Gernande, who bleeds her
for a year, though much less than his own wife, whom he
kills by over-bleeding. At Lyons she again fares ill, for she
comes upon the Count, and she also fares ill on the Dau-
phine road, for near Vienne she foolishly believes the
promises of a man named Roland, whom she rescues, not
knowing that she is going to accompany the head of a
band of coin counterfeiters into their hide-out in the Alps.
Worse treated than a beast of burden for some months, she
is at last arrested with the rest of the band and taken to
Grenoble, where she only escapes the scaffold by the eloquence of illustrious, kind-hearted Servan. Soon, however,
she gets mixed up in a new difficulty, for which reason she
proposes to leave Grenoble, and all but becomes the victim of a bishop who cuts off heads, when to have his
revenge the bishop charges her with incendiarism, theft
and murder. Imprisoned by him at Lyons, she is tortured
and condemned by a lying and debauched judge. Taken
to Paris to have the sentence of death carried out, she is
recognised at one of the halts *en route* by her sister Juliette
who has done well and whose rich lover intervenes. Saved
and rehabilitated at last, Justine should, one would think,
have the right to live happily in her sister's castle, but the
last word is with Heaven, and virtue is not left in peace.
The woman who is its incarnation dies at the age of 27,
struck by lightning during the frightful storm of July 13th
1788."

Despite the daring which the chain of incident of this story
reveals, the difference between the language of Laclos' *Liaisons
dangereuses* and the first *Justine* is not such as to exclude close
comparison, and the pre-eminence of both works when these in
turn are set beside the conventional fiction of the age lies, as
Heine well put it, in "a systematically pessimistic philosophy"
which inspires them both, an outlook which both writers base
on "serious knowledge of the world and of man". However,
one should also point out that quite apart from any aesthetic
consideration, this outlook is much less marked in Laclos's
work. In *Justine* it reaches the level of a dogma. The universe
is nothing but violence and cruelty, the author tells us. Thus

we see that quite apart from the sensual and positivistic attitude of the time, in the very first work which he published Sade took a stand diametrically opposed to the nature-loving optimism of his age, and was utterly original in his attitude. Six years later this initial statement was to grow into a monumental epic of evil, gushing forth, one might think, from the thought of Satan himself.

At the same time, those three thousand seven hundred pages of the *Nouvelle Justine* and *Juliette,* with all their descriptive and theoretical daring, and despite their poetic enthusiasm, frighten the reader rather than convince him. Precisely because of a measure of caution in the language and the utterly classical style of speech of the characters, who are reasonable beings, of all Sade's work the *Misfortunes of Virtue* remains the most insidious attack on the divine character of human nature. In his *Le Marquis de Sade et le Roman Noir* Heine points out the striking approximation of the dates of publication of Sade's works of horror in France and those of Anne Radcliffe in England and suggests the probability of *Justine* (1791) having influenced M. G. Lewis's *The Monk* (1796).

MINOR POLITICAL WORKS 1791-1793

Sade's minor political works belong rather to the story of his life than that of his works, and for this reason they have been mentioned in the preceding chapters. For the record, however, here are their titles and dates:

Adresse d'un citoyen de Paris au roi des François; June, 1791.

Observations Présentées à l'Assemblée Administrative des hôpitaux; October 28th 1792.

Idée sur le mode de la sanction des Lois; November 2nd 1729.

Pétition des sections de Paris à la Convention nationale;*

Discours aux mânes de Marat et de Le Pelletier; September 29th 1793.

---

*In July Sade had collaborated in two other works, or even may have been entirely responsible for them. These were: *Extrait des registres des délibérations a l'Assemblée générale et permanente de la Section des Piques* and *La Section des Piques à ses freres et amis de la Société de la Liberté et de l'Egalité, à Saintes.*

Pétition de la Section des Piques aux représentants du peuple français (November 15th 1793).*

ALINE ET VALCOUR—THE PHILOSOPHICAL NOVEL
(1795)

"The fruit of several sleepless years," *Aline et Valcour* must have been written, together with other works on a more modest scale, between November 28th 1785, when Sade completed the *120 Days of Sodom* and about October 1st 1788,** when Sade recorded the novel in his *Catalogue*. Whether it was still only in the state of corrected draft, or whether a fair copy had been made, we do not know. Either position would fit the date of the novel (1788) and the author's note: "Written in the Bastille, one Year before the French Revolution."

On March 6th 1791, we recall, Sade wrote to Reinaud that he was going to have his *Philosophical Novel* published at Easter. The following June 21st he spoke of the publication of *Justine* being imminent but because it was so spicy he was sending Reinaud the other book. But thirty months passed, and still *Aline et Valcour* was not off the press, for when on December 9th 1793 Commissioners Laurent and Juspel came to arrest Sade, what did he do but make them his messengers: he had had three pages of the novel back to make some changes, and he returned these to Girouard by courtesy of the Commissioners!

Sade went to prison, under the Terror, and while he was there, on January 8th 1794, Girouard his printer went to the guillotine. At the end of the year (December 5th 1794 to be exact) when he himself had been free for six weeks, Sade claimed from the authorities that part of his novel which was ready. He recovered one half, printed by Girouard before he was arrested. The following summer (August 1795) Sade was at last able to lock the dainty little volumes of *Aline et Valcour* in his library side by side with the first *Justine*, which had thus preceded it by four years. On August 26th he packed up two

*For the record one should also mention a little work which the Council of the Municipality asked for, on the changing of the names of certain streets, which never seems to have gone beyond manuscript form.

**At least we may be sure that he was already at work on it in November 1786.

copies for Gaufridy, one to pass on to his best friend, and on the following day with businesslike pen he drafted a circular designed for Provençal booksellers.

The four books of *Aline et Valcour,* each in two parts, were printed in four volumes in a format measuring about $3\frac{1}{8}$ in. by $5\frac{1}{8}$ in., approximating to a Royal $32°$. There were three different printings. The work began in 1791, was interrupted by the legalised murder of Girouard in 1794, and finally completed a year later. The only difference between the three editions, which may have been on sale simultaneously, is in the title-page—one of them even bears the date 1793—and in the number of engravings—fourteen in the first two editions, sixteen in the third. The books were paginated in pairs, and seven lines from Lucretius, Book IV, expressed the idea that children should be given bitter tonics—*nam veluti pueris absinthia tera medentes....*

To complete the account of this work's publication, one should add that one highly-coloured passage, the adventures of Sainville and Léonore, was the subject of two forgeries, *Valmor et Lydia* and *Alzonde et Loradin,* both of which the author denounced in a note in his *Crimes de l'amour.* Prohibited in 1815 and again in 1825, less for its immorality than for the boldness of the social theories which it contains, this book had only once been reprinted before the end of the nineteenth century.

*   *   *

This vast composition really consists of two works. First, there is the novel proper. (Far from feeling one should criticise the form of exchange of letters, one has to admit that this definitely serves to bring out the character's individuality.) We are told of the crimes of a cruel, depraved father, the president of the Blamont Assembly. To make sure of the possession of his own daughter, Aline, he tries to force her to marry Dolbourg the financier, an old rake like himself. He has already corrupted another wretched girl, Sophie, whom he believes to be his daughter too, and handed her over to his accomplice, but Aline's real sister is Leonore, taken to be the late Elizabeth de Kerneuil, a mix-up resulting from a double substitution of children by a dishonest wet-nurse.

Aline is a gentle, virtuous girl and she both loves Valcour and is loved by him. That sensitive, faultless model woman, Blamont's wife, whom only her rigid notions of the sanctity of the marriage bond keep loyal to her husband, would like the two young people to marry, despite Valcour's poverty—for his only fortune is his noble blood and the fine quality of his character (some extracts from Valcour's story of himself were given in Chapter Two). Blamont in vain tries to get rid of him, by offering him a large sum of money. Valcour refuses to give up Aline, and then one night in the *rue de Buci* is the object of an attack arranged by Blamont. Twice wounded by the assailant's sword, he escapes with his life because by lucky chance the night watch comes along at that moment.

Lady de Blamont is working to frustrate her husband's scurrilous plans, but he gets rid of his interfering wife by getting her maid Augustine to poison her. In despair at this terrible loss, to escape the dishonour which threatens her, caught between an incestuous father and a debauched husband, Aline writes a letter of farewell to the shades of her mother and to her beloved Valcour and with one blade of a pair of large scissors stabs herself three times and dies.

Artificially linked to this main story is the round-the-world pilgrimage of Sainville, searching for his wife Léonore, that is, Claire de Blamont, thought to be Elisabeth de Kerneuil, and the story of that young woman's adventures, exposed as she is to the lust of licentious men in every country. As she says, "I slipped out of the grasp of a Venetian noble, a Barbary pirate dared not make any attempt on my modesty, nor did it yield to the advances of a French consul. On the eve of being impaled at Sennar, saving my life at the cost of my honour, yet discovering the secret how to keep both the one and the other, I saw a cannibal emperor on his knees before me. I emerged intact from the hands of a young Portuguese, from those of an elderly Lisbon judge, and from that city's four worst rakes. Then a Gypsy girl, two monks and a brigand chief sighed for me in vain. And was I to undergo all that, Oh God, merely to become the prey of an Inquisitor?"*

---

*Léonore is a strong character, a forerunner of Juliette. She has a man's mind in a woman's body and though lustful herself, remains chaste from sheer pride.

Even briefly to analyse this double story would exceed the space available here, but it would be quite wrong not to mention the ethical paradise which Sainville visited. This was the Isle of Tamoé "where a government reigned fit to serve as model to every country of Europe", meant by the author to be in contrast to the man-eating kingdom of Butua, the frightful depravity of which is given a heated defence by the Portuguese Sarmiento, philosopher of the opportuneness of evil. The two descriptions are both excellent, but the former is without equal in Sade's pessimistic works, because it embraces a positive teaching of social and individual happiness being based on real knowledge of human nature, in harmony with the theories set forth in *Justine*. The outline of the views of the wise man Zamé constitutes a new *Esprit des Lois* of such genial inspiration that it may be compared in some of its utopian passages with that work of Montesquieu's and is throughout imbued with a sense of the ephemerality of institutions.

It is rather a tempting thought that it would be more suitable to publish these two stories separately, for they are organically separate, were it not that such treatment would rob of us a whole in which the scope of Sade's gifts gives us not merely a passionate ideological insight into the author's many-sided personality, but also a vivid picture of the emotional climate and ways of life of France prior to 1789. In a cross between sheer fancy and plain documentation of the ethics of a society we have many an astonishing episode, all interwoven by a masterly hand on a vast geographical background ranging from Venice to the Barbary states, from Lisbon and Toledo to the depths of black Africa. Sade was not in the least in error when in his publisher's note he said that "never were such strange contrasts drawn by the same brush" and that "bringing so many different characters together, constantly clashing one with the others, was bound to result in unprecedented, striking events."

* * *

Though the tale of *Aline and Valcour* together with the interwoven tale of Sainville and Léonore only at rare intervals offers such frightful scenes and such deliberately Sadistic professions of faith as those of the *Misfortunes of Virtue*, wicked characters of every kind abound in this work, and despite the moving figures of Aline de Blamont and her mother the problem of evil was set forth with quite sufficient detachment for the readers of the Year III of the Revolution to be given quite a shock. Was the Marquis' own reply to reproaches when his novel appeared merely a hypocritical manoeuvre intended to make it easier for people to swallow his disturbing pictures, or was there in it a hint of that "dialectical drama" which, according to the author of *My neighbour, Sade*, haunted Donatien Alphonse Françoise to his very end? "You say my brush strokes are too violent and that I give vice features which are too loathsome. Well, would you know why? I just don't want people to like it. . . . Nor shall I ever depict it but with the colours of hell, I want people to see it stark naked, I want people to fear it, loathe it, and I know no other way to achieve that end but to reveal it in all its repulsiveness. Cursed be they who deck it out with roses! Their aims are not nearly so clean, nor shall I ever follow their suit."

Aline et Valcour, a vision of morals and characters in which the viciousness of an incestuous father is drawn with exceptional vigour and a story of heroic comedy with adventures in all classes of society and all climes, with the sociology of a pioneer mingling with imaginary folklore systems, on many a page adumbrates the sensibility of our age, with pages teeming with unknown kingdoms and "voyages of discovery the story of which has never been told" evocative of Arthur Rimbaud in his *Alchimie du Verbe*. Were it not that the notoriety of the author's four-letter name made academic criticism blind to it, this novel, which throughout, despite the daring nature of the feelings described, never ceases to be decent, would long since have been listed among those works of imagination of universal significance which, like Don Quixote, the Decameron and Gulliver, have opened new realms to man's imagination.

PHILOSOPHY IN THE BOUDOIR (1795)

In the same years as *Aline et Valcour*, two little volumes which were disturbingly seductive appeared: the work was *Philosophy in the Boudoir* and the title page told the reader that this was a "Posthumous work of the Author of *Justine*" published "*A Londres, aux dépens de la Compagnie*"—in London, at the Company's expense.* The trickery was double. He was to use the device again. At one stroke it provided him with personal cover and tied the new book to a novel which was still selling vigorously after three years!

The sub-title of the 1805 edition, "or the Immoral Peda-gogues", almost certainly not added by Sade, who was now in-carcerated in Charenton asylum, exactly fits the work. For this boudoir philosophy, the plan of which clearly comes from *Aloisia Sigea*—that marvellous piece dictated to Nicolas Chorier by Venus's own lips—is in fact a scheme of erotic education for a girl.

The work is divided into seven dialogues, the language of which is completely unrestricted, the responses often turning into real treatises of metaphysics and morals and the actual tales are interwoven with sexology. The first dialogue is between Mme de Saint Ange, a young woman of extreme lubriciousness (in 12 years of marriage she has already slept with 12,000 men)! and her brother, young Lord de Mirvel, who, when he hears what she does reproves her for bringing cruelty into love-making. She then invites him to be present at some of the scenes which are to take place in her boudoir that same day, when Dormancé, "most corrupt and dangerous of men", and delight-ful young Eugénie de Mistival, a fifteen-year-old virgin, are to be present. "Dolmancé and I are going to fill that little head with the most unbridled principles of looseness, we are going to instil her with all our fire and feed her with our philosophy, inspire her with our desires, and as I want to combine a little practice with theory, I plan that you, my dear brother, shall harvest the myrtles of Cytherea while Dolmancé plucks the roses of Sodom. I shall have two forms of enjoyment simultaneously, that of personal enjoyment of these criminal delights and that of giving lessons in them and imbueing the charming innocent creature whom I am drawing into our snare with those same tastes."

The second dialogue is very short. It is between Mme de Saint Ange and Eugénie. Dolmancé comes in the third, the two next add Lord de Mirvel and Augustine the gardener's boy.

---

*Two volumes in 8°, of 180 and 240 pages, with an allegorical frontispiece and four erotic engravings.

The number of characters and the adaptability of their promptings make the most subtle erotic combinations feasible. As all this goes on, Mme de Saint Ange and Dolmancé work systematically to train out of the young girl all those notions of decent behaviour that her mother had originally taught her. Atheism, blasphemy, egoism, cruelty, theft and murder, adultery, incest and sodomy are lauded from one end to the other of this work, which is a veritable précis of Sade's teachings, given strange vividness by the dramatic form in which it is cast. The antisocial theories of the two leading characters are only once contradicted, though this most movingly, in the young knight's harangue which ends with the passage: "Let us shed all religious notions; very well, I agree, but do not let us turn our backs on those virtues which our own feelings inspire in us."

Eugénie at once proved to be the most eager of pupils, the one most worthy of praise. Never did she refuse a single one of her body's orifices, but allowed them all to be used for the daring practises of which the delights were praised to her. But when the frenzy of complete self-prostitution could no longer satisfy this disciple, she dreamt of making her own mother submit to some of the frightful things she had now learned about and which still made her imagination glow. And now it was Mme de Mistival, who had become worried by her daughter's lengthy absence, who appeared in the seventh and last dialogue to learn to a certain extent what a little monster of erotism her daughter has become in a single day. With the daughter taking part, mad with delight, all sorts of sexual violence were then done to Mme de Mistival, who was still lovely, in the autumn of her life. To crown it all, a footman named Lapierre, himself infected by this unquestionable evil, was called in to infect this new victim by normal and abnormal union. Then, before the meal which was intended to provide the actors in this orgy of debauch with new energy, Eugénie suggests that she herself would perform on her mother the torture of sewing up her genitals, an act that Mme de Saint Ange ordered.

The fifth dialogue of the Philosophy contains a long pamphlet entitled *Frenchmen, one more effort, if you want to be Republicans*! This Dolmancé reads out in a loud voice. Heine has summed the spirit of this up perfectly in a general appreciation of our author. Seating as he does in the individual—in the countless individuals into which human societies can be broken down—the only real, organic force which drives those societies, Sade maintains a merciless criticism of all the social constraints which in any way tend to reduce the uncoercible human element. As he sees it, solely the interest of the individual will counsel him to accept, not exactly a social contract, but rather a social compromise, one capable of being denounced and renewed at any moment. For him any society which fails to recognise this fundamental truth is oppressive and destined to perish."*

But however interesting this pamphlet may be in itself, some of the notions of the dialogues being given a sociological backing which lends them additional force, it remains none the less true that this long treatise, so arbitrarily inserted in a work which is otherwise so well constructed, to some extent spoils the balance. It may be that Sade had originally intended to publish it separately and only later thought of embodying it in his work in order to give an air of youth to both the story and its moral, which all smelled rather of the old régime.

Of all Sade's anonymous writings this work is by far the least cruel. Only rarely, apart from the final scene, where Mme de Mistival is tortured, is the reader shocked, as he may well be by the really horrible scenes depicted in *Nouvelle Justine* and *Juliette*. Despite their general definitely corrupting nature there are whole scenes of the dialogues which could be put on the stage without too much outcry. And more than once one of Sade's heroines seems like a sort of inverted Shakespearean mistress. More than any other of Sade's works this "Boudoir Philosophy", with its dialogue form, suggests such comparisons. There are for instance phrases of dazzling obscenity spoken by Mme de Saint Ange and Eugénie de Mistival which one might almost imagine to be uttered by Cressida or Rosalind at the height of love's enjoyment.

*Note in this pamphlet Sade's moving protest against the death penalty: "Cold itself, the law should never be touched by those feelings which in man himself may be held to justify the cruel act of murder; man is the recipient of natural impressions which may tend to make him forgive that act, but on the other hand, since it is always in opposition to nature and receives nothing from it, the law cannot be authorised to allow itself the same liberties, for since it has not the same motives, it is out of the question for it to claim the same rights."

THE NEW JUSTINE OR THE MISFORTUNES OF VIRTUE
FOLLOWED BY THE STORY OF JULIETTE, HER SISTER

A bogus *Publisher's Note* which heads *La Nouvelle Justine* informs us that a "disloyal friend", to whom the author, now dead, had confided the manuscript of his book, did not hesitate to make a summary "much below the quality of the original" (i.e., this refers to the *Justine* of 1791) and that authorship of that book was consistently denied by the author whose vigorous pen had drawn the portrait of the real *Justine* and her sister. . ." This commercial trickery should not surprise us, but it does not rob the works of their character of masterpieces. Both these novels were unquestionably a publisher's gamble based on the general licence which reigned during the *Directoire* period.

If we are to believe Restif de la Bretonne and Sébastien Mercier, these ten volumes, with their hundred and one obscene engravings, were on sale publicly in all the *Palais Royal* bookshops. There was no police seizure till a year later, though from then on anybody selling them was mercilessly tracked down, and on April 2nd 1801 it was as their author that Sade once again found himself behind iron bars.

Whether free or in prison, Sade always stubbornly maintained, against all appearances, that the *Misfortunes of Virtue* was not his work, neither in the earlier or the later form. On April 15th 1800 (26 Germinal, Year VI) the Journal de Paris took it upon itself to assert that everybody knew who had written "an obscene work entitled Justine". It was "a certain M. de Sade, whom the Revolution of July 14th released from the dungeons of the Bastille". Sade then sent in a vigorous protest and this appeared on April 18th:

"An article in your paper on the 26th Germinal, Citizens, insulted me personally, and I think I have a right to call on your columns, which have always seemed to me to be a resort to which a man might turn to seek defence against calumny which he has the misfortune to suffer, to beg you to make it known to the public that it is *false*, absolutely *false*, that I am the author of a book entitled *Justine ou les Malheurs de la vertu;* and as this slander, particularly of late, is pleased to throw its poison at me more violently than ever, I give notice that I am tired of this incessant and stupid gossip (although hitherto I have been content to treat it with the contempt it deserves) and I shall now on take most careful note of it and will attack, with all the means that justice offers a victim of slander, the first person who thinks himself authorised to name me again as the author of that rubbishy book.

(signed) Sade."

Another work, *The Author of the "Crimes of Love" to Ville- terque, Pamphleteer,* also contains a vigorous disavowal of the paternity of *Justine*. The Marquis calls on his slanderer to *prove* that he is the author of *that revolting work*. "It is only a slan- derer," he goes on, "who thus without any proof throws sus- picion on the probity of another person. . . . Now, Ville- terque denounces without offering proofs; without any explanation he holds a frightful suspicion over my head and never states it clearly, so Villeterque is a slanderer." Further, in a note in the same little work, our author furiously points to "that imbecilic defamatory rhapsody written by a certain Des- page who also made out that he was the author of that infamous book which in the very interests of public morals one should never even mention".

* * *

Maurice Heine has excellently drawn the distinction to be made between the very conceptions of the first and of the second *Justines*.

"In the first," he says, "it is the heroine herself who re- counts her misfortunes; yet, even in the most scabrous details Justine remains the very incarnation of virtue. No agonising experience, no infamy is capable of breaking the poor girl's will and to her very death, as tragic as her life, she remains a Christian martyr. In the 1797 version the narration becomes objective, Justine does not speak for herself. The most crudely obscene vocabulary takes the place of her chaste laments. At the same time the events which occur become more fantastic and the story in the

end gives the general impression of a brilliant 'instalment'
novel written for a daily paper, while in place of human
beings we have infuriated embodiments of the sexes let
loose on a crowd of victims."

The transformation from one version to the other is to some
extent given us by one hundred and eleven little slips of paper
in Sade's own handwriting, which have now been published.
Formerly (in 1933) only sixteen had appeared, with introduction and commentary by Heine. All the scenes sketched in these
notes "are additions to or developments of the 1791 novel, in
the form in which Sade apparently jotted them down as he
went through his earlier novel."

We refrain from giving the plot of the *Nouvelle Justine*. The
following excerpt from Heine's introduction to the notes will
give the reader a fair idea of it, when he refers back to
the author's résumé above of the 1791 novel.

"To accomplish the ruin of the wretched girl, at the very
outset we see Delmonse replaced by Harpin the miser.
And the adventures in the *Gothic château* of Bandole
'lost behind lofty hedges' come between those at Rodin's
place and the monastery. . . . Here we now have not a
mere four, but six monks, with a *seraglio* now, of no less
than eighteen boys and thirty girls—here it is easy to perceive a hint of the exaggerated fantasy of the *120 Days*. . . .
There seems no doubt but that Sade was trying to reconstitute some situations from memory. The speech given
Dom Severino, for instance, is clearly inspired by that of
the Duke de Blangis in the earlier work. When Justine
leaves the monastery, instead of her going straight to Gernande castle, there is an intermediate incident at the
Esterval couple's bloodstained inn, where she comes upon
Bressac, the whole company meeting Verneuil at Gernande for still more orgies, still more unrestrained. Later,
Justine is not merely robbed by the beggar-woman who
waylays her on the road. Following this woman, who is
named Séraphine, she finds herself in the beggars' cave
and there is forcibly initiated to their dissolute rites. The
further adventures which she endures are also modified

and intensified. In the end she escapes from the dungeons at Lyons with the assistance of a gaoler, and when she is found by her sister Juliette she is in the guise of a beggar-woman, not a prisoner, and as such is taken to the castle to hear the story of the *Prosperities of Vice,* a sub-title which we find on the end-paper of each volume of Juliette, but not on the title pages.

This profound work of revision has a triple result. First, the philosophical frame of the book and its interest in psychology are more developed. Secondly, by multiplying incident beyond the point of verisimilitude, there is perhaps a tendency to the excesses of the novel of adventure. Thirdly, in the tradition of the so-called *romans à tiroirs,*—novels within novels—to the main story he adds the personal confessions of both the monk Jérôme and the beggar-woman, Séraphine."

Now let us examine *Juliette or the Prosperities of Vice* in general outline. It is both a sequel to and the reverse of the heartbreaking Odyssey of virtue subjected to every sort of martyrdom. It is never less horrible than *La Nouvelle Justine* and one could scarcely find a better comment than these lines

> ... *I must talk of murders, rapes and massacres,*
> *Acts of black night, abominable deeds,*
> *Complots of mischief, treason, villanies,*
> *Ruthful to hear, yet piteously perform'd. ...*

The story is given to the heroine. First she tells of her life in Panthémont Nunnery. The abbess, Mme Delbène, indulges in refined and cruel orgies which send Juliette into raptures. After the bankruptcy and death of her parents, Juliette boards in Mme la Duvergier's bawdy house, where there are both professional prostitutes and society ladies who suffer from nymphomania and drop in there to prostitute themselves on the way home from mass. Here Juliette makes the acquaintance of the loathsome Noirceuil, who introduces Saint Fond, a minister, "most false, most treacherous, most depraved, most savage, of infinite hauteur, possessed of the art of robbing France to the highest degree". Enchanted by Juliette's criminal talents, he puts her in charge of his frightful indulgences. Saint Fond needs about thirty victims a month. He destroys them during his lecherous dinner parties. Thus young girls are roasted on the spit like chicken. On one occasion, having had Juliette poison her father, he organises a bout of sex at the dying man's bed-side. Among other monstrous deeds, he strangles the old man and buggers his own daughter, before handing her over to Noirceuil. When he recalls that act of debauch he cries: "I committed parricide, I murdered, I prostituted, I sodomised!" Soon a young English-woman, Lady Clairwil, is made Juliette's assistant, together with Delcour, who is the city executioner of Nantes.

The minister and his three assistants now proceed to the most incredible barbarities. A near relative of Saint Fond's is trapped, together with wife and daughter, and they are compelled to commit every possible incestuous combination together, after which all three are raped, tortured and one after the other put to death. Delcour is warned to cut the girl's throat as slowly as possible, so that Saint Fond, who is buggering her at the same time, can enjoy the double pleasure. A few days later, Juliette and Clairwil together blow out the brains of two men as they reach the point of orgasm in their arms. The Englishwoman introduces Juliette to the Society of the Friends of Crime, whose harems give them the fullest possible scope for more. Then Minister Saint Fond tells the heroine of his plan to dev-astate all France: he means to seize all foodstuffs and force two-thirds of the country to die of hunger. Notwithstanding her inborn wickedness, Juliette is really shaken by this. She shudders. This is her ruin. To escape from her infuriated pro-tector ("Oh, fateful virtue," is her comment, "you all but ruined me this time!") she goes to Angers to live. Here she marries the rich Count de Lorsange, and produces a daughter, to make sure of being her husband's inheritor, but as he is slow to die, she poisons him, then flees to Italy, still afraid lest Saint Fond finds her. In the "fatherland of the Neros and Messalinas" Juliette prostitutes herself to the top prelates and aristocrats, then forms a liaison with an adventurer named Sbrigani. The two commit one theft and atrocity after another in all the principal cities of the peninsula—Sade drawing freely on the fruits of his travels in Italy—then go to stay in the castle of a

Russian named Minskip who is a man-eating giant and the inventor of a machine which can stab or decapitate no less than sixteen people at a time.

In Rome Juliette is received in audience by Pope Pius VI, but he is unable to obtain her favours till he has celebrated black mass in St Peter's. Juliette then goes on to Naples, where she meets the Brigand chief Brisa Testa. He is the brother of Lady Clairwil, with whom he incestuously lives. This villain recounts to Juliette exploits in both England and Sweden, then at the court of Catherine II, in Siberia and among the Turks. In Naples Juliette enters into relations with King Ferdinand and his consort Caroline. Their favourite resorts for debauch are the ruins of Pompeii and Herculaneum. In his palace this ruler has had a unique theatre built. Seven different tortures are prepared on the stage: fire, scourge, noose, wheel, impaling, decapitation and quartering. The hall is decorated with the portraits of fifty of the handsomest young lads and girls. Merely by pulling the bell-rope which corresponds to his choice each member of the audience in turn can himself torture, or else hand over to the executioner, one of the victims, "naked and as lovely as Mars". There is also Vespoli, the King's confessor and director of his orgies. His form of pleasure is to dress in a tiger's skin and bugger mad people of either sex, especially those who think they are Christ or the Virgin. While out for a walk, Juliette and Lady Clairwil take their friend, the incendiarist, male-rôle Lesbian, Olympe Borghese, whom they knew in Rome, and throw her into the crater of Vesuvius.

Queen Caroline would now like to leave Italy with Juliette, after embezzling the Royal treasury, but Juliette denounces her and herself gets away with the huge fortune. Her story then continues with all manner of atrocity which would all take too long to list, and which ends in a terrible apotheosis with the death of her own daughter Marianne, whom after unspeakable tortures she throws into the flames.

"I confess, I love crime madly," says Juliette at the end of her story; "only crime can stir my feelings and I shall carry out its maxims to the last moment of my life. Free from any religious awe, so that I can put myself above any law, and with my judgement and my wealth, what power, divine or human, could constrain my desires? The past emboldens me, the present galvanises me, I have little fear of the future, so it is my hope that the remainder of my life will be very much more splendid than the wrongdoings of my youth. Nature only created man to find all the pleasure he can on earth. That is nature's most precious law and will ever be that of my heart. Bad luck indeed for the victims, because one must have victims. Without the profound laws of balance, everything would be destroyed in the world. It is only by wrongdoing that nature holds together, winning back those rights of which virtue robs it. So when we abandon ourselves to evil, we are obeying nature and resistance would be the only crime that nature could not forgive in us. Oh, my friends, let us all be convinced of those principles, for in their implementation is the only source of happiness that man can know."

But Justine was unable to hear her sister's terrible story without terror and tears and Juliette agrees with her hosts that they must get rid of this loathsome example of virtue at the earliest possible moment. But nature is to claim Justine as a victim. A terrible storm gathers. While they are chasing the wretched girl—just as she crosses the road past the castle, in fact—a fierce stroke of lightning pierces her through and through. The villains however are delighted. "Hurry, hurry, Madame, do come and see what lovely work heaven has done; come and see how heaven rewards virtue. Now is there really any sense in cherishing it when those who serve it best can themselves so cruelly become victims of fate themselves?"

Almost every one of the hellish orgies in this story of Justine and Juliette is preceded, interrupted or ended by a long moral or metaphysical disquisition, wonderfully eloquent, which Sade places in the lips of this or that hero, each of them resuming and building, sometimes to the point of delirium, upon the theories contained in Sade's earlier works. The principal aberrant of Sade's system, but also the seminal teaching which by close examination one can draw from it, have been admirably expressed by Maurice Blanchot.

"Sade," he says, "was brave enough to assert that by not flinching from accepting the peculiar tastes which were his and by taking them as the starting point and principle of all thought, he was offering philosophy the most sure foundation he could find and enabling it to interpret man's fate generally in a profound manner. . . . Now, it so happens that this is not a thought we can ignore, and in the heart of the contradictions in which it is involved . . . it does show us that when the choice is between a normal man with the sadist hopelessly locked within him and the sadist who makes that hopelessness an end in itself, it is the latter who sees more of the truth and logic of the situation and grasps it the more profoundly, to such a point that he is able to assist the normal man to understand himself and help him to modify the conditions of comprehension."

Pierre Klossowski's theory of spiritual interpretation is also worth noting: "Sade's whole work appears really to be one continued agonised lament, addressed to the image of an unattainable virginity, a cry which is wrapped and as it were set in a psalm of blasphemy. *I am excluded from purity because I want to possess the woman that is pure. I cannot help craving purity, but at the same time I am impure because I want to enjoy that purity which can never be enjoyed.*"

Indeed, the Marquis de Sade's philosophical epic would lose its richest meaning if one failed to see it simultaneously from three aspects—that of descriptive psychopathology, that of inverted humour and that of poetry.

Though in the novels that we are now considering, Sade's romantic invention goes infinitely farther than in the *120 Days of Sodom,* the consistency and unity of his scientific plan are no less clear. In a number of passages the author again takes up cases of perversion which he had already dealt with in the first of his large-scale erotic novels. Take necrophily. The case of the Duke of Florville in the *120 Days* is closely related to the Cordelli episode in *Juliette*; indeed, one finds identical turns of speech. To clinch the matter from the *Nouvelle Justine* we may observe that Sade never reached a greater height of enthusiasm, completely absorbed in the scientific task he began in the Bastille, which the loss of his marvellous roll (the *120 Days*) never for a moment hindered, than in these lines: "People just do not conceive how essential these pictures are to the development of man's heart. If we are still as ignorant as we are about this matter, this is only due to the stupid restraint of those who chose to write on such matters. Entrammelled by ridiculous fears as they are, all they discuss are childish things that any dolt knows, and they are afraid to thrust a fearless hand into the human heart and show us what monstrously wild things it is capable of."*

Sade revelled in Rabelais. Indeed, in some of his letters to his valet Carteron he tried to imitate him. But that "cheerful laughter of old France" had little in common with the inspiration behind *Juliette* and if one wanted to make a comparison between Sade and some divine forerunner clown, it would have to be Aristophanes. "You listen to me, you old baboon," cried Juliette to the Pope, in a dialogue without parallel in any literature, "my second desire is a philosophical dissertation on murder. I have many a time blotted my record with that act, and I want to know what my attitude towards it should be. What you will now tell me will determine my outlook for ever. Not that I believe in your infallibility, but I have confidence in the study you must have made, and as I am aware how much I am

---

*If the Marquis de Sade forestalled the Krafft-Ebings and Havelock Ellises in the domain of descriptive sexual pathology, he should also be considered as having been the first to indicate some of the fundamental notions which govern the Freudian system. As we know, the keystone of psycho-analysis is the notion of the pre-existence of erotic emotions in the infant. Freud has shown that the first sexual impressions of childhood direct and determine the nature of the final *libido*, and the suppression of this, under the control of social or ethical prohibitions, more or less seriously damages the mental balance of the adult. But what did the Marquis de Sade say at the close of the eighteenth century? "It is in the mother's womb that are formed those organs which are to make us responsive to this or that fancy; the first objects it comes in contact with and the first speech it hears complete the work of formation; tastes are now there, and nothing in the world can destroy them." (*Justine*, 1791 version I; 243). The child, Freud further notes, shows a natural trend towards incest and sadism. And what had the Marquis said before him? "Nature inspires a young boy to bugger his sister, and he does so, never guessing that there is a better passage. Frightful wickedness is thus conceived in the very bosom of innocence and nature, and he has his pleasure of his sister, and longs to beat her and *hurt her.*" (*La Nouvelle Justine* II;273).

Even hormone theory and physio-pathological anatomy found a precursor in Sade, who in the 1791 *Justine* wrote: "When the science of anatomy is perfected it will easily make clear the relationship of a man's structure and the tastes which govern his emotions. Pedants, executioners, ticket-men, legislators, all you of the tonsured rabble, what will you all do when we get so far? What will become of your laws, your morals, your religion, your gallows, your heavens, your Gods, your hells, when it is proved that this or that flow of juices, this or that sort of tissue, this or that degree of strength of the blood or other animal essences is enough to turn men into victims of your trials or your rewards?"

a philosopher, I am confident you would not dare deceive me."

In Juliette's utter lack of concealment we have all the women that history and fiction deliver to our magic embrace—Isabelle of Bavaria, Béatrix Cenci, Catherine Howard, Luisa Sigea, the *Marquise* de Merteuil, Pauline Borghèse. . . . Above even Sodom and superior to time, she makes the charms of any other woman risible. Tense with the shrill clamour of her youthful vigour, a maenad drunk with desire, she curves her loins and with mother-of-pearl fingers parts the lips of her vulva to soothe that never-quenchable thirst for knowledge. . . .

The realm in which Sade's supreme paean rings clear and his self-expression consumes the whole world about him as the monstrously swollen wheel of the sun consumes the planet Mercury, is desire, the image of erotic union, ever new in his eyes and of such intoxicating daring that he had no other course but to translate it into a fairyland of cruelty, a glorious dawn of torture. But his characters are endowed with language of such great charm that all one can hear of the frightful things they tell us is their music. "We will take her out of her tomb and there, on her delightful form, on that sweet head, where the shades of the grave which I have laid on her brow shall never fade, you shall b—— me. . . . Are you afraid?"

Everything on which Sade leaves his seal is—love.

OXTIERN OU LES MALHEURS DU LIBERTINAGE

(Year VIII)

This play has been discussed in Chapters Fourteen and Fifteen. It was published at Versailles by Blaisot in the Year VIII, a 48 page octavo volume entitled: *"Oxtiern ou les Malheurs du libertinage, drame en trois actes et en prose, par D. A. F. Sade. Représenté au Théâtre du Marais, à Paris, en 1791 et à Versailles, sur celui de la Société dramatique, le 22 frimaire, l'an VIII de la République."*

THE CRIMES OF LOVE, PRECEDED BY A REFLECTION ON NOVELS;

THE AUTHOR OF THE "CRIMES OF LOVE" TO VILLETERQUE,

JOURNALIST'S HACK (YEAR IX)

THE WORK OF THE STORY-TELLER

I

THE INITIAL SCHEME (1788)

"A note on the cover of the twentieth and last book of his autograph manuscript," Maurice Heine tells us, "informs us that Sade's work as story-teller consisted of some fifty stories. Sixteen of these, among the shorter or at least the more anecdotal, were intended to be entitled *Historiettes* (Anecdotes) and be part of a collection of two or three volumes of essays entitled *Le Portefeuille d'un Homme de Lettres*. Thirty others, alternately "cheerful" and "gloomy" and preceded by an author's note, were to have formed the four volumes of his *Contes et Fabliaux du XVIIIme Siècle par un Troubadour Provençal* (Stories and Legends of the Eighteenth Century by a Provençal Troubadour). Of the four that remained, one was kept in reserve (*Les Filous*—The Swindlers), another was made into a novel (The Adversities of Virtue) while the two others were scrapped (*Séide, conte moral et philosophique*—of which we have only the detailed plot—and *l'Époux complaisant*).

"All this material, written in the Bastille during 1787 and 1788, was in the form of revised rough draft in twenty notebooks, each of 48 pages, in a buff cover, eighteen of them being MS 4010, an important recent acquisition of the Bibliothéque Nationale. . . . At the present moment six anecdotes and five stories, which must have been in the two notebooks which are missing (numbers 2 and 7 of the series), are still to be found. . ."

Let us add that though the *Catalogue raisonné* of 1788 does not mention the title of this collection, there is at least Sade's initial scheme of it, for he made this note on the manuscript: "This work constitutes four volumes with a plate to each story; the stories are so placed that a cheerful and even boisterous story, though without ever departing from the rules of modesty or decency, comes next to a serious or tragic story."

II

THE CRIMES OF LOVE, PRECEDED BY A REFLECTION ON NOVELS (YEAR VIII)

Twelve years later, de Sade was to give up his first scheme.

Only eleven stories appeared during his lifetime, apart from a single story included in Volume III of *Aline et Valcour* (*Le Crime du Sentiment ou les Délires de l'amour*). This was a new collection, the *Crimes of Love,* from which he now excluded the cheerful stories, perhaps to fit the gloomy preoccupations of an unhappy period. If we exclude the *Double Épreuve* (The Double Test), "a superb literary tribute to the *fêtes galantes,* for all its fastidiousness—it ill fitted a collection of this sort, despite its ending with the death of the fair Dolsé—the ten other stories, all packed with horrific adventures, divide qualitatively into three groups. There are the rather mediocre stories on an historical background—*Juliette et Raunai, Rodrigue, Laurence et Antonio,* and *la Contesse de Sancerre,* rather reminiscent of the melodramatic stories of Baculard d'Arnaud, though the gloom is murkier and the imagination bolder. There are the contemporary stories, *Miss Henriette Stralson, Faxelange, Ernestine* and *Dorgeville,* in which Sade's vigorous originality shows in many a passage, despite the limits which restraint of language imposed on him. Finally, there were two stories which deserve to be placed among his masterpieces. These are *Florville et Courval ou le Fatalisme* and *Eugénie de Franval.*

Pierre Klossowski provides a very sound interpretation of the former. "Under the cover of exceptional warmth of heart Courval hides the sadistic satisfaction of knowing the secret which Florville does not seem to know, though in fact there is the Sadistic taint in the heroine herself, and Florville is an enigma to herself. . . ."

The other story might be sub-titled "the triumph of incest". Sade did not exaggerate at all when he said: "In all the literature of Europe there is no story or novel in which the dangers of loose living are more powerfully laid bare." Further, one cannot go better than the general judgment of the author of *My Neighbour, Sade* when he wrote of the best of the *Crimes of Love*: "Why is it that these tales, ostensibly moral, seem so dubious? It is because the rational morality which is their criterion presupposes a conscience and a human freedom of choice which are for ever submerged by the dark forces which are really involved." And Marie Constance Quesnet's opinion is most intriguing and worth quoting. It is Sade himself who gives it to us. *"Apropos* of the *Crimes of Love,* my dear one said that it was true, the stage often revealed features as terrible, but they were less dangerous played on the stage than when read in cold blood in a novel, and this was why she thought my book a dangerous one. Apart from that she thought my style simple, pleasant and not in the least affected."

The collection is preceded by a lively essay on the novel. After glancing at the most famous novels from the Greeks to Lewis, and extolling *Don Quichotte* ("the best of all novels") *Manon Lescaut* and *la Nouvelle Héloïse,* he also paid enthusiastic homage to the innovating brilliance of Richardson and Fielding. Sade outlined his view on works of imagination with a grandeur and sureness of which the following passage is a fine example:

". . . It must be admitted that in the stories you will now read the bold flights of imagination which the author has allowed himself are not always in harmony with the severity of the laws of art, but it is the author's hope that the extreme variety of the characters may serve as compensation; far stranger than our moralists would have it, nature is always breaking free from the dykes with which the policy of those gentry would like to hem her in; uniform in her schemes but irregular in results, her breast never calm, nature is like the heart of a volcano, whence from time to time gush forth either precious stones that serve man's sense of luxury, or balls of fire which destroy men; she is great when she peoples the world with Anthonys or Tituses, frightful when she belches forth Andronicuses or Neros, but yet all the time sublime, majestic, for ever worthy of our study, our brush and our respectful wonder, for her designs are hidden from us, and, slaves of her whims or her needs as we are, it is never on what these make us undergo that we should found our feelings regarding her, but on her grandeur, her energy, whatever these may lead to."

Heine has observed that this little work of Sade's on the theory of the novel offers the double merit of placing the author among his contemporaries and pointing the pre-romantic origins of his work.

III

A great aristocrat giving an insolent lackey a good whacking with his stick—that is the substance of this little work, published by Massé in Paris in the Year IX, a 12° booklet of 20 pages. It is Sade's response to a bitter attack on the *Crimes de l'Amour* in which he was by innuendo accused of being the author of *Justine*.

We should however note that there were also articles that praised Sade's book. On *6th Brumaire* there was an anonymous article in the *Journal de Paris* which was much more fair, speaking of the "fertility of the author's imagination" and the "great variety of the scenes". And if Eugénie de Franval was said to be "very gloomy", the critic found an alleviating circumstance for the author: "No doubt he considered that this atmosphere will be appropriate for us for some time yet, since in that respect reality with us still outdoes fiction."

IV

It was from that compendious *manuscript No. 4010* of the Bibliothèque Nationale that in 1926 Maurice Heine drew and for the first time published, under the title of *Anecdotes, Tales and Legends,** and in their original spelling, twenty-five of Sade's stories, which had remained unpublished because the author relinquished the original scheme of them. Later, as appendix, Heine added one more story. *Les Dangers de la Bien-*

---

*A Paris. Pour les membres de la Société du Roman philosophique. A quarto volume, limited edition of 233 copies. Historiettes: *Le Serpent; La Saillie gasconne; L'Heureuse Feinte; le M . . . puni; l'Évêque embourbé; Le Revenant; les Harangueurs provençaux; Attrapez-moi toujours du même; l'Époux complaisant; Aventure incompréhensible; Le Fleur du Châtaignier.* Contes et Fabliaux: *L'Instituteur philosophe; La Prude ou La Rencontre imprévu; Emilie et Tourville ou la Cruauté fraternelle; Augustine de Villebranche ou le Stratagème de l'amour; Soit fait ainsi qu'il est requis; Le Président mystifié; La Marquise de Thélème ou les Effets du libertinage* [fragments]; *Le Talon; Le Cocu de lui-même ou le Raccomodement imprévu; Il y a place pour deux; L'Epoux corrigé; Le Mari prêtre, conte provençal; La Châtelaine de Longevill ou la Femme vengée; Les Filous.* APPENDIX: *Les Dangers de la Bienfaisance*

faisance (The Dangers of Benevolence), otherwise known as *Dorci ou la Bizarrerie du sort* (Dorci or the Fitfulness of Fortune), which had been published as far back as 1881, though quite uncritically, by what Heine called "the rather malicious attentions of Anatole France".*

From this collection of stories, most of which are just entertaining, at least three masterpieces stand out. How could one fail to admire the delightful geniality and the Provençal humour which could thus flourish inside the grim walls of the Bastille? First there is *The Puzzled Chief Justice* in which we see the burlesque mishaps which befall one of those luminaries of the Aix bench who in 1772 treated Sade with such prejudice, but on whom he takes his revenge here with the most hilarious cruelty. Next comes *Augustine de Villebranche,* otherwise known as *the Converted Lesbian.* In the dialogue of the second part of this we are given a taste of what sort of plays Sade might have written had he not always been afraid to let himself go when he came to write for the stage. Finally, there is *Émilie de Tourville.* This is really one of the most tragic stories of the *Crimes of Love.* Heine wrote of it: "this story, full of puzzling restraint, needs to be read between the lines. It would lose a good deal of its meaning if one had not that key of Sade's to the conventional signs with which in his lists of his works he marked some titles. *Émilie* is *really concerned with sodomy,* and this alone gives a full explanation of the close solidarity of the brothers against their sister and their ferocity towards her, making the torture which they inflict on her a bloodstained seasoning to their own pleasures."

To Heine's choice we may add two other masterpieces drawn from the *Crimes of Love.* These are *Florville et Courval ou le Fatalisme* and *Eugénie de Franval.*

These five stories together would in their wonderful range make a little collection of stories unparalleled in French literature.

V

THE 1803-4 RE-ARRANGEMENT PLAN

Sade's *Notes littéraires,* written some time between June 1803 and March 1804, in Charenton Asylum, and published

*Paris; Charavay; 16°.

by the author in 1953, under the title *Cahiers personnels* (Private notebooks), contained a scheme for the re-arrangement of his work. Having first decided to alternate gloomy and cheerful stories, then (*Year VIII*) having decided on the contrary to include only "heroic" or "tragic" stories in his *Crimes of Love,* Sade now changed his mind yet again and returned to the original notion, adding ten stories to the *Crimes of Love* and compiling a companion volume, to be called *The French Boccaccio,* planned in the same way. This new arrangement he preceded by the plots of stories to be written or re-written—*Madame de Thélème, La Cruauté fraternelle, Les Inconvénients de la pitié, Aveuglement vaut mieux que lumière,* and *L'Ane sacristain.* It is not without interest to observe that *Madame de Thélème* and *Les Inconvénients de la pitié* were based on the new opportunities for murder and loose living provided by the sinister transformations of the revolutionary period. The hero of the first story is the Proconsul of Arras, Joseph le Bon, and Sade carefully noted that all the loathing the story was calculated to cause must be laid at the door of the leading character, who was "very real", and the whole purpose of such a story was to "make people loathe the crimes of the age".

This plan of rearrangement might well serve some day as foundation for a critical edition of Sade's stories, based on the author's latest intentions and would be able to include the various alternatives that *MS 4010* gives us.

LA MARQUISE DE GANGE (1813)

"*La Marquise de Gange,* though anonymous, can without question be taken to be by Sade, is a wonderful example of the psychological and descriptive detail that he could draw from a mere hint of history." Thus Heine, on a work which has become a great rarity, and although it deserved a better fate, was until 1957 almost as unknown as if it had never been published at all,* despite Heine's clear intention to publish it, which we can see from the numerous notes which he bequeathed to the Bibliothèque Nationale, including much information on the

---

*In 1957 a new edition, edited by the author, was published by Messrs. Pierre Amrot.

savage murder of one of the loveliest women of Louis XIV's time. Regarding the literary side of the work, Heine wrote: "The theme of unfortunate virtue and persecuted innocence haunted the Marquis de Sade throughout his literary career. Indeed, he began his work with that subject, when in the Bastille in 1787 he wrote *Les Infortunes de la vertu,* and he came back to it again with his last published novel, *La Marquise de Gange.* Alpha and Omega met. In Justine and Euphrasie* (the *Marquise*) we recognise sisters. And what moving victims we see in the course of development of the whole cycle! Need one recall Aline de Blamont, in *Aline et Valcour,* reduced to suicide by the incestuous demands of her father? Or Henriette Stralson, in the *Crimes of Love,* who stabs herself on the body of her murdered lover? Or Amélie de Sancerre, in the same work, so disloyally sacrificed by a rival who is none other than her own mother? . . ."

All bibliographers have attributed *la Marquise de Gange* to Sade. It was published anonymously in 1813 by the house of Béchet—two 12° volumes, of xi + 258 and 298 pages, and quite recently documentary proof came to light which supports this view: the inventory of Sade's effects made after his death at the Charenton home listed four çopies of the book. At the same time the internal proofs are so numerous that only a critical edition of the work could note them all. Here we have room for only two general observations, and a number of biographical details.

First, Sade's very personal style and train of thought immediately stand out in the ethical disquisitions of the characters, even when loyalty to the marriage bed or religion are the subjects. There is also an unquestionable relationship between episodes in some of his novels and stories and the imaginary adventures with which he fills out the story of his heroine. Further, on a different plane, there are the description of Avignon, the cradle of the Sade family, the lines devoted to Cadenet, and the roundabout itinerary from that village to the city of the Popes, by way of Durance bridge and Aix, which recalls the agitated days that the author himself once spent in that lovely countryside and could never forget. There is a passage in which

---

*The *Marquise* was in fact christened *Diane,* but no doubt Sade felt that Euphrasie sounded more romantic.

"a descendant of Laura, a fashionable poet" improvises a mad-
rigal, all very reminiscent of Sade's admiration for Petrarch's
mistress, and there is also a passage on dreams in which we have
Sade's thoughts of twenty-five years previously, partly in the
very same terms in which he told them to his wife—in a letter
which remained unpublished until 1948. The comparison of
these two documents is in itself sufficient most positively to
identify the author of *La Marquise de Gange*.

In the catalogue of his works which Sade drew up in 1804
the book is however not mentioned. But there had been the
exhausting work he had put in on the *Journées de Florbelle,*
which called for no less than one hundred notebooks and was
not complete till April 25th 1807. That alone left him no time
to begin the *Marquise de Gange* before that final date. And if
on the other hand we take it that *Adélaïde de Brunswick,*
which was begun on September 1st 1812, came after it, this
fixes the period between the spring of 1807 and the autumn of
1812 as the period of composition.

Though the work of a septuagenarian, this last of the novels
which Sade published shows no hint of the weaknesses of style
or form which make *Adélaïde de Brunswick* so disappointing.
It is equal in quality to the best of the *Crimes of Love,* which
were written in his prime, and is in the same *genre* of grimness
and eroticism, though *La Marquise* is wrapped in a cloak of
decency and the notions of good and evil are equally well defended by those that stand for one or the other. In this novel,
in short, we find all the resources of sheer skill which place
Sade in the front rank of French story-tellers. How lively the
tale is, what vigour there is in the dialogue, and with what a
pure style he depicts the horrors, how well this master of subtlety
knows how to play on our feelings!

However, in this work there is one marked difference. Apparently moved himself by the cruelty of his subject, Sade has
here given way much more noticeably than elsewhere to sensitivity and tears, and is far less indulgent than he usually is to
the exploits of the wicked. What is more, if he ventures to distort historical truth anywhere in his story, it is in that passage
in the novel in which he makes the Abbé de Gange come to a
bad end—"Die, monstrous rascal!" cries the imaginary instrument of justice and revenge, despite the fact that in that char-

acter he had his best historical proof of the rightness of the thesis of *Juliette,* that of vice invariably being recompensed and happiness dwelling in the practice of crime.

If the murder of the "fair maid of Provence"* by her two brothers-in-law, on May 16th 1667, was vile enough an act, one cannot but sense from the fragmentary evidence which has come down to us that the hearts of those two men were still more vile. Herein lay the interest of the case, both psychological and narrative. And by realising this and by his skill in clothing the scant details we find in *Causes célèbres* Sade created a most moving story, which if not one of his major works is none the less a little masterpiece, in which his Satanic genius lent pity a new colour altogether.

---

*Thus they called Lady de Gange when as wife of the Marquis Dominique de Castellane she appeared at Louis XIV's court. Of her we know that when she was widowed she inspired Christina of Sweden with Lesbian desires. "Oh, if only I were a man," Christine wrote in 1656, "I would fall at your feet, your slave, limp with love, and would spend my days and my nights gazing at your loveliness and offering you an affectionate, passionate, faithful heart . . . And now, without waiting for a delightful matempsychosis [*sic*] to change my sex, I must see you to worship you and tell you so at every moment . . ."

CHAPTER SEVENTEEN

St. Pelagie, Bicêtre and Charenton
(1810-14)

March 6th 1801 (5th Ventôse, Year IX). On this day police suddenly entered the offices of Nicolas Massé, publisher, when the Marquis de Sade was there on business. They made a search, discovering manuscripts in the handwriting of the Marquis (among those listed were *Juliette, The French Boccaccio, The Pastimes of a Rake or the Ninth of Cytherea,** and a political work, *My Whims (or. a little of everything)* as well as printed works containing additions and corrections in his hand—a copy of *La Nouvelle Justine* and the last volume of *Juliette.*)

At the same time, two other searches were made, one at the house of a friend of Sade's, where nothing suspicious was found, and the other at Saint Ouen, in the house of Marie Constance Quesnet, where the Marquis had "a secret study with licentious figurines" and a piece of tapestry "depicting the most obscene subjects, mostly drawn from that infamous novel, *Justine*". The tapestry was taken to the prefecture.

Apparently Sade had been denounced to the police by his own publisher, who for appearance' sake was also arrested—and held for twenty-four hours!

March 7th 1801 (16th Ventôse, Year IX). Sade and Massé

---

*In June, 1832 D. C. A. Sade, the Marquis' son, obtained permission to buy the manuscript of this work from the library, and then had it destroyed.

were cross-examined. Promised his liberty, the publisher revealed where the stock of *Juliette* was held.* The Marquis admitted to knowing the manuscript of the novel, but asserted that he was only the copyist.

April 2nd 1801 (12th Germinal, Year IX). After a number of discussions with the Minister of Police, Prefect Dubois agreed that a trial would cause an uproar which an exemplary punishment would still not make worth while. The thing to do was to "place" the Marquis in Sainte Pélagie prison "as administrative punishment" for being the author "of that infamous novel, *Justine*" and the "still more frightful work entitled *Juliette*".

April 3rd 1801 (13th Germinal, Year IX). Incarcerated in Sainte Pélagie, Sade was visited in the prison common-room by Mme Quesnet, who had obtained permission to visit him three times in every ten days.

A convent founded in 1662 by Lady de Miramion, Sainte Pélagie became a political prison during the Revolution. André Chénier, Roucher, the Sombreuils, Sartines' daughter, lovely Mme de Sainte Amaranthe, and Mme Roland were all held there. The building stood roughly where numbers 13 and 15 of the *rue Lacépède* now stand, overlooking then what were the *rue de la Clef* and the *Place du Puits de l'Hermite*.

* * *

All Sade's biographers have made the same grave error regarding the reason for the Marquis' arrest on *15th Ventôse, Year IX*. Without due checking they have adopted the view that it was *Zoloé et ses deux acolytes,* an anonymous pamphlet pillorying Josephine Buonaparte, Mme Tallien, Mme Visconti, Tallien, Barras and Napoleon himself, that was the reason for the arrest. It has been assumed that this pamphlet, which appeared in July, 1800, was Sade's work, and that to arrest him as the author of *Juliette* and *Justine* was merely a convenient cover for the vengeance of the First Consul, who found his marital honour deeply wounded by the pamphlet.

---

*One thousand copies, seized and destroyed. In the archives we also read of eleven records of searches or seizure of books at booksellers', printers' or binders' suspected of having copies of either *la Nouvelle Justine* or *Juliette* between 15th Ventôse and 17th Fructidor, Year IX.

But the available sources in no way justify this view. It was not till half a century after the publication of *Zoloé* that this erroneous notion arose, first in the *Biographie Michaud,* then, some years later, in G. Brunet's *Fantaisies bibliographiques.* Yet, as exhaustive research goes to show, in all the voluminous and most complete records of the whole matter there is not one single document about the Marquis which so much as mentions *Zoloé.*

In any case, the report which Dubois the Police Prefect made furnishes the following details:

(a) the arrest on *15th Ventôse* was made without any reference back to the Consuls. If the arrest really was due to the vicious satire on la Beauharnais, would not Napoleon have been the first to be informed?

(b) Supposing Dubois did make *Justine* and *Juliette* the excuse, to deceive public opinion, why was the fictitious reason never noted in the internal records? Besides, since administrative internment ruled out any appearances in court, why should this alleged fear of a scandal have arisen at all?

The whole story, as hitherto presented by Sade's biographers, depends on his having been the author of the lampoon. There is, however, not the slightest proof of this. In the absence of proofs, internal evidence might count for something. But however hard one strains one cannot trace any hint of Sade's style in the pamphlet. The very structure of the prose, as well as the vocabulary and the sheer movement of the style, the general management of the material, have nothing in common with Sade's style. The extreme untidiness and absolute flabbiness of the language are on the contrary typical professional libeller's work.

But though it was not on any personal order of the First Consul's that Sade underwent the horrors of a renewed imprisonment which was to last till his death, it remains none the less true that this arbitrary detention was the work of a régime in which one could already feel the growing tyranny of Napoleon, and it was by decisions signed personally by him in privy council on July 9th and 10th 1811 and April 19th and again May 3rd 1812 that Sade remained in prison.

May 20th 1802 (30th Floréeal, Year X). The prisoner wrote

to the Minister of Justice to say that he demanded freedom or a trial. He swore on oath that he was not the author of *Justine*.

Between February 20th and March 14th 1803 (Ventôse, Year XI). Sade was said to have tried to "satiate his bestial passion on some young scatterbrains who had been sent to Sainte Pélagie for a few days following rowdyism at the *Théâtre Français*", their cells being next to his.

March 14th 1803 (23rd Ventôse, Year XI). Following this outrageous incident, Sade was transferred to Bicêtre Prison, which under the old régime had been called "the mob's Bastille".

We have a description of Sade's appearance at this time—in fact, on the very morning when the author of *Juliette* was getting ready to leave for Bicêtre Prison—in the following striking lines of Charles Nodier's *Souvenirs*:

> "One of these gentlemen was up very early, because he was to be transferred and had been forewarned. All I at first noticed was a monstrous obesity which hampered his movements to such a point that he was unable to move with the same vestiges of charm and elegance which one could detect traces of in his general deportment. Yet his eyes still retain a hint of brilliancy and exquisiteness which glowed from time to time for a moment like the last spark of a dying ember."*

There is no reason to question—as does the author of one biography whose caution about documentary evidence of this sort might a hundred times better have been employed on something else—the authenticity of such a portrait, for it corresponds exactly to what Sade himself wrote about his fatness and also to what official records reveal of the delicacy of his features. And how could a man fail to recognise in Nodier's thumbnail sketch that outstanding radiance which expressed the man's real nature?

About April 15th 1803 (25th Germinal, Year XI). Sade's

Souvenirs, Épisodes et Portraits de la Révolution et de l'Empire. Further, Nodier goes on to say: "As I have said, I only caught a glimpse of him. All I recall is that he was courteous to the point of being obsequious, affable to the point of unctuousness, and spoke with respect of all that is accorded respect."

family now succeeded in persuading the Prefect of Police to transfer Sade from Bicêtre to the Charenton Asylum. The director of that establishment (M. de Coulmier) had a long talk with the head of the 5th Division of the Prefecture (J. B. Boucheseiche) and received instructions on the special measures to be taken to prevent any attempt at escape.

April 22nd 1803 (2nd Floréal, Year XI). On the eve of leaving the frightful prison he was in, to exchange it for the incomparably more comfortable régime of an asylum, the Marquis wrote to M. de Coulmier, promising to be deserving of his approval and to "deconvince" him of all the bad opinions his mind would have been filled with by others.

THE AGED INMATE OF CHARENTON SAINT MAURICE

April 27th 1803 (7th Floréal, Year XI). Sade was transferred under the charge of a policeman. His board, which the family had agreed to pay, was to be raised to the annual sum of three thousand francs.

Charenton Hospice or Asylum to which Sade had already once been transferred (July 4th 1789), had become empty in 1795. Two years later (June 15th 1797) the Directory ordered "all the necessary dispositions in the former house of the Brethren of Charity to establish there a complete course of treatment for cases of insanity". Lunatics of both sexes would be taken in and the establishment would be directly controlled by the Ministry of the Interior. This placed M. de Coulmier in charge. Coulmier was a former Father Superior of the Premonstrants, "a man of influence for his intelligence and his highly-placed contacts". He had sat in the Constituent Assembly. The other senior officers were M. Gastaldy (an acquaintance of Sade's), Chief Medical Officer, a former physician of the Avignon asylum, M. Bleynie, assistant Chief Medical Officer, who was to hold the post for fifty years, M. Deguise, surgeon, and M. Dumontier, chief steward. Instituted at first as an adjunct to the Bicêtre and Salpêtrière prisons, Charenton soon had civil boarders. Soldiers and sailors on active service and disabled men suffering from mental troubles were also sent there.

"Over it all M. de Coulmier ruled despotically, though

there was nothing austere or rigorous about his rule," wrote Dr Ramon, who became a doctor there in Sade's time, adding: "Everybody in the place liked him." We shall in due course see how kindly he treated the Marquis, steadfastly taking his part against the authorities, except during the first few months, when Sade was inclined to be obstreperous. What is more, his unquestionable grasp of certain aspects of Sade's genius is a particularly clear proof of his mental toughness. M. de Coulmier merits posterity's great respect.

April 13th 1804 (23rd Germinal, Year XII). Mme Quesnet wrote to the Minister of Justice to request Sade's release. (It seems that in 1806 she voluntarily joined Sade in the hospice. The *Personal Notebooks* contain many a reflection of their mutual affection, one of which is in particular most moving: "One day I reproached my dear one for being forgetful of my tastes, apropos of something she had offered me which I was not a lover of. *You are wrong,* she said, *to reproach me with forgetting your tastes; one thing is quite certain, I shall never forget that which you have for me.*" (9th Brumaire (October 31st), at Pélagie.)

May 1st 1804 (11th Floréal, Year XII). Either for this day or the next, the Prefect ordered an examination of Sade's papers and had Sade told that if continued to be rebellious he would be sent back to Bicêtre.

June 20th 1804 (1st Messidor, Year XII). Sade sent the Senatorial Commission for Individual Liberty, formed May 18th, a strongly-worded protest against his arbitrary detention. He said that now he had spent four years under "the most cruel and the most unjust constraint" without anybody being willing to let him stand his trial. He dared hope that he would see the end of his misfortunes in the new order of things which made the senators the arbiters of his fate.

August 12th 1804 (24th Thermidor, Year XII). Sade, Man of Letters, to Monseigneur Fouché, Minister of Police:

"Monseigneur,

I find myself without cause deprived of my liberty now nearly four years, and only a certain philosophic outlook has enabled me so far to suffer the various vexations to which I am submitted, on pretexts which are as frivolous as they are ludicrous.

The laws and regulations concerning individual liberty have never been as openly flouted as in my case, since it is *without any sentence or any other legal enactment* that they persist in keeping me under lock and key, allegedly because of an obscene work most mistakenly attributed to me and also because of some fables which they choose to suppose they can apply to my private life, *the whole thing without any foundation.*

In consequence, Monseigneur, I find myself obliged to have recourse to your authority and above all your sense of equity *to obtain my liberation,* since not only are all laws and commonsense ignored in my case, but also because *both the one and the other explicitly say I should be set free.*

I dare to hope, *Monseigneur,* that you will deign to take into consideration the justifiable application of a *sexagenarian* who will be indebted to you by all he holds dear.

I have the honour to be, with the most profound respect, Your Excellency's most humble and most obedient servant.
                                                    Sade."

August 28th 1804 (10th Fructidor, Year XII). Sade applied to Minister Fouché for permission to go to Paris on business whenever this became absolutely necessary. He pointed out to His Excellency that the régime at Charenton was the more suited to such a permission because such an institution was not looked upon as a prison.

September 8th 1804 (21st Fructidor, Year XII). The Prefect of Police, Dubois, and the Minister of Police produced a joint statement. It described Sade as "incorrigible". He was in a state of "incessant licentious insanity" and by character hostile to any form of constraint. The conclusion drawn was that there was good reason to leave him where he was. This was anyway what his family wanted, and it was they who provided for him.

April 14th 1805 (24th Germinal, Year XIII). This Easter Sunday Sade took communion in the parish church of Charenton Saint Maurice.

May 17th 1805 (27th Floréal, Year XIII). The Prefect wrote to M. de Coulmier:

"I am informed, Monsieur, that on Easter Sunday you allowed Mr Desade [sic], detained by governmental order in your establishment, to take Holy Communion in the parish church of Charenton. The only reason for which this individual was transferred from Bicêtre was to give his family opportunity to manage his affairs. He is your prisoner and you should not and in no case, under whatever pretext it may be, cannot allow him to go out, without out express formal authorisation from me. Did it not occur to you, moreover, that the presence of such a man would not fail to inspire horror and might cause public disorder?

Your excessive leniency towards M. Desade has all the more reason to astonish me since more than once you have complained bitterly about his conduct and above all his obstreperousness.

Monsieur, may I remind you of the orders given regarding him which I call upon you in future to carry out to the letter.

Yours truly,
Dubois."

August 24th 1805 (6th Fructidor, Year XIII). When, after long talks Sade's family proposed to purchase all his properties save the Saumane estate (with the house) for a life annuity of 5,000 francs a year, Sade sent them his own *memorandum* laying down the conditions to which they would have to agree, the principal aim of which was to guarantee Marie Constance Quesnet's interests.

December 22nd 1805 (1st Nivôse, Year XIV). Death of Dr Gastaldy, Chief Medical Officer of Charenton.

January 13th 1806. The Gregorian Calendar had been re-established on January 1st. On January 13th Antoine

Athanase Royer Collard was appointed to the late Dr Gastaldy's post. . . .

January 30th 1806. Sade drew up a last will and testament.

March 5th 1806. Sade began the fair copy of his *Histoire d'Emilie.*

August 6th 1806. The Apt Mortgage Depositary issued a certificate stating that there were nine mortgages on Sade's estates, totalling 715,367 *francs* 62 *centimes.* Among them were those of Lady de Sade for 199,037 *francs* 65 *centimes (8th Ventôse, Year IV)* and 347,456 *francs (3rd Germinal, Year XII)* and also one in the name of Marie Constance Quesnet, for 28,200 *francs (8th Germinal, Year VII).*

October 14th 1806. Louis Marie de Sade fought in the battle of Jena on General Beaumont's staff.

. . . 1806. Somewhere in this year should be placed a lengthy letter from Sade to Gaufridy. The end is most moving. Note in the postscript the imaginary address, to conceal the fact that Sade was interned at Charenton:

"And how is good, decent Mrs Gaufridy? And you, my dear lawyer, you, my life's contemporary, my boyhood pal, how are you yourself?

. . . Some details about La Coste, please, and those I was fond of, the Paulets and the rest.

Is it true that Madame Rovère is keeping the old house for herself? What sort of state is it in, I wonder? And my poor park, would I recognise any trace of myself in it?

My Apt relations, how are they?

Perhaps you would now like a word about myself? Right. *I am not happy,* but fairly well. That is all I can tell the friendship which, I hope, is still interested.

Yours till death.

Sade.

Please don't think the tardiness of our replies is due to laziness, the delay is merely caused by the long time it took your letter to reach us, seeing the number of times we have changed our home in the last five years and our time in the country three years since.

Our address is: care of M. de Coulmiers, Président du Canton et Membre de la Légion d'Honneur, Charenton Saint Maurice, Seine *département*."

By "our replies" and "our address" Sade clearly means jointly of himself and Mme Quesnet. From this letter, which makes many references to her, it is quite clear that in 1806 Sade had obtained the favour of having her live in the hospice, at the side of the man she loved.

April 25th 1807. After "thirteen months and twenty days' work" Sade completed revision of his *Histoire d'Émilie,* which filled seventy-two notebooks and formed the last four volumes of a large ten-volume work, the general title of which, "invariably accepted" today, is: *Les Journées de Florbelle ou la Nature dévoilée, suivie des Mémoires de l'abbé de Modose et des Aventures d'Émilie de Volnange servant de preuves aux assertions,*—"Florbelle's Days or Nature Unveiled, followed by the Reminiscences of the Abbé de Modose and the Adventures of Émilie de Volnange serving as proofs of the assertions."

June 5th 1807. The Minister of Police had "several manuscripts containing revolting reading-matter" seized in the Charenton prisoner's room. They were "a succession of obscenities, blasphemy and foulnesses beyond description". This must have been the manuscript of the *Journées de Florbelle,* which Sade was never to see again and which were burned very soon after his death.

June 14th 1807. Louis Marie de Sade, Captain of the 2nd Polish Infantry Regiment, Malezewski Column, at the time seconded to General Marcognet as *aide-de-camp,* was wounded in the street at Friedland. His conduct earned him mention in despatches.

June 17th 1808. Writing as father of a son who had distinguished himself fighting, Sade in a letter to Napoleon described his own poor physical condition, alleging it as a reason for his requesting liberation.

June 20th 1808. Sade declared that he refused to agree to his son Donatien's marrying his cousin, Louise Gabrielle Laure de

Sade d'Eyguières,* unless his son publicly agreed to certain conditions concerning his father's freedom and estates. As the son would not agree to these demands, and Sade was apprehensive lest after the marriage the family would have him shut up somewhere well away from Paris and his captivity would be made worse, he sent his son a formal letter protesting in advance against what they seemed to be proposing to do with him, which he said he would reveal to his elder son and to the other relations he had left. He would, he said, "and most vigorously, too, as loudly as he could, conjure them to preserve an unhappy old man from the gnawing anxieties with which they intended to surround his grave (and which would take him to it) and would consign the authors of such frightful perfidious acts to public hatred and execration".

June 21st 1808. Consulted by Lady de Sade and the younger son, the Chief Justice replied that being on a list of *émigrés* had meant Sade's loss of all civic rights. As Sade's wife, she no longer need seek any authority, and if the sons wished to marry they might do as they would were their father non-existent.

June 24th 1808. Sade's opposition to the marriage was indicated formally to Lady Laure de Sade d'Eyguières and to the Mayor of the Commune of Condé on the Aisne, where she was domiciled.

July 9th 1808. Jean Baptiste Joseph de Sade d'Eyguières,**

*We have to go back two hundred years to establish the degree of cousinship of this young lady to Donatien Claude Armand, for it was towards the close of the fifteenth century that Baltasar, in the main line of the family, the younger son of Girard de Sade, founded the junior branch line of Sade d'Eyguières. See also Chapter Two.

**On March 22nd 1770 he had married Marie Françoise Amélie de Bimard, issue being: Louise Gabrielle Laure, Généreuse Amélie, Françoise Xavier Joseph David, and another son whose name is unknown. On May 2nd 1778 he inherited the post of Lt-General of the Provinces of Bresse and Bugey. His property was sequestered at the beginning of the Revolution, then sacked and burned to the ground when he emigrated to Rome. In 1808 he was about fifty-nine. Jean Baptiste Joseph de Sade was the son of the Governor of Antibes, Jean Baptiste Joseph David, who defended the place for two months against Hungarian-Sardinian besiegers (December 9th 1745-February 2nd 1746), which conduct earned him the rank of Field-Marshal. It was thanks to this warrior that one of the streets of Antibes is called *rue de Sade*.

father of the girl (who, like his son-in-law to be, had been an *émigré*), informed the prefect that Donatien Claude Armand was going to apply to the courts, unless the Prefect could persuade Donatien's father to withdraw the objection "so foolishly" made, and in that way the name of the Marquis de Sade would not ring through the courts of justice, and so bring dishonour to both families.

August 2nd 1808. Royer-Collard, Chief Medical Officer of Charenton, put to the Minister of Police what great inconveniences followed from the presence of a man made "too famous" by his "brazen immorality". He considered it utterly scandalous that the "infamous author of *Justine*" should be organising a theatre and living with a woman whom he made out to be his daughter, and he requested the transfer of the Marquis de Sade to some prison or castle, to save the sick from the "incessant impression made by his profound corruptness".

August 5th 1808. The Minister of Police's principal undersecretary opened Dr Royer-Collard's letter. He immediately made a summary of it for the Minister, the Duke d'Otrante, minuting that the doctor could not reproach Sade with any of the facts which had led to his being transferred from Sainte Pélagie to Bicêtre. And since it was always possible that the real aim of the doctor's request was to go against M. de Coulmier "who had been making use of M. de Sade's lively imagination and mind" to entertain his patients, the chief undersecretary suggested to his minister that he should ask the Prefect to make discreet enquiry and give his opinion on the abuses which he denounced.

August 8th 1808. Donatien Claude Armand, *Chevalier* de Sade-Mazan, made a grant to the parish of Saint André d'Echauffour, the interest on which, fifteen *francs,* was after his death to pay in perpetuity for a Low Mass in his memory on every June 14th. At the same time, counting more on his solicitation of the Virgin's gratitude than on alleviating his father's sufferings, to attain Paradise, he offered the church a lamp, in honour of its patron saint, *Marie,* "to be lit during High Mass and Vespers at Christmas, Easter, Whitsun, the Holy Sacrament, All Saints', St Andrew's Day and on all feasts of the Virgin".

September 2nd 1808. The Prefect reported to the minister: it was true that M. de Sade was in charge of the elocution of the actors and actresses who acted on the stage which the director of Charenton Asylum had installed at the hospice. M. de Coulmier frankly said this was so. Indeed, "he even says that in this matter he is much obliged to de Sade, for, seeing in light drama a curative method for the mentally deranged, he thinks himself fortunate to have in the hospice a man capable of giving a stage training to the mentally deranged, whom he (M. de Coulmier) wishes to treat by this therapy". Nevertheless, having always held M. de Sade "to be in a habitual state of licentious insanity" the Prefect held that the residence at Charenton of a man "who has corrupted public morals by his impious, lascivious writings and has committed so many crimes" was "in the nature of a public scandal" and there were grounds for transferring this detainee to Ham Fortress or any other state prison.

The same day, having read the report, the Minister decided to transfer the Marquis to Ham Fortress.

September . . . 1808. Following further intervention by some member of the Marquis' family, and following a certificate appeal personally to the Minister to postpone the departure of his boarder and friend, de Sade, *sine die*.

September . . . 1808. Following further intervention by some member of the Marquis's family, and following a certificate issued by Dr Deguise, surgeon of the hospice, stating that in Sade's plethoric condition there would be danger of death if his way of life were changed, the transfer was postponed.

September 15th 1808. Donatien de Sade was married to Gabrielle Laure. . . .

November 11th 1808. Sade's family having requested postponement of the transfer to Ham till the end of the winter, the Minister agreed to fix the date at April 15th, 1809.

End of March 1809. As the fateful day drew near, the prisoner's niece, Lady Delphine de Talaru, approached the

Minister of Police to appeal to him to rescind the transfer order completely.*

April 21st 1809. The transfer was indefinitely postponed.

June 9th 1809. Louis Marie de Sade, Lieutenant in the 2nd Battalion, the Isembourg Regiment and author of a History of the French Nation (of which the first volume only had appeared four years before this) was ambushed by Neapolitan rebels near Mercugliano on the Otranto road, on his way to rejoin his regiment, and was killed.

Some days before May 28th 1810. Sade wrote to Mme Cochelet, Lady-in-waiting of the Queen of Holland, to ask her how many tickets she required for the next performance of his theatre. He was most grateful for the interest she took in their work.

* * *

Concerning these theatricals at Charenton, one cannot do better than quote again from Dr L. J. Ramon:

"Parties, balls, concerts and theatricals were organised. In this situation it was that Sade became an important figure at Charenton: parties, festivities, balls, shows, all were in his hands. He chose the plays, some of which were of his own composition,** he did the casting, he presided over it all and rehearsed the players. . . .

. . . . .

The rules of life were not at all strict—indeed they seem to have been very free and easy; as we have remarked, it was all festivities, balls, concerts, theatricals, to which a large number of outsiders were invited, a number of men of letters and many theatre celebrities, particularly chosen among the young actors and actresses of the *boulevard* theatres. The hero of the ball was above all the celebrated

---

*Louise Joséphine Delphine de Rozières-Sorans, widow of Count Stanislas de Clermont-Tonnerre, was the daughter of the Marquis de Sorans and Marie Louise Élisabeth de Maillé de Carman, second cousin of the Marquis' mother. In 1802 she had remarried, becoming the wife of Louis Justin Marie, Marquis de Talaru, born in 1769, whose family originated from the Lyonnais country, and who was allied or related to all the most noble families of the kingdom, the Béthunes, the Luxembourgs, the Montmorencys.

**For instance, *les Fêtes de l'amitié*, written in honour of M. de Coulmier.

Trénitz, choreographic luminary of the period, whom they decked out in the finest attire which it was not always easy to make him give up without some resistance or struggle. De Sade was the organiser of these festivities and shows. So it is not astonishing if among the shortcomings of the administration of Charenton prominence was given to the bond between the Director and de Sade."

Further, Alfred Bégis maintains—saying that it was Dr Ramon himself who told him—that on certain days Sade gave dinners in his quarters, to which he invited the better-known actors and actresses of Paris, among them being the charming Mlle de Sainte who had first appeared in 1783 at the Royal Academy of Music and now performed principally at the *Italian Theatre,* which she joined in 1788, acting in Favart's comedy *Annette et Lubin.*

July 7th 1810. Lady de Sade, who had been blind and obese for some considerable time, died at Echauffour Castle at about 10 a.m. In this house, inherited from her parents, she had resided with her daughter, Madeleine Laure.

In the new village graveyard, where they were removed at the beginning of this century, her mortal remains now lie, together with those of her daughter, marked by a rustically hewn gravestone and cross, and this inscription:

HERE
REPOSE THE MORTAL REMAINS
OF
MLLE LAURE MADELEINE DE SADE
WHO DIED AT THE CHATEAU
OF ECHAUFFOUR
JANUARY 18TH 1844
AGED 73
BURIED
BESIDE HER MOTHER
LADY RENEÉ PÉLAGIE
DE MONTREUIL, MARQUISE DE SADE,
BOTH OF THEM AS VIRTUOUS
AS THEY WERE BENEVOLENT.
PRAY TO THE LORD
FOR THE REPOSE OF THEIR SOULS.

August 28th 1810. Sade sold his Mazan estates to Calixte Antoine Alexandre Ripert for 56,462 *francs* 50 *centimes,* which sum was collected by the Marquis' children as heirs to their mother, in expectation of the same operation's being performed when the Malmaison, Granvilliers and Camargue properties were sold.

October 18th 1810. Count de Montalivet, Minister of the Interior, to M. de Coulmier:

> "Considering that M. de Sade, who has been put into Charenton, is suffering from the most dangerous of all insanities, that contact between him and the other inmates of the Home involves incalculable dangers, that his writings are no less demented than his speech and conduct, that these dangers are always latent among people whose imagination is already weakened or distraught, as Minister of the Interior I hereby order the following:
>
> Section 1. This M. de Sade is to be given completely separate lodging, so that any contact with other people, inside or outside, is prohibited, whatever the pretext. The greatest care is to be observed to prevent any use of pen, pencil or paper by him.
>
> Section 2. The Director of the Hospice shall by the 25th inst. at the last report to us on the steps he has taken to implement the present decision. He is personally responsible for its execution.
>
> Montalivet."

October 24th 1810. M. de Coulmier acknowledged receipt of the Minister's communication, but could not but request the transfer of M. de Sade, for he would be humiliated to be a gaoler or spend his time persecuting a fellow creature. He must point out to the Count de Montalivet that for a long time now his boarder, by his restrained conduct, had shown every intention to forget his past errors. At the moment, also, he was doubly distressed because he had been left without any resources by his children, who had taken advantage of his detention to completely denude him.

November ... 1810. Sade engaged one of his nieces (was it Lady de Talaru?) to call on the Minister of the Interior, who had issued the harsh order of October 18th, and this lady had assured the Count that he was most mistaken if he thought that the Marquis had ever dreamt of misusing the liberty he enjoyed to write again and have his works published in Leipsick (sic), and he had been blameless.

December 12th 1810. The prisoner's niece wrote to M. de Coulmier to say she had seen Count de Montalivet and the Count had agreed that her uncle might walk as much as he chose whenever the patients were not having their exercise, and the minister had found it quite right for M. de Sade to call on Mme Quesnet, provided there was no patient with her at the time. She requested de Coulmier to give Count de Montalivet the assurance he sought in this matter.

December . . . 1810. Sade to de Coulmier:

"I request M. de Coulmier:

1. to let me return the key of my room, except for being confined to the outer corridor from 10 p.m. to 7 a.m;

2. to let me take my walk *without being followed* at such hour of the day as suits me best, provided the garden is unlocked;

3. to be able to talk freely to the three persons hereunder indicated and this exclusively, in other words *I undertake to talk to nobody else* : Mme Blothière, my next door neighbour, M. de Savines, a relative of mine, and M. de Léon;

4. Finally, to have returned to me what was recently taken away, namely, both paper and pen."

February 6th 1811. Report of police officer La Chave against the booksellers Clémendot and Barba, who both in Paris and the provinces were selling *La Nouvelle Justine* and against Clémendot who, having come into possession of one hundred engravings for this work and *Juliette,* was secretly printing them and distributing them.

March 31st 1811. The Marquis was cross-examined by Count Jolivet, who gave him rather a bad time.

July 9th and 10th 1811. Napoleon, sitting in Privy Council, decided to keep Sade in detention at Charenton.

November 14th 1811. The Marquis was again cross-examined at Charenton, this time by Count Corvietto, who was "very gentle and decent".

November 16th 1811. Birth of Laure Émilie de Sade, first daughter of Donatien Claude Armand.

November 21st 1811. Sade informed Pépin, his bailiff at Saumane, that by an arrangement he had concluded with Donatien Claude Armand, the Saumane land would be his, together with the *château*.

This seems to indicate that Sade's "final proposals" of August 24th 1805 had at last borne fruit, though without Donatien Claude Armand's ever having kept his obligations, nor through his avarice and greed did he ever do so.

June 9th 1812. The Minister of Police informed M. de Coulmier that he might tell the person concerned that the Emperor in Privy Council on April 19th and May 3rd had decided to keep M. de Sade in confinement.

September 1st 1812. Sade began the rough draft of his novel entitled *Adélaïde de Brunswick, princesse de Saxe.*

October 4th 1812. Draft completed. He was to take a week correcting it.

October 6th 1812. Occasional verse written by Sade was sung to the tune of *From childhood on* ... (*Dè mon enfance* ...) to Milord the Cardinal Maury, Archbishop of Paris, when he visited Charenton Hospice. Here is a sample verse:

> *Like to a son of the Eternal*
> *By a kindness that is rare*
> *In mortal guise you come to us*
> *Those who are luckless to console;*
> *Of greatness ever full, your heart,*
> *Ever firm and ever fair,*
> *Beneath your pontifical purple*
> *Does not scorn misfortune.*

October 13th 1812. He began revision of *Adélaïde.*

November 21st 1812. He completed the work and revised it for thirteen days.

December 4th 1812. The work completed, he packed up the draft.

March 3rd 1813. Sade to de Coulmier:

> "*Monsieur,* I most pressingly request you to give Mme
> Quesnet the room above mine, *which you gave my son to
> hope you would,* my peace and my health depending on
> it. If you knew what I suffer when that room is occupied
> by people who (rightly) thinking themselves at home, con-
> sider they owe me no consideration ... yes, *Monsieur,* I
> make bold to assure you that if you knew what I suffer
> therefrom, I am sure that from the friendship you have
> always shown me you definitely would not do it.
>
> Therefore I beg you, pay attention to my application,
> and believe me to be Your most grateful and obedient
> servant
>
> Sade.
>
> Do not forget to send for the 1,500 *livres* that M.
> Boursier, Notary, rue Grenier St Lazare, has for you."

March 31st 1813. Third cross-examination, "very severe, but
very short" at Charenton by "Count Appelius or some such
name".

May 6th 1813. A Ministerial Order prohibited any theatricals
at Charenton. The Marquis was once again the obscure boarder
that he had been in 1803 and 1804.

May 19th 1813. Sade began to tidy up his *Histoire secrète
d'Isabelle de Bavière.*

September 24th 1813. The work was completed, though
twenty-six days later he made fresh emendations.

End of 1813. Sade sent his *Jeanne Laisné* to the *Comédie
Française.* He maintained that they had accepted it, subject to
corrections, in November 1791.

... 1813. The two *duodecimo* volumes of *La Marquise de
Gange,* an anonymous novel by Sade, was published by Béchet's
63, quai des Augustins.

January 22nd 1814. Sade handed the manuscripts of *Adélaïde de Brunswick* and *Isabelle de Bavière* to a Mr Paquet, who undertook to find a publisher for them.

February 20th 1814. A sarcastic reader's report reached the *Comédie Française* concerning *Jeanne Laisné,* and the play was not read to the committee.

April 11th 1814. Abdication of Napoleon.

May 3rd 1814. Louis XVIII's solemn entry into Paris.

May 31st 1814. M. de Coulmier's place was taken by Roulhac du Maupas, onetime lawyer, whom Dr Royer-Collard had recommended to the Ministry of the Interior.

September 7th 1814. M. Roulhac du Maupas called the attention of the Minister of the Interior, the Abbé de Montesquiou, to the necessity for removing the Marquis de Sade from the Royal Hospice of Charenton, where it was impossible to keep sufficient watch on him. He should be handed to the Director of Police, for that person to take charge of him and discover means matching security and public morals with the consideration due the age and infirmity of the detainee. The Director further remarked that despite engagements undertaken when the Marquis was transferred from Bicêtre to Charenton, M. de Sade junior refused to pay arrears of board amounting to 8,934 *francs,* or alternately had the effrontery to demand a considerable reduction of the sum, although he had acquired his father's properties which guaranteed the dowry of his late mother, and denied that he owed the Marquis' creditors anything, alleging that all these debts were posterior to his own mortgage undertaking.

October 21st 1814. The Minister of the Interior invited Count Beugnot, Director-General of Police, to take a decision about the Marquis de Sade, who could not remain at Charenton without the most grave consequences.

October 29th 1814. For the last time Sade revised the manuscript of *Isabelle de Bavière.*

November 5th 1814. The Marquis de Sade to M. Roulhac du Maupas:

"The Director of this establishment refuses to allow Mr Donge, head of the Lottery Office, to come and relieve Mme Quesnet's eyes and mine by reading us the newspaper, nothing more recondite. I am very far from wishing to infringe any rule. But this worthy lottery person undertook to copy out for me some dramatic works accepted at various theatres and all approved by the police and I urgently request that he be allowed to continue this work for both he and I would lose much were it to be broken off. I may add, in passing, that to go on with this work will not require Mr Donge to work more than one hour a week for only two months.

I present my respects to the Director, renewing my urgent request not to be inconvenienced by the refusal of this trifle. I shall write to my son as the Director wishes."

Thanks to the precious inventory made after his death, we are able to get a glimpse into the domestic circumstances in which the Marquis de Sade passed his final years and the furniture which stood about him when in large, dignified letters he copied out the rough draft of the *Secret Story of Isabelle de Bavaria* in large notebooks of fine laid paper.

His quarters were on the second floor, part of the right wing of the hospice. The main room and the little library adjoining it gave on to the garden on the Marne side. They were reached by a hall off which opened a cloakroom. The furniture was dilapidated and disseminated gloom. In the bedroom was a four-poster bed with white and calico curtains shot with red, one easy chair in yellow Utrecht plush, two rush-bottomed armchairs, a fumed oak bureau, a marble-topped commode, a mirror surmounted by a picture in grey framing, on the left of the fireplace a cupboard containing an elderly man's clothes —four coats, five waistcoats and six pairs of breeches, all of different cloths and colours. On the walls was an unframed portrait of his grandfather, the Marquis Gaspard François de Sade, and miniatures of his mother, his son Louis Marie and Lady Anne Prospère the Canoness, that sister-in-law whom he had loved so passionately. . . . The library contained a table and an armchair, and on three shelves and in a deal cupboard were some two hundred and fifty volumes, out of which at first glance stood the seventy volumes of Kehl's edition of Voltaire, and among the others: Seneca, Suetonius, Tacitus, Don Quixote, the *Princesse de Clèves,* La Fontaine's *Stories,* Newton's *Principia,* Condillac, *l'Émile, The Pornographer, Delphine,* Chateaubriand's *The Spirit of Christianity, l'Histoire des Indiens,* and the permitted works of the man himself— *Aline et Valcour, The Crimes of Love,* and four copies of his latest published novel, *La Marquise de Gange.*

Such was the dead man's dwelling when on January 2nd 1815, accompanied by lawyers Finot and Boursier, Registrar Decalonne and witnesses Heyl and Hordret, Donatien Claude Armand his son, entered it unmoved, to make an inventory of these magnificent possessions of the Marquis de Sade and therefrom, as required by the Director of Police, to extract those manuscripts "which concerned morals or religion".

CHAPTER EIGHTEEN

*Posthumous and Unpublished Works Written between 1801 and 1814**

NOTES LITTÉRAIRES (CAHIERS PERSONNELS)

EACH OF the two manuscripts in Sade's hand from which the author drew the contents of the *Personal Notebooks* (*Cahiers personnels*) published in October 1953,** is a slender paper-bound booklet measuring about $2\frac{3}{8}$ in. by $7\frac{1}{2}$ in., cut irregularly at the top, the covers being dark fawn laid paper bearing the words: *Notes littéraires* (literary notes).

Judging from a number of quotations from the *Journal des Débats* contained in these two manuscripts, ranging from issues of the 15th Messidor, Year XI to 4th Ventôse, Year XII, one may conclude that the *Notes littéraires* were written in the second half of 1803 and in January and February 1804. It would also seem from their contents that they were part of a collection of "five notebooks of jottings, reflections, songs and miscellaneous verse and prose" which the *Biographie Michaud* mentions as having been among those unpublished manuscripts of Sade's which remained in the hands of his family.

The reflections, jottings and schemes already published are only a trifle more than one-third of the two books which have been recovered. The present author's first impulse was to produce it all, then it seemed that there was some danger of Sade's

---

*The only work of this period published during Sade's lifetime was the *Marquise de Gange* (1811).
**Cahiers personnels* (1803-4), "published for the first time from the unpublished autograph manuscripts by Gilbert Lely, Paris; Corréa;" 12°.

own remarks being drowned under the quotations he made or else ruined by some fragments of most mediocre origin. However, in selecting among fragments of very unequal value, mostly hasty jottings, the least fragment capable of throwing some slight ray of light on his personality was preserved. The author's principal guiding thought in making his choice was to bring out the material which best helped to show us Sade's principal preoccupations in the sixty-third year of his life, and at the dawn of the new century, of which he was to see only ten more years.

* * *

Considerable space in Sade's second notebook is given to a recapitulation of the works he admitted were his, whether published or still only in manuscript (all with a view to a collected edition) and to notes and arguments connected with recasting his stories. This notebook is a companion book to the *Catalogue raisonné* of 1788. It contains four new titles: the author's *Confessions* (to include, as frontispiece, his portrait), a *Refutation of Fénelon,* and two novels—*Conrad or the Delirious Jealous Man,* taken from the story of the Albigenses, and *Marcel or the Cordelier.* The manuscripts which were probably destroyed on Sade's death* would probably have been those for a new edition of *Aline and Valcour,* the enlarged *Crimes of Love* and *The French Boccaccio,* amounting to some thirty duodecimo volumes.**

Among the literary schemes which Sade's notebooks contained was the *Plot of a novel in letters* (No. 24) which calls for special notice. But first some general remarks.

In the preface to the *Crimes of Love,* the *Idée sur les romans,* which is an exposition of his views on works of fiction and a review of the most famous of them from antiquity to the end of the 18th century, Sade did not even mention Laclos's *Liaisons dangereuses,* however close to his own work this was, and

---

*They were probably the "ten volumes of various works" mentioned in the inventory made after Sade's death, which, together with "twenty-four notebooks in manuscript entitled diaries" were taken from Sade's trunk and handed to M. Rivière, Master of Requests in the State Council, as they were held to touch on "morals and religion."

***Aline et Valcour,* 6 Vols.; *Les Crimes de l'amour,* 6 vols.; *Le Boccace, Française,* 2 vols.; *Théâtre,* 2 vols.; *Le Portefeuille d'un homme de lettres,* 3 vols.; *Conrad,* 4 vols.; *Marcel ou le Cordelier,* 4 vols.; *Réfutation de Fénelon* 1 vol.; *Confessions,* 2 vols.

notwithstanding that he cannot have failed to recognise what a masterpiece this was. How are we to understand what must surely have been a deliberate omission? Two explanations come to mind at once, neither exclusive of the other. The first is that although Sade had so little to envy Laclos for, and in some aspects was so much his equal, he left the other writer out for some reason of personal jealousy. The second explanation is based on a coincidence which has not hitherto been noted. From the end of March to mid-October 1794 both Sade and Choderlos de Laclos were detainees in the same Picpus establishment. It is inconceivable that during seven months' joint captivity the two men did not sooner or later come into contact. That being so—till we have more information—it seems most plausible to assume (especially bearing in mind Sade's touchiness) that the two writers made each other's acquaintance only to fall out again, and when Sade wrote his *Crimes of Love* preface this still smarted.

Now, though the *Plot of a novel in letters,* the main features of which recall the subject of the *Liaisons dangereuses,* is not sufficient to justify the hypothesis of jealousy, it does at least seem to hint at Sade's complex reaction to a publishing success which he himself never attained.

The character of Théodorine, "a corrupted woman" who "pretends virtue" to young Clémence, while planning her dishonour and ruin, certainly seems to be a reincarnation of the *Marquise* de Merteuil, just as Delville, her accomplice, "an immoral man . . . a rake and a villain", seems to be a counterpart of the Viscount de Valmont. Sade's Clémence, alone in the book, seems meant to evoke pity, whereas in the *Liaisons dangereuses* Mlle de Volanges does not enjoy this feature alone, but has to share it with lovely Lady de Tourvel, and it seems clear that Clémence, as the "innocent young maid" seduced by Delville after Théodorine has robbed her of her own admirer, is definitely Mlle de Volange's counterpart. This is not the only parallel in the scheme. But though his plot is the same, Sade otherwise differs from his predecessor. Moreover, this is to his disadvantage—at least in theory, since we cannot know how Sade would have developed his theme because of the banality of the criminal subterfuges which he ascribes to Théodorine, whereas in Laclos's story the psychology of the *Marquise* de

Merteuil is brilliant in conception. There is however no reason to question that the apparently over-simple motivation of Théodorine's conduct, as "a relative of Clémence's whose death would bring her a fortune and enable her to marry Delville" was the fruit in Juliette's apologian of the words he placed on that heroine's lips: "Whatever the passion that was its inspiration, no crime was ever suggested that did not send the subtle fire of lubricity coursing through my veins, and lying, blasphemy, slander, rascality, hard-heartedness or even gluttony always affected me in the same way."*

Complete objectivity rules out the thesis that this sort of copying of Laclos's argument—however close it may have appeared in general outline—really justifies any suggestion of Sade's having been envious of Laclos. Yet it still seems reasonable to suggest that for a moment Sade had played with the idea of *rewriting* the *Liaisons dangereuses*. If this was the case, did he perhaps not feel that Laclos's fame encroached on a domain which he believed to be his own special field, and that for this reason meant to challenge his rival in the only way which in his opinion would enable the reading public to make a definitive comparison? It is not only the choice of letter form that seems to indicate Sade's intention to enter the lists against Laclos.

However, the author of *Juliette* and *Aline and Valcour* has numerous enough claims to our admiration, especially the magnificent originality of his gifts, for us to feel any risk of degrading him if we put onto his lips the following lapidary pronouncement: Why, but I could have written *Les Liaisons dangereuses* myself!

*   *   *   ·

The sensual philosophy of Mme de Staël's *L'Influence des passions,* her marked attachment to the philosophy of the eighteenth century, her warm-hearted outbursts during the

*In *Aline et Valcour* Sade recorded the exact opposite. "I have sometimes noticed that the narrow-minded type of woman has to be aroused by her own secret desires before she will take part in excesses of this kind. Once they are aroused, however, it is incredible how far one can go with them. Their spirit is closer to that state of evil for which Nature intended them and they more readily agree to whatever fresh atrocity one may find it necessary to suggest to them."

first horrors of the French Revolution, her fearless opposition
to Napoleon's growing tyrany—in a word, her complete dedication to the "consolidating and extending of the influence of
liberty", which is so clearly to be seen in all she wrote and did,
particularly in *Delphine,* which had only recently appeared,
could not fail to attract Sade's curiosity, without any ideological obstacle in it diminishing the remarkable sensitivity of
thought and expression which he must have seen in it.

So one should not be surprised to find that a large part of
Notebook A (folios 18-28) is devoted to a transcription of no
less than forty-two excerpts from *Delphine!* However justified
one may be in cutting nearly all of them out of the volume
entitled *Personal Notebooks,* (for they would clearly have upset
the balance and were not Sade's own thoughts), one can
scarcely pass them over in silence. The choice of the quotations,
made with such obvious fellow-feeling, from Mme de Staël's
work is most moving evidence of Sade's state of mind in the
first months of the new captivity which was to last for the rest
of his life. Almost exclusively the extracts from *Delphine* concern two subjects only, adversity and the discomforts of old
age. Both together are summed up in one single quotation:
"It is horrible to see the circle of the years closing in on oneself
without ever having enjoyed happiness." At the same time, a
number of less gloomy quotations, which refer to the existence
of a beloved woman, are expressive of the only consolation of
this period—the affection of Mme Quesnet, the loyal figure of
whom we find in all her charm in autobiographical notes *14*
and *25.*

*   *   *

It is an exquisite pleasure indeed to picture the Marquis de
Sade for the first time turning the pages of Chateaubriand's
Génie du Christianisme. What cries of sheer rage those sub-
titles must have called forth? *"The Existence of God Proved by
Nature"* ... *"The Immortality of the Soul Proved by Morals
and the Emotions".* In the notebooks we find Chateaubriand
insultingly spoken of as "a toady of the tonsured" and classed
ignominiously among third-rank authors such as Legouvé and
de Lancival.

At the end of April 1802, a few days before this work of Chateaubriand's was published, a solemn *Te Deum* in Notre Dame marked the promulgation of the Concordat. It was at about this time that Sade's anti-religious passion inspired him with the idea of compiling a methodical exposé of all the arguments that his own atheism had suggested to him, from the *Dialogue between a Priest and a Dying Man* to the *Histoire de Juliette*.

Of the *Refutation of Fénelon* we would know only the title referred to in the 1803-4 general catalogue, did not the notebooks give us the fragment (No. 7) entitled *Phantoms* (Fantômes). "Execrable abortion," cries Sade, addressing God, "I would have left you to yourself, delivered you over to the scorn which you alone inspire and refrained from once again combatting with you in Fénelon's meditations. But I have promised to do so and shall keep my word. . . ."*

. The *Note concerning my imprisonment* (No. 22), which gives us some new details of the moral sufferings which the prisoner of Vincennes and the Bastille endured, is followed by reflections of exceptional interest concerning the first *Justine*. As we know, Sade consistently denied being the author of that novel. In 1803 he had more reason than ever to do so, since it was as the author of such a work that he had spent two and a half years in confinement. But *Notebook A* contains arguments of such outstanding interest, so vividly put, so breathless with their sincerity of feelings that the more one examines them the more reason one has to believe that here, at the beginning of the nineteenth century, with the first signs of a priests' revenge, Sade cursed himself for having by sheer clumsiness served the defenders of God by publishing that novel *Justine* in which all the corrupt characters were also atheistic philosophers.

> "Read [*Justine*] carefully and it is clear that by unpardonable clumsiness, by a plan well devised (as happened) to embroil the author with both wise men and fools, with good and evil alike, all the philosopher characters in the book are rotten with wickedness. Yet I am a philosopher;

* Let us note in passing that this vigorous fragment is somewhat reminiscent of certain passages in an episode of the *Songs of Maldoror* in which the Count de Lautréaumont challenges the Creator.

nobody who knows me could doubt that this is my pride
and my faith. ... And could anybody for an instant suspect, unless they thought me mad, could it, I say, be believed for a minute, that I would willingly befoul the character which I consider my greatest claim to distinction
with horror and with cursing? What would you say of the
man who purposely dipped the coat he liked best, and
was most vain about, in the filth? Is such ineptness conceivable? Are such things to be seen in my other works?. . .
So it is not true that *Justine* is by me. I will add here something stronger still—that it is strange that all that godfearing rabble, all your Geoffroys, Genlis, Legouvés,
Chateaubriands, La Harpes, the Luces de Lancival, the
Villeterques, all those fine lackeys of the tonsure raised a
hue and cry against *Justine,* when that book simply played
into their hands. Even had they paid to have such a work
written, so well calculated to denigrate a philosophy, they
could not have had it. I swear on all that I hold most
sacred in the world that I would never forgive myself for
having helped creatures whom I so tremendously despise."

*   *   *

But though, more than ever infuriated by the idea of a God,
Sade may have regretted having written *Justine,* to the extent
to which that work was calculated by ricochet to furnish the
godfearing rabble with ammunition, he none the less never
gave up those ideas of the erotic and the cruel, all those things
which he "summoned to his aid when he wished to dull his
mind to his situation", those "delightful details", as he called
them, which so greatly mitigated his misfortunes when he let
his imagination play on them. There are places in the notebooks which dispel any shadow of doubt on the steadfastness
of his curiosity about details of lascivious living to be found in
chronicles ancient and modern and likely to feed his restless
meditations as well as to build up that psycho-sexual store
which was indispensable to his work. Thus we find him carefully noting down the title of the work "containing Procopius'
secret tales about Theodora" (*No. 13*) or, reading in de Thou
the historian that the morning after St Bartholemew's night

the ladies of the French court emerged from the Louvre "to gaze at the naked bodies of the Huguenots killed and stripped under the palace walls". He remarks that in the evening of August 10th 1792 "the women of Paris came to stare at the naked bodies of the Swiss guards" as they lay massacred in the Tuileries gardens (No. 4). In another place he seems to wish to give a tacit justification of the bold pictures of *Justine* and *Juliette,* when he remarks that just like the Juvenals, Suetoniuses and Dion Cassiuses the fathers of the church too did not shrink from "painting vice in the most brilliant colours". (No. 12). And as corollary to this, in item No. 6 we find him waxing indignant against dull moralisers who would like to destroy in the writer "the vigour he has from nature", with their demand that neither his works nor his own morals should be such as to earn him the disrespect of virtuous folk. "It is the man of natural talent that I want in a writer, whatever his morals or his character," cried the one-time hero of Arceuil and Marseilles, "because it is not with him that I want to live, but with his works, and all I want in what he gives me is truth."

However, these notes and thoughts, however indicative they may be, are still only an aid to our picture of Sade's literary preoccupations round about 1804. For the material in his two books of notes deals exclusively with his acknowledged plans. Their contents could not reveal that at this very time he was also thinking of refashioning and expanding quite encyclopedically the erotic manuscript of the *Conversations du Château de Charmelle,* which the police seized at the premises of Massé the publisher on the *15th Ventôse, Year IX,* and which was never to be seen again. With which we come to the new version of that work, which was destroyed after his death in 1814, *Florbelle Days.*

A SODOM DESTROYED : FLORBELLE DAYS OR NATURE UNVEILED (LES JOURNÉES DE FLORBELLE OU LA NATURE DÉVOILÉE)

All that can be learned of *Florbelle Days* we have in a photographic reproduction of a slender unpublished notebook of notes in Sade's handwriting, the original of which, last in the hands of Jean Desbordes, vanished during the recent war. The

owner, Viscount Charles de Noailles, had prior to this handed
it to Maurice Heine, and it was he who took the precaution
of photographing it and. making a description, accompanied
by a partial decipherment of certain words or portions of phrase
the reading of which presented difficulties.*

While the *Final analyses and final observations on this great
work*—that is the title of the document in question—give us
some indication of what was in the book, from a note made by
its first owner, M. de Monmerqué, we learn that this "dis-
graceful" novel—as he called it—the fair copy of which was
contained in some hundred and eight notebooks,** together
with the rough draft, was after the author's death committed
to the flames by Police Prefect Delavau acting on the request
of Sade's son Donatien, who was present. (By all appearances
the book about Florbelle had been seized in June 1807, two
months after completion.) This notebook, the only surviving
piece of all Sade's enormous work, was offered to de Monmerqué "as a curiosity" by the Prefect's personal secretary, a
certain M. Du Plessis, who had extracted it and some other
pieces from among the papers condemned to be burned.

What can we discover in this unique source-document which
would have followed the rest into nothingness—after one hundred and twenty-five years—had not Heine had it photo-
graphed?

The whole title of this enormous composition "finally decided upon on April 29th 1807, upon completing the work",
one which shows very clearly what it was about, is : *Les Journées de Florbelle ou la Nature dévoilée, suivies des Mémoires
de l'abbé de Modose et des Aventures d'Émilie de Volnange
servant de preuves aux assertions.* (Florbelle Days or Nature
Unveiled, followed by the Reminiscences of the Abbé de
Modose and the Adventures of Emilie de Volnange serving as
proofs of the assertions.) There is a pugnacious epigraph taken
from Seneca: "True liberty consists in fearing neither men nor
the gods," words which might serve as key to the story of Sade's

---

*At the moment of writing all this material, now in the hands of the
Bibliothèque Nationale, was with the binder!

**The author makes this suggestion concerning the three parts of the
novel on the basis of the 68 books of the *Aventures d'Émilie*, which were
two-fifths of the complete work.

life itself, for, as we see, however hard despotism struck, Sade never once in any field betrayed the pride and sanity of his rebellion.

The original title had been: *Valrose ou les Écarts* [or *Égarements*] *du libertinage*—Valrose or the Byways of a Libertine's Life—which was then transformed into : *Mémoires d'Emilie de Valrose ou les Égarements du libertinage*—The Reminiscences of Valrose or the Byways of a Libertine's Life. This had the following as epigraph: "It is by showing vice naked that one leads to virtue." The author then made a marginal note that his heroine would change from Valrose to Volnange. Finally, we may note that before adopting the final title, Sade had a shot in a very different direction: *Les Entretiens du château de Florbelle, ouvrage moral et philosophique suivi de la sainte Histoire du bienheureux abbé de Modose et des Mémoires pieux d'Émilie de Volnange, ornés de gravures édifiantes.*

In fact the notebook contained no analysis of the *Reminiscences of the Abbé of Modose.* The fourteen notes touching on this part are too detailed to tell us anything about the whole. But we have the contents of several episodes of the *Adventures of Émilie de Volnange,* in some fifty notes and observations. It would seem that the heroine was a reincarnation of Juliette and the author brought in historical figures of the old régime, Louis XV, the Cardinal de Fleury, Count de Charolais and Marshal de Soubise.

When exactly was it written? The only indications concern the third part of the work, *Emilie's Adventures.* Sade began the revision March 5th 1806 and finished it April 25th 1807, taking thirteen months, twenty days over it. (The first volume was completed by July 10th 1806.)

However, by means of the various summaries, notes and other indications in Sade's notebook, all very fragmentary and often confusing, it is possible to reconstitute the plot. The result is a sufficiently clear picture to make it most regrettable that a work of such powerful, many-sided imagination should be lost. How it was written we cannot know, but that it was a grand summing up of Sade's thought there is no doubt.

THE PLOT OF DAYS AT FLORBELLE RECONSTITUTED

VOLUME I

Explanation of the frontispiece. Publisher's note, blurb and indication that he was the author of *Justine*. Author's preface to libertines of whatever sex or age. Dedication to God. Introduction. Names of characters in the dialogues : Émilie, 32; Modose, her lover, 38; Eugénie and Flavie, his children by Mme de Mistival, a character in the *Philosopher in the Boudoir,* 15 and 16; Augustin, his valet, 19; Eudoxie, daughter of a rich business man of Marseilles, Émilie's girl friend, 17; a hermit; Mme de Mistival (who appears only in the eighth dialogue), which according to *Les Aventures d'Émilie de Volnange* concludes the book.

First Day

Dialogue I. Treatise on Religion, by the Abbé de Modose, Dialogue II.

Second Day

Dissertation on the Soul. Dialogue III.

Third Day

Treatise on God by the Abbé de Modose. Dialogue IV.

VOLUME 2

Fourth Day

(Placed in a shrubbery of myrtles and roses). Treatise on Morals. Dialogue V "containing the adventure of the poor forester; here the murder of the hermit is planned and to this end he is taken to the castle prison (Florbelle)."

Fifth Day

Shameless Venus or the Art of Love. Introduction; Sections 1 —viii and beginning of ix-th.

VOLUME 3

Sixth Day

Continuation and end of the Shameless Venus, namely: *Plan for Thirty-two Houses of Prostitution in Paris*. Section X, first part: *Treatise on the Antiphysical*;* *Treatise on Tastes*. "This disquisition ends with the cries of the hermit," (He is in fact being tortured in prison). Dialogue VI: "In this dialogue, Eudoxie is energetically threatened by Modose; Modose's children prove very licentious; Eudoxie is whipped. Here comes the cross-examination of the hermit, who is made to suffer countless horrors; Flavie's death proves to be very cruel; his agony lasts seven hours. Eudoxie is still alive. She has been manhandled, but she is still quite well and maintains her prejudices.

VOLUME 4

Seventh Day

Reminiscences of the Abbé de Modose, Chapters I-XIV.

VOLUME 5

Eighth Day

Ibid, Chapters XV-XXVI.

VOLUME 6

Ninth Day

Ibid, Chapters XXVII to XXXIV (end).

VOLUME 7

Tenth Day

Dialogue VII: "Eudoxie's death under a rare and terrible torture." After this dialogue, Modose gets Émilie to tell the story of her life. *Adventures of Émilie de Volnange*, Chapters I, II, III.

*Meaning no doubt heterosexual and homosexual sodomy and Lesbianism.

VOLUME 8

Eleventh Day

Adventures of Émilie, Chapter IV.

VOLUME 9

Twelfth Day

Ibid, continuation. (How many chapters this and the preceding volume contained we do not know.)

VOLUME 10—LAST VOLUME

Ibid, concluded. *Dialogue VIII,* "taken from the end of the second volume of the *Philosophy in the Boudoir* (torture of Mme de Mistival) also containing "the details of her death, over which a veil had been drawn".

The scarlet walls of the tales of Modose and Émilie; the four towers at the corners of the dissertations on Religion, the Soul, the Creator and Morals; the eight flanking towers of the Dialogues; the diabolical chapel of the Epistle dedicating it to God, the dungeon of shameless Venus complete with its three corner turrets : the brothels scene, the treatise on the "anti-physical" and the treatise on tastes; at the summit the oriflame and identity of the author . . . this was the edifice that rose into the peerless empyrean of murder and erotic corruption, this was the monstrous Sodom of "Nature Unveiled".

ADÉLAÏDE DE BRUNSWICK, PRINCESSE DE SAXE

Here is a description of the manuscript of this novel (in Sade's own hand) in the *X. de Sade Collection*:

Adélaide de Brunswick, princesse de Saxe, événement du XIe century—Paris 1813.

There are two notebooks, $7\frac{1}{4}$ in. $\times$ $9\frac{1}{2}$ in. of two hundred and fourteen and two hundred and seventy-five pages, in soft, greenish marbled cardboard covers. The paper is medium weight, off-white laid. Every page, of 18 to 20 lines, contains some 150 words. There are very many corrections. Large chunks are stuck on to recast passages. There are jagged remains where pages have been torn out (though the numeration is complete). In Volume 1 there is a map of the Electorate of Saxony, drawn in Indian ink.

On a loose sheet attached to Volume III, with a list of the characters on the reverse, Sade has jotted the following time-table details: "I began this work on September 1st 1812; the draft was finished October 4th; I spent a week correcting the draft, which brought me to October 12th, when I began the fair copy (October 13th 1812), which I finished November 21st. Thirty-nine days copying. It was on December 4th that it was all completely ready and I packed up the draft. In all three months, four days."

A "publisher's note" at the end of the manuscript tells us that this eleventh century story was "founded in fact". As written by Sade the story of the love and misadventures of the Princess of Saxony is, like some of the *Crimes of Love*, of the "heroic order".

Shortly after her marriage to Frederick, Prince of Saxony, Adelaide, daughter of the Duke of Brunswick, was falsely accused by traitorous Mersbourg of having become young Kaunitz's lover. In reality she was in love with Louis de Thuringia, who loved her in return. Their love, however, remained chaste. Locked up on the Prince's orders in Torgau Fortress, the Princess succeeded in escaping. The greater part of the novel consists in her adventures as a fugitive and those of Frederick who is in pursuit in various countries, not to assuage his vengeance, but to obtain the forgiveness of the woman he loves, despite the jealousy with which she has rent his heart. At last, having found his wife, the Prince is killed in a duel with the Marquis of Thuringia, who succeeds him to the throne. But then Adelaide retires to a convent, soon to die of consumption.

Taken as a whole, this work, one must admit, hardly rises above mediocrity. Despite a rather brilliant opening, which for a moment gives rise to hopes of another *Princesse de Clèves*, the slight verisimilitude of the characters is only here and there redeemed by romantic fancy. If one excepts several passages in which descriptions of jealousy are coloured by a preromantic sensitivity, there is very little to repay one for the monotony of most unrewarding reading. Two strange features, moreover, merit mention. One is a most edifying praise of monastic life, which comes strangely from the pen of the author of *Juliette*. The other is the presence of episodes clearly related to the *Misfortunes of Virtue,* which are however in a mutilated form. Thus we are given a picture of the princess in the hands of a brigand chief on the point of ignoring any vestige of modesty in his captive, but at the last moment there is no rape, for a most unexpected access of gratitude suddenly prevents completion of the act!

Nor is the fact that this novel about her, which was never published in its original tongue but translated into English and published in Washington in 1954, the least singular of the facts about the Princess of Saxony.*

THE SECRET HISTORY OF ISABELLE OF BAVARIA QUEEN OF FRANCE**

There seems no question but that originally the Marquis de Sade as writer, felt an interest in history. For instance, in 1764 and 1765 we see him tearing himself from the arms of his mistresses to go delving into the medieval collections of the library of the Carthusians of Dijon. On June 26th, we recall, he addressed the high court of Burgundy on the occasion of being accepted as Lieutenant General of Bresse and Bugey, and in May 1765, travelling to Avignon with la Beauvoisin, he passed through Dijon—and halted there. He had a precise reason: the capital of Jean the Fearless might well contain some unpublished document which would add something to the scant information on the political part that Isabelle of Bavaria played. Not that Sade's interest in that intriguing personality, as interesting for "her personal charms" as for "her mind, and the grandeur of her titles", is our only proof of that attraction to the historical which was to show again while he was in Vincennes and the Bastille. In September 1783 Sade spoke to his wife of three literary projects which he intended to occupy his time

*Adelaide of Brunswick, by Donatien Alphonse François, Count [*sic*] de Sade, translated by Professor Hobart Ryland, University of Kentucky; Washington; The Scarecrow Press; 8°, pp. 168. (Limited Edition).

**Histoire secréte d'Isabelle de Baviére, reine de France, dans laquelle se trouvent des faits rares, inconnus ou restés dans l'oubli jusqu'à ce jour, et soigneusement étayés de documents authentiques, allemands, anglais et latins. Published by Gallimard in 1953, 16°, edited with an introduction by the author. The present essay replaces the original introduction.

with. The second of these was a *Eulogy of King François I*
(never carried through) while the third was to make a fair copy
of some "ten or twelve" notebooks full of stories covering the
history of France. Let us also note that the second volume of
the *Portfolio of a man of letters,* one of the lost works, contained
ninety fragments which Sade had written of history of all the
nations. These were jotted down in his own peculiar manner,
intermingled with comments. In the rough as they were in October 1788 they were intended to be used in the French anecdotes to which reference has just been made. They were not to
go beyond the reign of Charles IX. Here, however, nothing
of any length was in mind, and it was not till the end of his life,
about his seventy-second year, that Sade undertook a more
ambitious piece of work which was to give scope to the leanings
of half a century, first towards history generally, but in particular concerning the consort of an insane monarch.

The autograph manuscript of *Isabelle de Bavière* consists of
three thick notebooks of fine white laid paper, bound in soft
green marbled card, containing 625, 753 and 771 pages, size
$6\frac{5}{8}$ in. $\times$ $8\frac{5}{8}$ in. There are no more than eleven lines or forty
words to a page and the writing is not less than $\frac{3}{8}$ in. high, in a
grand style. The second volume contains an inset map showing
the situation of Barbette House.

From notes at the end of each volume it would seem that the
book was commenced on May 19th 1813 and completed on
September 24th, the final revision being completed on November 20th. There is however an additional note showing that on
October 29th 1814, just over a month before he died, Sade
proposed to make yet another revision. There is another version of the book in M. Xavier de Sade's library. This is the work
of a professional copyist. It contains a number of emendations,
not one of which is in Sade's hand. The only autograph entry
here is on the fly-leaf of Volume 3: "The corrections in this
book were commenced in the evening of December 13th."
Comparison shows that quite a large number of alterations
which are in the original manuscript had not been made in the
copyist's version, but were added later by a second copyist.

Although in the *Biographie universelle* both this work and
Adélaïde Brunswick are characterised as "black and terrible"
it is also remarked that there is in it "nothing objectionable

regarding either morals or religion". And indeed, the inmate of Charenton was so sure that he had said nothing to offend that he seriously hoped to find a publisher for the work, as we see from a receipt listed in the inventory made after his death.

Sade informs us that all he wished to achieve in *Isabelle de Bavière* was "a sound if rare use of the novel form". If in the style of ancient historians he thought fit to put words into the mouths of his characters, he did so merely to add force to the truth of the facts. He had also thought it right to weave the history of France into that of his heroine. Isabelle's own fortunes were too inextricably linked with the vicissitudes of France for these to be left unmentioned. Ten years earlier than Augustin Thierry, Sade in his preface attacked what he called the "apathy" of the historians who made mere compilations of facts of the 17th and 18th centuries, thinking of such as Mézerai Anquetil, the Abbé Velly and his successor Villaret. He also attacked their ignorance of prime sources and their lack of the critical spirit.

Sade above all found it inexcusable in those who had studied the reign of Charles VI to have produced no "reason for it", a "negligence", he said, "which made that astonishing reign so fabulous that it loses the great interest which it should excite. Countless attacks are made on Queen Isabelle without anybody taking the trouble to tell us what that extraordinary woman did to deserve them. The little knowledge one had of her resulted in her being regarded as a merely episodic figure, even in the events in which she played the principal part. . . . It was considered that everything had been said, whereas the truth, meaning the most vital part of history, had not even been touched upon."

And how did Sade claim to have discovered this truth, which he maintained was "remarkable"? It was from unpublished sources which had remained unknown and "chance, or rather, a number of journeys of a literary nature", had allowed him to discover. In 1770 in the Royal Library of Londre he found material relating to the trial of Richard II, Isabelle's brother-in-law; he also examined a manuscript of Joan of Arc's trial which he maintained was not the "apocryphal" document which the historians had quoted from. But it was at the Carthusian Priory of Dijon in 1764 and 1765 that—or at least, so he said—Sade succeeded in discovering unparalleled archives which were fifty years later to be the corner stone of his work. This was the cross-examination, lasting several days, of the Louis de Bourdon, *knight,* the Queen's factotum,* whom Charles VI condemned to death. He under torture revealed "the part played by Isabelle in all the crimes of the reign".

Now, this alleged document is no longer in existence. Sade himself recorded that when the old régime collapsed the library of the "worthy monks" was destroyed "by the imbecile barbarity of the Vandals of the 18th century", whom in another place he calls the "sinister Ostrogoths of the French Revolution".

In 1814, when Sade was looking for a publisher for his book, this story of the Dijon manuscript was already regarded with suspicion. In fact, there were doubters who called on the Marquis to deposit his supporting evidence with some lawyer. And after another century and a half we have to put the question flatly: what proof did Sade give that in 1764 the Carthusians possessed those documents? Though in many places there is a footnote and reference to some folio of the fourteen "bundles of papers" recording that cross-examination of Louis de Bourbon, there is not a single quotation from the alleged original statements!** Though Sade maintained that he had made extracts, he refrained from producing any. It seemed pointless to him to do so. "From the very circumstance that it was I myself that copied them will not those who question everything, being made incapable of believing anything, deduce the objection that what I say is no more reliable than what I offer as proof?" This sarcasm makes Sade's argument frivolous and suggests a certain embarrassment. For if those extracts really existed, he could only have gained by letting people see them. Such a linguistic expert as Raynouard, for instance,*** could well have adjudged whether they were authentic or not.

*That such a person existed, whom Sade calls Bois-Bourdon, is confirmed by the chroniclers. See *Chronique du Religieux de Saint-Denis,* Paris, 1852, vol. VI, p. 71 *et seq.*
**Except on p. 109 three lines in old French. But why did Sade limit himself to that specimen, too slight to be any proof?
***Author of plays and learned works on the language of the troubadours, who had just published a collection of historical documents concerning the condemnation of the Knights Templars and the abolition of their order.

Here we may add that Sade was as a rule far from reluctant to produce supporting evidence. His tragedy, *Jeanne Laisné*, was followed by letters patent which Louis XI issued to the warrior girl of Beauvais. And his letter to the *Journal de Paris* on the subject was written partly to boast of having by those letters "made immortal" the real name of Jeanne Hachette,—Laisné. What rare satisfaction he was depriving himself of in not publishing, not merely extracts, but the whole cross-examination! It seems quite conceivable that among the criminal acts of that rascal of the feminine court of Vincennes Louis Bourbon did sully the Royal bed. Though Chapter 167 of Monstrelet's *Chronicles* does not list the charges of the indictment, it does at least indicate a causal connection between whatever the man confessed to and the rigorous exile of the Queen. So one may imagine what unusual interest the publication of such a document would have caused, especially since it might have been presumed that to preserve the honour of his name Charles VI would have taken care to have the shocking documentary evidence destroyed. Now, apart from having waited half a century to make use of it, we have to ask why Sade chose to use his evidence in this less convincing way.

When one examines certain passages of the chroniclers (the priest of Jacques Legrand, quoted by the Monk of St Denis, the allegories of the *Songe véritable* and Pastorelet's stories and pictures), there remains little doubt as to Isabelle's lascivious nature or her adulterous relation with the Duke d'Orléans. Nor can one help remembering Charles VII's concern as to the legitimacy of his birth. But neither Isabelle's misconduct nor the political crimes which history places at her door were sufficient alone to fire Sade's imagination. It was essential to have these rather humdrum details reinforced by "the most infamous acts of betrayal, sacrilege, depravity, infanticide and murder".

"Not a drop of blood was shed during that terrible reign," he says in his preface, "that Isabelle was not guilty of . . . not a crime was committed but she was either the cause or the object."

Alas, there is no confirmation of this. Sade's thesis of Isabelle's universal guilt corresponds to no verifiable source, and the charges made by this peculiar historian of ours still rest uniquely on the alleged contents of Louis de Bourbon's cross-examination or, concerning the years following 1417, on letters clearly written by Bourbon or other such surprising evidence, the originals of which one seeks in vain.

Let us glance at some of the shameless acts which Sade without the least compunction ascribed to Isabelle in the fifty years between her marriage and her death. To bribe him to murder the Constable of Clisson, she prostituted herself to Craon. She conjured up the ghost of Mans Wood, organised a ball of nobles disguised as savages and forced them so to behave; the King, also dressed as a savage, only escaped being roasted alive by a hairsbreadth. She supported Bolingbroke's conspiracy against her brother-in-law, Richard II. She gave herself to Jean the Fearless and then, that Royal personage's accomplice in the trap laid in the Barbette quarter, kept Louis d'Orléans with her for two lascivious days, up to the moment planned for his murder. She then added the murder of his wife, and slept with her victims' son. During the Caboche rebellion she harangued and egged on the rascals who were flaying men alive. Disguising herself as a public prostitute, she frequented brothels, to couple with thieves and murderers. She poisoned three of her children, Louis the crown prince, Jean the crown prince, and Michelle Duchess of Burgundy and on the eve of the Montereau meeting urged Jean the Fearless to slay the crown prince Charles. Finally, she handed Joan of Arc over to the Holy Office and persuaded the Duke of Bedford himself to examine Joan's sex.* What a close relation there is between the Bavarian woman as Sade saw her and that monster of horror, Juliette!

But though under the cover of non-existent documents Sade thus in many a passage offers us as factual evidence promptings and causes drawn from his own algolagneic imagination, nevertheless at the same time by the use of real sources masterly

*On p. 312 Sade remarks that "it was God's will that this treacherous woman Isabelle, soaked in crime, should die a peaceful death at an advanced age, while he had Joan of Arc killed at the stake in the flower of her age, the most decent, most courageous and most astonishing woman of her time." A remarkable passage for two reasons—not merely because we have Sade thus honouring the Maid of Orleans, but because we have the author of *Justine* and *Juliette* now trying by an example drawn from history to support his theory of virtue punished and vice rewarded.

used he does also give a broad and striking canvas of the reign of Charles VI. By the vigorous flow and vivid quality of the narration, the boldness of the invention and the subtlety with which this is fitted into the undeniable facts, the profundity of reflections on both individual and mass psychology, also by those disturbing dark hues with which he so skilfully painted the portrait of the Queen herself, the author of *Isabelle de Bavière* well merits a prominent place among the authors of that hybrid form which though far removed from the novel, has certain of its features, and though in Clio's vein, is still not quite history.

After that impoverished story, *Adélaïde de Brunswick,* the production of such a work as *Isabelle* at the age of seventy-one is amazing for the vigour and the brilliance which in it he again attained, even though the rather heavy gravity of expression here and there does movingly suggest the ponderous gait of that elderly "haughty and morose nobleman" whom Dr Ramon used to meet in the corridors of Charenton Asylum in 1814.

Among the finest passages of the work, the portrait of the Queen herself is worthy of mention, for here the last rays of Sade's genius lingered, before being quenched for ever:

"To the graces and charms which are natural enough at that age, Isabelle's features added a sort of pride which is rare indeed at sixteen. In those very large, very black eyes there was more of *hauteur* than that sensitivity which is so sweet and attractive in any young girl's glance. Her bearing was eloquent of both dignity and sublety, her gestures were very definite, her gait bold, her voice rather hard, her speech tending to curtness. There was in her great loftiness of temperament and not a hint of that gentle humanity which is the property of kindly souls and which, when it brings its owner to the throne, consoles her for the painful elevation which fate has forced on her. There was already indifference regarding morals or the faith which supports them; an unconquerable aversion from anything that ran counter to her tastes; an inflexibility in her moods and an impetuosity in her desires, a dangerous tendency to be revengeful and a great readiness to find faults in those about her. She was as prompt to suspect as to punish, as quick to cause evil deeds as to contemplate them unmoved, and she had certain traits which indicated that whenever passion fired her heart she would yield to it to the full and make it her only real aim. Both mean and prodigal, craving everything, seizing everything, ready to sacrifice any interest, even that of the State, to her own interests, she rejoiced in the position to which fate had brought her, not to use it for good but so that she might find impunity for evil in it; in short, she was endowed with all the vices and redeemed by no virtue."

One word more, to complete this examination, in which praise had inevitably to yield place to revelation of a culpable piece of literary fraud: throughout this work on Isabelle of Bavaria Sade never let slip an opportunity for the pronouncement of moral judgments which, coming from the pen of the author of the *Philosopher in the Boudoir,* may at first surprise. But quite apart from his probable anxiety to increase his chances of being published, and the fact that in places his most daring works contain similar passages, why should one not consider such thoughts about *Justine* and *Juliette* in the light of that union of contradictions which sheds its glow alike over the *Chants de Maldoror* and the *Preface to an Unwritten Work?*

CHAPTER NINETEEN

Death

(December 2nd 1814)

WHEN ON Saturday November 11th 1814 L. J. Ramon, medical student, aged nineteen, newly appointed principal student-doctor to do his hospital training at Charenton, arrived to begin work and first met an elderly gentleman in the corridor, how could it have occurred to the Marquis that this young stranger was marked by fate to watch over his last moments and close his eyes for ever?

Fifty-three years later, beginning his brief account of what he recalled of the famous inmate of Charenton, Dr L. J. Ramon wrote: "I often used to meet him, walking all by himself, with heavy, dragging step, most carelessly attired, in the corridor off which his apartments opened; never once did I catch him talking to anybody. As I passed I would bow and he would respond with that chill courtesy which excludes any thought of entering into conversation. . . . Nothing could have led me to suspect that this was the author of *Justine* and *Juliette*; the only impression he produced on me was that of a haughty, morose elderly gentleman."

It was this same day, November 11th, that Sade wrote to M. Pépin, his Saumane tenant, one of the last of the countless letters he wrote in his long life. He said how anxious he was to know if the Garrigue wood-cutting had been done properly, in the way that he had indicated in the instructions he had sent Maître Roze, Notary of Isle sur Sorgue, more than six weeks earlier. He would like part of the proceeds of the sale of this timber to be used on urgent repairs to the Saumane manor house (the only property still his). The rest was to be sent him without delay, he had "inexpressible need of it".

Thursday, December 1st the Marquis lost the use of his legs. He had been failing for some time. He was taken to a two-roomed apartment, no doubt more comfortable than his own, and a servant assigned to look after him. In no document later than November 5th, is there any mention whatsoever of Mme Quesnet, whom one would have expected now, of all times, to be at her dear friend's side. To what her absence was due we do not know. It is hard to believe that M. Roulhac du Maupas was so hard-hearted as to have expelled the only person still interested in the Marquis' well-being.

On the Saturday—December 2nd—in the afternoon, Donatien Claude Armand visited his father, and asked M. Ramon to spend the night in the old man's room. Late in the evening, on his way there, young Ramon met the Abbé Geoffrey, the Charenton almoner, as he came out of Sade's room. The Abbé had had the impression that "if not greatly edified, the Marquis was at least pleased by the visit".

The young doctor sat down at Sade's bedside and a number of times helped him to take a few sips of a herbal tea and some other medicine prescribed "to ease the pulmonary congestion", of an asthmatical nature, from which Sade was suffering. The Marquis' respiration was "noisy and laboured". He was finding it increasingly difficult to get his breath.

At a little before ten, proposing to give the patient a drink, M. Ramon "could hear no sound and, surprised by the stillness" went to the bedside. The old man was dead.

The following day, M. Roulhac du Maupas informed the Director of Police and remarked that it had hardly seemed necessary to seal the room, since he "could presume M. de Sade *junior* to be honest enough to suppress any dangerous papers, if his father had any".

A little before midday two men, Demoustier and Dubuisson, no doubt on the staff at Charenton, went to the municipality to make the usual declaration. Midday was being struck as the death certificate was issued:

"On December 3rd, at midday, 1814, before us, Mayor of the Commune of Charenton Saint Maurice, Messrs Jean Pierre Demoustier, aged fifty-five and Marie Victoire François Dubuisson, aged fifty-seven, both domiciled at the said Charenton Saint Maurice Hospice, appeared before me and did declare that yesterday the Second of the present month of December in this commune at about ten p.m. M. Donatien Alphonse François Count *Desade,* man of letters, aged seventy-four, dwelling at the said Charenton Saint Maurice Hospice died, and the said persons declaring this have signed the present death certificate together with us. Read and duly signed, Demoustier, Dubuisson and Finot, Mayor."

The Marquis de Sade had drawn up a will on January 30th 1806. This was first published in the original French edition of the present work. All that had previously been known was the fifth paragraph, which had aroused admiration by the wild grandeur of it, which seemed to ring with the tones of Alfred de Vigny. Now it was seen to contain not merely stark pessimism, but also touching evidence of gratitude and affection, in the paragraphs which begin with praise of Mme Quesnet, whose "courageous efforts" had saved the Marquis from the "revolutionary scythe". Here we see Sade solely preoccupied with how to assure his Marie Constance a revenue which would suffice "for her maintenance and upkeep", and to place any books and manuscripts he might leave in her good hands.

Here is the famous fifth paragraph: "I categorically forbid the dissection of my body for any purpose whatsoever; I must pressingly request that it be kept for forty-eight hours in the room in which I die, in a wooden coffin not nailed down till the forty-eight hours here prescribed have elapsed, after which it shall be nailed. During this time an express messenger shall be sent to M. Le Normand, firewood merchant 101, *Boulevard de l'Egalité,* Versailles, to request him to come himself, with a waggon, to take my body and in his care transport it in the said firewood waggon to the woods on my Malmaison property in the commune of Émancé near Épernon, where I wish it to be placed, without any sort of ceremony, in the first thicket on the right in those woods as you enter past the old manor house by the main drive which divides the estate in two. The grave shall be dug by the Malmaison farmer under M. Le Normand's supervision, who shall not leave my body till he has placed it in this grave. If he wishes he may have with him those of my relatives and friends who, without any sort of display, would like to show me that last mark of affection. Once the grave is filled in, acorns are to be scattered over it, so that in time the grave is again overgrown, and when the undergrowth is grown as it was before, the traces of my grave will vanish from the face of the earth as I like to think memory of me will be effaced from men's minds, save for the tiny band of those who were kind enough to be fond of me to the end and of whom I carry a very warm memory to the grave."

Was Sade's son really brazen enough to contest the legacy of 80,000 *livres* which warm-hearted Mme Quesnet by her never-failing loyalty so deserved? That bigoted miser, who had already given proof of his slickness after his mother's death, when he had taken advantage of his father's detention to rob him without shame, would certainly have made no bones about seizing the money of a defenceless woman. But the will was categorical, and as he and his sister in the end gave up their claim to the Marquis' estate, there is every reason to believe that Mme Quesnet received what was her due, and the sale of Saumane provided enough to guarantee it. Nevertheless, this conclusion remains mere conjecture, and we do not know for certain if Marie Constance ever received Sade's library. The manuscripts were certainly shared between the police and the family, the former to burn their share, the latter to pack them away in a chest, from which they were not to be extracted till the fifth generation! It will ever be to the honour of the Marquis Xavier de Sade to have responded to the present author's request and allowed publication of those masterpieces, the letters which his ancestor wrote while in Vincennes prison and the *Secret History of Isabelle of Bavaria*.

As has already been noted, the son in September 1814 despite precise undertakings refused to pay arrears of board demanded by the Charenton establishment. On December 24th 1817, three years after the Marquis' death, M. Roulhac de Maupas complained again to the Prefect that "the shameless

heir" had again refused to "pay the sacred debt for board supplied to his father". For fourteen years Charenton in vain
claimed 7,534 *livres,* which included 2,877 silver *livres* advanced to Sade between 1803 and 1808. Of a totally different
order of scurrility, this impious son not only requested the
police to burn the manuscript of *Florbelle Days,* but was himself actually present at the act of vandalism.

Only one act of filial piety can be set to the credit of that
dismal, greedy creature. He persuaded the head of Charenton
not to have Sade's body dissected. But on the other hand, Sade's
other requests about disposal of his body were ignored, and it
was subjected to religious burial in the Charenton cemetery.

The burial, with a plain stone cross and no inscription, cost
65 *livres*; 10 for the coffin, 6 to the chapel, 9 for candles, 6 for
the almoner, 8 for the bearers, 6 for the gravedigger, 20 for
the cross. Exactly when Sade was buried we do not know, nor
who followed him to his last prison.

Thus was engulfed in silent night the man who, as Guillaume
Apollinaire put it, twenty-eight years a prisoner, remained "the
freest soul that ever existed". Never will his rebelliousness be
dead. Quite apart from those works which are less disturbing,
but sufficient to make a man famous, such as the *Dialogue* or
Aline and Valcour—or his letters—his vigorous yet graceful
genius, in *Sodom, La Nouvelle Justine* and *Juliette,* lifted to
their greatest heights the frenzy of language and the tragic
glories of scholarship.

Index